English B

FOR THE
IB DIPLOMA

English B

Mark McGowan
Hyun Jung Owen
Aaron Deupree

HODDER
EDUCATION
AN HACHETTE UK COMPANY

Although every effort has been made to ensure that website addresses are correct at time of going to press, Hodder Education cannot be held responsible for the content of any website mentioned in this book. It is sometimes possible to find a relocated web page by typing in the address of the home page for a website in the URL window of your browser.

Hachette UK's policy is to use papers that are natural, renewable and recyclable products and made from wood grown in well-managed forests and other controlled sources. The logging and manufacturing processes are expected to conform to the environmental regulations of the country of origin.

Orders: please contact Bookpoint Ltd, 130 Park Drive, Milton Park, Abingdon, Oxon OX14 4SE. Telephone: +44 (0)1235 827827. Fax: +44 (0)1235 400401. Email education@bookpoint.co.uk. Lines are open from 9 a.m. to 5 p.m., Monday to Saturday, with a 24-hour message answering service. You can also order through our website: www.hoddereducation.com

ISBN: 978 1 5104 4657 1

© Mark McGowan, Hyun Jung Owen and Aaron Deupree 2019

First published in 2019 by

Hodder Education,

An Hachette UK Company

Carmelite House

50 Victoria Embankment

London EC4Y 0DZ

www.hoddereducation.com

Impression number   10 9 8 7 6 5 4 3 2 1

Year   2023 2022 2021 2020 2019

Cover photo © sebastiangora/Shutterstock.com

Illustrations by Integra Software Services Pvt. Ltd., Pondicherry, India

Typeset in India by Integra Software Services Pvt. Ltd., Pondicherry, India

Printed in Slovenia

A catalogue record for this title is available from the British Library.

Contents

Introduction vi

Theme 1 Social organization 1

UNIT 1 Social relationships 1
Population change 1
Social services 5
Inequalities 9
Literature: *Animal Farm* 13

UNIT 2 Education 15
Early years education 15
Language and education 19
Graduation 25
Literature: *Narrative of the Life of Frederick Douglass, an
American slave* 28

UNIT 3 Law and order 30
Crime 31
Discrimination and the law 34
Imprisonment 38
Literature: *Want You Dead* 42

Theme 2 Experiences 44

UNIT 4 Leisure and holidays 44
Hobbies 45
Tourism 50
Sports 57
Literature: *Notes from a Small Island* 64

UNIT 5 Life stories 67
Professions 68
Migration 74
Trauma 80
Literature: *The Kite Runner* 87

UNIT 6 Customs and traditions 89
Traditions 89
Social norms and taboos 96
Dress codes and uniforms 101
Literature: *Dead Men's Path* 107

Theme 3 Identities 110

UNIT 7   Lifestyles 110
          Health 111
          Physical well-being 116
          Mental health 121
          Literature: *Wonder* 125

UNIT 8   Beliefs and values 127
          Culture (the influence of culture on identity) 128
          Values 133
          Beliefs 136
          Literature: *The Curious Incident of the Dog in the Night-Time* 140

UNIT 9   Language and identity 142
          The benefits of bilingualism 143
          English as a global language 147
          Gender and identity 152
          Literature: *The Other Hand* 156

Theme 4 Human ingenuity 158

UNIT 10   Artistic expression 158
          Expression through culture 158
          Expression through movement 162
          Expression through images 166
          Literature: *Sonny's Blues* 170

UNIT 11   Communication and media 172
          Mobility 173
          Social media 177
          Entertainment 180
          Literature: *The Ballad of the Landlord* 185

UNIT 12   Innovation in science and technology 186
          Benefits to society 187
          Privacy 191
          The future 195
          Literature: *The War of the Worlds* 199

Theme 5 Sharing the planet 201

UNIT 13 The environment 201
Green power 201
Plastic pollution 206
Climate change 211
Literature: *The Coming Race* 217

UNIT 14 Human rights 220
Freedom of speech 221
Children's rights 226
Women's rights 232
Literature: *1984* 238

UNIT 15 Globalization 240
Cultural globalization 241
Trade globalization 245
Environmental globalization 250
Literature: *Of Mice and Men* 254

Grammar summary 256

Introduction

This book will help you to achieve three things:

1 To be a confident and creative linguist

To be proficient in English at Diploma level you need to gradually build up your level of skill in reading, listening to, speaking and writing the language.

- This new book will steer you along the path to proficiency by offering a range of texts and tasks that will provoke your curiosity, stimulate you to think and challenge you to be creative with the language.

- As you work through the course, you will acquire strategies for writing. In doing so, you will learn to be a good **communicator**, a key attribute of the IB learner profile. In keeping with the aims of the IB, our book also explores concepts and issues that will enable you to become more **knowledgeable**, make you a more **open-minded** student of other cultures, and turn you into a more **reflective** learner.

- We introduce and remind you of the 'nuts and bolts' of English language in regular **Grammar** features; these are linked to a **grammar summary** at the end of the book that covers all the key structures you need to know.

- The core of the new syllabus includes **Theory of Knowledge (TOK)** and **Creativity, Activity, Service** and these are woven into each unit. Listening comprehension now forms part of the assessment in Paper 2 and you will find listening comprehension exercises in every unit, some of which include videos or audios for added interest.

- Speaking activities such as role plays and debates are opportunities to be creative in the language.

2 To score the highest grades in IB English Language B

The activities in this course will prepare you thoroughly for the IB examination.

- Coverage of the prescribed IB themes is extensive. Each of the five themes, **Social organization**, **Experiences**, **Identities**, **Human ingenuity** and **Sharing the planet**, has three units dedicated to it. This book incorporates new texts that are up to date and cover a range of issues past and present.

- Reading and writing activities will prepare you for the examination by familiarizing you with a range of task types.

- Listening passages, photographs and a variety of speaking activities will help you prepare for your listening and oral exams.

- We link the topic content with both the **Theory of Knowledge (TOK)** and **Creativity, Activity, Service** to give you lots of practice in discussing ideas related to these important IB aspects of the Diploma programme.

- If you are studying at higher level, we feature a dedicated literature section in every unit, with topic-related extracts for you to enjoy, analyse and reflect on, from a wide range of notable English-language writers. Your acquaintance with the work of these writers will help you to prepare for your oral discussion of one of the two literary works you will study.

3 To appreciate the range of English culture

English culture is international: many countries around the world are bound together by the common thread of the English language, yet they also vary in culture and language. We have reflected that range in this book.

- The English in the texts and listening extracts is authentic and contains a range of local vocabulary and usage; this will help you to become familiar with the language of different countries in the English-speaking world.
- Many of the passages show the interconnectedness of the different countries that make up the Anglophone world, reinforcing the aim of the IB to give you a greater understanding of cultural diversity.

Finally…

To get the most out of this course make sure you:

- read and listen to English regularly, even if it is only for a short while
- contribute fully to class discussion in English; this is how you will build up confidence in using the language
- explore English language and culture for yourself – discovery is an essential part of learning!

Based on an introduction by Mike Thacker & Sebastián Bianchi

Key to icons used in this book

| | Reading | | Listening | V | Vocabulary |
| Writing | | Speaking | | G | Grammar |

The audio and transcripts for texts with a Listening icon and track number can be found at www.hoddereducation.com/IBextras

UNIT 1 Social relationships

REFLECTION

- Above are three images connected to social relationships. What is each image trying to communicate? Why is it necessary for people to understand these issues?
- Think of a problem or difficulty that a group of people have in the world today. With a partner, create an image that would communicate this difficulty to others. Explain your image to the class.

1 Population change

In small groups, discuss the following two questions:

1 What are the causes of the increases or decreases of certain age groups in a country's population?

2 What are some advantages and disadvantages of this?

One person should take notes on your responses and then share them with the rest of the class.

Australia at 24 million: The challenges facing a growing and ageing nation

This week Australia's population will reach 24 million. It's a demographic marker sure to trigger debate about the future – some will argue for a much bigger Australia, others want far slower population growth. But the milestone draws attention to the changing profile of the population, not just the total. There's much to celebrate in Australia's demographic data but it foreshadows big challenges as well.

Let's start with some positives. Maybe the brightest spot of all is our longevity. Improvements in living conditions, rising incomes and medical advances have combined to increase life expectancy at birth by about 33 years since Federation in 1901. Even since the mid-1970s life expectancy has improved by 10 years.

Females born in Australia can now expect to live 84.4 years and males 80.3 years. The Bureau of Statistics points out this is one the highest life expectancies in the world. On current trends it's likely that one in three children born today will live to 100.

The news is especially good for men. While they still have a lower life expectancy than women, the gender gap has been getting smaller. Since the turn of the century life expectancy for men has risen by 3.7 years compared with a 2.4 year improvement for women. Economic change, especially the nature of work, has contributed to this trend. Improved safety standards have lowered the death rate in relatively dangerous, male-dominated industries such as agriculture, mining, manufacturing and construction. Also, a larger proportion of men now work in knowledge-based office jobs where the risk of early death is low. The compulsory use of seat belts has also been a factor.

Australia's growing longevity is a decisive indicator of national progress. But longer life spans are contributing to a major challenge that officials have been warning us about for years: the ageing of the population.

In 1968, when Australia's population was half what it is today, just over 1 million people were aged over 65 – about 8 per cent of the total. But the number of [1]_____ 65s has now swelled to 3.57 million, or 15 per cent of the population. Meanwhile, the proportion of the [2]_____ aged 14 years and under has fallen from 29 per cent to 19 per cent in that period. [3]_____ mid-century one in four Australians will be aged over 65 and about one in 14 people will be aged over 85, up from one in 50 now.

One big policy response to Australia's changing demographic profile is the government's plan to [4]_____ lift the retirement age, now 65, in a bid to contain spending [5]_____ the age pension.

That raises an important question: will people be healthy enough to keep working into their late 60s or early 70s?

Economists have been investigating. This month America's National Bureau of Economic Research published research assessing the capacity of older people to work longer in a dozen developed countries including the US, UK, Canada, Japan and Spain. Overall the news is good. The researchers found 'substantial' additional work capacity among older people in all the countries studied, especially among 65- to 69-year-olds. In the United States, for example, economists Courtney Coile, Kevin Milligan and David Wise found the share of the population with the health capacity to work at ages 60 to 64 is about 17 per cent higher than the current level. But between the ages of 65 and 69, the difference was about 31 per cent.

'As people live longer and healthier lives, it may be appropriate for policymakers to consider how these gains in life expectancy should be divided between years of work and retirement,' the study concluded.

But that assumes there will be demand for employees in their 60s and beyond. Advocates for older workers claim that bias against those aged over 50 in the jobs market is endemic. This week's demographic landmark is a reminder that will have to change.

Matt Wade
www.smh.com.au/opinion/australia-at-24-million-high-points-and-hazards-in-the-demographic-data-20160212-gmszk2.htmlchange

A Match the start of each sentence with the correct ending

1 Maybe the brightest spot of all
2 While they still have a lower life expectancy than women,
3 Also, a larger proportion of men
4 One big policy response to Australia's changing demographic profile
5 The researchers found 'substantial' additional work capacity

a among older people in all the countries studied.
b the gender gap has been getting smaller.
c is our longevity.
d is the government's plan to gradually lift the retirement age.
e now work in knowledge-based office jobs.

B Choose a word from the box below to fill in the blank spaces numbered 1–5 in the text.

a pensions	**c** by	**e** over	**g** sometimes	**i** in
b gradually	**d** while	**f** population	**h** on	**j** under

Grammar

Prepositions and conjunctions of time

For

We use **for** with a period of time to say how long something happened. For example:

- **for** a week
- **for** a long time
- **for** the summer

During

We use **during** with a noun to explain when something happened:

- **during** class
- **during** my summer holiday
- She received a call **during** the speech.

While

We use **while** with a subject and a verb:

- I was listening to the radio **while** I was cleaning.
- **While** you were having fun, I was studying.
- We visited a lot of museums **while** we were in Italy.

By

Using **by** in reference to time means 'no later than':

- The new shopping centre should open **by** the end of June.
- We will complete the project **by** Monday.
- **By** the time you arrive, the game will be over.

Until

We use **until** to explain how long something continues:

- People must work **until** they are 65 years old.
- **Until** a new law is passed, people will continue to suffer.
- You can use my car **until** yours is fixed.

C Use *for*, *during*, *while*, *by* or *until* to fill in the blanks in the following sentences:

1 _____ you were at work, I was looking for an apartment for us to live in.
2 I want to arrive in London _____ 1 August.
3 The teacher became angry because a student was eating _____ the lesson.
4 _____ the winter break, I went skiing.
5 You will continue to make mistakes _____ you listen to instructions.
6 We will be finished decorating the house _____ the time Tina arrives.
7 They have been repairing that road _____ three months.
8 The road will be blocked _____ the damaged cars are removed.
9 _____ your eyes are closed, I want you to imagine that you are on a sunny beach.
10 _____ an hour, you have done nothing but complain.

D The words listed below are often used in relation to an aging population. Copy and complete the table by writing the meaning of each word in your own words. If you do not know the meaning, look it up. Then to solidify your knowledge, write your own sentences about an aging population, where you use each of the words in the table. Try to use more than one of the words in one sentence, when you can.

Word / Phrase	Meaning
1 demographic	
2 life expectancy	
3 gender gap	
4 pension	
5 retirement	

E Go to https://n.pr/2fGeClf and listen to the audio. You will hear a radio report on the lack of housing for a Native American community living on an Indian reservation in Wyoming. Copy and complete the table by matching the name of the correct person with each statement on the left.

Statement	Lynell Shakespeare	Patrick Goggles	Heidi Frechette	Vonda Wells
1 They do not have the money to build more homes.				
2 People are spending more money on repairing existing homes.				
3 It's difficult for children to learn in school when they live in such conditions.				
4 They do not have money to pay for electricity.				
5 Crowded homes can cause violence.				
6 Cultural values enhance their family life.				

F Choose a city or country where English is the native language. Research the changes in population there over the last 30–50 years. Look for the causes and effects of those changes. Create a chart or a graph of certain changes and present it to the class.

G Use the information you have gained in Question F above on the changing population of a city or country and write an article based on this information. Use your graph or chart as a visual aid and analyse the data. Use subheadings for short sections of the article, such as:

- 1990 to the present
- Causes
- Effects
- Recent developments
- Problems
- Solutions

■ TOK Links

To what extent does 'indigenous knowledge' change over time?

To what extent do 'areas of knowledge' increase our understanding of social change?

CREATIVITY, ACTIVITY, SERVICE

For a 'super project', organize a group of students to work with elderly people or an indigenous population in your community.

2 Social services

1   In the box below, there is a list of problems that can destroy a community. If you had to organize those problems into a list of which to solve first, what would your list look like? In small groups, organize the list below from 1 to 5, where #1 is the most important problem to solve first and #5 is the least important problem to solve, in comparison to the others.

    poor housing   poor medical services
    lack of electricity   unemployment
    lack of clean water

2   Below is a list of personal qualities. If a person were working to solve the problems listed in Question 1 above, which qualities would be most important for them to have to be successful? Again, in your group, create a list from 1 to 5 of the most important personal qualities to have to fight social problems.

    reliable   persistent
    efficient   passionate
    responsible

Interview with Sarah Soloane

The author interviews a social entrepreneur and promoter of off-grid renewable energy solutions, to learn more about what has made her successful and how others can learn from her experiences

Ken Fullerton, a field specialist at PlaNet Finance and based in Johannesburg, South Africa, works in the field of sustainable development. He recently caught up with Sarah Soloane, a social entrepreneur, EnerGcare Independent Distributor, promoter of off-grid renewable energy solutions and winner of the Renewable Energy Prize at the International Micro Entrepreneurship Awards held in Paris, France in December 2014 to learn more about what has made her successful and how others can learn from her experiences and lessons.

What does your role as an EnerGcare Independent Distributor entail?

My role involves helping people in my community to have reliable access to energy, help overcome unemployment and other social problems. The EnerGcare products are affordable to many people. I am responsible for marketing and selling off-grid clean energy products and I use many different approaches to do this.

[1] _____

When I first started I wanted to grow myself and help people in my community. One day I want to have my own shop where I sell my products and continue to serve my community. I also wanted my people to learn about energy saving products and why they should buy and use them.

[2] _____

I particularly wish to serve the youth and women in my community and help to uplift their lives so that they can stand for themselves and do something for a better life. Many of my people live in bad conditions in shacks and do not have basic services. By helping them with such products I want people to learn from me, improve their knowledge and encourage them to work for themselves and be ambitious.

[3] _____

There are a wide range of EnerGcare products. There are products for lighting, cooking and for charging your cell phone. The product that I have been the most successful at promoting is the EcoZoom efficient cook stove. All the products are easy and safe to use, help the user save money because they are efficient, they are healthier than many of the products currently being used (such as candles, paraffin / kerosene and brazier cook stoves) and they are reliable. They are socially beneficial because they are helping people overcome many of the energy challenges being faced in South Africa such as no electricity connection, high electricity, paraffin and oil costs, and power cuts.

[4] _____

I use a variety of different strategies and I understand that sometimes different ones are more likely to work than others. In order to market and sell my products I make use of a wide range of marketing materials provided to me (such as EnerGcare branded banners, clothing, flyers and posters) and I use demonstration products to explain to people how a product actually works and what its benefits are. I market products in different locations such as through my church network, by going house to house and door knocking, by distributing marketing materials and through family and friends. Because of the hard work I have already put in and the efforts I have made, I am now starting to get referrals where potential new customers phone me after having heard about me from an existing customer. This shows that interest is growing and people are looking for affordable new solutions to the energy challenges they face.

[5] _____

My personality and who I am today has been largely influenced by my background. I grew up in a rural village and saw first-hand how hard my parents had to work to look after me. My mother regularly had to walk long distances to fetch water and collect firewood, it was difficult for me to learn due to a lack of electricity and my family had very little money to purchase candles. Since my youth I have always maintained a strong desire to help other people particularly because many families are still living in the dark.

[6] _____

I feel that my community thinks that they are very lucky to have me as I share knowledge and information with them and bring them solutions to their energy problems. Women, in particular, appreciate the role I play because I am sharing history with them and together we can turn the old history into the new future. After returning from Paris with my International Micro Entrepreneurships Award many of the ladies in my church group took me out to lunch to congratulate me. I found that very special.

[7] _____

People must do something to support and stand up for themselves if they are unable to find a job. They should not just wait for the government to do something for them as this sets a bad example to others and might not ever happen. The South African government is currently overwhelmed trying to rectify many socio-economic development challenges. I am willing to give further advice and support if people contact me like I did when I was a panel speaker at the recently held Citi Micro Entrepreneurship Awards event in Johannesburg. People can sell anything that can help them in life as they must want to support themselves and their families properly.

[8] _____

It was excellent, it was wonderful! Never in a million years did I ever think that I would be invited abroad and get to go to Paris to receive an award at an international ceremony. I thank God for the chance to be selected as an entrepreneur and to show everyone the potential I have to grow and continue succeeding by helping others. I will never forget the memory.

Sarah, do you have any final advice or thoughts to share?

My advice is that to be an entrepreneur you don't always need to have a formal education. You need to have the desire to help yourself and others around you. You also need to be persistent and believe in yourself as you are likely to have challenges along the way.

Ken Fullerton is a field specialist at PlaNet Finance, based in Johannesburg. This interview first appeared on the Energy Blog. www.ngopulse.org/article/2015/05/13/interview-sarah-soloane

A **Some of the interviewer's questions have been removed from the text and are listed below. Choose the correct question for the blanks numbered 1–8. There are more choices than questions asked.**

a What has been your biggest success so far?

b How would you describe the market for sustainable solutions in South Africa?

c What would your advice be to other aspiring social entrepreneurs looking to make a positive impact on their communities?

d How was the experience of attending the International Micro Entrepreneurship Awards ceremony in Paris? It must have been amazing!

e How has South Africa changed since you became a social entrepreneur?

f What role can women play in your community?

g Tell us a bit more about the range of products you promote. Why are they socially beneficial to others?

h What strategies and techniques do you use to market and sell these energy-efficient products to potential customers?

i When you first started, what were your expectations?

j Are there any key features, techniques or aspects that you believe define you as a social entrepreneur rather than just a 'regular' one?

k How does your community feel about what you are doing and the products you are providing? Have you had positive reactions from them?

l Why do you consider yourself to be a social entrepreneur?

B **Words are best understood when you can see their 'roots' or 'related forms'.**

The root of a word is the word it comes from. For example, the root of 'disadvantaged' is 'advantage'. *Dis* means 'not having'. A related form is a change in a word to make it a different part of speech. For example, a related form of 'advantage' is 'advantageous'.

The words listed below were used in the interview. Copy the table and, for each word, write the root of one of the words, or a related form. Then explain how the word is connected to the text. The first one is done for you.

Word / Phrase	Root / Related form	Use in the text
1 social entrepreneur	society	Sarah Soloane is a social entrepreneur who created her own business to help society.
2 renewable energy		
3 sustainable development		
4 reliable		
5 unemployment		
6 responsible		
7 efficient		
8 strategies		
9 benefits		
10 potential		

C Write answers to the following questions using *would*, *will* or *would have*:

1 Where would you like to go to university?
2 When will the next Olympic games be?
3 What would you have done if you were the only person who came to English class yesterday?
4 You are afraid of heights and your friend wants you to go with him to the top of the Eiffel Tower. What would you say?

Rewrite this sentence using *would*:

5 'I will wait until your train arrives,' Nancy said.

Grammar

Would

We use **would**:

• when we imagine something:

   I **would** like to become a doctor.

• when we can't do something:

   I **would** go to the party, but I can't.

• sometimes as the past tense of 'will':

   'I will drive you to the cinema.' – Jack said he **would** drive us to the cinema.

We use **would have** when we imagine actions in the past:

• I **would have** done my homework earlier, but I had tennis practice after school.

 D Go to www.ted.com/talks/mitchell_besser_mothers_helping_mothers_fight_hiv#t-325705 and play the video. Cover the screen or turn it away so you cannot see it – this will help you prepare for the listening part of the exam. You will hear a TED Talk on AIDS in Africa. Listen to the talk up to 4:23 and answer the questions below.

1 What is 'the picture' of that he describes seeing at the beginning of his talk?
2 How many people are living with AIDS in sub-Saharan Africa?
3 Why does the speaker compare the United States to a hospital in South Africa?
4 What is the assumption about pregnant women with HIV?
5 What is the reality of pregnant mothers infecting their children in the United States?
6 What are two differences between pregnant mothers' treatment in the United States and South Africa?
7 When did treatment for AIDS begin in the United States?
8 How many babies are born with HIV in the United States each day?

 E In groups of three or four, create a podcast of a 3–5 minute report on people in need of assistance. Have a reporter introduce the story, interview people and tie the story together. Record your podcast and play it for the class.

 F Write an interview with someone who has worked to help improve the lives of people in a certain area of the world. Give a short introduction that includes background information on that person, then include the questions and answers.

To what extent is knowledge accessible to everyone?

To what extent can the natural sciences contribute to social change?

CREATIVITY, ACTIVITY, SERVICE

Create a website to inform your school community about communities in need of social services, such as: health care; heat and electricity; housing; employment; education. Tell people's stories, raise awareness and attempt to get students engaged in helping these communities.

3 Inequalities

Albert Einstein said 'A human being is part of a whole'. What he meant was that human beings are inter-connected and that we must understand this circle of connection. What does this mean as far as inequalities in societies are concerned? Draw a picture that demonstrates how human beings are part of a whole and then explain your picture to a classmate.

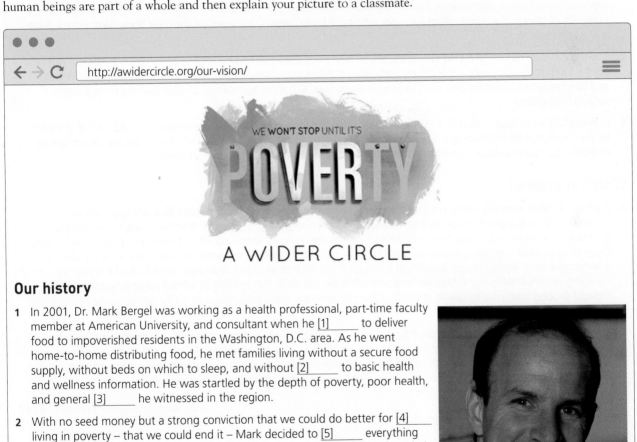

http://awidercircle.org/our-vision/

WE WON'T STOP UNTIL IT'S

POVERTY

A WIDER CIRCLE

Our history

1   In 2001, Dr. Mark Bergel was working as a health professional, part-time faculty member at American University, and consultant when he [1]_____ to deliver food to impoverished residents in the Washington, D.C. area. As he went home-to-home distributing food, he met families living without a secure food supply, without beds on which to sleep, and without [2]_____ to basic health and wellness information. He was startled by the depth of poverty, poor health, and general [3]_____ he witnessed in the region.

2   With no seed money but a strong conviction that we could do better for [4]_____ living in poverty – that we could end it – Mark decided to [5]_____ everything else in his life and converted his living room into a nonprofit office. He founded A Wider Circle with the mission of helping children and adults lift themselves out of poverty. His goal was to create an organization that [6]_____ address 'the whole person' – with programs that would not only tend to people's tangible needs but also to their 'inner needs.'

3   Using donated furniture and a handful of [7]_____ volunteers and health professionals, A Wider Circle furnished the homes of 774 children and adults and delivered 33 educational workshops at local shelters in [8]_____ first year of service. He met with social workers, shelter managers, school personnel, and nonprofit leaders in the region, exploring how to best reverse the trends of more people getting into poverty than finding a path out of it. Interns from local universities – and soon universities from across the country – joined the team each season. With each passing year, the organization became a larger and larger [9]_____ of the solution.

4   Today, A Wider Circle operates out of a 38,000 square-foot center, [10]_____ it purchased in May 2015. The organization has 50 staff members, 15 university interns, and more than 15,000 volunteers each year. It is their energy and [11]_____ that allows A Wider Circle to now furnish the homes of more than 16,000 children and adults each year and deliver [12]_____ programs to thousands of men, women, and children.

5   Though A Wider Circle has [13]_____ served more than 160,000 children and adults – through its educational programs and the provision of urgently needed beds, dressers, cribs, and more – Mark does not go to sleep each night on a bed of his own. Rather, he ends his 15-hour workdays by collapsing onto his couch or floor, pledging not to sleep in a bed until every child and adult in this country has a bed in which to sleep. Since A Wider Circle moved to its current location in 2008, Mark has worked seven days a week, [14]_____ week of the year.

6   Mark has been known to say that 'as one of us goes, so go all of us.' [15]_____ this is a powerful idea that many of us espouse, few of us live and breathe it each day. Mark's pledge to give up his own bed means that he can say to the hundreds of men and women calling each day who have been sleeping for years on the bare floor, 'I know how hard it is' – and mean it.

7   The organization has come a long way since 2001 – and even since the first handful of years when it was run out of Mark's living room with only a few interns each season. More than 500 calls per day now come in from individuals and families in need, people who want to help in some way, and from agencies of all sizes looking for assistance in serving their clients.

8   A Wider Circle has been called 'the quintessential grassroots movement' and has been twice named 'one of the best' by the Catalogue for Philanthropy. The organization is poised today to be a major part of the national movement to end poverty, to bring about an end to poverty for one individual and one family after another.

What's in a name?

9   It's more difficult than you might imagine to come up with the name for an organization that you hope will be responsible for helping millions of children and adults lift themselves out of poverty. That has always been the true goal here – however long it may take. And to do that, we are going to need each of us to shift our focus more toward those of us in need than we currently do. We know we can end poverty. If we were told that our lives depended on it, we would do it. Many lives do depend on it; in fact, I believe that all of our lives depend on it. And it is only by widening our understanding of how we exist and what we can do in this world that we will make it happen. That thought process made the following quote by Albert Einstein the appropriate place to go for selecting the name of the organization:

A human being is part of a whole, called by us Universe, a part limited in time and space. We experience ourselves, our thoughts and feelings, as something separate from the rest – a kind of optical delusion of our consciousness. This delusion is a kind of prison for us, restricting us to our personal desires and to affection for a few persons nearest us. Our task must be to free ourselves from this prison by widening our circles of compassion...

Mark Bergel, Founder, President & CEO

A **Choose the word that best fits the blank spaces 1–15.**

	a		b		c	
1	a	volunteers	b	volunteered	c	volunteer
2	a	access	b	potential	c	success
3	a	inequalities	b	disproportionate	c	services
4	a	these	b	them	c	those
5	a	add	b	hold	c	drop
6	a	will	b	would	c	wouldn't
7	a	dedicated	b	questionable	c	helping
8	a	their	b	its	c	those
9	a	work	b	whole	c	part
10	a	which	b	where	c	that
11	a	inspired	b	commitment	c	education
12	a	educational	b	educated	c	educate
13	a	too	b	been	c	already
14	a	fifty-two	b	all	c	every
15	a	Though	b	However	c	Nonetheless

B **Choose the correct answer for Questions 1–5.**

1 What was Dr. Bergel doing before he founded A Wider Circle?
   a Converting his living room into an office
   b Teaching at American University
   c Living in poverty
   d Doing research on inequality in society

2 How does A Wider Circle find furniture for people living in poverty?
   a It is given to them as donations
   b Social workers organize it
   c University interns are responsible for obtaining it
   d It is purchased through funding projects

3 To what is the phrase 'I know how hard it is' referring?
   a Being a volunteer
   b Having 500 calls a day
   c Developing an organization
   d Living without a bed

4 Which definition is closest in meaning to 'come a long way' as it is used in paragraph 7?
   a Taken a long time
   b Was far away
   c Developed significantly
   d Created more phone calls

5 How is Albert Einstein connected to the organization's name?
   a He also helped millions of children and adults in poverty
   b He talked about widening our circle of compassion
   c He said we are all limited by time and space
   d He was as famous as the organization wants to be

Grammar

For and *since*

We use *for* and *since* to say how long something happened.

- We use *for* for a period of time:

  *I have lived here **for** seven years.*

- We use *since* with the start of a period of time:

  *I have lived here **since** 2005.*

For and *since* are used with the present perfect:

*I have been playing football **since** I was young.*

*I have played the saxophone **for** years.*

C Use *for* or *since* with the words below to make a complete sentence. The first one is done for you.

It / raining / yesterday

It has been raining since yesterday.

1 Stephen / absent / work / a few days

2 / I / changed careers I / become a new person

3 Airplanes / existed / 1903

4 We / waiting / her / hours

5 I / played piano / I / very young

D Go to www.bbc.co.uk/programmes/b09v32jk and click 'Play'. You will hear a podcast about the inequality in pay between men and women in the United Kingdom. Listen to the podcast up to 3:20 and answer the following questions:

1 Why does the speaker begin the podcast by listing men's names?
   a Because they all contributed to Parliament square
   b Because they all contributed to women's right to vote
   c Because they are important and from different countries
   d Because a statue of an early feminist is about to be built next to them

2 Why does she read out a quotation from 1918?
   a Because women are still struggling to get equal pay in the workplace
   b Because it was exactly 100 years ago
   c Because it was important for women getting the right to vote
   d Because it was written in an economic journal

3 What has Sam Smithers noticed over the last three years?
   a You cannot picture the pay gap
   b The pay gap between men and women has not changed
   c Progress has been made
   d Her research has helped close the pay gap

4 Which reason is **not** given for the pay gap, according to Sam?
   a Part-time work
   b The number of hours worked
   c Women who are fired from their job
   d The work culture

5 How do 'the kinds of jobs' women are employed in contribute to the pay gap?
   a They are lower paid
   b They are valued less
   c They combine to give us the gender pay gap
   d They are connected with science and technology

E In small groups, role play a guided tour in a city or town where important social changes have taken place throughout its history. One person can act as the guide, highlighting important monuments or sites, while the others act as tourists who ask questions.

 F Create a website for a non-profit organization. List the tabs at the top, such as:

- About us
- History
- Testimonials
- Quick links

- Volunteer
- Help us
- Contact

Highlight one of those tabs and write the content for that page, including photos or images to complement the text.

■ TOK Links

How can we know what is ethical?

To what extent is 'shared knowledge' biased?

CREATIVITY, ACTIVITY, SERVICE

Organize a collection of unused items in your school and donate them to a community in need.

Organize an event at your school that promotes awareness of inequality. This could include TED-style speeches, round-table discussions and workshops.

■ Literature

HIGHER LEVEL

4 Animal Farm

Animal Farm, written by George Orwell in 1945, is the story of a group of animals that rebel and take control from the human owners of Manor Farm. The novel is written from the point of view of the animals, and it is a satire on the Russian Revolution of 1917. Through the actions of the animals, Orwell tries to show how the original ideas of the Russian Revolution were ignored and led to the dictatorship of Joseph Stalin. This excerpt depicts the moment when the animals rebel and take over the farm.

Now, as it turned out, the Rebellion was achieved much earlier and more easily than anyone had expected. In the past years Mr. Jones, although a hard master, had been a
5 capable farmer, but of late he had fallen on evil days. He had become much disheartened after losing money in a lawsuit, and had taken to drinking more than was good for him. For whole days at a time he would lounge
10 in his Windsor chair in the kitchen, reading the newspapers, drinking, and occasionally feeding Moses on crusts of bread soaked in beer. His men were idle and dishonest, the fields were full of weeds, the buildings
15 wanted roofing, the hedges were neglected, and the animals were underfed.

June came and the day was almost ready for cutting. On Midsummer's Eve, which was a

Saturday, Mr. Jones went into Willingdon and
20 got so drunk at the Red Lion that he did not come back till midday on Sunday. The men had milked the cows in the early morning and then had gone out rabbiting, without bothering to feed the animals. When Mr.
25 Jones got back he immediately went to sleep on the drawing-room sofa with the *News of the World* over his face, so that when evening came, the animals were still unfed. At last they could stand it no longer. One of the
30 cows broke in the door of the store-shed with her horn and all the animals began to help themselves from the bins. It was just then that Mr. Jones woke up. The next moment he and his four men were in the store-shed
35 with whips in their hands, lashing out in all directions. This was more than the hungry

animals could bear. With one accord, though nothing of the kind had been planned beforehand, they flung themselves
40 upon their tormentors. Jones and his men suddenly found themselves being butted and kicked from all sides. The situation was quite out of their control. They had never seen animals behave like this before, and
45 this sudden uprising of creatures whom they were used to thrashing and maltreating just as they chose, frightened them almost out of their wits. A minute later all five of them were in full flight down the cart-track
50 that led to the main road, with the animals pursuing them in triumph.

Mrs. Jones looked out of the bedroom window, saw what was happening, hurriedly flung a few possessions into a carpet bag,
55 and slipped out of the farm by another way. Moses sprang off his perch and flapped after her, croaking loudly. Meanwhile the animals had chased Jones and his men out on to the road and slammed the five-barred gate
60 behind them. And so, almost before they knew what was happening, the Rebellion had been successfully carried through: Jones was expelled, and the Manor Farm was theirs.

For the first few minutes the animals could
65 hardly believe in their good fortune. Their first act was to gallop in a body right round the boundaries of the farm, as though to make quite sure that no human being was hiding anywhere upon it; then they raced
70 back to the farm buildings to wipe out the last traces of Jones's hated reign. The harness-room at the end of the stables was broken open; the bits, the nose-rings, the dog-chains, the cruel knives with which Mr. Jones had
75 been used to castrate the pigs and lambs, were all flung down the well. The reins, the halters, the blinkers, the degrading nosebags, were thrown on to the rubbish fire which was burning in the yard. So were the whips. All
80 the animals capered with joy when they saw the whips going up in flames. Snowball also threw on to the fire the ribbons with which the horses' manes and tails had usually been decorated on market days.

85 "Ribbons," he said, "should be considered as clothes, which are the mark of a human being. All animals should go naked."

When Boxer heard this he fetched the small straw hat which he wore in summer to keep
90 the flies out of his ears, and flung it on to the fire with the rest.

Excerpt from Animal Farm *by George Orwell*

Answer the following questions:

1 What led to Mr Jones drinking more?
2 What are two examples of Mr Jones's neglect of the farm?
3 How were the animals able to get food on their own?
4 Why were Jones and his men surprised?
5 What kind of animal is Moses?
6 What was the first thing the animals did when they gained their freedom?
7 What does 'wipe out the last traces' mean in lines 70–71?
8 Which phrase shows the animals' excitement in lines 30–39?
9 Why did Boxer go to get his hat?

UNIT **2** Education

REFLECTION

- Create a caption for the picture above. Explain your decision.
- In groups or as a class, discuss the following questions:
  How has technology changed learning in the classroom?
  Should mobile phones be banned in the classroom?
  Do you think technology has had a negative or positive effect on students' learning?
  How must education change to meet the needs created by the changes in society today?

1 Early years education

In small groups, imagine that you have been asked to create a new school. What would the school buildings look like? What would you have children learn in elementary school, middle school and high school? Explain your decisions to the rest of the class.

First day of school: It's the parents crying – not the children

Mothers and fathers dabbed their eyes as children got stuck into their school day

■ Balbriggan's Educate Together opened their doors for a new year of junior infants and there were tears and laughter as the new students grappled with the curriculum

There [1] was / were tears and sniffles aplenty on the first day of school – but that [2] was / were just the parents. Most junior infants, well-versed to a world of pre-schools and childcare, eased into their new classrooms, oblivious to much of the fuss around them.

Parents dabbed their eyes and lingered at the door for a final glimpse of their little ones, before being gently reminded [3] with / by teachers to move on. That was the scene played out [4] in / at Balbriggan Educate Together National School in Co. Dublin and repeated in many other primary schools as the new academic year got under way.

Sarah McCormack and Julie Kells admitted that most of the morning [5] had been / has been spent trying to hide their tears from their children who were both starting school today.

"I messaged Julie this morning saying, '[6] Are / Were you crying?' And she replied 'Yes: for the fifth time'," she said.

"When they're at home, you're protecting them and now we're sending them off into the world. You [7] will be / won't be there for them. You hope they mix well and they listen to the teacher."

Princess

Sarah's daughter, Madison (4), meanwhile, bounced into class. She gave [8] the / a twirl as she showed off the princess dress she wanted to wear for [9] an / the occasion.

"She looks like she's going to a wedding," Ms McCormack laughed. "Tomorrow, she'll be in leggings and a T-shirt."

It was a morning of high emotion for Sorcha Maguire's parents. She was born with Down Syndrome and congenital heart disease, [10] who / which required two open-heart surgeries when she was still an infant.

"We weren't sure we'd ever see this day," said her mother, Collette Maguire. "Her cardiologist said at one point that it's only her fight that's keeping her alive… and it's what has her here today. She wants to be [11] as / like everyone else."

Sorcha, carrying her favourite Mr Tumble schoolbag, giggled and played with her older brother's hair as she waited to enter her new classroom.

"[12] There's been / It's been lots of emotion and excitement at home this morning," said Collette. "The school has been great and worked closely with us to make sure it all goes smoothly. She's more than ready. She's the [13] most / more sociable child. She'll be an asset to the class and loves mixing with kids."

Anna Alecsandrescu, originally from Romania, felt conflicted as she waved goodbye to her twin daughters, Jamine and Daphne.

"I'm a bit emotional, yes. But I'm happy [14] for / to see them in junior infants. I like this school and what it stands for."

The twins played happily with colouring books as she left. Another parent, Alexander Kuksjonok, lingered by the door of the classroom to see how his daughter Alisa was faring without him. She sat colouring in a workbook, seemingly without [15] a / the care in the world.

"I'm happy to see that she looks happy," he said.

Routine

The fact that parents are [16] more / most likely than pupils to break into tears these days is a change [17] which / who junior infants teacher Bronagh Lavin-Dixon has witnessed over recent years.

"The children [18] have / has nearly all been to pre-school before. They are used to the routine, to sitting down, to getting into a line, asking to go to the toilet which wasn't the case, say, 10 years ago," she said. "The separation [19] from / to parents can still be an issue and parents can help by showing there's nothing to be scared of, that it is a safe space and they will be back."

Balbriggan Educate Together, like many other schools around the country, has witnessed startling changes over the past decade. It opened in 2005, just when a crisis was blowing up in the town over a shortage [20] of / with school places for foreign nationals. Many non-Irish, who [21] found / find themselves frozen out of the education system, flocked to the new primary school, along with other multi-denominational schools built in the following years. School principal Fintan McCutcheon says local Irish families were initially reluctant to send their children [22] to / in the school.

"They were fearful of their children being in a minority. They were fearful [23] for / of low standards, such as whether not having English as a first language was a dominant thing in the classroom. They felt it was too much of a gamble."

Those concerns [24] have / had since melted away, said Mr McCutcheon. Today, the school has a mix of Irish and non-Irish which reflects the community. It is also well-resourced and benefits from being part of the Deis scheme for disadvantaged schools.

"Our children want for nothing," Mr McCutcheon said. "We are as well resourced a school as St Gerard's in Bray, and that's without taking any voluntary contributions. Our standardised attainment scores equate [25] with / to

the most middle-class areas in Dublin or elsewhere... We're hugely oversubscribed with 346 applications for 48 places this year."

Meanwhile, it's back to the job of settling in the newcomers: there are nerves to be soothed and worries to be addressed. He heads off, not to the classroom, but to a coffee morning upstairs for frazzled parents of junior infants.

"The first day of school is not quite as daunting as it used to be for children," he said. "That said, there can still be the odd tear or two."

Carl O'Brien

www.irishtimes.com/news/education/first-day-of-school-it-s-the-parents-crying-not-the-children-1.3203368

 A Select the correct option for each of the 25 pairs of underlined words in the article.

 B Based on the information given in the article, which of the following statements are true and which are false?

1 Parents were allowed to spend the first day at school with their children to help them adjust.
2 Children today are better prepared for primary school because they have attended pre-schools.
3 One little girl wore a wedding dress to school.
4 The parents worry about how they will mix with others.
5 Parents can help by showing there is nothing to be afraid of.
6 Since 2005, the Balbriggan school has remained the only one of its kind.
7 Irish parents were hesitant to send their children to the Balbriggan school.
8 The mix of students at the school reflects the area that surrounds the school.
9 The Balbriggan school is not as well resourced as other schools.

 C Match the quotation on the left with the person who said it on the right.

Quotation

1 "I like this school and what it stands for."
2 "We weren't sure we'd ever see this day."
3 "You hope they mix well and they listen to the teacher."
4 "I'm happy to see that she looks happy."
5 "They were fearful of low standards, such as whether not having English as a first language was a dominant thing in the classroom. They felt it was too much of a gamble."

Person

a Alexander Kuksjonok
b Sarah McCormack
c Fintan McCutcheon
d Collette Maguire
e Anna Alecsandrescu

Grammar

A / an and *the*

- We use **a** when we are talking about one item, event or action:
  *He bought **a** litre of milk.*
- We use **an** when it precedes a word beginning with a vowel:
  ***An** elephant likes to eat hay.*
- We use **a** when it is the first time we mention something:
  ***A** man approached me and asked me for directions.*
- We use **the** after the first time we mention something:
  ***The** man needed directions because he had never been to New York.*
- We use **the** when referring to something specific:
  *You will find an extra blanket in **the** closet.*
- We use **the** when we are familiar with the person, place or thing:
  ***The** floor needs to be cleaned.*
- We use **the** with the verb forms of *go to*:
  *He went to **the** bank to deposit some money.*

D **Fill in the blanks with either *a, an* or *the*.**

Last night, I went for [1]_____ walk. It was late and I couldn't see [2]_____ fence they had put up around the park, so I walked right into it. I cut my arm and knew I had to see [3]_____ doctor. There was no one around to ask for help and I did not have [4]_____ phone. Luckily, I remembered that [5]_____ old friend of mine lived near [6]_____ park, and so I walked to his house. When I rang [7]_____ doorbell at his house, I heard [8]_____ dog barking inside. [9]_____ dog's voice sounded like it was from [10]_____ very large dog, but when my friend opened the door, he laughed and said he didn't have [11]_____ dog. Instead of [12]_____ sound of [13]_____ bell, [14]_____ doorbell made [15]_____ sound of [16]_____ dog barking.

E **Go to https://n.pr/1ZfIZzs and click 'Play'. You are going to hear a radio broadcast on the importance of recess for young children. Listen to the report and answer the questions below.**

1 Where is the elementary school that is being talked about in the report?
2 How often do kindergarteners and first graders get recess at Eagle Mountain Elementary School?

Copy and complete the table and identify who says which of the following statements:

Statement	Debbie Rhea	Cathy Wells	Bob Murray
1 We don't need to control children.			
2 They are sharpening pencils less.			
3 Finnish children are healthier in many regards.			
4 Some schools cut recess for more academic work.			
5 Children are absorbing more information faster in the classroom.			
6 Children are developing better socially and emotionally with longer recess.			
7 Positive behaviour is also being worked on, in addition to recess.			

F To what extent is Mandela's statement below true?

 Education is the most powerful weapon which you can use to change the world.

Nelson Mandela

Why and how is education important? Make notes on your thoughts about this. Then, in groups of four or five, have a round-table discussion about the topic. Consider the following:

- Pre-school and primary school education
- High-school programmes
- University education
- Education outside the classroom
- Preparation for the real world
- Inequality in educational opportunities

G **Look again at the article on the first day of school. What do you notice about the way it was written? What is different about a newspaper article such as this one and another form of writing?**

Imagine that you are a reporter for your school's newspaper and you have been asked to write an article on the first day of school. Interview three or four people about their experiences on the first day at a new school. Use the information you gather to write your article. Take notes so that you can include quotations from the people you speak to. Remember:

- Give the article a heading.
- Start with a description of a scene then explain the topic of the article.
- Use a mixture of quotations and explanation to develop the article's ideas.
- End the article with something that refers back to your beginning.

■ TOK Links

To what extent does emotion affect our ability to acquire knowledge?

Where do 'personal knowledge' and 'shared knowledge' overlap in schools?

CREATIVITY, ACTIVITY, SERVICE

What type of 'super project' could a student organize with the primary section at his / her own school? What type of problems might children in that community face that older students could assist them with?

2 Language and education

1 Write the following words in your native language:
- night
- water
- mother
- home
- family

2 Share your words with other students and look for similarities and differences. Discuss why those similarities and differences might exist. What are other similarities and differences between your mother tongue and the English language?

Why learning a language is hard & how to make it easier

If you're struggling to learn a new language, *breathe*, you're not alone. Adults famously find language learning more difficult than children, whose super-flexible brains actually grow the connections necessary to learn an additional language.

But, why is it so hard to learn a foreign language, anyway? Put simply, it's hard because it challenges both your mind (your brain has to construct new cognitive frameworks) and time (it requires sustained, consistent practice). But there's more to it than that.

In this article we'll explore three major factors that make language learning difficult – and give you six tips to make it that much easier; to put a little spring in your language learning step!

The brain itself

Have you ever wondered why some people sail through Spanish and others can barely mutter 'hola'? Well, there is research which suggests that our own brain's unique wiring can pre-determine language success. In a study conducted at McGill University, participants' brains were scanned before and after undergoing an intensive 12-week French course. Researchers [1]_____ that stronger connections between brain centers involved in speaking and reading were seen in the better-performing participants. While this could [2]____ that some people are simply cognitively better equipped for language learning, it doesn't mean that everyone shouldn't try (and yes, it really is that good for you)!

[Example]_____

After-work classes, studying abroad, apps, talking with your foreign partner, working overseas, taking an intensive language [3]_____ – there are so many ways to learn a language. However, it's clear that because adults have to, you know, *be adults*, we simply can't learn 'implicitly' as young children do, by following around a nurturing native speaker

all day. Unfortunately, our more sophisticated grown-up brains [4]_____ in the way of learning.

As adults, we tend to learn by accumulating vocabulary, but often don't know how each piece interacts to form grammatically correct language. Research from MIT even suggests that adults' tendency to over-analyze hinders their ability to pick [5]_____ a foreign language's subtle nuances, and that straining harder and harder will not result in better outcomes.

Voxy's Katie Nielson blames this on the idea of 'language as object'. 'In history class, you start chronologically and you use dates in order of how things happened. That's just not how language-learning works,' she says. 'You can't memorize a bunch of words and rules and expect to speak the language. Then what you have is knowledge of "language as object". You can describe the language, but you can't use it.'

It's better, she says, to consider the process 'skill learning' (something you do), rather than 'object learning' (something you know). The remedy? Lose the perfection. Get messy in your learning – whether via app, class or travel – be happy to make mistakes and realize that you *will* feel silly at times.

[A]_____

We empathize! It's not easy to learn a language vastly different than your own (think English speakers struggling with Korean, or a Thai native wrestling with Arabic). Interestingly, studies show that these difficulties are not due to personal aversions to challenge, but rather, to neurological preferences. Research at Donders Institute and Max Planck Institute for Psycholinguistics indicates that our brains are not indifferent to the similarities between languages, and will reuse our native tongue's grammar and characteristics to make sense of a similarly-structured foreign language. Professor of psycholinguistics Nuria Sagarra agrees that learners of vastly differing languages have a greater challenge ahead: 'If your native language is more similar to the foreign language (e.g. your native language has rich morphology and you are learning a different rich morphology, such as a Russian learning Spanish), things will be easier.'

[B]_____

While learning a language will never be 100 per cent easy – nothing truly worthwhile is – it can definitely be enjoyable and successful. So what can you do? Luckily, a lot!

[C]_____

Why are you learning this language? For professional reasons? Pleasure? To communicate with family? With your goal in mind, actively search for opportunities to learn what *you* need and filter out what you don't (for example, vocabulary for talking about your work is very different to that necessary to navigate North America on a road trip). Focusing on your overall learning goal will help you combat burnout when it comes.

[D] _____

While our brains are no longer as flexible as kids' are, we *can* be as curious as them! Immersion and play are key, and for adults excellent approaches are taking a class in your language (French cooking in French or salsa in Spanish) or going on a study abroad program that combines language learning with travel and cultural immersion.

[E] _____

Already know one foreign language? Give yourself a head start by diving into a relatively (or very!) similar one (e.g., Portuguese / Spanish or Dutch / German or Norwegian / Swedish / Danish). Your previous learning experience will help you filter this new language more effectively.

[F] _____

'You need motivation to repeatedly seek out new language learning experiences, and motivation has been consistently

tied to language learning success,' says Angela Grant, from Pennsylvania State University. Find yours by buying your plane tickets right away, having a lovely notebook for class, exploring your city with a language exchange partner or making a ritual of doing your homework in a favorite coffee shop.

[G] _____

Come face to face with new input as much as possible! Change the language on your social media accounts, computer and phone. Download movies, listen to music and podcasts; read novels, non-fiction and magazines; watch documentaries and cook from foreign recipes.

[H] _____

Remember, you're learning a skill, not an object. Relish the ridiculous moments, especially during the first months, and do not fear failure or embarrassment. Make peace with the fact that your accent isn't perfect and you don't understand everything. None of this matters in the long run. What matters is commitment!

Erin
www.ef.com/blog/language/why-learning-a-language-is-hard

A The blog is separated into sections with subheadings. All of those headings have been removed, except for the first one, 'The brain itself'. Match each heading below to the section of the blog you feel is the best fit. The first one is done for you.

0   *How we learn = Example*
1   Know your goals and yourself
2   Two for one
3   Get surrounded
4   Realize that it's messy
5   Similarities between languages
6   Tips to make your journey easier
7   Find child-like joy
8   Motivate yourself

B Individual words have been removed from sentences in paragraphs 4–6. Choose the correct word from the box below to insert into each blank space. There are more words in the box than necessary to complete the exercise.

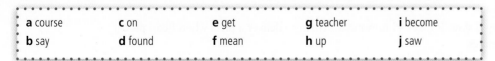

a course	**c** on	**e** get	**g** teacher	**i** become
b say	**d** found	**f** mean	**h** up	**j** saw

C Answer the following questions about the blog:

1 Why does the writer say 'breathe' in line 1?
   a To explain their nervousness
   b To ease people's fears
   c To make people read on
   d To try to be funny

2 Why is it easier for children than adults to learn a language?
   a Because they can follow around native speakers all day
   b Because they use the language when they play
   c Because their brains are different
   d Because they have more of a need to learn a language

3 What are two reasons it is difficult to learn a language as an adult?
   a Your mind and time
   b Your mind and money
   c Your native language and grammar
   d Your native language and travel

4 Why is it easier to learn a language similar to your mother tongue?
   a Because you can empathize
   b Because of research done at the Donders Institute
   c Because our brains are different
   d Because of a similar language structure

5 What does 'filter out' mean in the paragraph headed 'C'?
   a Eliminate
   b Exit
   c Create
   d Hesitate

D Read the completed sentences below, and then use the information given to complete each sentence starter using the comparative form *-er* or *more*. For example:

Jack can run a mile in 6 minutes and 4 seconds.
Ron can run a mile in 5 minutes and 53 seconds.

Ron is faster than Jack.

1 I tied the boat tightly to the dock, but the captain said it was not tight enough.
   The captain wanted me to…

2 Some people find chess boring. They prefer playing cards.
   Some people…

3 On Wednesday, the weather was not nice. On Thursday, it was very nice.
   The weather…

4 My maths exam was difficult and my French exam was easy.
   My maths exam…

5 Pizza delivery is slow. It takes 45 minutes for them to deliver a pizza when I can pick it up in 20 minutes.
   It is…

Grammar

Comparatives with *-er* or *more*

When we want to **compare two things**, in general we add *-er* to a short word of one syllable and we use *more* for words with two or more syllables. For example:

-er	*more*
fast – faster	slowly – more slowly
kind – kinder	interesting – more interesting
big – bigger	enjoyable – more enjoyable

'Spoken word' poetry is an oral reading of a poem, where emphasis is placed on word play, intonation and use of voice. It can become more of a dramatic reading, or a performance. In the 1980s, spoken word poetry grew in popularity with the founding of 'poetry slams'. Poetry slams are open competitions of dramatic readings of poems where people compete for the best reading of a poem. Listen to Taylor Mali's well-known spoken word poem 'What Teachers Make'. Mali is a former middle school teacher who wrote the poem in response to a comment he heard at a dinner party where someone repeated an old cliché: 'Those who can, do; those who can't, teach.'

Listen to the poem at https://youtu.be/RGKm201n-U4 and then answer the questions that follow.

1 What does Taylor Mali mean when he says 'I decide to bite my tongue'?
   a Not to become a lawyer
   b Not to eat any more
   c Not say anything in response
   d Not to continue being a teacher

2 When the lawyer asks Taylor 'What do you make?', what does he mean?
   a How much money do you make?
   b How much of a difference do you make?
   c How do you make students learn?
   d What do you make of my job?

3 When Taylor says he can make 'an A– feel like a slap in the face', what does he want from his students?
   a He wants them to behave
   b He wants them not to like him
   c He wants them to be honest
   d He wants them to feel they can do better

4 Why does he say he makes students 'apologize and mean it'?
   a Students are often mean
   b Students often criticize others
   c Students sometimes apologize and don't mean it
   d Students would rather say it than write it

5 What does he mean when he says 'Let me break it down for you'?
   a That the educational system is broken
   b That he wants to say it simply
   c He wants everyone to make a difference
   d That he is frustrated

 Work with a partner to create a dialogue where one person interviews the other about one of the following topics:

- The importance of learning other languages

- The difficulties of learning another language

- The importance of one's language to his / her culture

- The power of words

- Tips and tricks to learning a language

G **Choose one of the following writing exercises:**

1 Write a blog for people who want to learn English.

- Create an introduction on the importance of learning English.
- Write four headings that highlight important points to consider when learning a language.
- Finish with a small paragraph offering encouragement.

2 Write and deliver a spoken word poem on one of the following:

- The importance of school for everyone
- Racism in school
- Bullying in school
- The importance of a good teacher
- The importance of a good subject
- The difficulty, or beauty, of a particular subject
- The importance of working together
- What learning means

You could follow Taylor Mali's structure, where you begin with what someone has said about the topic, and then your response. Think of the following questions about your chosen topic to generate ideas:

- Why is this important?
- What are good examples of this topic?
- What creates problems?
- How can we solve them?
- What are the key words related to this topic?
- Remember to write it like a poem, with lines and stanzas, and possibly rhyme, but also think about how you would read it; which words you would emphasize and where you would pause.

■ TOK Links

To what extent does language shape our reasoning?

To what extent does language create bias?

CREATIVITY, ACTIVITY, SERVICE

Is there a group of people in the city or town where you live that you and other students could go to and help them learn English?

Are there opportunities for groups of people to come to your school and engage in or observe activities or performances that they would enjoy and would enable them to enhance their English?

How could social media or technology be used in your school to help people learn English?

3 Graduation

Why do you think students graduating from certain schools wear caps and gowns? How are graduation ceremonies different in different countries? Look up the reasons behind one of these traditions and share them with the class.

J.K. Rowling's Harvard Commencement speech

1 President Faust, members of the Harvard Corporation and the Board of Overseers, members of the faculty, proud parents, and, above all, graduates.

2 The first thing I would like to say is 'thank you.' Not only has Harvard given me an extraordinary honour, but the weeks of fear and nausea I have endured at the thought of giving this Commencement address have made me lose weight. A win–win situation! Now all I have to do is take deep breaths, squint at the red banners and convince myself that I am at the world's largest Gryffindor reunion.

3 Delivering a Commencement address is a great responsibility; or so I thought until I cast my mind back to my own graduation. The Commencement speaker that day was the distinguished British philosopher Baroness Mary Warnock. Reflecting on her speech has helped me enormously in writing this one, because it turns out that I can't remember a single word she said. This liberating discovery enables me to proceed without any fear that I might inadvertently influence you to abandon promising careers in business, the law or politics for the giddy delights of becoming a gay wizard.

4 You see? If all you remember in years to come is the 'gay wizard' joke, I've come out ahead of Baroness Mary Warnock. Achievable goals: the first step to self improvement.

5 Actually, I have wracked my mind and heart for what I [1] _____ to say to you today. I have asked myself what I [2] _____ I had known at my own graduation, and what important lessons I have learned in the 21 years that have expired [3] _____ that day and this.

6 I have come up with two answers. On this wonderful day when we are [4] _____ together to celebrate your academic success, I [5] _____ decided to talk to you about the benefits of failure. And as you stand on the threshold of what is sometimes called 'real life', I want to extol the crucial importance of imagination.

7 These may seem quixotic or paradoxical choices, but please bear with me.

8 Looking back at the 21-year-old that I was at graduation, is a slightly uncomfortable experience for the 42-year-old that she has become. Half my lifetime ago, I was striking an uneasy balance between the ambition I had for myself, and what those closest to me expected of me.

9 I was convinced that the only thing I wanted to do, ever, was to write novels. However, my parents, both of whom came from impoverished backgrounds and neither of whom had been to college, took the view that my overactive imagination was an amusing personal quirk that would never pay a mortgage, or secure a pension. I know that the irony strikes with the force of a cartoon anvil, now.

10 So they hoped that I would take a vocational degree; I wanted to study English Literature. A compromise was reached that in retrospect satisfied nobody, and I went up to study Modern Languages. Hardly had my parents' car rounded the corner at the end of the road than I ditched German and scuttled off down the Classics corridor.

****

11 Ultimately, we all have to decide for ourselves what constitutes failure, but the world is quite eager to give you a set of criteria if you let it. So I think it fair to say that by any conventional measure, a mere seven years after my graduation day, I had failed on an epic scale. An exceptionally short-lived marriage had imploded, and I was jobless, a lone parent, and as poor as it is possible to be in modern Britain, without being homeless. The fears that my parents had had for me, and that I had had for myself, had both come to pass, and by every usual standard, I was the biggest failure I knew.

12 So why do I talk about the benefits of failure? Simply because failure meant a stripping away of the inessential. I stopped pretending to myself that I was anything other than what I was, and began to direct all my energy into finishing the only work that mattered to me. Had I really succeeded at anything else, I might never have found the determination to succeed in the one arena I believed I truly belonged.

https://news.harvard.edu/gazette/story/2008/06/text-of-j-k-rowling-speech/

A Some of the following words have been removed from the text. Choose the word that best fits each blank space (1–5), both in meaning and grammatically.

a had	**c** gathered	**e** also	**g** wish	**i** ought
b between	**d** have	**f** probably	**h** for	**j** between

B Answer the following questions:

1 Why does J.K. Rowling say it's a 'win–win situation' in the second paragraph?
2 How did Baroness Mary Warnock's speech help J.K. Rowling's?
3 Which word in paragraph 4 or 5 means 'searched'?
4 Which word in paragraph 7 or 8 is closest in meaning to 'goals'?
5 How did failure actually help J.K. Rowling?

C Match each beginning of a sentence on the left with the correct ending on the right. There are more endings than necessary.

1 I was striking an uneasy balance between…
2 The world is quite eager…
3 A compromise was reached that…
4 I was convinced that…
5 Failure meant…

a in retrospect satisfied no one.
b satisfied my parents.
c what I wanted to do and what I thought I should do.
d I was a failure.
e the only thing I wanted to do was write novels.
f that period of my life was a dark one.
g the ambition I had for myself and what those closest to me expected.
h to give you a set of criteria if you let it.
i a stripping away of the inessential.
j to see you fail

Grammar

Parallelism

Parallelism is used to balance the structure of a sentence so that pairs or groups of words are written in a similar form.

Parallelism is used in a list or a series:

• **Incorrect:** *Sofia likes to ride a bike, play the piano and talking to her friends.*

  The verbs have to follow the same pattern: *to ride … play … and talk.*

• **Correct:** *Sofia likes to **ride** a bike, **play** the piano and **talk** to her friends.*

Parallelism is also used when things are compared:

• **Incorrect:** *He is more interested in acting in a play than he is to play basketball.*

• **Correct:** *He **is** more **interested in acting** in a play than he **is in playing** basketball.*

Parallelism is used with linking words that connect two ideas, such as: *not only … but also; Although…; Even though…;* and *Despite the fact that…*:

• **Incorrect:** *Margaret not only sings in a choir, but she is also organizing two after-school clubs.*

• **Correct:** *Margaret not only **sings** in a choir, but she also **organizes** two after-school clubs.*

D Write three of your own sentences where you practise parallel structure. Write one sentence similar to each of the examples above: one with a list of actions, one that includes comparison and one that uses one of the linking words listed above.

E Listen to Larissa Martinez's 2016 high-school graduation speech at https://youtu.be/k2rNCD2e1P8, from 2:43 to 6:00, and say which of the following statements are true and which are false:

1 The speaker now lives outside the United States.
2 She was born in McKinney.
3 She took care of her sister at a young age.
4 She had a washing machine and the internet, just like other children.
5 Her father was abusive.
6 Most people don't want to keep their struggles behind closed doors.
7 Her intelligence was questioned.
8 She is not a legal American citizen.
9 Her family became wealthy in the United States.
10 She talks about expectations and reality.

 F In groups of two or three, identify a video of a speech that you find impressive and prepare to analyse it for the class.

1 Before showing it to the class, explain what they are about to see and why it is impressive.
2 Show the speech to the class.
3 After viewing the speech, have each student in the group explain one or two important speaking techniques used, such as structure, word choice, body language, anecdote, direct address, repetition and / or rhetorical questions.

 G Imagine you are graduating from high school and you have been asked to give a graduation speech. Write your speech. Remember:

■ Address the audience.
■ Refer to the moments that were important.
■ Tell a short story.
■ Ask a question or two.
■ Mention what you hope for everyone for the future.

■ TOK Links

From the speeches of J.K. Rowling and Larissa Martinez, what can be considered 'shared knowledge' and 'personal knowledge'?

How can imagination play a role in our acquisition or transmission of knowledge?

CREATIVITY, ACTIVITY, SERVICE

Create a video, a website, posters or a podcast on the truths / myths about immigration, and share it with the school community.

■ **Literature**

4 Narrative of the Life of Frederick Douglass, an American slave

Frederick Douglass was a former slave who lived from 1818 to 1895. He was born into slavery in the United States, and at a very young age he learned the importance of reading. His slave owners would not let him learn how to read because they did not want him to become educated and to demand his freedom. So, young Frederick found a way to get other young white boys to teach him to read, which is described in this extract. Douglas escaped from his slave owners and moved to the north of the United States, where he became a spokesperson against slavery. He wrote a memoir of his life, called the *Narrative of the Life of Frederick Douglass*, which was published in 1845. The following is an excerpt from that memoir.

My mistress was, as I have said, a kind and tender-hearted woman; and in the simplicity of her soul she commenced, [1]_____ I first went to live with her, to treat me as she
5 supposed one human being ought to treat another. In entering upon the duties of a slaveholder, she did not seem to perceive that I sustained to her the relation of a mere chattel, and that [2]_____ her to treat
10 me as a human being was not only wrong, but dangerously so. Slavery proved [3]_____ injurious to her as it did to me. When I went there, she was a pious, warm, and tender-hearted woman. There was no sorrow or [4]_____
15 for which she had not a tear. She had bread for the hungry, clothes for the naked, and comfort for every mourner that came within her reach. Slavery soon proved its ability to divest her of these heavenly qualities. Under
20 its influence, the tender heart [5]_____ stone, and the lamblike disposition gave way to one of tiger-like fierceness. The first step in her downward course was in her ceasing to instruct me. She now commenced to practise
25 her husband's precepts. She finally became even more violent in her opposition than her husband himself. She was not satisfied with simply doing as well as he had commanded; she seemed anxious to do better. Nothing
30 seemed to make her more angry than to see me with a newspaper. She seemed to think that here lay the danger. I have had her rush at me with a face made all up of fury, and snatch from me a newspaper, in a manner
35 that fully revealed her apprehension. She was an apt woman; and a little experience soon demonstrated, to her satisfaction, that education and slavery were incompatible with each other. From this time I was most
40 narrowly watched. If I was in a separate room

any considerable length of time, I was sure to be suspected of having a book, and was at once called to give an account of myself. All this, however, was too late. The first step
45 had been taken. Mistress, in teaching me the alphabet, had given me the inch, and no precaution could prevent me from taking the ell. The plan which I adopted, and the one by which I was most successful, was that
50 of making friends of all the little white boys whom I met in the street. As many of these as I could, I converted into teachers. With their kindly aid, obtained at different times and in different places, I finally succeeded in learning
55 to read. When I was sent of errands, I always took my book with me, and by going one part of my errand quickly, I found time to get a lesson before my return. I used also to carry bread with me, enough of which was always
60 in the house, and to which I was always welcome; for I was much better off in this regard than many of the poor white children in our neighborhood. This bread I used to bestow upon the hungry little urchins, who,
65 in return, would give me that more valuable bread of knowledge. I am strongly tempted to give the names of two or three of those little boys, as a testimonial of the gratitude and affection I bear them; but prudence
70 forbids;—not that it would injure me, but it might embarrass them; for it is almost an unpardonable offence to teach slaves to read in this Christian country. It is enough to say of the dear little fellows, that they lived on
75 Philpot Street, very near Durgin and Bailey's shipyard. I used to talk this matter of slavery over with them. I would sometimes say to them, I wished I could be as free as they would be when they got to be men. "You will
80 be free as soon as you are twenty-one, but I

am a slave for life! Have not I as good a right to be free as you have?" These words used to trouble them; they would express for me the liveliest sympathy, and console me with the 85 hope that something would occur by which I might be free. I was now about twelve years old, and the thought of being a slave for life began to bear heavily upon my heart.

Excerpt from Narrative of the Life of Frederick Douglass, an American slave *by Frederick Douglass*
www.ibiblio.org/ebooks/Douglass/Narrative/Douglass_Narrative.pdf

A **Select the right answer to each of the following questions:**

1 How did the mistress change from when the narrator first went to live with her?
   a She changed from being kind to being aggressive
   b She changed from giving clothes to the poor to taking them away
   c She changed from listening to her husband to disobeying him
   d She changed from treating the narrator as a slave to treating him as a human being

2 Why did the mistress not want the narrator to read the newspaper?
   a Because the news stories made her angry
   b Because the news stories were all about slavery
   c Because she did not want him educated
   d Because she did not want him to avoid his work

3 How did the narrator learn to read?
   a His mistress taught him
   b He learned from boys on the street
   c He taught himself
   d He learned from his teachers at school

4 Why did the white boys want the narrator's bread?
   a They did not want slaves to have bread
   b They preferred bread to reading
   c They were embarrassed by where they lived
   d They were poor and hungry

5 How did the white boys react to the narrator's thoughts about him never being free?
   a They were heavy-hearted
   b They were annoyed
   c They were sympathetic
   d They were pessimistic

B **Use the words in the box to fill in the missing words for numbers 1–5 in lines 3–20.**

a however	c to	e just	g terror	i became
b as	d when	f was	h for	j suffering

C **Answer the following questions:**

1 Which word in lines 20–25 means 'teach'?
2 Which word in lines 30–35 means 'grab'?
3 Which phrase in lines 40–45 most nearly means 'explain'?
4 To what is the narrator referring when he says the 'bread of knowledge' (line 66)?
5 What idea is the writer referring to when he says 'bear heavily upon my heart' (last line)?

UNIT **3** Law and order

REFLECTION

Above are seven screenshots from the 1963 film *Charade*.
- Look at each of the first three pictures. What do you think the filmmaker was trying to communicate with each image? Why do you think this?
- Look at images 4–7. With a partner, use these shots to imagine the story of the film. Tell your story to the class.
- With a partner, discuss the following questions:
  Why do people commit crimes?
  What are the best ways to reduce crime?
  How and why are innocent people sometimes imprisoned?
  When and why should laws change?
  Why do people seem so fascinated with films or series about crime, police work or lawyers?

1 Crime

If you had to create a graph, with crime on one side and a factor influencing crime on the other, what would that other factor be? Draw the graph where you depict the relationship of that factor to crime over a certain period of time, in a particular country. Do not look up real facts. Draw the graph based on what you imagine to be true. When you are finished, you can look up the true facts and see how close you were to the truth. Share your discovery with the class.

The truth about criminal cases

The purpose of this page is to shed some light on how long it typically takes between an offence being committed and the case being resolved in a criminal court.

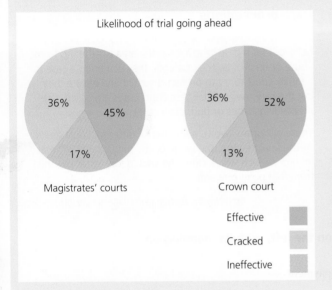

Likelihood of trial going ahead

Magistrates' courts — 36%, 45%, 17%

Crown court — 36%, 52%, 13%

Effective
Cracked
Ineffective

Magistrates' or Crown Court?

All criminal cases start in the magistrates' court. Depending on the seriousness of the crime the case will either take place in a magistrates' court from start to finish, or will be referred from a magistrates' court to a higher court, usually the Crown Court.

Over half of all criminal court trials don't go ahead as [1] planned, which uses up court time. Some, called 'cracked' cases, don't go ahead on the intended date at very short notice but don't need rescheduling – this might be because the [2] defendant entered a guilty plea, or the case is dropped by the prosecution. But other trials that don't go ahead and do need rescheduling are called 'ineffective' – this might be because the prosecution or the defence aren't ready to begin the trial, or the defendant doesn't attend as instructed. Those cases that do go ahead are said to be 'effective'.

How the courts work

There are different [3] types of courts in England and Wales which cover between them all legal disputes, from defendants accused of crimes, consumers in debt, children at risk of harm, businesses involved in commercial disputes or individuals asserting their employment rights. The main three types of court are:
- criminal courts – dealing with all cases where a crime has been committed and there is enough evidence [4] gathered against the alleged offender for there to be a reasonable chance of a conviction
- civil courts – dealing with disputes between private individuals and/or organisations, such as the non-repayment of a debt, personal injury, the breach of a contract concerning goods or property, housing disputes, bankruptcy or insolvency
- family courts – dealing with disputes relating to family matters including divorces, [5] disputes about financial issues or custody of the children following the breakdown of a relationship, domestic violence, adoption or protection of children from abuse or neglect.

Criminal cases

Just 19% of a criminal case on average is spent in court.

All criminal court cases start in a magistrates' court, and the vast majority will finish there. A small number will be referred to a higher court, usually the Crown Court.

Cases at magistrates' courts

Some offences, such as motoring [6] offences or disorderly behaviour, are dealt with only by magistrates' courts. They are known as summary offences. The maximum punishment for a single summary offence is six months in prison, and/or a [7] fine of up to £5,000.

About 1.5 million to 2 million criminal cases go through the magistrates' courts each year.

Serious cases

The most serious offences like murder, robbery or rape can only be dealt with in the Crown Court, which is able to hand out more [8] severe sentences. A number of crimes, including certain drug offences and serious fraud offences, can be dealt with by either magistrates' courts or the Crown Court – these are called either-way offences

About 100,000 cases per year are passed to the Crown Court to be tried. A further 40,000 cases are also passed to the Crown Court because the punishment the magistrates' court thinks the defendant deserves is more than it can give.

Civil cases

In England and Wales, civil disputes – those not relating to family disputes or the committing of a crime – are usually dealt with at the county courts, sometimes called the small claims courts.

Bringing a case to court

Civil disputes which are brought to court are called claims. Once a claimant has brought a case to court, the defendant – the person or organisation against whom they are bringing the case – has 14 days to decide what to do in response. They can:

- do nothing
- settle the dispute by coming to an agreement with the claimant
- challenge the case, also called 'making a defence'.

If the defendant does nothing, then the claimant can ask the court to order the defendant to pay the amount claimed. If the defendant continues to challenge the case and cannot reach a [9] settlement with the claimant, then the case will be decided in court at a hearing.

Types of cases

Civil hearings are presided over by a single judge, without juries. There are two main types:

- small claims hearings – usually where the value being disputed is less than £5,000
- trials – usually where the value being disputed is greater than £5,000.

About 1.5 million to 2 million civil claims are brought to the county courts each year. But not all civil disputes are dealt with at the county courts. Particularly important, complex or substantial cases are instead [10] dealt with in the High Court. Cases relating to a failure to pay council tax or child maintenance are dealt with at magistrates' courts.

Family courts

In England and Wales, disputes relating to family matters are dealt with in the single family court. Before 22nd April 2014, family cases were dealt with at Family Proceedings Courts (part of magistrates' courts) or at County Courts.

Family court cases are presided over either by magistrates or judges and are without juries.

Care proceedings

Where the social services department of a local authority believes that a child who lives in the area is suffering from abuse or neglect by their parents, they can bring a case to a family court to try to protect the child and ensure they get the care they need. These court cases are called care proceedings cases or public law cases.

These will often involve a number of different court hearings. At the final hearing, the judge or the magistrates will make an order which will decide who should look after the child from that point onwards.

http://open.justice.gov.uk/courts/criminal-cases

 A **Match the word from the text (numbers 1–10) on the left, with its meaning on the right (a–j).**

1	planned	a	payment
2	defendant	b	serious
3	types	c	collected
4	gathered	d	accused
5	disputes	e	agreement
6	offences	f	taken care of
7	fine	g	scheduled
8	severe	h	kinds
9	settlement	i	disagreements
10	dealt with	j	crimes

 B **Is each of the following sentences true or false?**

1 17% of cases going ahead in the Crown Court are labelled 'ineffective'.
2 In 'care proceedings' the judge or magistrate decides who will take care of children in child abuse cases.
3 A civil hearing will go to trial if the value of the dispute is greater than £5000.
4 Cases dealing with disputes over money will go to the civil courts.
5 Cases dealing with family matters are presided over by juries.
6 The 'defendant' is the person who brings the claim to a court.
7 Cases involving disorderly behaviour can result in either a prison sentence of a fine.
8 An ineffective case needs rescheduling.
9 The majority of court cases are referred to the Crown Court.
10 Court cases that do not go ahead as planned are called 'cracked cases'.

Grammar

Direct and indirect (or reported) speech

- When **dialogue** is written, or a journalist quotes someone, the speaker's words are put in quotation marks ('…' or "…") and it is noted who said it. For example:

  'I saw a man wearing a green hat enter the building,' the witness said.

  Notice there is a comma inside the quotation mark, before 'the witness said'. You always use a comma before indicating who spoke.

- **Indirect, or reported, speech** is when someone retells, or reports, what was said. For example:

  The witness said that he saw a man wearing a green hat enter the building.

  Often this form begins with a structure like 'He said that…'.

- Note that when someone speaks in the present tense in a quotation, the verb of the reported speech is changed to the past tense. Reported speech is always in the past tense. For example:

  Direct speech: *'I'm going to the cinema,' she said.*

  Reported speech: *She said that she was going to the cinema.*

C Change the following examples of direct speech into reported speech:

1 'I want to improve my English,' Alya said.
2 'We will clean our rooms,' the children said.
3 'Vijay is a close friend of mine,' Asha said.
4 'That couch is expensive and I don't have enough money to buy it,' he said.
5 'John and Carol are going to adopt a child,' she said.

D Go to https://n.pr/2FUodlx and press 'Play'. You will hear an interview with Patrick Sharkey, who has written a book on the decline of violence in American cities. Listen to the interview and answer the questions below.

Complete the following gaps. You will need no more than three words for each gap.

1 Chicago had a _____ last year to 650 homicides.
2 Sharkey says the country saw violence as a _____ and began to mobilize.
3 More police is a reason crime fell but it also brought some of _____.
4 Sharkey has looked at how changes in population have affected _____.
5 Poor families in Cleveland, Detroit and Baltimore are _____ because of increased rents.

Answer the following questions:

6 When did crime start falling in the United States, according to Sharkey?
7 What, does the presenter suggest, might 'push out' poor families from certain city neighbourhoods?
8 According to Sharkey, 25 years ago what was the biggest problem in cities, aside from violence?
9 What are two effects of lower homicide rates in big cities?

In small groups, conduct a debate on one of the following statements:

- 'Guns don't kill, people do.'
- 'The possession of a firearm is a person's right.'
- 'All guns should be illegal in the United States.'
- 'Racial profiling is unethical.'
- 'The pursuit of justice is more often racist, than not.'

Do some research on the topic. Give each group member a role:

- One member introduces the topic and explains the group's position on it. That same person can also give the concluding remarks.
- Each group member takes a turn giving one point with one supporting example.

There can be organized time for rebuttal from both sides, but each student should be able to present his / her prepared points.

 Write an opinion piece for the school newspaper on crime, guns or violence.

- Begin with a short story, an interesting quotation or a question, to grab the reader's attention.
- Continue by giving your argument, point by point.
- Include quotations or statistics to support your argument.
- Include the opposing point of view and give your response to it.
- End with a memorable sentence or quotation that might be connected to how you began the opinion piece (that is, your opening quotation, question or story).

■ TOK Links

To what extent can the human sciences increase our knowledge?

To what extent is our perception biased?

CREATIVITY, ACTIVITY, SERVICE

Create a club at your school where you raise awareness about violence or crime in the local or global community.

2 Discrimination and the law

Discuss the following questions as a class:

1 Why were people discriminated against in the past in certain countries?
2 What did people do to fight against that discrimination?
3 How are people still discriminated against today?
4 What can be done to fight this form of discrimination?

Screenplay of 12 Angry Men

Below is an excerpt from the screenplay for the film *12 Angry Men*. The scene describes a discussion between jury members of a murder trial. None of the members of the jury has a name. Instead, they are called No. 1, No. 2, No. 3, and so on.

FOREMAN

All right. Now, you gentlemen can handle this any way you want to. I mean, I'm not going to make any rules. If we want to discuss it first and then vote, that's one way. Or we can vote right now to see how we stand.

NO.7

Let's vote now. Who knows, [1] _____ we can all go home.

NO. 10

Yeah. Let's see who's where.

NO. 3

Right. Let's vote now.

FOREMAN

Anybody doesn't want to vote?

(*He looks around the table. There is no answer.*)

Okay, all those voting guilty [2] _____ your hands.

[*Seven or eight hands go up immediately. Several others go up more slowly. Everyone looks around the table.*]

[*There are two hands not raised, NO. 9's and NO. 8's. NO. 9's hand goes up slowly now as the foreman counts.*]

FOREMAN

Nine... ten... eleven... That's eleven for guilty. Okay. Not guilty?

(*NO. 8's hand is raised.*)

One. Right. Okay. Eleven to one, guilty. Now we know where we are.

NO. 3

(*Sarcastically*)

Somebody's in left field.

(*To NO. 8*)

You think he's not guilty?

NO. 8

(*Quietly*)

I don't know.

NO. 3

I never saw a guiltier man in my life. You sat right in court and heard the same thing I did. The man's a dangerous killer. You could see it.

NO. 8

He's nineteen years old.

NO. 3

That's old enough. He knifed his own father, four inches into the chest. An innocent little nineteen-year-old kid. They proved it a dozen different ways. Do you want me to list them?

NO. 8

No.

NO. 10

(*To NO. 8*)

Well, do you [3] _____ his story?

NO. 8

I don't know whether I believe it or not. Maybe I don't.

NO. 7

So what'd you vote not [4] _____ for?

NO. 8

There were eleven votes for guilty. It's not so easy for me to raise my hand and send a boy off to die without talking about it first.

NO. 7

Who says it's easy for [5] _____ ?

NO. 8

No one.

NO. 7

What, just because I voted fast? I think the guy's guilty. You [6] _____ change my mind if you talked for a hundred years.

NO. 8

I don't want to change your mind. I just want to talk for a while. Look, this boy's been kicked around all his life. You know, living in a slum, his mother dead since he was nine. That's not a very good head start. He's a tough, angry kid. You know why slum kids get that way? Because we knock 'em on the head once a day, [7]_____ day. I think maybe we owe him a few words. That's all.

[*He looks around the table. Some of them look back coldly. Some cannot look at him. Only NO. 9 nods slowly. NO. 12 doodles steadily. NO. 4 begins to comb his hair.*]

NO. 10

I don't mind telling you this, mister. We don't owe him a [8]_____. He got a fair trial, didn't he? You know what that trial cost? He's lucky he got it. Look, we're all grown-ups here. You're not going to tell us that we're supposed to believe him, knowing what he is. I've lived among 'em all my life. You can't believe a [9]_____ they say. You know that.

NO. 9

(*To NO. 10 very slowly*)

I don't know that. What a terrible thing for a man to believe! Since when is dishonesty a group characteristic? You have no monopoly on the truth.

NO. 3

(*Interrupting*)

All right. It's not Sunday. We don't need a sermon.

NO. 9

What this man says is very dangerous.

[*NO. 8 puts his hand on NO. 9's arm and stops him. Somehow this touch and his gentle expression calm the old man. He draws a deep breath and relaxes.*]

NO.4

I don't see any need for arguing like this. I think we ought to be able to behave like gentlemen.

NO.7

Right!

NO. 4

If we're going to discuss this case, let's discuss the [10]_____.

FOREMAN

I think that's a good point. We have a job to do. Let's do it.

Excerpt from 12 Angry Men, *screenplay by Reginald Rose*
www.scripts.com/script.php?id=12_angry_men_58&p=5

A Fill in each blank (numbered 1–10) with one of the words listed below.

a every	**f** word
b thing	**g** couldn't
c me	**h** raise
d guilty	**i** maybe
e facts	**j** believe

B Make a copy of the table below and put a tick next to the name of the person who said or did the following:

Questions	Foreman	No. 3	No. 4	No. 7	No. 8	No. 9	No. 10
1 Who votes not guilty?							
2 Who thinks the boy got a fair trial?							
3 Who combs his hair?							
4 Who counted the votes?							
5 Who discusses life in a slum?							
6 Who thinks No. 10 is dangerous?							
7 Who says you couldn't change his mind?							
8 Who says they should behave like gentlemen?							
9 Who calms down No. 9?							
10 Who is sarcastic?							

Grammar

Verbs with the prepositions *about*, *for* and *of*

Many English verbs are joined with prepositions to create new meanings of those verbs, for example 'to care **for** someone' or 'to care **about** them'.

C Below is a list of verbs that can be used with *about*, *for* or *of*. Choose one of these prepositions for each verb and write a sentence where the meaning of the words is clear. For example:

care + about: *Parents care about their children's education because they want them to have a successful future.*

1 accuse
2 talk
3 apply
4 dream
5 think
6 remind
7 complain
8 ask
9 wait
10 search

D Go to www.bbc.co.uk/programmes/b09tds71 and click 'Play'. You will hear a BBC podcast on sex discrimination and the law. Listen to the podcast up to 3:30 and decide which of the statements below are true and which are false.

1 Ms Brearley believed the company had 'gotten rid of her' because of her pregnancy because things had been going really well.

2 Ms Brearley set up a website because she realized that many women had encountered similar situations.

3 It is less than 40 years since parliament passed its first sex discrimination law.

4 The website does not let women tell their stories anonymously.

5 Ms Brearley was told by voicemail that her contract had ended.

6 Ms Brearley's first action was to write her employer a letter herself.

7 The employer ignored Ms Brearley's lawyer's letter.

8 Ms Brearley dropped the case because she discovered she had a high-risk pregnancy.

9 There was a doubt in Ms Brearley's mind that she may have lost her position because she was not doing her job properly.

10 The programme will also discuss how graffiti artists were awarded money for damage caused to their art.

 E Role play a court case for someone accused of sexual discrimination, racism or 'disturbing the peace' by protesting. Have each student play a role such as a lawyer, a judge, a witness and / or the accused.

 F Choose one of the following:

■ Write a letter from the point of view of someone who has been discriminated against. Think about whom they are writing to and why.

■ Write a letter to someone who has been in jail for his / her actions and include his / her response to you.

■ **TOK Links**

To what extent does history affect our beliefs?

To what extent can we have faith in the legal system?

CREATIVITY, ACTIVITY, SERVICE

Create a 'speaker's series' at your school, where once a month you have someone speak on topical issues, such as social justice.

---

3 Imprisonment

Look at the words in the box below. Write a story that is only three sentences long. Try to use as many of the words in the box as you can in only three sentences.

law	prison	court	rights	suspect
lawyer	witness	police	cell	handcuffs

www.leighsprague.com/

One year down

Thinking of freedom

After a long, partially self-imposed silence, I decided to write this overdue post in honor of May 5, otherwise known as Leigh Sprague Incarceration Day. No, it's not a national holiday (at least not yet), but rather the anniversary of that awful day exactly one year ago when I 'checked myself' in to Lompoc Prison Camp for a 50-month, all-expense paid stay. [1]_____ the big day, a friend of mine here 'inside' brought me (unbidden, I might add) a can of Diet Coke together with half a lime that he happened to stumble across.

Ahh, the simple pleasures I once took for granted.

Seriously, though, I'm not sure if this is an anniversary to be celebrated or mourned. But either way [2]_____ to me. Most importantly, it means that half of my sentence, after being adjusted for good time and drug treatment (RDAP) time off, has passed. The 50% mark. As one old-timer told me: 'It's all downhill from here.' Some days another year seems like an eternity. But when I think about how quickly the first year passed, release seems so close that I can almost taste it. Can't let my mind go there too often though or it starts to play tricks on me.

This has been an eventful year [3]_____. A year to remember. A year that will go down in infamy. Sorry, I realize that I'm getting over-dramatic. But I shudder to think back to that first day, how scared I was, how disoriented, how depressed. Over time, though, I've gradually adjusted, adapted, acclimated. For better or for worse, this life of mine here in prison has become more-or-less normal…

Or maybe better to say not entirely abnormal.

I have my bunk, I have my locker, I have my things. I have my acquaintances and I have my schedule. I walk 10 miles a day around the prison track and [4]_____ taco day in the Chow Hall. In that way life is normal; I guess you could say I'm a teeny-tiny bit institutionalized. Many of the things that caused me stress in the real world – job and taxes and bills and shopping – are no longer a part of my life. But I still think about my kids and family constantly, missing them [5]_____ of every day. I still gaze out at the road that passes within feet of the track, enviously watching free people freely driving free cars down the free street. I picture myself behind the wheel, maybe going nowhere but, at the same time, going everywhere.

I want that person to be me.

I want to be free.

My prison experience has benefited from my 9 months here at RDAP, the residential drug treatment and behavioral modification program that, once I complete it next month, will shave one year off my sentence. At first I suffered in the program, bucking at all the rules and resenting its focus on group work and change.

But [6]_____ many inmates' prison experiences – which for the most part consist of [7]_____ in front of the TV and on the weight pile – I've gained a lot from the program. I recognized the errors in my thinking that made me a criminal just [8]_____ my drug-dealer bunkie. I'm glad to be at the finish line but feel like a much better person now than the broken man that walked through RDAP's doors last July. The 'new improved' me. All thanks to the kind-ol' BoP.

So that's all for now. I've had some issues with freedom of expression so can't promise when I'll write next other than to say that it will be before my next anniversary: that day when I walk [9]_____ through these doors to the Greyhound station in nearby Santa Maria.

Until then, keep well and keep in touch. And promise me not to [10]_____ that most special of gifts: freedom; freedom to be with your loved ones, freedom to go where you want, freedom to say and be and do whatever you happen to choose. I once took those freedoms for granted. But I never will again.

A Fill in the blanks 1–10 with one of the phrases below.

> **a** every minute
> **b** take for granted
> **c** wasting time
> **d** as much as
>
> **e** once-and-for-all
> **f** in honor of
> **g** it means a lot
>
> **h** to say the least
> **i** look forward to
> **j** in comparison to

 B Complete the sentences 1–5 with the most appropriate ending from a–j.

1 The writer decided to break his silence and write this post…

2 The writer seems comforted by the fact that the first year…

3 Over time, the writer's life in prison has…

4 He is no longer stressed by…

5 He feels different from other inmates…

a become adjusted.
b went by so quickly.
c because he does not waste time.
d should be celebrated or mourned.
e become normal.
f to celebrate the one-year anniversary of his incarceration.
g because he has gained a lot from the programme.
h missing his kids and family.
i in honour of his one-year silence.
j taxes and bills.

 C Use *still*, *yet* or *already* to join the pairs of sentences below. For example:

We moved over a year ago. My sister is homesick.

*We moved over a year ago and my sister is **still** homesick.*

1 I have waited for two weeks. I haven't received my results.

2 They said it would take three years to build the skyscraper. They finished it in two years.

3 When I left work, my boss was there. When I returned an hour later, he was there.

4 My mother has been in the hospital for three days. The doctor said she could not go home.

5 The semester went by fast. It is winter break.

6 Derek wants to go to a concert. He hasn't asked his parents' permission.

7 Aadi asked me if I wanted to go to dinner. I have more work to do.

8 You live in an apartment. You have been talking about moving out for over a year.

9 I changed my university studies from English literature to law. I enjoy reading novels in my free time.

10 I wanted to tell Joe what happened. He knew.

Grammar

Still, yet and already

- We use *still* to say that a situation or action is ongoing and has not stopped. For example:
  *He is **still** in the library.*

- We use *yet* to mean *until now*. For example:
  *Have you finished your homework **yet**?*

- It can be used in negative sentences:
  *He hasn't answered my email **yet**.*

- *Still* can also be used in negative sentences, but it usually shows more surprise or impatience than *yet*. For example:
  *He hasn't arrived **yet**, and I'm worried.*
  *He **still** hasn't arrived, and I'm upset.*

- We use *already* to say that something has happened, sometimes sooner than expected. For example:
  *He has **already** finished all of the tasks I assigned him. I'm really impressed.*

D Go to www.ted.com/talks/salil_dudani_how_jails_extort_the_poor/
transcript#t-108415 and click to play the video 'How jails extort the poor'.
Cover the screen or turn it away so you cannot see it – this will help you
prepare for the listening part of the exam. You will hear a TED Talk about a
man who was falsely arrested in the United States. Listen to the talk up to 4:50
and answer the following questions:

1 Why was Mr Dudani originally at the police station?

2 What showed his fear?

3 What was strange to Mr Dudani about the police description of him?

4 What are two things the police did to check his background?

5 Why did the police officer 'scan the side of the police station'?

6 What does the speaker say is the real point of his talk?

7 Why does he use the example of receiving a parking ticket?

8 What does he say most people think of when they think of Ferguson?

9 What was the interesting fact he found about the police arrest warrants in Ferguson?

E Role play an interview with someone who has committed a crime and spent
time in prison. Discuss why he / she committed the crime, the lessons they
learned in jail and what they hope for the future.

F Write the beginning of a crime story. Make sure that you:

- Describe the setting.
- Create suspense.
- Include dialogue.
- End with a dramatic action that either completes the scene or leaves the reader
wanting to know what will happen next.

■ TOK Links

To what extent does memory contribute to our personal and shared knowledge?

To what extent are mathematical models accurate in depicting social problems?

CREATIVITY, ACTIVITY, SERVICE

Organize an art exhibit or a theatrical performance that highlights the causes and effects of
crime in a particular area.

4 Want You Dead

Peter James has sold millions of copies of his crime stories, and his famous detective, Roy Grace, is on the case again in *Want You Dead*, the tenth book in the series, where he tries to stop Red Westwood's ex-boyfriend from committing more murders. James's novel is centred around the life of Red, a beautiful real estate agent who has started a new romance with Dr Karl Murphy. The only problem is that Red's ex-boyfriend is jealous and has promised her that if he can't have her, then no one can. In this extract, we read about how Karl Murphy was on his way to meet Red for a date, when something very unexpected happened.

Karl Murphy was a decent and kind man, a family doctor with two small children [1] that / whom he was bringing up on his own. He worked long hours, and did his very best
5 for his growing list of patients. The last two years [2] have been / had been tough since his beloved wife, Ingrid, had died, and there [3] was / were some aspects of his work he found really hard, particularly having to
10 break news to patients who were terminally ill. But it [4] always / never occurred to him that he might have made enemies – and certainly not that there might be someone who hated him so much he wanted him
15 dead.

And was planning to kill him tonight.

Sure, okay, however hard you tried, you [5] wouldn't / couldn't please everyone, and boy, did he see that at work some
20 days. Most of his patients were pleasant, but a few of them tested him and the staff in his medical practice to the limit. [6] And / But he still tried to treat them all equally.

25 [7] When / As he stood at the clubhouse bar on this late October evening, showered and changed out of his golfing clothes, politely drinking his second pint of lime and lemonade with his partners in the
30 tournament and glancing discreetly at his watch, anxious to make his escape, he realized [8] for / at the first time in a long, long while he was feeling happy – and excited. There was a new lady in his life.
35 They hadn't been dating for long, but already he [9] grew / had grown extremely fond of her. To the point that he had thought today, out on the golf course, that he was falling in love with her. But being a
40 very private man, he said nothing of this to his companions.

Shortly after 6pm he downed the remains of his drink, anxious about the time, quite unaware that there [10] is / was a man
45 waiting outside in the blustery darkness.

His sister, Stefanie, had picked the kids [11] up / after from school today and would be staying with them at his home until he arrived with the babysitter. But she had to
50 leave by 6:45pm latest, to go [12] on / to a business dinner with her husband, and Karl could not make her late for that. He thanked his host for the charity golf day, and [13] his / their fellow teammates in
55 turn congratulated him for playing so well, [14] then / as he slipped eagerly away from the nineteenth-hole drinking session that looked set to go on late into the night. He had something that he wanted to do very
60 much [15] other / more than get smashed with a bunch of fellow golfers, however pleasant they were. He had a date. A very hot date, and the prospect of [16] seeing / having seen her, after three days apart,
65 was giving him the kind of butterflies he'd not had since his teens.

He hurried across the car park, [17] with / through the wind and rain, to the far end where he had parked his car, popped
70 open the boot, and slung his golf bag inside it. Then he zipped the small silver trophy he had won into a side pocket of the bag, totally preoccupied with thoughts of the evening ahead. God, what a ray
75 of sunshine she had brought into his life! These [18] past / passed two years since Ingrid had died had been hell and now, finally, he was coming through it. In the long, bleak period [19] from / since her
80 death, he had not thought that would ever be possible.

He didn't notice the motionless figure, all in black, who lay beneath the tartan dog rug on the rear seat, [20] neither / nor did he think it odd that the interior lights failed to [21] come / be on when he opened the driver's door. It seemed that almost every day another bit of the ageing Audi ceased working, or, like the fuel gauge, only functioned intermittently. He had a new A6 on order, and would be taking delivery in a few weeks' [22] period / time.

He settled behind the wheel, pulled [23] up / on his seat belt, started the engine and switched on the headlights. Then he switched [24] the / a radio from Classic FM to Radio 4, to catch the second half of the news, drove out of the car park, and along the narrow road beside the eighteenth fairway of Haywards Heath Golf Club. Headlights were coming the [25] one / other way, and he pulled over to the side to let the car pass. As he was about to accelerate forward he heard a sudden movement behind him, then something damp and acrid was clamped over his mouth and nose.

Chloroform, he recognised from his medical training, in the fleeting instant that he tried to resist, before his brain went muzzy and his feet came off the pedals, and his hands lost their grip on the wheel.

Excerpt from Want You Dead *by Peter James*
https://crimefictionlover.com/2014/11/free-extract-from-peter-james-want-you-dead

A Choose the correct option for each of the 25 pairs of underlined words to complete each sentence.

B Choose the correct answer for each of the questions below:

1 Which aspect of his work was Karl finding particularly difficult?
   a His wife's death
   b That some people wanted to kill him
   c Telling patients they were going to die
   d Playing golf with his colleagues

2 What did Karl's companions think of Karl's new girlfriend?
   a They were anxious about Karl's happiness
   b They didn't know about her
   c They knew Karl kept her private
   d They were secretly in love with her

3 How did Karl feel about his date that evening?
   a He felt like a teenager
   b He didn't want to be late for it
   c He was thankful that he could leave early
   d His sister made him anxious about the date

4 Why was his new girlfriend like 'a ray of sunshine'?
   a Because the weather was so bad that night
   b Because his wife had always been so unhappy
   c Because he had felt sad for a long time
   d Because she was so warm

5 How did Karl lose his grip on the wheel?
   a He was blinded by the headlights of another car
   b He was thinking of medical school
   c He was thinking of his date that evening
   d He had been drugged with chloroform

UNIT **4** Leisure and holidays

REFLECTION

Think individually about the questions below. Then pair with a partner and discuss the questions. Share your ideas with the rest of the class.

- What do you like to do in your leisure time?
- What influences your choice of leisure activities?
- What types of holidays can you think of?
- What influences your holiday destination or the type of holiday you choose?
- When was the last time you went on holiday? Where did you go? Whom did you go with? What did you do?
- Have you ever had a nightmare holiday? If so, what happened?
- What sports do you play or watch?
- What is the difference between a sport and a game?
- Do you ever visit art galleries, museums or exhibitions? When was the last time you visited one?
- What makes an excellent experience at a gallery, museum or exhibition?

1 Hobbies

Studying for the diploma course can be challenging and stressful. There are so many things to do, and you don't have enough time: homework deadlines, internal assessments, Extended Essay, CAS activities… When it gets too much, what do you do? How do you deal with stress? Do you watch TV? Or go out with your friends?

Most hobbies not only help you reduce your stress level, but also require creativity, which helps you develop creative thinking skills in your studies. Giving your brain a break by taking some time off will help you refocus your energy when you come back to your studies. Hobbies can build confidence, as being good at something or learning something new is very rewarding. Hobbies also help you socialize. The internet provides endless ways to connect with people who do the same things as you. If you join a club, you can meet new people. We often bond easily when we have the same interest.

What does the following proverb mean?

All work and no play makes Jack a dull boy.

Discuss with a partner.

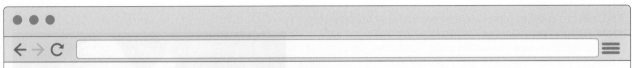

How Successful People Spend Their Spare Time

Finding time for yourself away from work can often be a challenge. Many of us tend to put our personal pursuits and hobbies aside for other responsibilities we think are more important. But even the most highly motivated and successful people can find time out to unwind – after all, there is more to life than just working and sleeping! Doing an activity you love can even contribute to success in your career or studies. Playing an instrument, writing stories, participating in team sport or learning how to bake are all hobbies that stimulate the mind through creativity, analysis, communication, social skills, focus and coordination.

Here are some ways that successful people spend their time to give you inspiration.

Mark Zuckerberg

The Facebook CEO Mark Zuckerberg has spoken often about the importance he places on having a hobby – incredibly, Facebook was created from one of his side projects while he was at Harvard. Speaking in 2017 he said, 'At Facebook we often ask [job candidates], "What is something that you've built that is outside of the jobs you've done?" Often that's one of the best ways people can show passion and leadership'. Zuckerberg himself enjoys keeping fit and is a keen runner. In 2016 he set himself a challenge of running 365 miles in a year and completed it by July! He reasoned, 'Doing anything well requires energy, and you just have a lot more energy when you're fit.'

Richard Branson

The billionaire businessman Richard Branson has been pictured many times enjoying outdoor adventure sports, particularly kitesurfing, but states his great passion is sitting down to a game of chess. 'I think chess may just be the best game in the world,' he told the Virgin blog. 'It combines the greatest aspects of many different sports – tactics, planning, bravery and risk-taking.'

Kate Middleton

In her spare time it is thought that Kate Middleton enjoys adult colouring books, helping her to relax and be creative. At university she studied Art History and she is royal patron of the National Portrait Gallery in London, showing her hobby to be an extension of her academic and philanthropic interests.

Tom Hanks

Tom Hanks has been avidly collecting typewriters since the 1970s and has over 100 in his collection. He uses one almost every day and explained in an article he wrote for The New York Times in 2013 that it's the sounds of typewriters he loves: 'The sound of typing is one reason to own a vintage manual typewriter… In addition to sound, there is the sheer physical pleasure of typing; it feels just as good as it sounds.' His hobby led him to writing a book about typewriters entitled *Uncommon Type*, which he published in 2017.

Petr Čech

Petr Čech is one of the world's most successful goalkeepers and is top of the leader board for keeping the most clean sheets in the Premier League era. In his spare time, Čech is a keen drummer and attributes his drumming skills to helping him improve as a goalkeeper. He says, 'There are so many things I learn on the drums that I can use in goalkeeping as well, because the hand-eye co-ordination and the independence on each of the limbs is helpful. It gives you a routine and a new structure to practice. I enjoy it and for me to sit and play along with a song I enjoy to listen to, it really relaxes me.'

Julia Roberts

Julia Roberts is a keen knitter and often utilises the downtime on movie sets to knit and relax. While filming Larry Crowne with Tom Hanks in 2011, the actor played a prank on his co-star by buying enough yarn and knitting needles to occupy the whole crew when Roberts arrived on set! Knitting has also proved to be a popular on-set hobby with other famous actors such as Meryl Streep, Amanda Seyfried and Ryan Gosling.

Bill Gates

Bill Gates has come to appreciate the importance of hobbies later in life. He told Time magazine, 'When I was in my 20s and early 30s, my whole life was focused on work. These days, I'm better at balancing the work that I love to do with my foundation and taking time off to spend with family and friends.' Among his hobbies and interests, Gates cites playing Bridge, reading a book per week, travelling and playing tennis as his favourite pastimes – he even played against Roger Federer in a charity match in 2017.

Warren Buffett

Warren Buffet, one of America's most successful investors, manages to pursue many hobbies in his spare time. Like Bill Gates, he is a keen Bridge player and sees lessons in business mirrored in the game, telling CBS News, 'You have to look at all the facts. You have to draw inferences from what you've seen, what you've heard.' He has also stated that he reads up to 500 pages per day to keep his brain fresh. But perhaps his most surprising hobby is playing the ukulele. In 2012 he duetted with Jon Bon Jovi to perform one of their songs for charity.

1. According to Mark Zuckerberg, what is one of the best ways to show passion and leadership?
2. According to Richard Branson, what are the benefits of playing chess as a hobby?
3. What does Tom Hanks love most about typewriters?
4. The paragraph about Kate Middleton says: 'At university she studied Art History and she is royal patron of The National Portrait Gallery in London, showing her hobby to be an extension of her academic and philanthropic interests.' Which word is closest in meaning to 'philanthropic'?
   a charitable
   b complicated
   c educational
   d personal
5. How does drumming help Petr Čech as a goalkeeper?
6. Which two people from the extract share the same hobby?
7. How many pages does Warren Buffet read per day?

Grammar

Present simple, past simple and present perfect

Notice the tenses in the following sentences.

Present simple tense:

We use the **present simple tense** when you talk about something habitual.

* She **collects** knives with her family.
* He **dons** a suit and **walks** through Central Park to get there.
* In his spare time, the Google cofounder **likes** to push his body to the limit in any way he can.

Past simple tense:

we use the **past simple tense** when you describe an event that happened in the past.

* Her mom **introduced** her to daggers.
* Bush **took** up painting after leaving office in 2009.
* The Project Runway co-host and mentor **told** The New York Times that he spends every Sunday at the Metropolitan Museum.

Present perfect tense:

The **present perfect tense** is used to describe something that happened in the past, but the exact time it happened is not important. It has a relationship with the present.

* Branson says he **has** likely **played** thousands of games in his lifetime.
* The actor and filmmaker **has been collecting** vintage typewriters since 1978.
* The Yahoo CEO tells San Francisco magazine that she **has** always **loved** baking.

B **Choose the correct verb forms.**

1 She go / goes / went / has gone to Australia in 1994 and she liked it very much.

2 My father usually like / likes / liked / has liked his steak well-done.

3 Last week I am / was / have been very busy and I don't have / didn't have / haven't had the time to do a lot in the household.

4 Tomorrow some friends are coming over. I don't see / didn't see / haven't seen them for ages and they are never / were never / have never been to my place before.

5 The gentleman speak / speaks / spoke / has spoken to his servant two hours ago.

6 My aunt live / lives / lived / has lived all her life in London, and doesn't travel / didn't travel / hasn't travelled much since her husband died.

7 The kangaroo always carry / carries / carried / has carried its baby.

8 My uncle die / dies / died / has died of lung cancer last year, but he never smokes / never smoked / has never smoked in his life.

Are you surprised by any of the hobbies that highly successful people practise in their free time? Or do you think their hobbies match their profiles? If you have a hobby, how did you choose it? Did your family introduce you to it? Or did your friends? If you were to take up a new hobby, how would you choose one?

According to the highly successful people in the article, hobbies not only help you relax and re-focus your energy, but also develop skills that you would not learn elsewhere. Could your hobbies help you further develop the IB learner profile attributes? With your partner, discuss what hobbies could help develop which IB learner attributes. Fill in a table like the one below, and share your ideas with the class.

IB learner profile	Hobbies
Inquirers	
Knowledgeable	
Thinkers	
Communicators	
Principled	
Open-minded	
Caring	
Risk-takers	
Balanced	
Reflective	

● ● ●

← → C   www.theguardian.com/lifeandstyle/2014/nov/09/why-do-we-collect-things-love-anxiety-or-desire   ≡

Why do we collect things? Love, anxiety or desire

About a third of people in the UK collect something. Their reasons and manner vary hugely. For some, like the football fan who collects club memorabilia, it is a way to express loyalty; for others, like the stamp collector proud of rare finds, there can be an obsessive streak.

One psychoanalytical explanation for collecting is that unloved children learn to seek comfort in accumulating belongings; another is that collecting is motivated by existential anxieties – the collection, an extension of our identity, lives on, even though we do not. More recently, evolutionary theorists suggested that a collection was a way for a man to attract potential mates by signalling his ability to accumulate resources.

Humans are unique in the way we collect items purely for the satisfaction of seeking and owning them. The desire to collect only became possible about 12,000 years ago, once our ancestors gave up their nomadic lifestyles and settled down in one location.

Christian Jarrett

Have you ever wondered why we collect things? Read the short article above.

 Now watch the TedEd video entitled 'Why are we so attached to our things? – Christian Jarrett' at https://ed.ted.com/lessons/why-are-we-so-attached-to-our-things-christian-jarrett and answer these questions:

1 What does Jean Piaget, a founding father of child psychology, observe about human nature?

2 What is the endowment effect?

3 Three psychological experiments are provided to validate the endowment effect. Briefly explain what these experiments are.

4 Why do some people pay a lot of money to buy items that were previously owned by celebrities?

5 Why do we feel reluctant to part with our family heirlooms?

6 What could explain the cause of hoarding disorder?

7 Is each of the following sentences true or false?

   a From a young age, we believe our possessions have a unique essence.

   b When a child is given a brand-new version of their favourite toy, he / she has a tendency to get excited about the new toy.

   c We often grow out of our sense of attachment to objects as we grow older.

   d The concept of contagion – some collectors are attracted to celebrity belongings because these objects are seen as being infused with the essence of the person who owned them – can even alter our perception of the physical world and change our athletic abilities.

   e The endowment effect has been globally demonstrated, and people in every culture exhibit this effect.

   f We can conclude that we have less of a sense of ownership in an egalitarian society where almost everything is shared.

   g Some people believe that the nature of our relationship with our possessions will change with the rise of digital technologies.

Task 1: To write a blog entry

 Do you have any hobbies? If you don't have one, would you like to take up a new hobby? Write a blog entry about a hobby or two. In the blog, you should introduce the hobby / hobbies, and state the benefits of them. A blog is your own website where you share your thoughts and ideas with the world. When writing a blog entry, it is important that you demonstrate your awareness of the audience. Use the following checklist:

- An eye-catching title
- An introduction
- Body paragraphs
- A conclusion
- Coherence
- Awareness of the audience

Task 2: To write a letter to your friend

Imagine you are a member of a hobby club. Write an informal letter to your friend to invite him / her to your club. Decide what kind of hobby club you are in. Your club members share their ideas and experiences online, and get together every month. This month they are planning for something special, and you think your friend would really enjoy this event. In your letter, provide as much detail as possible about all the benefits of your hobby and your excitement about the upcoming event. Use the following checklist:

- Conventions of an informal letter
- Paragraphs (first paragraph: general chat; body paragraphs: details about your hobby and the event; last paragraph: invitation, closure to the letter)
- Informal register
- All the relevant information
- Coherence

■ TOK Links

While there are arguably many ways of knowing, the TOK course identifies eight specific ways of knowing. They are:

- Language
- Sense perception
- Emotion
- Reason
- Imagination
- Faith
- Intuition
- Memory

How does the endowment effect affect our ways of knowing? The endowment effect explains some unreasonable human behaviours. Is it possible to make an objective judgment on our sense of selves or our own work / knowledge? Do we value personal knowledge more than shared knowledge? How do we make sure that our personal knowledge is unbiased?

CREATIVITY, ACTIVITY, SERVICE

What about taking up a new hobby for CAS? Most hobbies require creative thinking skills, which is perfect for the Creativity strand of CAS. There are many approaches to creativity, such as ongoing creativity, school-based creativity, community-based creativity and individual creativity. Hobbies can be a good starting point. Remember to set yourself appropriate targets and challenges. Ensure that your hobbies take place over an extended duration of time. You may showcase your creation / performance in a variety of ways, for example through a recording, a presentation, an exhibition, social media or shared discussion.

2 Tourism

We love travelling, whether camping in our own country or staying in a luxurious hotel in an exotic place abroad. Globalization has enabled us to travel further and more often every year. Tourism has been a source of national revenues for many countries, and has been encouraged by travel companies, airlines, tourists and the media. We are on a mission to leave our country every summer.

Locals of popular holiday destinations are now suffering from mass tourism. It is not surprising to see graffiti that reads 'Tourist you are the terrorist' in Barcelona in the height of summer.

Discuss the following questions with a partner.

- Have we gone too far?
- Is it time to actively promote responsible tourism that minimizes negative economic, environmental and social impacts, and makes positive contributions to the conservation of natural and cultural heritage?
- How do we ensure responsible tourism in every corner of the world?

A **Before reading the article below, discuss the meaning of the following words:**

- infestation
- depredation
- mass tourism
- stress-inducing
- simultaneously

- relentless
- disembark
- humiliation
- inflict
- carbon footprint

- mitigate
- irk
- restraint

Grammar

Compound adjectives

Stress-inducing is a **compound adjective**, as two words, *stress* (mental or emotional strain or tension) and *induce* (to bring about), are combined to create a new adjective. It is often very easy to guess what these compound adjectives mean. Have a go at the following:

- an **English-speaking** country
- a **time-saving** gadget
- a **well-known** writer
- a **short-sighted** man

Try creating a few of your own compound adjectives and share them with your class.

Mass tourism is at a tipping point – but we're all part of the problem

1 Nearly 30 years ago, researching for a *Guardian* series on global population pressures, I interviewed the zoologist Desmond Morris. During that interview, Morris said something that was hard to forget. "We have to recognise," he said, "that human beings may be becoming an infestation on the planet."

2 Those words came back to me as reports came in about the increasing reaction in many parts of Europe against the depredations of mass tourism. Last week I read a stress-inducing story in *The Times* about appalling passport-check delays at Milan Airport; three days later, I walked through those same passport gates with only a brief and courteous check.

3 Nevertheless, when places from the Mediterranean to the Isle of Skye all start complaining more or less simultaneously about the sheer pressure of tourist numbers in their streets and beauty spots, as has happened this August, it feels as if the always uneasy balance between the visited and the visitors has gone beyond a tipping point.

4 Pictures of a wall in Barcelona saying, "Tourist Go Home", or of protesters in Palma saying, "Tourism Kills Mallorca", should touch an uneasy nerve in anyone whose summer getaway has taken them to places such as San Sebastián, Dubrovnik, Florence, Venice and – further afield – New Orleans and Thailand. For all of these have either taken or are considering measures to limit the relentless pressure from mass tourism by people like you and me.

5 Predictably, Venice is one of the most agonisingly pressured of all. It embodies the increasingly irreconcilable forces of vernacular life, tourism and sustainability in historic parts of Europe. But that doesn't stop the millions arriving all the time – 28 million this year, in a city with a population of 55,000, many disembarking from monstrous cruise ships that dwarf the ancient city as they approach the Grand Canal. Each day in summer is a humiliation of most of the things the world treasures about Venice. Not surprisingly, many locals have had enough.

6 It's a pattern that is replaying in different ways in other much-visited parts of Europe and beyond. Anarchists in Barcelona captured the headlines by holding up tourist buses in protest against the cost of living that they say is inflicted by tourism, especially by short-term-let companies such as Airbnb, which drive up housing costs.

7 But these are only the hot spots. The tourism problem runs far wider. Human beings across the world make more than a billion foreign trips a year, twice as many as 20 years ago. In Britain, statistics this week show we took 45 million foreign holidays last year, a 68 per cent increase on 1996. The problem shows itself in both supply and demand. There isn't enough room for the many to walk through the centre of Dubrovnik, or enough public loos on Skye for the visitors. But the number of people wanting to visit such places is rising all the time, fed by greater global prosperity, cheaper air travel and increased overall provision of hotels worldwide. Tourism is now the largest employer on the planet. One in every 11 people relies on the industry for work. Unsurprisingly, few governments want to put a squeeze on such a source of wealth.

8   There are multiple genuinely difficult issues involved in mass tourism. The biggest, in a global sense, is the rise of Chinese tourism. But why should Chinese people be denied the rewards – for they certainly exist – of travel? The tourism industry's <u>carbon footprint</u> is equally problematic. But if people want to take the planes, and the planes are available, who is to say that this should stop? Closer to home, it is <u>beyond question</u> that many British tourists behave badly abroad. The stag-do and hen-do* culture is out of hand. But you can't restrict access to Italy to those who know their Giotto from their Duccio.

9   Writing a few days ago, the writer Elizabeth Becker argued that only governments can handle runaway tourism. Governments can control entry to their countries, she said, can regulate airlines and ships, prevent inappropriate hotel development, and use taxes to shape visitor demand and benefit local people, place limits on rip-off prices that distort markets. Yet even Becker admits that most governments prefer things as they are. The prospect of truly effective coordination by governments remains distant.

10 It would be wonderful if governments could find effective ways to at least <u>mitigate</u> the worst problems. Some, such as those of Thailand and Bhutan, have been bold, even though most restrictions hit hardest at the less well-off and are most easily circumvented by the rich. The role of government action to ensure adequate and appropriate infrastructure in tourist areas is indisputable.

11 In the end, though, I think we have to take greater individual responsibility too. This will <u>irk</u> those who think of themselves as independent travellers rather than members of tourist herds, but unless we embrace individual and collective <u>restraint</u> more seriously, the destruction and damage to cities such as Venice or beauty spots such as Glen Brittle will simply grow.

12 We have to re-examine the idea that we enjoy an <u>unfettered</u> liberty to travel at will or for pleasure. We have to rethink the impulse that says a holiday from work – or retirement from work – is an open sesame to exploring the world. We should learn from Henry David Thoreau that one can travel as much – and develop as much as a human being – in one's own locality as in the far-flung and exotic corners of the globe.

13 Travel broadens the mind, they say. But is the person whose air-conditioned tour bus whisks them to a distant glacier in Patagonia or to the Mona Lisa for a quick selfie before depositing them at a characterless international hotel richer in experience than the one who spends the same amount of time watching the birds or the butterflies in the back garden? I doubt it. We may not be an infestation yet. But we are a problem. Travel can narrow the mind too.

*A stag-do and a hen-do are a big party arranged for a groom-to-be (stag) and a bride-to-be (hen) before their wedding day. In Britain, these parties often involve going abroad with your friends and having a laugh with a few drinks.

Martin Kettle

www.theguardian.com/commentisfree/2017/aug/11/tourism-tipping-point-travel-less-damage-destruction

B   **Read the article and answer the following questions:**

1   In paragraph 1, what word does Desmond Morris use to emphasize global population pressures?

2   What is the main problem with current tourism?

3   Give a word from paragraph 5 that describes the ugliness of mass tourism in Venice.

4   What is one of the biggest problems caused by tourism in Barcelona?

5   What three elements feed into the global tourism problem?

6   Why don't governments do more to tackle the tourism problem?

7   Which of the following words is the closest in meaning to the phrase 'beyond question' in paragraph 8?
   a   impossible
   b   questionable
   c   certain
   d   probable

8   According to Elizabeth Becker, what can governments do to handle runaway tourism? List at least three.

9 The writer thinks that we have to take greater individual responsibility, while he discusses the importance of government action to ensure sustainable tourism. What does he encourage individuals to do?

10 Which of the following is the synonym of 'unfettered' in paragraph 12?

a unlimited

b unbiased

c unaffordable

d unacceptable

11 The writer thinks that 'travel can narrow the mind'. Why does he think so?

Grammar

Modals

A **modal verb** is a verb used with another verb to express an idea such as possibility that is not expressed by the main verb. The modal verbs in English are:

- *can*
- *could*
- *may*
- *might*
- *must*
- *ought*
- *shall*
- *should*
- *will*
- *would*

Modal verbs are useful when you express your opinion.

Notice the modal verbs used in the following sentences:

- *I think we **must** (have to) take greater individual responsibility.*
  Meaning: *Must* and *have to* are both used to express obligation.
- *We **may** not be an infestation yet.*
  Meaning: *May* is used to express possibility.*
- *Travel **can** narrow the mind too.*
  Meaning: *Can* is used to express possibility.**

May can also be used to express permission, for example: *You **may** borrow my computer.*

Can* is also used to express permission, for example: ***Can I have some more water, please?*

Note: Although *may* and *can* are interchangeable when used for permission, *may* is more polite than *can*.

 C **Choose the correct modal verb for each sentence.**

1 You <u>must / can / may</u> be 17 to get a driving licence in the UK.

2 There is no dress code for this event. You <u>must / may / can't</u> wear whatever suits you.

3 For your safety, you <u>may / must / may not</u> wear a helmet when you enter this area.

4 To ensure the better future of the Earth, I think we <u>don't have to / have to / can</u> take greater care when dealing with nature.

5 You <u>don't have to / have to / can</u> bring money as we will provide everything for you.

6 <u>Can / Would / Must</u> I bring a dog to your house party? Is anyone allergic to dog hair?

7 You <u>can / may / must</u> bring a passport to the airport if you take an international flight.

8 You <u>mustn't / don't have to / can't</u> bring a passport to the airport if you take a domestic flight.

D In the Language B SL internal assessment, you are to describe a visual stimulus and relate it to the relevant theme and the target culture(s) for 3–4 minutes, followed by a 4–5 minute follow-up discussion and a 5–6 minute general discussion.

Work with a partner for this exercise. The visual stimuli below are all related to the topic 'Leisure and holidays'.

Student A: Choose one of the photos, and prepare your talk for 15 minutes. When you are ready, talk to your partner about the stimulus for 3–4 minutes.

Student B: Prepare questions related to the stimulus and the theme for 15 minutes. When your partner's talk is finished, ask questions to follow up.

Swap roles, and repeat the process.

 E Watch the YouTube video entitled 'The Future of Tourism: Ian Yeoman at TEDxGroningen' at https://youtu.be/IRv1-6Y9N2A and answer these questions:

1 To what effect does Ian Yeoman mention Sunderland at the beginning?

2 According to Ian Yeoman, what elements of tourism will not have changed by 2050?

3 Today approximately 1 billion people go on an international holiday. How many people went on an international holiday in 1950?

4 What are the three main causes of the increase in international travel?

5 According to the UN World Tourism Organization, how many people are predicted to take a holiday in the year 2050?

6   To know the future of tourism, what do we have to understand?

7   Which country currently takes the most holidays in the world?

8   How would an aging society affect the world of tourism?

9   How would technology affect the world of tourism?

10 Throughout the talk, Ian Yeoman is…

    a   challenging

    b   neutral

    c   humorous

F   ■ Task 1: To write a brochure

Write a travel brochure of your favourite holiday destination or your home town. Choose a place you want to write a brochure about. Find out as much as you can about the place. Your brochure should be informative and persuasive. Try to be concise and accurate. The text should be written in short sentences with positive language and use the active voice. Start planning to write your brochure. Use the following checklist:

- Heading / subheadings / bullet points
- Specific, attractive and powerful words
- Short sentences with positive language
- Clarity / accessibility (Is your brochure clear and easy to understand?)
- Contact details (phone number, website, map, how to get there, and so on)

■ Task 2: To write a journal entry

Imagine you keep a travel journal. You recently went on a holiday where you experienced mass tourism and its negative impact. Write a journal entry about your experience. Provide as much detail as possible. Write it in an engaging style, remembering that some people publish their travel journal. Use the following checklist:

- Date of entry
- Well-elaborated paragraphs
- Descriptions and opinions
- Coherence
- Engaging style of writing

■ TOK Links

Memory is the facility of the mind to encode, store and retrieve information. Memory is vital to personal knowledge. Without memory, we would not remember our past and we wouldn't even know whom we are. Therefore, memory is a critical element to our identity. Which of your memories would you say are central to your sense of whom you are and which are peripheral?

We write journals and take photos to keep records of our holiday experiences. If we don't take photos or write journals, how much do you think we remember of our experiences? How accurate are our memories? What role do photos play in the preservation of personal memories? How can they distort such memories?

When you say 'I know exactly what happened', do you really remember everything exactly as it was? How reliable is our memory? What interferes with our memory? If two people give different accounts of the same holiday, does it necessarily follow that one of them is lying, or could each of them simply have a different memory of the same holiday?

You may think it would be a dream come true if you had a photographic memory and remembered many things in great detail. However, photographic memory has troubling implications for our social relationships. Would you always be happy with a friend who remembers everything about you or your shared experiences? If you made a terrible mistake or had a bad experience, would you not be pleased that we are able to forget and move on? Sometimes we *need* to forget to move forward. They say 'Time heals everything', but does it? Or does it just replace memories?

CREATIVITY, ACTIVITY, SERVICE

Along with many human activities that are harmful to our Mother Earth, mass tourism has damaged much of our coastlines and the oceans. Plastic-infested seawater is harmful not only to marine life but also to humans who consume seafood. Countless marine animals and birds have been found dead with plastic in their stomachs. Can we do something about this disaster?

Yes, there are many organizations that realize the seriousness of marine pollution and try to clean up the coastlines and oceans. Check out the following websites. There is an International Coastal Clean-up day every year. You can find a clean-up activity near you and participate in this meaningful community activity.

- https://oceanconservancy.org/trash-free-seas/international-coastal-cleanup/
- www.theoceancleanup.com

You can also **create a brochure** about responsible tourism, using the knowledge you have gained in this unit. Find out more about responsible tourism at the following website: http://responsibletourismpartnership.org/what-is-responsible-tourism/

3 Sports

What makes a sport? Sport often sparks all kinds of debate for many people, whether they are supporting a favourite team, watching an elite competition such as the Olympics or competing for fun against friends and peers. But at the heart of the debate is the question: *when is a sport not a sport?* Does sport require stamina and physicality? Does it require technical skill and high levels of concentration? The criteria you need to tick off to officially label something a sport can change from person to person.

The Council of Europe charter on sport uses the following definition: `Sport means all forms of physical activity which, through casual or organised participation, aim at expressing or improving physical fitness and mental well-being, forming social relationships or obtaining results in competition at all levels'. Many funding bodies will consult this criteria when deciding whether or not to label something as a sport. But the debate goes on …

In your opinion, what makes an activity a sport? Is participation more important than competition? Do you play sports for your physical fitness and mental well-being? What sports do you play? What sports do you watch?

Sport has been a big part of human history. The history of sports goes as far back as the beginnings of military training, with competition used as a means to determine whether individuals were fit and useful for service. The competitive spirit of sport has caused many negative consequences in modern-day society, including substance abuse, cheating, inequality and hooliganism. Have you ever had a negative experience in sport?

A Before reading the article below, discuss the meaning of the following words:

- pressure
- fair play
- manipulate
- banned
- guidelines
- puberty

- weight loss / weight gain
- influence
- percentile
- spectrum
- restriction

- stimulant
- excessive
- diet
- paediatrician
- supplements
- side effects

Weigh-ins, weight gain & rules for teen athletes

Has your child talked about losing or gaining weight for his or her sport? Such practices start young, and the pressure can be intense.

For example, instead of competing at their natural weight, many wrestlers attempt to lose weight rapidly and believe a lower weight class will give them an edge during competition – which can be as soon as the very next day. Dancers and gymnasts often feel that they will be judged more favourably if they have a thinner physique. With other sports, like football and weight-lifting, some young athletes seek to gain weight and add muscle mass. As a result, many of these young athletes put their bodies through extremes to change their weight – using methods that have the potential to cause serious health problems.

[1] _____

Weight classifications in sports (e.g. football, wrestling, rowing, boxing) were designed to ensure healthy, safe, and fair play. While that is the concept, it is far from the reality due to the number of young athletes who try to manipulate the system.

How national sports governing bodies have tried to address the issue

- The National Collegiate Athletic Association (NCAA) instituted updated rules to curb dangerous weight-loss practices in wrestling. It banned the use of diuretics, impermeable suits, and saunas for weight loss and decreased the amount of time between "weigh-ins" and competition. Additionally, the NCAA established a system of setting a minimum weight for competition during the wrestling season – using a calculation that incorporates hydration status, weight, and body composition.
- In 2006, the National Federation of State High School Associations adopted similar guidelines (i.e. body composition, weigh-in procedures, and hydration status) for determining minimum body weights in high school wrestlers. However, the body fat minimums were higher (≥7% in males, ≥12% in females) than the levels for collegiate athletes determined by the NCAA. These differences were implemented to address growth needs of teens during puberty and sex differences.

The establishment of minimum competition weight rules has led to a decrease in the practice of rapid weight loss before competition. However, not all sports or activities in which weight might play a role in performance use a weight classification system. For example, in dance, distance running, gymnastics, and cycling, weight and body composition are believed to influence physical performance and the aesthetics of performance. Yet the governing organizations of these activities have no mandated weight-control practices.

[2] _____

Body fat percentage varies by age, and weight is not an accurate indicator of body fat or lean muscle mass.

- Use of body mass index (BMI) in athletes is not recommended, because it falsely classifies some teens who are of normal weight as being overweight.
- BMI can also be falsely elevated in an athlete or nonathlete with a muscular build, as well as in someone who has a high torso-to-leg ratio.
- Body composition measurements (body fat and lean muscle mass) in addition to height-for-weight for age measurements can be much more useful in determining an athlete's physical status.
- Lean muscle mass should be greater than 25th percentile in most well-nourished athletes.

[3] _____

At one end of the spectrum are those with mild energy imbalance. At the other end of the spectrum are athletes who try to lose weight (and subsequently maintain that lower weight) with dangerous techniques that may actually hurt athletic performance, increase injury, and cause medical complications.

If your child plays a sport that emphasizes thinness, leanness, and / or competing at the lowest possible weight, be on the lookout for any of the following:

- Fasting / calorie restriction
- Restricting intake of liquids
- Use of laxatives, diuretics, or stimulant medications
- Excessive exercise to promote sweating
- Use of saunas to promote sweating
- Vomiting after eating

Tips for parents

- Emphasize to the athlete that gradual weight loss is best: No more than 1.5% of total body weight or 1 to 2 pounds each week is recommended.

- Calorie requirements depend mainly on the size of the athlete and the caloric expenditure during exercise. The appropriate <u>diet</u> for most young athletes is 2,000–3,500 calories per day, divided as follows:
  □ Carbohydrates: 55% to 65%
  □ Protein: 15% to 20%
  □ Fat: 20% to 30%
- Except in sports requiring mandatory weigh-ins, your child's coach should not be discussing weight or weight loss.
- Talk with your <u>pediatrician</u> to determine if weight loss is appropriate for your child, and if so, how to develop a safe and effective diet and exercise program to achieve a healthy weight. Your pediatrician may refer you to a registered dietitian or nutritionist for advice on an appropriate diet.
- Children and teens should avoid cycling between high and low weights but should attempt to maintain an appropriate weight.

[4] _____

Some sports – such as football, rugby, and weightlifting – value a muscular physique for improved power and strength. This may cause some children and teens to try to gain weight. However, simply increasing the amount of food one eats may lead to increasing body fat without an increase in muscle mass and strength. Increased or unhealthy body weight may put certain athletes at higher risk of injury and heat illness. <u>Supplements</u> used to increase muscle mass have the potential to be associated with unfavourable side effects. Contrary to popular belief, eating more protein by itself will not lead to increased production of muscle.

Tips for parents

- Emphasize to the athlete that gradual weight gain is best. Gaining an excess of 1.5% of body weight per week may result in unwanted fat.
- Talk with your pediatrician to determine if weight gain is appropriate for your child. Discuss how to develop a safe and effective diet and exercise program to increase lean body mass. Your pediatrician may refer you to a registered dietitian or nutritionist for advice on an appropriate diet.
- Child and adolescent athletes can participate in strength training. They should begin by learning proper technique under the supervision of a knowledgeable adult. Weight loads should be increased gradually; programs should incorporate 2 to 3 sets of 8 to 15 repetitions with the athlete maintaining proper technique. Young athletes who have not finished puberty yet should be aware that, while weight training will improve strength, they might not see an increase in muscle bulk.

[5] _____

As a parent, the most important thing you can do is surround your child with a community of coaches and teammates who care more about his or her long-term health than short-term accomplishments. While an Olympian may say great achievements take great sacrifice, your teen is a teen first and an athlete second. When it comes to your child's long-term health, how much sacrifice is just too much?

Rebecca L. Carl, MD, MS, FAAP

www.healthychildren.org/English/healthy-living/sports/Pages/Weigh-Ins-Weight-Gain-Rules-for-Teen-Athletes.aspx

---

B **After reading the article, answer the following questions:**

1 Read the text and choose an appropriate heading from the list below for each of the paragraphs numbered 1–5.
  a The continuum of unhealthy weight loss
  b Regulations – what's in the rule book?
  c Kids first. Athletes second.
  d Why athletes shouldn't focus on BMI
  e Unhealthy weight gain

2 Is each of the following sentences true or false?
  a Using extreme methods to change your weight has the potential to cause serious health problems.
  b When setting a minimum weight for competition the NCAA recommends using a calculation that incorporates hydration status, body composition and weigh-in procedure.
  c The establishment of minimum competition weight rules has led to a decrease in the practice of rapid weight loss in all competitive sports.
  d Body mass index (BMI) is not an accurate indicator of body fat or lean muscle mass.
  e Parents are advised to speak to their paediatrician to discuss a safe and effective diet and exercise programme for their child.
  f Teenage athletes are not allowed to participate in strength training.
  g If you want to lose weight in a short time, you are advised to eat healthy food and use saunas to sweat out any excessive fat.
  h The appropriate diet for most young athletes is 2000–3500 calories per day, regardless of their size.

3 Find the words that complete the following sentences. Answer using words as they appear in the 'Tips for parents' section and the final paragraph.
   a Excessive weight gain may result in _____.
   b To get advice on an appropriate diet, your paediatrician may ask you to speak to _____.
   c Adult supervision is required for child and adolescent athletes' _____.
   d For parents, their child's long-term health is more important than _____.

Grammar

Passive voice

Notice how the **passive voice** is used in the following sentences:

* *For example, in dance, distance running, gymnastics and cycling, weight and body composition **are believed to** influence physical performance and the aesthetics of performance.*
* *Use of body mass index (BMI) in athletes **is not recommended**, because it falsely classifies some teens who are of normal weight as being overweight.*

We use the passive voice when we want to focus attention on the person or thing affected by the action. Normally, we use the passive voice when the performer of the action, or the *agent*, is too obvious or ambiguous or not important enough to be mentioned.

The passive forms are made up of the verb **be** with a **past participle**:

	be	*Past participle*	
English	*is*	*spoken*	*all over the world.*
Apples	*have been*	*grown*	*for many years in Asia and Europe.*
The room	*was being*	*cleaned.*	
The work	*will be*	*finished*	*soon.*
You	*must have been*	*invited*	*to the party.*

C **Complete the sentences with the correct tenses, in the active or passive voice, as appropriate.**

Hadrian's Wall

1 In the year 122 AD, the Roman Emperor Hadrian <u>visit</u> his provinces in Britain.

2 On his visit, the Roman soldiers <u>tell</u> him that Pictish tribes from Britain's north <u>attack</u> them.

3 So Hadrian <u>give</u> the order to build a protective wall across one of the narrowest parts of the country.

4 After 6 years of hard work, the Wall <u>finish</u> in 128.

5 It <u>be</u> 117 kilometres long and about 4 metres high.

6 The Wall <u>guard</u> by 15,000 Roman soldiers.

7 Every 8 kilometres there <u>be</u> a large fort in which up to 1000 soldiers <u>find</u> shelter.

8 The soldiers <u>watch</u> over the frontier to the north and <u>check</u> the people who <u>want</u> to enter or leave Roman Britain.

9 In order to pass through the Wall, people <u>must go</u> to one of the small forts that <u>serve</u> as gateways.

10 Those forts <u>call</u> milecastles because the distance from one fort to another <u>be</u> one Roman mile (about 1500 metres).

11 Between the milecastles there <u>be</u> two turrets from which the soldiers <u>guard</u> the Wall.

12 If the Wall <u>attack</u> by enemies, the soldiers at the turrets <u>run</u> to the nearest milecastle for help or <u>light</u> a fire that <u>can see</u> by the soldiers in the milecastle.

13 In 383 Hadrian's Wall <u>abandon</u>.

14 Today Hadrian's Wall <u>be</u> the most popular tourist attraction in northern England.

15 In 1987, it <u>become</u> a UNESCO World Heritage Site.

www.ego4u.com/en/cram-up/tests/hadrians-wall

D ■ Task 1: Discussion

With your partner or in a small group, discuss the following questions:

- ■ What is sport?
- ■ Should hunting be banned as a sport?
- ■ What do you think is the most popular sport in the world?
- ■ What do you think the top five most watched sports are in the world?
- ■ What is the most dangerous sport?
- ■ Which new sports should be included in the Olympics?
- ■ Do you think professional athletes earn too much money? Why or why not? The athletes from which sport do you think earn the most money?
- ■ What are some of the benefits of sports?
- ■ What can your school do to help students stay healthy and fit?

■ Task 2: Role play

In pairs, choose role A or B and act out a conversation in which you try to persuade the other person.

Role A	Role B
You are a child who wants to play a sport that your parent does not approve of. You decide which sport. Think of the benefits of this sport. Try to convince your parent to support you.	You are a parent, and your child wants to play a sport that you do not think is appropriate for him or her. Think of reasons why you don't approve of this sport. Try to convince your child to change his or her mind.

E Watch the video clip entitled 'Taylor Townsend – Tennis – Highlights / Interview – Sports Stars of Tomorrow' at www.sportsstarsoftomorrow.tv/video/taylor-townsend-tennis-highlights-interview-sports-stars-of-tomorrow/ and answer these questions:

1 What is the state of Florida widely known for?

2 What is the USTA training centre for?

3 What three elements did Ola Malmqvist (USTA Head of Women's Tennis) look for when he selected Taylor Townsend?

4 Choose the five true statements from the following:

a Taylor was born and brought up in South Florida.

b She discovered a love for tennis when she became a teenager.

c The selection process of the USTA training centre is tough.

d Taylor found adjusting to her new routine in the USTA training centre extremely challenging.

e Her fitness training helps her develop endurance and quick movement.

f Fitness level is not as important as the ability to play tennis well.

g Taylor spends several hours a day playing tennis.

h Her biggest victory is the Junior Australian Open's singles championship.

i She became a professional tennis player in 2013.

j Her ambition is to be as successful as the Williams sisters.

5 Ola Mamqvist thinks Taylor Townsend's future career is…

a challenging

b promising

c plateaued

F ■ Task 1: To write an interview

Imagine you are a journalist who has interviewed a famous sports star. Write the interview for a sports magazine. Before you write, read 'Interview: Sania Mirza and the challenges of making a dream come true' on FirstPost at www.firstpost.com/sports/interview-sania-mirza-and-the-challenges-of-making-a-dream-come-true-2229090.html. Then use the following checklist:

- Heading, byline, date
- An engaging introduction
- Carefully designed questions
- Detailed answers (that are not too long or too short)
- A semi-formal register (with a hint of informal register in answers)

■ Task 2: To write an article

Write a sports article based on either the previous interview or a recent sporting event. While an interview and an article have a similar audience and purpose, the format of these two text types is quite different. Questions and answers are distinctively written in an interview, whereas an article is written in the journalist's words, with comments from other people included. Before you start writing, read one of the sports articles on this website: www.telegraph.co.uk/sport. Then use the following checklist:

- Heading, byline, date
- An engaging introduction, answering the questions: who, what, when, where?
- Paragraphs explaining why and how, with the important details first
- Main facts followed up with additional information
- Direct quotations from one or two reliable sources
- An effective conclusion

■ TOK Links

One of the most famous and scandalous sports stars is Lance Armstrong, an American former professional road racing cyclist. Armstrong was the 1993 professional world champion, and won the Tour de France a record seven consecutive times from 1999 to 2005. However, in 2012 he was banned from sanctioned Olympic sports for life as a result of long-term doping offences. As part of those sanctions, all results going back to August 1998, including his seven Tour wins, were voided.

In an interview with Oprah Winfrey in 2013, Armstrong admitted he used performance-enhancing drugs during all seven of his Tour de France wins after years of denials. Upon being asked whether he felt in any way that he was cheating while taking banned drugs, Armstrong replied:

> At the time, no. I kept hearing I'm a drug cheat, I'm a cheat, I'm a cheater. I went in and just looked up the definition of cheat and the definition of cheat is to gain an advantage on a rival or foe that they don't have. I didn't view it that way. I viewed it as a level playing field.

Although it is illegal to take banned performance-enhancing substances, it is obvious that Armstrong's judgments were not clear due to his circumstances. Our moral values and judgments are often influenced by others around us. You know cheating on a test is wrong. However, if you believe it's something everyone else does in your community, would you still be able to hold your moral high ground and be the only one who doesn't cheat on a test? Or would you do the same as the others? Knowing that cheating is wrong, would you feel less guilty if everyone else was doing it?

Sometimes what's right or wrong is not a clear cut. What is legal and morally right in one country or one era might be completely illegal and immoral in another country or another era. In our history, we have seen many unsettling practices that are considered morally wrong and illegal now: keeping slaves, killing adulterers, female genital mutilation, and so on.

Some famous examples of moral dilemmas may seem far-fetched and unrealistic. However, these moral dilemmas help us understand the nature of morality and ethics. These dilemmas cannot be resolved, but they make us think...

The 'trolley problem' (originally posed by Philippa Foot in 1967) is a good example of this. If there is an oncoming train heading for five people tied to one track, would you divert it to the opposite track even if you know there is also one person tied to that one? In other words, would you kill one person in order to save the lives of five? The debate becomes more interesting if the single person is related to the person switching the tracks in some way (i.e. a son or daughter).

CREATIVITY, ACTIVITY, SERVICE

CAS helps students to 'recognize and consider the ethics of choices and actions' (learning outcome 7), in accordance with the ethical principles stated in the IB mission statement and the IB learner profile. This involves exploring values, attitudes and behaviours as students undertake enterprises with significant outcomes. Various ethical issues will arise naturally in the course of CAS experiences, and may be seen as challenges to a student's preconceived ideas and instinctive responses or ways of behaving.

If you come across any moral or ethical issues in your CAS experiences, make sure that you speak to your CAS coordinator who will give you advice that is in line with the IB learner profile.

On 18 December 2017, there was a news report concerning misuse of anabolic steroids by hundreds of thousands of people, many of whom are young adults. They often use anabolic steroids to build bigger muscles. However, they should be aware that anabolic steroids cause an imbalance of hormones that can damage many organs, in particular the heart. Read the full article here: www.bbc.co.uk/newsbeat/article/42391438/steroid-abuse-raising-health-risk-for-thousands

For your CAS experience, create a brochure for your school community explaining the dangers of using anabolic steroids and suggesting alternative ways to build bigger muscles. You can work with your friends to further develop your collaborative skills. Research information about anabolic steroids, and think of ways to make positive influences on your school community.

■ Literature

4 Notes from a Small Island

Bill Bryson (born 8 December 1951) is an American author of non-fiction books who is known for his humorous style of writing. *Notes from a Small Island* is his travel journal of Britain. In this book, Bryson arrives in England on a ferry at midnight in March 1973. He spends his first night on a bench, having found it impossible to find a hotel room in the middle of the night. He then wakes up early the next morning and finds a room that suits his needs. The following passage is about his experience of meeting the proprietress of his first guesthouse in England.

I didn't know how early one could decently begin asking for a room in England, so I thought I would leave it till mid-morning. With time on my hands, I made a thorough
5 search for a guesthouse that looked attractive and quiet, but friendly and not too expensive, and at the stroke of ten o'clock presented myself on the doorstep of the one I had carefully selected, taking care
10 not to discompose the milk bottles. It was a small hotel that was really a guesthouse, indeed was really a boarding-house.

I don't remember its name, but I well recall the proprietress, a formidable creature of
15 late middle years called Mrs Smegma, who showed me to a room, then gave me a tour of the facilities and outlined the many complicated rules for residing there – when breakfast was served, how to turn on the
20 heater for the bath, which hours of the day I would have to vacate the premises and during which brief period a bath was permitted (these seemed, oddly, to coincide), how much notice I should give if I intended
25 to receive a phone call or remain out after 10 p.m., how to flush the loo and use the loo brush, which materials were permitted in the bedroom waste-basket and which had to be carefully conveyed to the outside dustbin,
30 where and how to wipe my feet at each point of entry, how to operate the three-bar fire in my bedroom and when that would be permitted (essentially, during an Ice Age). This was all bewilderingly new to me. Where
35 I came from, you got a room in a motel, spent ten hours making a lavish and possibly irredeemable mess of it, and left early the next morning. This was like joining the Army.

'The minimum stay,' Mrs Smegma went
40 on, 'is five nights at one pound a night, including full English breakfast.'

'Five nights?' I said in a small gasp. I'd only intended to stay the one. What on earth was I going to do with myself in Dover for five
45 days?

Mrs Smegma arched an eyebrow. 'Were you hoping to stay longer?'

'No,' I said. 'No. As a matter of –'

'Good, because we have a party of Scottish
50 pensioners coming for the weekend and it would have been awkward. Actually, quite impossible.' She surveyed me critically, as she might a carpet stain, and considered if there was anything else she could do to make my
55 life wretched. There was. 'I'm going out shortly, so may I ask that you vacate your room within quarter of an hour?'

I was confused again. 'I'm sorry, you want me to leave? I've just got here.'

60 'As per the house rules. You may return at four.' She made to depart but then turned back. 'Oh, and do be so good, would you, as to remove your counterpane each night. We've had some unfortunate occurrences
65 with stains. If you do damage the counterpane, I will have to charge you. You do understand, of course?'

I nodded dumbly. And with that she was gone. I stood there, feeling lost and weary
70 and far from home. I'd spent a hysterically uncomfortable night out of doors. My muscles ached, I was dented all over from sleeping on bolt heads, and my skin was lightly oiled with the dirt and grit of two
75 nations. I had sustained myself to this point

with the thought that soon I would be <u>immersed</u> in a hot, soothing bath, followed by about fourteen hours of deep, peaceful, wallowing sleep, on plump pillows under a
80 downy comforter.

As I stood there <u>absorbing</u> the realization that my nightmare, far from drawing to a close, was only just beginning, the door opened and Mrs Smegma was striding across
85 the room to the strip light above the sink. She had shown me the correct method for turning it on – 'There's no need to yank it. A gentle tug is sufficient' – and evidently remembered that she had left it burning.
90 She turned it off now with what seemed to me a sharp <u>yank</u>, then gave me and the room a final suspicious once-over, and departed again.

Excerpt from Notes from a Small Island *by Bill Bryson*

Read the extract and answer the following questions:

1 List three things from lines 1–7 that Bill Bryson looks for in a guesthouse or hotel.

2 Which of the following words best describes Mrs Smegma?

   a quiet

   b complex

   c forbidding

   d hospitable

3 Which phrase in the second paragraph indicates the season?

4 In line 34, to what does *this* in 'This was all bewilderingly new to me' refer?

5 In line 38, Bryson says 'This was like joining the Army' because…

   a Mrs Smegma reminded him of his Army service

   b the guest house rules were so rigid and complicated

   c staying in the guest house was similar to joining the Army

   d you had to go through a complicated procedure to join the Army

6 Which phrase between lines 49 and 55 describes the manner in which Mrs Smegma scrutinized Bryson?

7 Which of the following is true about Mrs Smegma and her guesthouse?

   a Mrs Smegma's guesthouse was friendly but too expensive

   b Mrs Smegma charges guests for any damage they make to the guesthouse

   c A bath is always permitted in Mrs Smegma's guesthouse

   d Mrs Smegma is a complicated person

8 Which of the following is **not** true about Bryson?

   a He had previously spent a very uncomfortable night outdoors

   b He was in physical pain

   c He felt unwashed and unclean

   d He was overjoyed as soon as Mrs Smegma was gone

9 The idea of staying in this guesthouse…

   a utterly consumed Bryson

   b nearly fascinated Bryson

   c mildly interested Bryson

   d hardly attracted Bryson

10 What do the following words mean in the text? Choose the appropriate words from the list.

a discompose (line 10)

b wretched (line 55)

c immersed (line 77)

d absorbing (line 81)

e yank (line 91)

i tug

ii push

iii plunged

iv snatched

v taking in

vi discomfort

vii miserable

viii delightful

ix pulling down

x disarrange

UNIT 5 Life stories

When I look back on all these worries I remember the story of the old man who said on his deathbed that he had had a lot of trouble in his life, most of which had never happened.

Winston Churchill

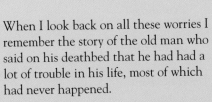

Elon Musk's 10 Rules for Success

1 Never give up
2 Really like what you do
3 Don't listen to the #littleman
4 Take a risk
5 Do something important

6 Focus on signal over noise
7 Look for problem solvers
8 Attract great people
9 Have a great product
10 Work super hard

REFLECTION

Think individually about the questions below. Then pair with a partner and discuss the questions. Share your ideas with the rest of the class.

- Does anyone in your family have an interesting / inspiring / memorable life story? What did they experience?
- Where and when were you born? What is your first, most vivid memory?
- Who is stricter: your mother or your father? Do you have a vivid memory of something you did that you were disciplined for?
- What have you liked best about your life so far? What is your happiest or proudest moment?
- What is the most challenging thing that has ever happened in your life? How did you deal with it?
- If you were writing the story of your life, how would you divide it into chapters?
- In your opinion, what is the best job in the world? Why do you think so?
- How do you define a 'good life' or a 'successful life'?
- Do you think a person needs to overcome serious setbacks or challenges to be truly successful?
- How do you think your experience of moving to another country and studying at an IB school will influence your future life?

1 Professions

According to the Cambridge dictionary, *profession* means 'any type of work that needs special training or a particular skill, often one that is respected because it involves a high level of education'. After graduating from the IB DP course, you will choose either to go to university or to train to become a professional in your chosen field. Have you decided which career path you will pursue? There are many factors that will influence your choice of career, and it is a life-determining, tough decision.

You may think that you can always change your career path after you graduate from university or after you start one career. Yes, this is true! There are many people who change their career path several times in their lifetime. If you do so, you gain many experiences and broad knowledge. That said, it is undeniable that you should be committed and dedicated to your work to be truly successful at what you do, for example Elon Musk, CEO of leading electric car company Tesla and private space transport company SpaceX, is said to be working an impressive 85 to 100 hours per week to achieve his goals.

Success in life, however, means much more than success in career. We all know that just because you are successful in your career doesn't mean you are successful in your life. What would make your life successful?

Discuss the meaning of the following quotations:

Choose a job you love, and you will never have to work a day in your life.

Confucius

It's not what you achieve, it's what you overcome. That's what defines your career.

Carlton Fisk

Work to become, not to acquire.

Elbert Hubbard

Find out what you like doing best and get someone to pay you for doing it.

Katherine Whitehorn

I've missed more than 9000 shots in my career. I've lost almost 300 games. 26 times, I've been trusted to take the game winning shot and missed. I've failed over and over and over again in my life. And that is why I succeed.

Michael Jordan

The following article is an interview with Bruce Daisley, Vice President of Twitter Europe, about modern work culture. It is taken from Lecture in Progress, an online creative careers resource. Its aim is to inspire and inform the next generation of talent by providing insight into the creative industry.

A **Before reading the article below, discuss the meaning of the following words:**

- manifesto
- automation
- receptive
- millennials
- sustainable
- mantra
- instinct
- cognitive
- finite

- ethics
- demotivate
- inflame
- flexibility
- heighten
- infantilise
- intuition
- depict

Be happy at work: Bruce Daisley, Vice President of Twitter Europe

Achieving true happiness and balance in your working life can seem like a never-ending challenge. This is something that Twitter's Vice President Bruce Daisley knows only too well, having dedicated much time and thought to exploring the ways that work and working cultures impact our well-being. On top of his podcast Eat Sleep Work Repeat, he launched The New Work Manifesto with Sue Todd, an eight-point proposal to make work healthier and more fun. As part of our Insight Report, we spoke to Bruce about his findings, including the ways we can prepare for the future of work.

What drove you to create The New Work Manifesto?

We employ several hundred people in the Twitter London office and we've always been aware that it's been a positive environment. I used to think that as long as we preserved that, we'd be in a good place. But what we found as time went on, was that work everywhere, not just here, was becoming more stressful and demanding. I started noticing that people were showing the signs of that. I was interested in learning what we could do to make work less demanding, to make it a place where you can laugh. So the manifesto came from those discussions.

Why do you think happiness is a topic that all companies should really be embracing at the moment?

The critical thing is that we're currently in the mix of two broad trends. The first is the arrival of email everywhere. It's such a given now that we don't even think about it, but it's only happened in the last 15 years. In that time, the average working day has gone up from seven and a half working hours a day to nine and a half hours a day. In fact, in America there's an expectation in some places for employees to stay online, connected to their work, for 70 hours a week.

The working day is getting longer, and the reason that matters is because half of those who check emails outside of work show signs of high stress levels. That's particularly relevant if we look at what's going to happen to the nature of work, with the automation of some jobs, principally those with no creativity – repetitive, manual jobs. So if we want to remain part of the workforce, the jobs we need to ready ourselves for will demand us to be at our most creative.

There's no shortage of neuroscience, psychological and organisational behaviour studies that show that stress kills creativity. Put these things together and you realise that although emailing outside of work hours feels like people are getting the job done, what they're actually doing is leaving themselves unable to be at their most creative.

Will any of those issues especially affect new graduates?

New grads are brilliantly receptive. The reason why millennials often get bad press is because they question the things organisations do, and hold the mirror up to some of our practices. The critical thing is that new staff in the workplace need to find a way to add value, while feeling like they're being their best selves.

The danger is that when you're new to a role, you might expect to do what you did at college – work late nights, cram and work harder and longer to get things done. The evidence suggests that we need to find a way to do sustainable work. That means trying to be productive within a short (or manageable) working week. One of the best things anyone can do, and something new graduates are good at, is maintaining a sense of outside interests. It leaves you ready and willing to contribute more in the workplace.

Why is flexible working in such demand right now?

If you speak to elite sports people, they say their goal is to have maximum impact in the time you're at it. The mantra of the GB cycling team is, 'Never stand when you can sit. Never sit when you can lie down.' That's interesting as, for most of us, if we were training for a big race our natural instinct would be to walk up stairs as much as possible, but it's the opposite of what elite athletes do. We do the same at work – we work continuously and think breaks are for wimps. We're not thinking about the way our brains work.

As cognitive psychologist Daniel Levitin points out: 'Our brains are configured to make a certain number of decisions a day. Once we reach that limit, we can't make any more regardless of how important they are.' This is based on academic research where students watched clips and then made decisions. What they found is that your brain has an almost finite amount of gunpowder it can pop a certain number of times a day. Then you think about the way we work. About 40% of our time is spent emailing; between two to three days a week goes on meetings. We're largely using this finite resource (our attention) on rubbish. Finding a way to spend less time on unproductive things is really critical.

You mention the importance of company ethics in the manifesto. Are you seeing ethics featuring higher up on job hunters' priorities?

Definitely. And if people take a job that doesn't reflect them, they feel anxious about it. In Daniel Cable's book Alive At Work, one of the things he found was that people who take big rewards for jobs they find boring or demotivating actually end up making themselves ill. They inflame their immune systems. While a few of us might take a job with a company whose ethics we don't necessarily agree with as a short-term thing, this actually has a consequence on our body that's far more significant.

What advice do you have for managers and senior staff wanting to improve workplace culture within their companies?

The most important thing is a degree of flexibility. There's a lot of proven science around the benefits of coming in to work, where we tend to be more collectively and individually productive. But people should have the flexibility to work in different ways. A lot of people struggle with open-plan offices. If you've got to finish a document or a presentation, stepping away from your desk can be really productive. But if your boss says, 'Where are you? Why are you not at your desk?' it actually ends up heightening anxiety, because now you're concerned that you're upsetting your boss. There's so much about modern work that infantilises us. Time and timeagain, bad managers and bad work turns us into children.

How can grads work out whether a company's culture is a good fit for them?

Some of it is going to be intuition. Did the interviewer smile, laugh or appear to value questions about personality? Sometimes you get a sense from the way current employees depict themselves on LinkedIn, Twitter and Facebook, plus how they interact with each other. Ask about the things the team does together to build culture, and how they feel it has evolved in the last two or three years.

Lecture in Progress is an online creative careers resource. Its aim is to inspire and inform the next generation of talent by providing insight into the creative industry. Laura Snoad https://lectureinprogress.com/journal/bruce-daisley

B **To whom or to what do the underlined words refer? Answer using words as they appear in the text.**

1 I used to think that as long as we preserved <u>that</u> … (paragraph 2)

2 … we don't even think about <u>it</u> … (paragraph 3)

3 Put <u>these things</u> together … (paragraphs 3–5)

4 …they feel anxious about <u>it</u>. (paragraph 10)

Is each of the following sentences true or false?

5 The New Work Manifesto is an eight-point proposal to prepare you for the future of work.

6 The average working day has increased from 7.5 hours to 9.5 hours.

7 Checking email outside of work can cause high stress levels, which kills creativity.

8 Graduates lose their interests outside of work quickly.

9 There is a limit to how many decisions our brains can make effectively.

10 Bruce Daisley thinks we are already using our time effectively, but we can find ways to work harder.

11 Doing work that is demotivating is boring but necessary.

12 Bad managers can be a cause of workplace anxiety.

13 Asking how a team builds their culture is a good way of finding out whether you are a good fit for the company.

14 This article is mainly aimed at managers and bosses of big corporations.

Grammar

Verb + -*ing* or verb + infinitive

Have a look at the following sentences:

• *Even people who **want to go** to heaven don't **want to die** to get there.*

• ***Keep looking** until you find it.*

Have you noticed that we use the **-*ing*** form after certain verbs and the **infinitive** after other verbs? Sometimes we can use either form and there is no change in meaning. Occasionally we can use either form and there is a change in meaning. So what's the rule for whether we use the -*ing* form or the infinitive? Sorry, there isn't a rule. You have to learn which verbs go with which pattern.

Verbs followed by -*ing* include:

• *stop*
• *finish*
• *practice*
• *suggest*
• *allow*
• *avoid*
• *mind*
• *miss*
• *urge*
• *enjoy*

Verbs followed by the infinitive include:

- *hope*
- *need*
- *fail*
- *agree*
- *forget*

- *say*
- *learn*
- *afford*
- *wait*
- *ask*

- *seem*
- *would like*
- *choose*
- *hurry*
- *promise*

- *want*
- *invite*

The following verbs can be followed by either form:

- *start*
- *bother*
- *love*
- *like*

There are some more verbs that can be followed by *-ing* or the infinitive, but **the two options have different meanings**, for example *remember* and *stop*:

- I **forgot to meet** my friend on her birthday.

  (forget + infinitive = didn't remember to do something you needed to)

- I **forgot meeting** my friend on her birthday.

  (forgot + -ing = to have no memory of something you have done)

- She **stopped drinking coffee** six weeks ago.

  (stop + -ing = to not do something anymore)

- It was raining, so we **stopped to** find some shelter. (we stopped walking in the rain)

  (stop + infinitive = to not do something in order to do something else)

 C **Complete the sentences with the correct form of the underlined verb.**

1 I don't like <u>drink</u> coffee late in the evening.
2 Don't forget <u>feed</u> the dogs while I'm away.
3 Remember <u>lock</u> the door when you leave.
4 Do you remember <u>come</u> here when you were a child?
5 He stopped <u>smoke</u> when he started training for the marathon.
6 He chose <u>study</u> economics in university.
7 I suggest <u>go</u> to the cinema.
8 Do you mind <u>open</u> the door for me please?

D **Working with a partner, imagine that you are having a job interview or a university interview. Student A is an interviewer and asks questions. Student B answers the questions and sells himself / herself! Once the interview is finished, reverse your roles and do the same activity again. You can create your own interview questions or use some of the following common interview questions.**

10 common university interview questions:

1 Tell me about yourself.
2 What do you do in your spare time?
3 What is your school like?
4 What do you enjoy most about school and what frustrates you most about it?
5 Why do you want to do this degree?
6 Why this university?
7 Why should we offer you a place?
8 Give an example of a time when you worked in a team.
9 Give an example of a time when you showed leadership skills.
10 What is your primary motivation for going to university?

10 common job interview questions:

1 Tell me about yourself.
2 Where do you see yourself in five years?
3 Why should we hire you?
4 Why do you want to work here?
5 What do you know about us?
6 How do people describe you?
7 What is your greatest strength / greatest weakness?
8 How did you find this job?
9 Why do you want this job?
10 Do you have any questions?

 E Watch the video clip on YouTube entitled '10 Questions for Elon Musk' at https://youtu.be/UwT3Y0lkYaQ and answer the questions below. Watch the clip only twice.

Complete the following gaps. Use no more than three words for each gap.

1 Tesla Motors was awarded $465 million in a loan from _____.
2 Elon Musk says that we're living in times where _____ is extremely difficult.
3 Elon Musk thinks that within 20 years a majority of new cars manufactured will be _____.
4 Elon Musk is planning to create a _____ by combining the knowledge sets from SpaceX and Tesla.

Answer the following questions:

5 How many companies has Elon Musk successfully founded?
6 According to Elon Musk, what do we have to create to achieve our goal of becoming a spacefaring civilization?

Choose the correct answer.

7 Which of the following is **not** a piece of advice from Elon Musk to a new entrepreneur?
   a Listen to any positive and negative feedback
   b Reflect on all information you receive
   c Organize groups of people into a company
8 From the interview, we know that:
   a Congress is fully supportive of commercial rocket travel
   b Falcon 9 successfully launched
   c Elon Musk thinks that commercial rocket travel is achievable within 20 years
9 Throughout the interview, Elon Musk's attitude towards the future is…
   a optimistic
   b indifferent
   c concerning

F ■ Task 1: To write a diary entry

You recently did work experience at Tesla or SpaceX (or another company of your choice) for a week. You were very impressed with the company: the way it operated and the way it organized work-experience programmes. Write a diary entry in which you reflect on your work experience. A diary is a personal text where you should be descriptive and honest about your experience and feelings. Use the following checklist:

■ Date of entry

■ Descriptions of experience

■ Reflections (thoughts and feelings)

■ Informal register

■ Coherently organized paragraphs

■ Task 2: To write an editorial

You recently did work experience at a company of your choice for a week. Although the work the company did was innovative, you felt that it had a long way to go before it achieved gender equality at its workplace. You learned that male and female workers have different salaries. Male and female work-experience students were also treated differently. Write an editorial in which you express your opinions about gender equality at work. Use the following checklist:

■ Heading

■ Introduction, body and conclusion

■ An objective explanation of the issue

■ Opinions from the opposing viewpoint

■ A solid and concise conclusion

■ Formal or semi-formal register

■ TOK Links

Intuition

When considering whether a company's culture is a good fit, Bruce Daisley encourages new graduates to follow their intuition. What does he mean by this?

Intuition is one of the ways of knowing in Theory of Knowledge. What is intuition? According to the Cambridge dictionary, *intuition* is '(knowledge from) an ability to understand or know something immediately based on your feelings rather than facts'. Knowing that intuition is more based on feelings than facts, how reliable do you think our intuition is? Where does our intuition come from?

Our brain is constantly assessing and gathering information – some of which we do with conscious awareness, while some is gathered completely unintentionally. The gathered information is stored as 'patterns' of information and becomes tacit knowledge. Our intuition comes from this tacit knowledge – often in the form of gut feelings.

We rely on our gut feelings (our intuitive automatic system) to make hundreds of routine judgments and decisions every day. However, if you are to make an important decision – for example as a member of a jury deciding if a defendant is guilty or not – you will need more evidence and careful thinking to make a decision.

Intuition is certainly a way of thinking and knowing. However, we cannot fully rely on our intuition as it is not always logical or reasonable. It is good to question our intuitions – especially if they conflict with reason, experience and other people's intuitions.

Have you ever had an experience where you followed your heart and intuition and received good outcomes? If so, share your experience with your class.

2 Migration

Ever since the beginning of our history, people have moved to start new lives elsewhere for various reasons. Starting a new life in an unfamiliar place can be exciting and daunting at the same time. Regardless of the distance you move, a new place will form a new experience, which will in turn shape your identity.

Moving to another country is quite a common experience for an IB student. Have you moved to another country? If so, what was your experience? If you were to write an autobiography, how important do you think is your experience of settling in another country, on a scale of 1–10? Why?

Did you know that early human migrations are thought to have begun when Homo erectus first migrated out of Africa to Eurasia around 1.8 million years ago? Why do you think Homo erectus decided to migrate to Eurasia? When we decide to move away from the place where we were born, what life experience do we anticipate?

Discuss the meaning of the following words:

- migration
- immigration
- emigration

A **Before reading the story below, discuss the meaning of the following words:**

- prodigy
- crinkly
- lament
- lop off
- assure
- at a slant

- fame
- adore
- reproach
- accusation
- betrayal
- inevitable

Two Kinds

My mother believed you could be anything you wanted to be in America. You could open a restaurant. You could work for the government and get good retirement. You could buy a house with almost no money down. You could become rich. You could become instantly famous.

'Of course you can be <u>prodigy</u>, too,' my mother told me when I was nine. 'You can be best anything. What does Auntie Lindo know? Her daughter, she is only best tricky.'

America was where all my mother's hopes lay. <u>She had come here in 1949</u> after losing everything in China: her mother and father, her family home, her first husband, and two daughters, twin baby girls. But she never looked back with regret. There were so many ways for things to get better.

We didn't immediately pick the right kind of prodigy. At first my mother thought I could be a Chinese Shirley Temple. We'd watch Shirley's old movies on TV as though they were

training films. My mother would poke my arm and say, '*Ni kan*' – You watch. And I would see Shirley tapping her feet, or singing a sailor song, or pursing her lips into a very round O while saying, 'Oh my goodness.'

'*Ni kan,*' said my mother as Shirley's eyes flooded with tears. 'You already know how. Don't need talent for crying!'

Soon after my mother got this idea about Shirley Temple, she took me to a beauty training school in the Mission district and put me in the hands of a student who could barely hold scissors without shaking. Instead of getting big fat curls, I emerged with an uneven mass of <u>crinkly</u> black fuzz. My mother dragged me off to the bathroom and tried to wet down my hair.

'You look like Negro Chinese,' she <u>lamented</u>, <u>as if I had done this on purpose</u>.

The instructor of the beauty training school had to <u>lop off</u> these soggy clumps to make my hair even again. 'Peter Pan is very popular these days,' the instructor <u>assured</u> my mother. I now had hair the length of a boy's, with straight-across bangs that hung <u>at a slant</u> two inches above my eyebrows. I liked the haircut and <u>it made me actually look forward to my future</u> fame.

In fact, in the beginning, I was just as excited as my mother, maybe even more so. I pictured this prodigy part of me as many different images, trying each one on for size. I was a dainty ballerina girl standing by the curtains, waiting to hear the right music that would send me floating on my tiptoes. I was like the Christ child lifted out of the straw manger, crying with holy indignity. I was Cinderella stepping from her pumpkin carriage with sparkly cartoon music filling the air.

In all of my imaginings, I was filled with a sense that I would soon become *perfect*. My mother and father would <u>adore</u> me. I would be beyond <u>reproach</u>. I would never feel the need to sulk for anything.

But sometimes the prodigy in me became impatient. '<u>If you don't hurry up and get me out of here</u>, I'm disappearing for good,' it warned. 'And then you'll always be nothing.'

[...]

It was not the only disappointment my mother felt in me. In the years that followed, I failed her so many times, each time asserting my own will, my right to fall short of expectations. I didn't get straight As. I didn't become class president. I didn't get into Stanford. I dropped out of college.

For unlike my mother, I did not believe I could be anything I wanted to be. I could only be me.

And for all those years, we never talked about the disaster at the recital or my terrible <u>accusations</u> afterward at the piano bench. All that remained unchecked, like a <u>betrayal</u> that was now unspeakable. So I never found a way to ask her why she had hoped for something so large that failure was <u>inevitable</u>.

And even worse, I never asked her what frightened me the most: Why had she given up hope?

For after our struggle at the piano, she never mentioned my playing again. The lessons stopped. The lid to the piano was closed, shutting out the dust, my misery, and her dreams.

So she surprised me. A few years ago, she offered to give me the piano, for my thirtieth birthday. I had not played in all those years. I saw the offer as a sign of forgiveness, a tremendous burden removed.

'Are you sure?' I asked shyly. 'I mean, won't you and Dad miss it?'

'No, this your piano,' she said firmly. 'Always your piano. You only one can play.'

'Well, I probably can't play anymore,' I said. 'It's been years.'

'You pick up fast,' said my mother, as if she knew this was certain. 'You have natural talent. You could been genius if want to.'

'No, I couldn't.'

'You just not trying,' said my mother. And she was neither angry nor sad. She said it as if to announce a fact that could never been disproved. 'Take it,' she said.

But I didn't at first. <u>It was enough that she had offered it to me</u>. And after that, every time I saw it in my parents' living room, standing in front of the bay windows, it made me feel proud, as if it were a shiny trophy I had won back.

'Two Kinds' by Amy Tan

B **Choose the correct answer.**

1 The narrator's mother was…
   a pessimistic
   b optimistic
   c unrealistic
   d eccentric

2 The narrator watched Shirley Temple's old movies because…
   a her mother wanted the narrator to have the same hair style as Shirley Temple
   b her mother loved Shirley Temple's works
   c her mother thought Shirley Temple was the best actress
   d her mother thought the narrator could become a child prodigy

To whom or to what do the underlined words refer? Answer using words as they appear in the text, for example:

<u>She</u> had come here in 1949…

My mother

3 … as if I had done <u>this</u> on purpose.

4 … <u>it</u> made me actually look forward to my future fame.

5 If you don't hurry up and get <u>me</u> out of here,…

6 It was enough that she had offered <u>it</u> to me.

Is each of the following sentences true or false? Justify your answers by quoting a relevant phrase from the text.

7 My mother believed in the American dream.

8 I was never excited about the American dream.

9 I failed my mother's expectations more than once.

Grammar

The conditionals

The following sentences are taken from the text 'Two Kinds'. Discuss the meaning of the sentences.

- *It made me feel proud, **as if** it **were** a shiny trophy I had won back.*
- *She lamented, **as if** I **had done** this on purpose.*

We use *if* + past simple to talk about imaginary or hypothetical situations in the present or future.

We use *if* + past perfect to talk about situations that did not happen in the past. The situation described is often the opposite of what really happened.

C Write the correct form of each of the underlined verbs. Use the past simple or *would*.

1 **A:** If you are coming tonight, can you bring your car?

   B: Sorry, if I <u>have</u> it, I <u>bring</u> it, but I've lent it to Zara.

2 **A:** What <u>you do</u>, if you <u>be</u> me?

   B: I think I <u>accept</u> the job, but only if they <u>offer</u> to give me a pay rise!

3 **A:** If you know where he is, please tell me.

   B: But I don't know! Honestly, if I <u>know</u> where he <u>be</u>, you <u>be</u> the first person I'd tell.

Write the correct form of each of the underlined verbs.

4 **A:** You missed a good concert last night. You really should have been there.

   B: But I was!

   A: If you <u>be</u> there, why <u>I / not / see</u> you?

   B: I was in the gallery. If you <u>look</u> up, you <u>see</u> me. I waved at you, but you didn't wave back.

   A: If I <u>not wave</u> back, it <u>be</u> because I couldn't see you! Why didn't you text me or something? If you <u>send</u> a text, we <u>go</u> out for a drink or something.

   B: I tried, but my phone had no signal. And anyway, I had to go home early.

Practical Grammar by John Hughes and Ceri Jones

D Choose one of the following role play sets and act it out with your partner:

Scenario	Role A	Role B
1	You are a 32-year-old female lawyer. Six months ago, you gave birth to a daughter. In a couple of months, you are planning to go back to work. Today your husband tells you that he will be transferred to Croatia. He wants to go, but you don't want to. You are worried about your and your daughter's future.	You are a 32-year-old male geologist. You have been successfully working on a project, and your project manager has asked you to go to Croatia for this project. You will get a pay rise, and you think it is a great opportunity for you and your family to explore a new culture. Persuade your wife to come with you to Croatia.
2	You are a 45-year-old Polish mother who immigrated to Britain 20 years ago. You think it is important to teach your son the Polish culture and language. You have found a school where he can learn traditional Polish dance and language. Persuade your son to go to this school on Saturdays.	You are a 15-year-old boy who was born and brought up in Britain. Your parents are from Poland and you speak Polish at home. However, your mother thinks your Polish is not fluent enough and you are slowly losing your connection with the Polish culture. She is asking you to join a Saturday Polish school where you can learn Polish dance and language. You do not think it is necessary for you to go to this school, and you have better things to do on a Saturday.
3	You are a 47-year-old engineer. You live in New York as a single father. You have been offered a job in Paris. The prospect of this new job is too good to turn down. You need to tell your daughter that you want to move to Paris with her.	You are a 17-year-old girl, living in New York with your father. Your father tells you that he's found a new job in Paris. He tells you this will be a great opportunity for you to experience a new culture and learn the French language. He says he is planning to be in Paris for 3 years. You do not want to go, as this is an important time in your life and you don't want to leave your friends behind.
4	You are a 50-year-old professor from Australia. You and your family have been living abroad over the last 20 years. You have lived in Britain, America, Africa, Spain and Denmark. This year you have found an opportunity to go back to your home country. You want to go back to Australia and spend the rest of your life there. Persuade your child to come with you.	You are an 18-year-old university student in Denmark. Your parents are from Australia and you have an Australian passport. You were born in Britain and have lived in five different countries since birth. You are a true global nomad. Your parents tell you that they plan to go back to Australia for good. You don't think it's a good idea. You are worried about the reverse culture shock that they may experience once they go back. You certainly don't want to go to Australia for good.
5	You are a student from Japan in Britain. You are talking to your British friend about the culture shock you experienced when you first came to Britain.	Your Japanese friend tells you about the culture shock she experienced when she first came to Britain. Whenever she talks about differences she observed, you want to tell her that there are more similarities than differences between cultures, according to your experience.

E Ask two students to read aloud the transcript of Dana Gioia's interview with Amy Tan www.the-american-interest.com/2007/05/01/a-conversation-with-amy-tan/.

Choose the correct answer to each question.

1 As she was growing up, Amy was…
   a fully bilingual in Chinese and English
   b a lover of fairy tales
   c forced to speak Mandarin at home

2 For Amy, reading was…
   a a magical world to escape to from reality
   b where she found a resolution to her problems
   c all about dangers and tensions

3 When Amy was growing up, her parents did not talk about China because…
   a they didn't want to be mistaken for communists
   b they didn't want to talk about the Second World War in China
   c they wanted Amy to stay ignorant of China

4 The novel *The Joy Luck Club* is…
   a not related to Amy's family's past
   b about gambling and investment
   c somewhat based on Amy's past

5 When she was in higher education, Amy was…
  a obedient to her parents
  b rebellious to her parents
  c agreeable to her parents

6 Choose the five true statements.
  a All Amy's family members immigrated to America.
  b It is implied that Amy was a lonely child.
  c Amy's parents believed in the American dream.
  d The history of China was very important to Amy as she was growing up.
  e Amy thinks that joy and luck are specific to Chinese culture.
  f Amy's parents believed artists do not make enough money.
  g Amy's ambition to be a writer was fully supported by her parents.
  h Amy's parents started the Joy Luck Club.
  i The word 'luck' is prevalent in China.
  j Amy believes that she was lucky because she chased luck.

F ■ Task 1: To write an informal email

Imagine you have recently moved to Australia from Singapore. Since your arrival, you have observed many differences and similarities between the two cultures. Write an informal email to your friend in Britain about your experience of moving to and settling in Australia. Use the following checklist:

■ Conventions of an informal email

■ Paragraphs (first paragraph: general chat; body paragraphs: details about your experience; last paragraph: closure to the email)

■ Informal register

■ Coherence

■ Cohesive devices

■ Task 2: To write a set of guidelines

Imagine a group of students from another country is planning to visit your school for two weeks. They will be staying with a host family for the duration of their stay. To help them adjust to the new culture as quickly as possible, write a set of guidelines about the cultural norms / etiquettes at school and at a host family's house. Use the following checklist:

■ Title / heading

■ Subheadings

■ Logical order of information

■ Short sentences and paragraphs

■ Supportive and sympathetic tone (don't be too bossy!)

■ TOK Links

Stereotypes

A stereotype is a fixed, oversimplified and usually negative picture of an individual or group based on their membership of that group. It arises when we make assumptions about a group of people purely on the basis of their membership of that group. The use of stereotypes is particularly apparent in the case of nationality. Since Giovanni is Italian, he must love wine, pasta and ice cream, throw his hands around when he talks and enjoy opera. And since Fritz is German, he must love beer, sausages and sauerkraut, work hard and be very serious.

Theory of knowledge for the IB Diploma *by Richard van de Lagemaat*

Are you annoyed by stereotypes of your nationality? If so, why? Do you think these stereotypes have an element of truth in them?

We classify and generalize a lot to make things easier for communication. We use generalized language to make our communication easier, for example if we didn't have the common noun 'cat' in our language, it would be time-consuming and difficult to describe your cat to somebody who doesn't know your cat. Generalization is often efficient and economical.

However, generalization can lead to stereotypes that often exaggerate the negative features of a group and assume that these features are possessed by all members of the group. As these stereotypes are based on prejudice rather than fact, they have disadvantages over our perception.

What common stereotypes exist in your culture? To what extent do you think they affect the way people see things?

CREATIVITY, ACTIVITY, SERVICE

Every year, millions of people make difficult and often dangerous treks from their home country to a new nation. Motivations for leaving are as varied as the immigrants themselves: some leave for opportunity, some for adventure and some to escape oppressive regimes that threaten their rights or religions. When they don't have a choice but to leave their own country, they often risk their lives to come to a new country. Even if they make it to a new country, they face huge challenges.

When you moved to a new country, how difficult was it for you to get used to the new environment? Moving to another country is a huge upheaval, regardless of your circumstances. Some people have to go through this upheaval on their own without much help from anyone else. But there are some charity organizations that have been established to help such migrants and refugees. Why not volunteer your service to these organizations? Below are some UK charity organizations:

- Migrant's Organise: www.migrantsorganise.org
- Refugee Action: www.refugee-action.org.uk
- Migrant Help: www.migranthelpuk.org
- Joint Council for the Welfare of Immigrants: www.jcwi.org.uk

3 Trauma

Trauma means 'a deeply distressing or disturbing experience'. Have you ever experienced trauma? If so, how did you deal with it? A traumatic experience such as a car accident or a natural disaster may last only for a short time, while other traumatic experiences such as war, persecution, bullying, discrimination, and so on can last for a long time. One thing in common for all these traumatic experiences is the lasting effect. People who have experienced a form of trauma often have to deal with their pain for a long time afterwards. The damaging effect of trauma may lead people to change their identity.

Post-traumatic stress disorder (PTSD) is an anxiety disorder caused by very stressful, frightening or distressing events, or trauma. Someone with PTSD often relives the traumatic event through nightmares and flashbacks, and may experience feelings of isolation, irritability and guilt. They may also have problems sleeping (insomnia) and find concentrating difficult. These symptoms are often severe and persistent enough to have a significant impact on the person's day-to-day life.

Here are some types of events that can cause PTSD:

- Serious road accidents
- Violent personal assaults, such as sexual assault, mugging or robbery
- Prolonged sexual abuse, violence or severe neglect
- Witnessing violent deaths
- Military combat
- Being held hostage
- Terrorist attacks
- Natural disasters, such as severe floods, earthquakes or tsunamis

Do you know anyone who has experienced any of the above? How can you help someone who has suffered trauma?

 Before reading the article, discuss the meaning of the following words:

■ unconscious	■ helter-skelter
■ convenience	■ Urdu
■ reunited	■ threat
■ procession	■ stinky
■ rickshaws	■ sprout
■ ornamented	

The day my world changed

1 I come from a country which was created at midnight. [1] Before / When / After I almost died it was just after midday.

2 One year ago, I left my home for school and never returned. I was shot by a Taliban bullet [2] and / so / but was flown out of Pakistan unconscious. Some people say I will never return home but I believe firmly in my heart [3] what / if / that I will. To be torn from the country that you love is not something to wish on anyone.

3 Now, every morning [4] when / that / which I open my eyes, I long to see my old room full of my things, my clothes all over the floor and my school prizes on the shelves. Instead I am in a country [5] why / which / what is five hours behind my beloved homeland Pakistan and my home in the Swat Valley. [6] But / So / And my country is centuries behind this one. Here there is any convenience you can imagine. Water running from every tap, hot or cold as you wish; lights at the flick of a switch, day and night, no need for oil lamps; ovens to cook on that don't need anyone to go and fetch gas cylinders from the bazaar. Here everything is so modern one can even find food ready cooked in packets.

4 [7] Before / After / When I stand in front of my window and look out, I see tall buildings, long roads full of vehicles moving in orderly lines, neat green hedges and lawns, and tidy pavements to walk on. I close my eyes and for a moment I am back in my valley – the high snow-topped mountains, green waving fields and fresh blue rivers – and my heart smiles when it looks at the people of Swat. My mind transports me back to my school and there I am reunited with my friends and teachers. I meet my best friend Moniba and we sit together, talking and joking [8] even if / as if / after I had never left. Then I remember I am in Birmingham, England.

5 The day when everything changed was Tuesday, 9 October 2012. It wasn't the best of days to start with as it was the middle of school exams, [9] because / which / though as a bookish girl I didn't mind them as much as some of my classmates.

6 That morning we arrived in the narrow mud lane off Haji Baba Road in our usual procession of brightly painted rickshaws, sputtering diesel fumes, each one crammed with five or six girls. [10] Since / Before / Because the time of the Taliban our school has had no sign and the ornamented brass door in a white wall across from the woodcutter's yard gives no hint of what lies beyond.

7 For us girls that doorway was like a magical entrance to our own special world. [11] Though / As / Because we skipped through, we cast off our head-scarves like winds puffing away clouds to make way for the sun then ran helter-skelter up the steps. At the top of the steps was an open courtyard with doors to all the classrooms. We dumped our backpacks in our rooms then gathered for morning assembly under the sky, our backs to the mountains as we stood to attention. One girl commanded, 'Assaan bash!' or 'Stand at ease!' and we clicked our heels and responded, 'Allah.' Then she said, 'Hoo she yar!' or 'Attention!' and we clicked our heels again. 'Allah.'

8 The school was founded by my father before I was born, and on the wall above us KHUSHAL SCHOOL was painted proudly in red and white letters. We went to school six mornings a week and as a fifteen-year-old in Year 9 my classes were spent chanting chemical equations or studying Urdu grammar; writing stories in English with morals like 'Haste makes waste' or drawing diagrams of blood circulation – most of my classmates wanted to be doctors. It's hard to imagine that anyone would see that as a threat. [12] Just / Yet / In fact, outside the door to the school lay not only the noise and craziness of Mingora, the main city of Swat, but also those like the Taliban who think girls should not go to school.

9 The school was not far from my home and I used to walk, but [13] for / before / since the start of last year I had been going with other girls in a rickshaw and coming home by bus. It was a journey of just five minutes along the stinky stream, past the giant billboard for Dr Humayun's Hair Transplant Institute [14] where / when / that we joked that one of our bald male teachers must have gone when he suddenly started to sprout hair. I liked the bus because I didn't get as sweaty as when I walked, and I could chat with my friends and gossip with Usman Ali, the driver, [15] which / who / whose we called Bhai Jan, or 'Brother'. He made us all laugh with his crazy stories.

10 I had started taking the bus [16] as though / because / unless my mother was scared of me walking on my own. We had been getting threats all year. Some were in the newspapers, some were notes or messages passed on by people. My mother was worried about me, but the Taliban had never come for a girl and I was more concerned they would target my father [17] as / until / while he was always speaking out against them. His close friend and fellow campaigner Zahid Khan had been shot in the face in August on his way to prayers and I knew everyone was telling my father, 'Take care, you'll be next.'

Modified from I Am Malala *by Malala Yousafzai with Christina Lamb*

B the article and answer the following questions:

1 For each of the gaps marked 1–17 in the text, choose one word or phrase from the options provided that renders each sentence meaningful.

2 To whom or to what do the underlined words below refer? Answer using words as they appear in the text, for example:

… when <u>it</u> looks at the people of Swat…

My *heart*
a … I didn't mind <u>them</u> as much as…
b … <u>each one</u> crammed with five or six girls.
c … that anyone would see <u>that</u> as a threat.
d … all laugh with <u>his</u> crazy stories.
e … on <u>his</u> way to prayers…

3 Based on the text, answer the following questions:
a Why was Malala flown out of Pakistan?
b Which of the following is **not** one of the modern conveniences in England that she does not have in her home country?
   i   Cold and hot water taps
   ii   Readymade food in packets
   iii National Grid-supplied gas
   iv   Oil lamps
c Which word between paragraphs 4 and 6 indicates that Malala was a studious girl?
d Which word in the seventh paragraph indicates that the girls moved about in a disorderly way?
e Name four subjects mentioned in the eighth paragraph.
f Why had Malala's family been getting threats all year?
g Why did Malala think the Taliban would target her father?

Grammar

Used to / be used to / get used to

We use **used to** to talk about past habits, and situations or states:
- *The school was not far from my home and I **used to** walk.* (habit)
- *I **used to** live in Swat.* (situation)
- *She **didn't use to** like the country lifestyle.* (state)

We use **be used to** to explain that someone is familiar with a situation or a routine:
- *I **am used to** staying in bed late.*

We use **get used to** in the present continuous to explain that someone is in the process of becoming familiar with a situation:
- *I **am getting used to** working early in the morning.*

Use the past simple to show that the process is complete:
- *I quickly **got used to** the new routine.*

C **Complete the dialogue with the correct form of *used to*, *be used to* or *get used to*.**

A: So, what did you [1]_____ do before you became a teacher?

B: I [2]_____ work as a banker in the City, in London.

A: Why did you decide to become a teacher?

B: My working life [3]_____ be very stressful. I [4]_____ working ten to twelve hours a day and was under a lot of pressure. It was very tiring and I decided it was time for a change.

A: Was it difficult to [5]_____ your new lifestyle?

B: Well, I [6]_____ earning a lot more money, so it took me a bit of time to [7]_____ living on a teacher's salary! And I was not [8]_____ working with kids, but now I'm slowly [9]_____ the role of teacher and I'm loving every minute of it – well, almost!

A: And what about your new working routine?

B: I [10]_____ the shorter working hours and the longer holidays very quickly! I only [11]_____ take ten or fifteen days' holiday a year when I was a banker. Now I have six weeks' holidays in the summer alone. That's great.

Practical Grammar Level 3 *by John Hughes and Ceri Jones*

D ■ **Standard level**

For this task, you'll be working in pairs. The visual stimuli below are all related to the theme 'Experiences'.

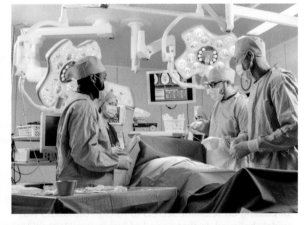

A Answer the following questions:

1. Which phrase between lines 10 and 20 indicates that the narrator did something terrible in the past and has done nothing to make amends?

2. Find the words or phrase between lines 25 and 35 that indicates Hassan's very distinctive physical feature.

3. Find a phrase between lines 65 and 74 that indicates Hassan's unwavering loyalty to the narrator.

4. Which phrase between lines 65 and 74 indicates Hassan's talent?

5. Find a word that describes Ali's personality.

B Choose the correct answer to each question.

1. The narrator is...
   a. glad that San Francisco is where he lives now
   b. profoundly guilty of what he did in the winter of 1975
   c. grateful that Rahim Khan rang him
   d. sorry about the absence of Hassan for the last 26 years

2. In 'how you can bury it' (line 9), the word 'it' refers to...
   a. the winter
   b. the alley
   c. the precise moment
   d. the past

C What do the following words mean in the text? Choose the appropriate words from the box.

1. crouching (line 5)
2. propelled (line 22)
3. pelted (line 53)
4. flickering (line 55)
5. chiselled (line 57)

a teasing	c attacked	e waiting	g pushed	i mashed
b cowering	d stolen	f flown	h carved	j quivering

UNIT **6** Customs and traditions

Think individually about the questions below. Then pair with a partner and discuss the questions. Share your ideas with the rest of the class.

- What are some of the most important customs and traditions in your country? Do you follow all your country's traditional customs?
- What are some strange customs that you have heard of? Are there any customs in your country that visitors might find strange?
- If you could change one element of your country's traditions, what would you change?
- What taboos exist in your culture?
- What do you think would happen if you broke one of the taboos you just discussed?
- What are social norms? How do we learn social norms? What are positive and negative aspects of social norms?
- Do you wear school uniform? If so, do you like wearing it? Why or why not? If you don't, would you like to wear school uniform? Why or why not?
- Are there any dress codes in workplaces in your country? Do you think dress codes are effective?

1 Traditions

All cultures have their own traditions and customs. Some traditions are quite universal, for example in most cultures it is considered conventional to respect elderly people, marry at a certain age, go to school, and so on. Other traditions are quite unique to their own culture. Did you know the following rather unique and somewhat strange traditions around the world?

- **Teeth tossing in Greece:** Some cultures pop children's teeth under their pillows and wait for a swap with cold hard cash by a fairy. Others throw a baby's recently liberated tooth on their roofs.

■ **Avoiding using red ink in South Korea:** Based on their history and customs, red ink was used to write down names of dead people. It is therefore considered a taboo to write someone's name in red.

■ **Tomato craze in Spain:** La Tomatina is the biggest tomato fight that exists. It is a unique culture among the Valencians in Buñol where tomatoes are used as weapons.

https://garfors.com/2016/12/25-strange-customs-and-traditions-html

A lot of these quirky traditions started for a reason. However, most of the origins have been lost, and no one knows why we have such traditions. The things is, though, these traditions create a sense of belonging. It is almost like having inside knowledge! Such traditions not only belong to a national culture, but also to a family or community culture. Is there a unique tradition that belongs to your family? Do you know how it all started?

As valued as it is, tradition can also pose limits on our thinking. Discuss the meaning of the following quotation:

> 'The thinking [person] must oppose all cruel customs, no matter how deeply rooted in tradition and surrounded by a halo. When we have a choice, we must avoid bringing torment and injury into the life of another.'

Albert Schweitzer

Can you think of any examples in history where we had to break traditions and customs to establish a more equitable society?

A **Before reading the article below, discuss the meaning of the following words:**

■ wacky	■ humdingers	■ vie
■ eccentric	■ Solstice	■ bog
■ antiquity	■ bonfire	■ don
■ daredevil	■ attest	■ peat
■ impulse	■ tussle	■ submerged

8 best weird and wacky British traditions

The British are masters of the weird and wacky. From cheese rolling in Gloucestershire and fireball whirling in Scotland, to Morris Men dancing and banging sticks, or hobby horses terrorizing villages on May Day, there are wonderfully eccentric traditions all over the British Isles. Most have origins lost in antiquity. No one cares how they got going – the point is to have a good time.

1 Cheese rolling in Gloucestershire

Cheese rolling on Cooper's Hill in Gloucestershire may not sound dangerous but this annual event (which local authorities keep trying to ban) is no walk in the park. Once a year, as they have done for hundreds of years, daredevil young men and women hurl themselves down a hill so steep that it is impossible to remain standing, in pursuit of a seven or eight pound wheel of locally made Double Gloucester cheese. There is simply no way participants can come down Cooper's Hill on their feet. Spectators who get too close to the edge have been known to tumble over and join the race involuntarily. And the prize? The wheel of cheese, of course.

2 The best winter fire festivals in Scotland

There's no denying that the Scots love to party through the night. When you combine those high spirits with the primitive northern impulse to light up the long nights and the ancient idea that fire purifies and chases away evil spirits, you end up with some of the best mid-winter celebrations in Europe. At one time, most Scottish towns celebrated the New Year with huge bonfires and torchlight processions. Most have now disappeared, but those that are left are real humdingers.

3 The Burning of the Clocks

The Winter <u>Solstice</u> – the longest night of the year – marks the end of shortening days and, at last, the sun shines a little bit longer every day. Brighton celebrates the lengthening days with its own local twist on a typical Northern fire festival – the Burning of the Clocks. The event includes a themed parade with as many as 1,000 participants. The 2017 theme was simply 'East' and saw children and adults parading with lanterns shaped as lotus flowers, available as kits purchased in local shops. After the parade, the paper and willow lanterns are burned on the beach and there's a spectacular firework show.

4 Guy Fawkes or Bonfire Night

Guy Fawkes, also called <u>Bonfire</u> Night, is a uniquely British festival that commemorates a historic attempt to blow up Parliament. It's combined with bonfire celebrations that reach back to the Celtic harvest festival of Samhain. Though not a UK national holiday, Bonfire Night is a deep-seated tradition and is marked by public and private fireworks displays and huge public bonfires all over the UK. In fact, many people say that 5 November, Bonfire Night, is the smokiest night in the realm.

5 Summer Solstice at Stonehenge

The Summer Solstice at Stonehenge is a magical new age party – an ad hoc celebration that brings together neo-druids, neo-pagans and Wiccans with ordinary families, travelers and party people. For many the impulse to arrive at Stonehenge in time for the Solstice is a little like all those people drawn to the strange rock in *Close Encounters of the Third Kind*. It's akin to a spiritual experience. Anyone who has witnessed the crowd become silent as the sky begins to brighten can <u>attest</u> to that. Interestingly, while the Summer Solstice is when all the Druids come out to play, the latest research suggests the Winter Solstice was far more important here.

6 The Rochester Sweeps

Up until the mid-19th century, children worked as chimney sweeps. When summer came they had a lot to celebrate as they could resume their trade. Today in Rochester, a Kentish town associated with Charles Dickens, the Sweeps Festival, a modern revival of an old tradition, commemorates those celebrations with three days of Morris Dancing in the streets.

7 The Haxey Hood

Seven hundred years ago, Lady de Mowbray lost her silken hood to a gust of wind and various brave locals took off after it. In gratitude for the adventure, she created the celebration, named all the participants – The Fool, The Boggins and The Lord of the Hood, and gave all the participants a strip of land. At least that's the story of how the Haxey Hood, a rugby-like <u>tussle</u> between Haxey and Westwoodside in North Lincolnshire, got started. Sounds like a lot of fuss over a hat to me. Today crowds of gigantic men <u>vie</u> for possession of the hood in what looks like a precursor to rubby on mega steroids.

8 Bog snorkeling in Wales

The Waen Rhydd <u>Bog</u>, near Llanwrtyd Wells, Britain's smallest town, is the scene of one of the country's most bizarre sporting events. Bog snorkeling probably began as a way to get a bit of tourism attention for this tiny place. But now it has grown into an international event with world records recorded by the man from Guinness and everything. Anyone 14 years or older can <u>don</u> a mask, snorkel and flippers and swim back and forth the length of a 60-foot channel cut in a <u>peat</u> bog. Any stroke is allowed but the snorkeler has to keep his or her head <u>submerged</u> in the muddy water and make way through the reeds and peat. They also do a Bog Triathlon.

Ferne Arfin
www.tripsavvy.com/weird-and-wacky-british-traditions-1661724

B Answer the following questions:

1 According to the writer, what is the purpose of these wonderfully eccentric traditions all over the British Isles?

2 Which word in section 1 indicates that this event takes place once a year?

3 Which phrase in section 1 indicates that this tradition has a long history?

4 What are the two main reasons that the Scots ended up with some of the best mid-winter celebrations in Europe?

5 How did most Scottish towns celebrate the New Year in the past?

6 What is the Winter Solstice?

7 List three elements that are included in the Burning of the Clocks in Brighton.

8 What is celebrated on Guy Fawkes (Bonfire) Night?

9 How is Guy Fawkes Night celebrated?

10 There are two types of solstice festivals at Stonehenge. According to the text, which is more important?

Find the words that complete the following sentences. Answer using words as they appear in sections 5 to 8.

11 For many people, the Summer Solstice at Stonehenge feels similar to _____.

12 The Rochester Sweeps are celebrated with _____.

13 According to the Haxey Hood story, Lady de Mowbray rewarded all the brave participants who went after her lost silken hood with _____.

14 Bog snorkeling in Wales got started to _____.

15 There are two bog-related events in Wales: _____ and _____.

Grammar

Adjectives or adverbs?

Have a look again at the following sentences from the text '8 best weird and wacky British traditions':

- *There are **wonderfully** **eccentric** traditions all over the British Isles.*
- *Spectators join the race **involuntarily**.*
- *There is a **spectacular** firework show.*

We use **adjectives** to describe **nouns**. They come before the noun or after a copular verb, for example:

- *appear*
- *be*
- *become*
- *get*
- *feel*
- *seem*
- *sound*
- *look*
- *taste*
- *smell*

We use **adverbs** to describe **verbs**, **adjectives** and other **adverbs**.

Some words can be used as both adjectives and adverbs, for example:

- *clean*
- *daily*
- *deep*
- *early*
- *far*
- *fast*
- *free*
- *high*
- *hourly*
- *late*
- *loud*
- *hard*
- *weekly*
- *well*
- *yearly*

- *The test was **hard**.* (adjective: it describes the test)
- *He works **hard**.* (adverb: it describes the way he works)
- *You don't look **well**.* (adjective: well = in good health)
- *She plays the piano **well**.* (adverb: it describes how she plays the piano)

Hardly and lately:

The adverbs *late* and *hard* have a different meaning from the adverbs *lately* and *hardly*. **Lately** means 'recently'. **Hardly** means 'almost not / almost never'.

- *I worked **late** last night.*
- *I've been doing a lot of work **lately**.*
- *He worked **hard** for his exam.*
- *He **hardly** did any work for his exam.*

C   Choose the correct options.

The father looked [1] close / closely at his son. Was he being
[2] honest / honestly? Or was he just giving his usual, [3] easy / easily
answer? His son stared back at him [4] defiant / defiantly. He knew
his [5] terrible / terribly test mark was going to get him into trouble.
He knew his father was going to get really [6] angry / angrily. But still
he stared at his father. His father sighed [7] quiet / quietly. With a
[8] tired / tiredly look on his face, he took the test paper from his son's
hand. The boy waited [9] anxious / anxiously for the [10] inevitable /
inevitably explosion. Nothing came. The father looked [11] sad / sadly
at his son, shook his head and walked [12] slow / slowly away.

Practical Grammar Level 3 by John Hughes and Ceri Jones

Complete the following sentences using appropriate adjectives or adverbs:

1   If you work too _____, you will fall ill.
   a   hard
   b   hardly

2   The country received _____ any rainfall this year.
   a   hard
   b   hardly

3   In a democratic country, everyone has the right to speak _____.
   a   free
   b   freely

4   He hit the nail _____.
   a   hard
   b   hardly

5   The show was _____ amusing.
   a   high
   b   highly

6   Throw it as _____ as you can.
   a   high
   b   highly

7   He has _____ arrived.
   a   just
   b   justly

8   All criminals must be _____ punished for their crimes.
   a   just
   b   justly

9   He is never _____ for work.
   a   late
   b   lately

10   I haven't been to the theatre much _____.
   a   late
   b   lately

www.englishgrammar.orgladjective-adverb-grammar-exercise

Discussion

1 You have read the article '8 best weird and wacky British traditions'. Which one of the weird events would you like to participate in? Why?

2 Do you know any weird and wacky traditional events in your home country or in any other countries where you have lived? Tell your partner details of the event.

3 Do you agree or disagree with each of the following statements? Explain your reasons.

'You do not understand your own tradition if you do not see it in relation to others.'

John Searle

'Tradition becomes our security, and when the mind is secure it is in decay.'

Jiddu Krishnamurti

'Tradition is a guide and not a jailer.'

W. Somerset Maugham

'Half of tradition is a lie'

Stephen Crane

 Listen to the dialogue between two colleagues (available at www. hoddereducation.co.uk/ib-extras) and answer the following questions.

Track 1

1 Choose the five true statements.

a Riya's favourite part of the nuptial was the Mehndi ceremony.
b Only the bride's friends are invited to the Mehndi ceremony.
c The deeper colour of henna means the stronger bond of the newly wedded couple.
d The bride's henna artwork should be designed by her mother.
e It takes no time for the bride's henna to dry.
f The henna artists are expected to include the names of the bride and groom in the henna artwork.
g It brings bad luck if the groom cannot find the names in the henna artwork.
h A fire is an essential part of a traditional Indian wedding.
i Riya is not sure whether she would want a traditional wedding.
j Riya does not think family traditions are important.

2 How long does the traditional Indian nuptial usually last?
3 When does the Mehndi ceremony take place?
4 In what is the groom meant to find the names of the bride and groom?
5 What do the bride and groom walk around in the traditional Indian wedding?
6 What do Indians believe that the god of fire does?
7 According to Fiona, what is the distinctive feature of the Scottish wedding?
8 Which one of the two – Riya or Fiona – thinks that we spend too much money on a wedding?

  ■ **Task 1: To write a review of an event**

You have recently been to a weird and wacky traditional event. Write a review of the event for your school newspaper. The purpose of an event review is to inform the reader of the event in an engaging way. You want to offer enough information so that the reader makes an informed decision on whether to pay a visit or not, but you do not want to offer too much information so that the reader feels like he / she has been there after reading your review! It's a fine balance you have to ensure. Most of all, make it interesting to read; otherwise, your review will not be read! Use the following checklist:

■ A headline

■ Appropriate register for the target audience (semi-formal for the school newspaper)

- Engaging / attention-grabbing first paragraph
- Clear and well-developed paragraphs
- Clear viewpoint on the event
- Use of humour (it is quite tricky to master, but worth trying!)

■ Task 2: To write a blog entry

Write a blog entry about weird and wacky traditional events in your country. The format of this should be very similar to the text you've read in this chapter '8 best weird and wacky British traditions'. You may want to do some research to find out more about the events you would like to write about. Use the following checklist:

- An eye-catching title
- An introduction
- Subheadings
- Body paragraphs
- Awareness of the audience
- Use of humour (it is quite tricky to master, but worth trying!)

■ TOK Links

Tradition is formed by shared beliefs and practices. It is a shared knowledge within a culture. Does this mean that everyone in a culture agrees on a particular tradition? In the past, it was a long British tradition that women had no political power. If everyone agreed on this long tradition, we wouldn't have come to the day when women are allowed to vote and be elected as political leaders. Therefore, we have to admit that not all traditions are or should be valued, which leads to the next question: When should we question our tradition?

Discuss the following traditions that exist in some cultures but not in all. Should we question these traditions?

- We always have a cut evergreen tree in our living room for Christmas.
- When we are introduced to someone, we kiss them on both cheeks.
- We never ask a lady how old she is.
- It is okay to arrive at a dinner party fashionably late.
- When your senior is talking to you, you should never look him / her in the eye.
- When a woman gets married, she should adopt her husband's surname.

CREATIVITY, ACTIVITY, SERVICE

For a Creativity project, why not display some traditional dance? If you are not familiar with your own country's traditional dance, it would be great if you could learn a routine for a project.

There are also indigenous cultures of which you may wish to raise awareness by staging some of their dances in your school community. Below are examples of indigenous dances from Anglophone countries:

- New Zealand: The haka is a type of ancient Māori war dance traditionally used on the battlefield, as well as when groups came together in peace. Haka are a fierce display of a tribe's pride, strength and unity. Actions include violent foot-stamping, tongue protrusions and rhythmic body slapping to accompany a loud chant. You can see haka performed by the All Blacks at rugby matches.
- Australia: Traditional Aboriginal ceremonial dance is performed in parts of Australia to this day. Ceremonies contrast in different territories and regions and are an important part of the education of the young. Some ceremonies are a rite of passage for young people aged between 10 and 16, representing a point of transition from childhood to adulthood. Most ceremonies combine dance, song, rituals and often elaborate body decoration and costume. The Elders organize and run ceremonies that are designed to teach particular aspects of the lore of their people, spiritual beliefs and survival skills.

2 Social norms and taboos

Social norms are the unwritten rules of behaviour that are considered acceptable in a group or society. Norms function to provide order and predictability in society. On the whole, people want approval, they want to belong, and those who do not follow the norms may suffer disapproval or even be outcast from the group. Norms can change according to the environment, situation and culture in which they are found, and people's behaviour changes accordingly. Social norms may also change or be modified over time.

Taboos are the opposite of social norms. A taboo is an activity that is forbidden or restricted based on religious beliefs or morals. Breaking a taboo is extremely objectionable. Just the same as social norms, an act may be taboo in one culture and not in another.

Discuss the following social norms. Do these social norms apply to your society?

- Shake hands when you meet someone.
- Make direct eye contact with the person you are speaking with.
- Do not stand too close to a stranger. Don't invade someone's personal space.
- Be kind to elderly people, for example by opening a door or giving up your seat.

Discuss the following taboos. Do these taboos apply to your society?

- Giving an even number of flowers is taboo in Russia because they are for the dead.
- Marriage between people who are closely related is taboo. (It may even be illegal in some countries.)
- Adultery (sexual intercourse with someone other than your spouse) is taboo.
- In India, it is taboo to give and receive something using the left hand.

A Before reading the article below, discuss the meaning of the following words:

- well-equipped
- well catered for
- Code of Conduct
- harassment
- adhere
- demonstrate
- ridicule
- etiquette

- enhance
- banter
- intimidating
- aggressive
- ban
- bureaucratic
- regulatory

Bramble Park Golf and Country Club

Bramble Park boasts one of the best-maintained and enjoyable courses in the area. Established in 1972, it stands out for its variety and scenery, nestled among the rolling green hills in the south of England. With experienced, qualified professionals and a well-equipped Pro Shop, you will find all you need for an enjoyable game of golf at our club.

There is also plenty on offer besides the beautiful game. Enjoy a drink or relaxing meal in our Members' Bar or join us on one of our many social events for members. Memberships are available for Gentlemen, Ladies and Juniors and you might be surprised how affordable a basic membership is – enquire with us at the Club today.

Code of Conduct

Bramble Park Golf and Country Club is committed to welcoming all players to a friendly and accepting atmosphere that does not discriminate on the bases of gender, religion, age, sexual orientation, disability or race. All members, guests and visitors must adhere to our code of conduct at all times in and around the Club, maintaining an acceptable level of behaviour and demonstrating fair sporting values while enjoying the benefits of the course, the restaurant and social club.

On the course

All golfers must respect the course and their fellow members and visitors at all times. Mobile phones should be switched off or on silent mode so as not to disrupt other golfers. Adhere to the dress code and observe proper golf etiquette upon entering the Club. Avoid slow play, apply fair golfing principles and always allow other golfers to overtake when necessary in order to keep up speed of play. When searching for lost balls, it might be necessary to cede your place in the order of play. All staff members of the Club are entitled to fair treatment and respect and should not feel intimidated or harassed by members and visitors. When working on the course, golf course staff always have priority – do not play your ball if there is any risk to them or their equipment. The standard and appearance of the course should always be maintained; replace divots, rake bunkers, fix pitch marks etc.

Behave in a sporting way and refrain from cheating, aggressive behaviour, deliberately obstructing play, foul language, throwing golf clubs in frustration and do not take performance-enhancing drugs.

In the Clubhouse

The use of abusive, disrespectful or bad language is not permitted within the Clubhouse and any member heard engaging in this behaviour will be immediately warned. Members consistently using offensive or improper language may have their membership revoked. Visitors and other members should not feel intimidated or made to hear language that would make them uncomfortable or that they would not personally use. Discrimination or harassment on the basis of gender, religion, age, sexual orientation, disability or race will not be tolerated. The Club takes this very seriously. Smoking on the premises is banned. Any taking of illegal substances on the premises will result in an automatic ban and further action may be taken. Mobile phones should be switched to silent and no phone calls are permitted within the Clubhouse unless in an emergency.

This Code of Conduct is here to protect the values and beliefs of the Club and safeguard others. It is not designed to be unnecessarily prohibitive or bureaucratic. We believe that the traditions and sporting values of golf should be fully respected despite its growing populism and transformation into a multi-billion-dollar industry.

B To whom or to what do the underlined words below refer? Answer using the words as they appear in the text, for example:

...it stands out for its variety and scenery... *Bramble Park golf course*

1   ...if there is any risk to them...
2   The club takes this very seriously.
3   It is not designed to be unnecessarily prohibitive...
4   ...despite its growing populism...

Is each of the following sentences true or false? Justify your answers by quoting a relevant phrase from the text.

5   Non-members can participate in social events at the club.
6   An acceptable standard of behaviour is expected only on the course and in the clubhouse.
7   There is a strict dress code at Bramble Park.
8   Golfers are expected to repair pitch marks.
9   You are at liberty to take as much time as you wish when playing.
10 If you use offensive language, you can be chucked out of the clubhouse.

Answer the following questions:

11 In what ways can Bramble Park offer an enjoyable game of golf?
12 What is the consequence of the use of illegal substances in the clubhouse?
13 What is not permitted in the clubhouse or on the course except for emergency use?
14 With the Code of Conduct, what do they wish to protect and respect?
15 According to the text, how is golf changing?

Grammar

Verbs and dependent prepositions

Some verbs are usually followed by prepositions before the object of the verb. These are called **dependent prepositions** and they are followed by a noun or a gerund (*-ing* form).

- *All golfers must* **adhere to** *the dress code.* (*to* is the dependent preposition for *adhere*)
- *Members, guests and visitors are reminded not to* **engage in** *any form of sexual, racial or religious discrimination or harassment.* (*in* is the dependent preposition for *engage*)

Here are some other verbs with their dependent prepositions.

For:

- *He* **apologized for** *being late.* (You can also 'apologize to' someone.)
- *I* **applied for** *the job but I didn't get it.*
- *How do you* **ask for** *a coffee in Polish?*
- *She spent many years* **caring for** *her aged parents.*
- *I can't go out tonight because I have to* **prepare for** *my interview tomorrow.*

From:

- *This spray should* **protect** *you* **from** *mosquitoes.*
- *Has he* **recovered from** *his illness yet?*
- *He won an award because he* **saved** *someone* **from** *drowning.*
- *I* **suffer from** *hay fever.*

In:

- *She* **believes in** *ghosts.*
- *Our company* **specializes in** *computer software.*
- *You have to work hard if you want to* **succeed in** *life.*

Of:

- *I don't* **approve of** *your language, young man.*
- *Our dog* **died of** *old age.*
- *This shampoo* **smells of** *bananas.*

On:

- *The film is* **based on** *the novel by Boris Pasternak.*
- *If you make so much noise I can't* **concentrate on** *my work.*
- *Come on! We're* **relying on** *you!*
- *We don't* **agree on** *anything but we're good friends.*

To:

- *Can I* **introduce** *you* **to** *my wife?*
- *Please* **refer to** *the notes at the end for more information.*
- *Nobody* **responded to** *my complaint.*

With:

- *I* **agree with** *everything you've said.*
- *My secretary will* **provide** *you* **with** *more information if you need it.*

There are many more verb + dependent preposition combinations – make a note of them as you meet them.

https://learnenglish.britishcouncil.org/en/quick-grammar/ verbs-prepositions

---

 C Match the two halves of the sentences.

1 I totally forgot…
2 Has Pete recovered…
3 Are you sure you're prepared…
4 We usually disagree…
5 I know I can depend…
6 You really should apologize…
7 We're hoping…
8 Can you deal…

a about most things.
b about Keira's birthday.
c for better weather next weekend.
d for your exams?
e for your mistakes.
f from the flu yet?
g on you.
h with this problem please?

 D Have you heard of the game 'Taboo'? It's a word guessing game for parties. Below are the rules and what you need. Have fun!

What you need:

- Cards with three taboo words and the key word that has to be explained
- Timer

Rules:

1. Divide the class into two teams.
2. Players take turns as the 'giver', who attempts to prompt his / her teammates to guess as many keywords as possible in the allotted time.
3. Each card also has 'taboo' (forbidden) words listed, which may not be said.
4. If the giver says a 'taboo' word, their team gets one penalty point.
5. The giver must not say a part of a taboo word or use any form of a taboo word, for example if the key word is 'wedding' and the taboo words are 'marriage', 'bride', 'groom', the words 'marry' and 'bridal' would not be allowed.
6. The giver may use only speech to prompt his / her teammates; gestures, sounds (such as barking) and drawings are not allowed.
7. Singing is permitted, provided the singer is singing words rather than humming or whistling a tune.
8. The giver's hints may rhyme with a taboo word or be an abbreviation of a taboo word.
9. The teammates may make as many guesses as they want with no penalties for wrong guesses.
10. The playing team receives one point for each correct guess.

 E **Watch the video entitled 'Taboos Around the World' at www.theinfographicsshow.com/taboos-around-world/. Watch twice without subtitles and answer the questions below.**

Is each of the following sentences true or false?

1. The word 'taboo' was imported into the English language by British explorer James Cook in the 18th century.
2. For the Korowai tribe in Western New Guinea, it is taboo to consume the carcass of a deceased ancestor.
3. An incestuous relationship is taboo in almost every culture.
4. When The Mamas & Papas band leader John Phillips confessed his intimate relationship with his sister, the world was hostile towards them.
5. Charles Darwin's marriage to his first cousin was illegal in the UK at the time.
6. In Asia, it is considered rude to hold up your forefinger and index finger with the palm turned inwards.
7. Holding up two fingers in the UK is equivalent to showing a middle finger in the USA.
8. A thumbs-up gesture is considered offensive in Israel.
9. In most of Asia, the foot is seen as dirty and the head is seen as sacred.
10. The Chinese make slurping noises when eating to show their appreciation of the food.
11. Writing in red ink is associated with death in some Asian cultures.
12. Taboo foods such as dog and cat meat are only eaten in some parts of Asia.
13. It is considered polite in China, India and Afghanistan to leave a little bit of food on the plate.
14. In the West, it is considered polite to clean up your dishes after a meal.
15. Insulting someone's mother or father is a universal taboo.

 F ■ **Task 1: To write an email**

Your friend, whom you met during your overseas studies or at your international school, is coming to visit you in your home country. He / She has never been to your country. Write an email to your friend explaining social norms and taboos in your culture. Use the following checklist:

■ Conventions of an email

- Paragraphs (first paragraph: general chat; body paragraphs: details about social norms and taboos in your culture; last paragraph: closure to the email)
- Informal register
- Friendly and supportive tone
- Reference to your shared experience (optional)

■ Task 2: To write a set of guidelines

You have been asked to write a set of guidelines to help new students settle into your school. You should explain the social norms and taboos of your school and local community. Use the following checklist:

- Title / heading
- Subheadings
- Logical order of information
- Short sentences and paragraphs
- Supportive and sympathetic tone (don't be too bossy!)

■ TOK Links

Taboos are often established based on religious beliefs. As there are many different religions around the world, taboos are understandably specific to a culture or religion, and the sacredness of religion prevents us from questioning unreasonable taboos.

Religion has a special place in us human beings as we seek the purpose of life in religion. We find the answers to our eternal questions such as 'What is the meaning of life?' and 'Is death the end of our being?' in our own religion and find peace with the 'knowledge' offered by our religion. Due to the nature of religion, people choose to believe what they believe and do not question their beliefs. This nature of religion creates some practices or taboos that are not logically understood. To challenge such practices or taboos needs knowledge, conviction and courage.

For example, a menstrual taboo is any social taboo concerned with menstruation. In some societies it involves menstruation being perceived as unclean and embarrassing, inhibiting even the mention of menstruation in public or in private. Due to this taboo, girls have reportedly been banned by authorities from crossing a river while menstruating in a central district of Ghana. As a result, they are said to miss 20 out of 60 days of their school classes. What do you think of this taboo? Would you challenge the authorities? Or would you abide by the rules?

CREATIVITY, ACTIVITY, SERVICE

For centuries around the world, it was a long-held belief that women were born inferior to men. As a result of this belief, there were many limitations on women in terms of education, political involvement, career choice and property ownership. Fortunately, this has changed for many women. Although not completely equal, many of us now live in a society where women and men have equal access to opportunities.

Not for all, though. More than 130 million girls are denied an education around the world. Can we do something about this? There are organizations that work every day to ensure that more girls are educated so that they are not marginalized for being born a girl:

- www.onegirl.org.au
- https://camfed.org
- https://africaeducationaltrust.org/girls-and-women
- www.malala.org/girls-education
- www.care.org/work/education/girls-education

Why not get involved?

3 Dress codes and uniforms

School uniforms have been worn in many countries for many decades around the world. Contrary to the belief that uniforms are to homogenize all members and minimize their individuality, there are many practical benefits of school uniforms. Discuss the following benefits of schools having a uniform:

- Reduces distractions
- Improves community and school spirit
- Helps prevent bullying
- Prevents on-campus violence
- Streamlines morning routines
- Lowers clothing costs
- Encourages other ways to express oneself

A **Before reading the article below, discuss the meaning of the following words:**

- fetching
- tartan-patterned
- revolution
- soared
- attire
- fall foul of
- utmost
- isolation

- detention
- sarcastic
- literally
- injustice
- controversial
- economical
- searing

Teenage boys wear skirts to school to protest against 'no shorts' policy

Dozens of pupils at Isca Academy in Exeter stage uniform protest after school insists they wear trousers despite heatwave

1 Some had borrowed from girlfriends, others from sisters. A few had gone the extra mile and shaved their legs. When the Isca Academy in Devon opened on Thursday morning, an estimated 30 boys arrived for lessons, heads held high, in fetching tartan-patterned skirts. The hottest June days since 1976 had led to a bare-legged revolution at the secondary school in Exeter.

2 As the temperature soared past 30°C earlier this week, the teenage boys had asked their teachers if they could swap their long trousers for shorts. They were told no – shorts weren't permitted under the school's uniform policy.

3 When they protested that the girls were allowed bare legs, the school – no doubt joking – said the boys were free to wear skirts too if they chose. So on Wednesday, a handful braved the giggles and did so. The scale of the rebellion increased on Thursday, when at least 30 boys opted for the attire.

4 "Quite refreshing" was how one of the boys described the experience, pointing out that if even Royal Ascot had allowed racegoers in the royal enclosure to remove their jackets, then the school ought to relax its dress code. Another said he rather enjoyed the "nice breeze" his skirt had afforded him.

5 A third, tall boy said he was told his short skirt exposed too much hairy leg. Some of the boys visited a shop on their way to Isca – the name the Romans gave to Exeter – to pick up razors to make sure they did not <u>fall foul of</u> any beauty police.

6 Ironically, the temperature had dropped in Exeter to a more manageable 20°C, but some boys said they had enjoyed the freedom afforded by the skirts and that they might continue.

7 The school said it was prepared to think again in the long term. The headteacher, Aimee Mitchell, said: "We recognise that the last few days have been <u>exceptionally</u> hot and we are doing our <u>utmost</u> to enable both students and staff to remain as comfortable as possible.

8 "Shorts are not currently part of our uniform for boys, and I would not want to make any changes without consulting both students and their families. However, with hotter weather becoming more normal, I would be happy to consider a change for the future."

9 It was too late. The revolution was picked up by media organisations across the globe, and Devon County Council was forced to help the school out with inquiries. A spokesperson said: "About 30 boys arrived at school this morning wearing school skirts. None of the boys has been penalised – no one was put in <u>isolation</u> or <u>detention</u> for wearing a skirt."

10 The mother of one of the boys who began the protest said she was proud of him. Claire Lambeth, 43, said her son Ryan, 15, had come home earlier in the week complaining about the heat. "He said it was <u>unbearable</u>. I spoke to a teacher to ask about shorts and she said it was school policy [that they could not be worn]. I did say this was exceptional weather, but they were having none of it. If girls can wear skirts, why can't boys wear shorts?

11 "Ryan came up with the idea of wearing a skirt, so that evening we borrowed one. He wore it the next day – as did five other boys. Then this morning … I didn't expect it to <u>take off</u> like that. The school is being silly really – this is exceptional weather. I was very proud of Ryan. I think it was a great idea."

12 Another mother said: "My 14-year-old son wanted to wear shorts. The headteacher told them: 'Well, you can wear a skirt if you like' – but I think she was being <u>sarcastic</u>. However, children tend to take you <u>literally</u>, and because she told them it was OK, there was nothing she could do as long as they were school skirts."

13 A third mother said: "Children also don't like <u>injustice</u>. The boys see the female teachers in sandals and nice cool skirts and tops while they are wearing long trousers and shoes and the older boys have to wear blazers. They just think it's unfair that they can't wear shorts in this heat."

14 There were signs that the revolution might be spreading. The *Guardian* has heard of at least one more school in Wiltshire where one boy turned up in a skirt, although it did not go down quite so well with his friends.

15 And schoolboys were not the only ones making <u>controversial</u> dress choices because of the heat. Michael Wood, who works as a porter at Watford General Hospital, claimed he was facing <u>disciplinary action</u> from his employers Medirest for rolling his trousers up to try to cool down. A spokesperson for the company declined to comment on the case, but said: "The health and safety of our colleagues is always our number one priority."

16 What happened to summer school uniforms? Matthew Easter, managing director of the schoolwear supplier Trutex, said they had become less popular for reasons of economy. "It's really up to the individual school to decide, but the headteacher is in a difficult position. A decade or so ago, summer wear was more popular, but there's been a change recently to try to make uniforms as <u>economical</u> as possible. Summer uniforms are only worn for a matter of weeks.

17 "If parents haven't bought uniform shorts, then some children may feel disadvantaged, so perhaps the decision in this case is simply down to fairness."

18 It may be that the weather will solve the problem for the school. The Exeter-based Met Office – situated up the road from the school – predicts pleasant, but not <u>searing</u>, temperatures over the coming week.

Steven Morris

www.theguardian.com/education/2017/jun/22/teenage-boys-wear-skirts-to-school-protest-no-shorts-uniform-policy

B Choose the correct answer from a, b or c to replace each word or phrase below.

1 gone the extra mile (paragraph 1)
   a taken the long route
   b made an extra effort
   c made a detour

2 swap (paragraph 2)
   a exchange
   b shorten
   c make

3 exceptionally (paragraph 7)
   a extremely
   b unusually
   c unimaginably

4 unbearable (paragraph 10)
   a impermissible
   b unforgettable
   c intolerable

5 take off (paragraph 11)
   a remove
   b achieve sudden success
   c become airborne

6 disciplinary action (paragraph 15)
   a inappropriate action
   b dismissal
   c punitive measures

Based on the information in the text, match the first part of sentences 7–11 with the appropriate endings a–j.

7 About 30 boys at the Isca Academy arrived at school in uniform skirts…

8 The boys had been told…

9 The boys made a mockery of the school's uniform policy…

10 The school said it was going to…

11 Claire Lambeth, Ryan's mother, was proud…

a review the policy in the long term.
b to protest against the school's uniform policy.
c that they had to go home and get changed into trousers.
d change the policy temporarily.
e to concentrate on their studies.
f because they thought it was unfair.
g that the other boys followed Ryan's example.
h that shorts weren't permitted under the school's uniform policy.
i because they felt rebellious.
j that Ryan came up with the idea.

Is each of the following sentences true or false? Justify your answers by quoting a relevant phrase from the text.

12 The boys enjoyed wearing skirts.

13 The boys received disciplinary action from the school.

14 According to the article, this is an isolated singular incident where boys decided to protest against their dress codes.

15 Continuous hot weather has been forecast for the foreseeable future.

Grammar

Past perfect simple and past perfect continuous

We use the **past perfect simple** to talk about:

- single, complete events:
  *A few **had gone** the extra mile and **shaved** their legs.*

- repeated actions when we give the number of times the action is repeated:
  *He **had done** a lot of different jobs in his lifetime.*

We use the **past perfect continuous** to talk about how long an action, or a series of actions, was in progress:

- *He **had been working** hard all his life.*
- *He **had been riding** his bike for five hours without stopping.*

C **Complete the text using the past perfect simple or past perfect continuous form of the underlined verbs.**

We [1] work for the same company for a couple of months. I [2] see her in the distance and I [3] notice how attractive she was, but we [4] never speak. Then, while we [5] do a training course together, we finally got to know each other. We [6] have a drink with the other people on the course at the end of the first day, and we [7] all talk about how difficult it was. I [8] not notice that she was standing just behind me. I laughed at one of the jokes, stepped back and spilt her drink down her dress! I [9] never feel so embarrassed in my life. But she was really nice about it. I bought her another drink and we got talking. She told me she [10] just buy a house on my street and that she [11] spend her weekends painting and decorating. I offered to help her. That's how it all started!

Practical Grammar Level 3 by John Hughes and Ceri Jones

D **In the Language B SL internal assessment, you are to describe a visual stimulus and relate it to the relevant theme and target culture(s) for 3–4 minutes, followed by a 4–5 minute follow-up discussion and a 5–6 minute general discussion.**

For this task, you'll be working in pairs. The visual stimuli below are all related to the topic 'Customs and traditions'.

Student A: Choose one of the visual stimuli, and prepare your talk for 15 minutes. Once ready, talk to your partner about the stimulus for 3–4 minutes.

Student B: Prepare questions related to the stimulus and the theme for 15 minutes. When your partner's talk is finished, ask questions to follow up. Include a general discussion on at least one additional theme from the five themes (Social organization, Experiences, Identities, Human ingenuity, Sharing the planet). Note that the topic 'Customs and traditions' belongs to 'Experiences'. This follow-up and general discussion should last about 9–11 minutes.

Swap roles and repeat the process.

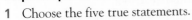

E **Listen twice to the news report on Starbucks' new dress code at https://n.pr/2acm6vO and answer the following questions:**

1 Choose the five true statements.
   a Starbucks has a 15-page long dress code to ensure that all baristas look neat.
   b The labour union requested that Starbucks relax its dress policy.
   c The strict dress code is mainly due to food hygiene issues.
   d Until now, baristas were not allowed to have artificial hair colours.
   e Starbucks baristas are not allowed to wear leggings.
   f Neon-coloured socks can be worn on specific days.
   g Starbucks has run a tight ship on its dress policy.
   h Most consumers of Starbucks' coffee think that such a strict dress policy is necessary in the service industry.
   i Baristas welcome the relaxation of their dress code.
   j Baristas' individuality is prohibited at Starbucks.

2 Which of the following items of clothing are still **not** permitted according to the Starbucks dress code? Choose **three** items.
   a Hats
   b Sweatshirt hoodies
   c Baseball caps
   d Hair dye
   e Wrinkled shirts
   f Baggy pants
   g Tights
   h Shorts

3 Starbucks' customers' reaction to the new dress code is…
   a varied
   b indifferent
   c surprising

4 Leon, a Starbucks coffee shop manager, thinks the changes are good…
   a for company management
   b for customers
   c for investors

5 According to Leon, the changes will promote…
   a attitude
   b food safety
   c individuality

F 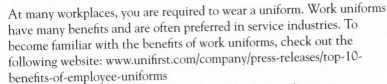 ## Task 1: To write a proposal

At many workplaces, you are required to wear a uniform. Work uniforms have many benefits and are often preferred in service industries. To become familiar with the benefits of work uniforms, check out the following website: www.unifirst.com/company/press-releases/top-10-benefits-of-employee-uniforms

Imagine that you work in a hotel and your uniform is the one in the image. You think this uniform is impractical, old-fashioned and gender-biased, and does not match the image of the hotel you work at. Write a proposal to improve the design of your work uniform. Use the following checklist:

■ Title

■ Subheadings

■ The problem and solution clearly explained

■ A formal register

■ A positive tone (focus on the benefits of your proposal)

■ Task 2: To write a speech

Write a speech about school uniforms. You can go either with the opinion that school uniforms are conducive to learning and therefore we should wear school uniforms, or with the opinion that school uniforms are outdated and therefore we should not wear them. Make sure your opinion is clear in your speech and make it as convincing as possible. You can learn more about the pros and cons of school uniforms at the following website: https://school-uniforms.procon.org. Use the following checklist:

- ■ An engaging introduction
- ■ Rhetorical devices
- ■ Clear development of your ideas

- ■ A semi-formal register
- ■ Awareness of the audience
- ■ A strong impression at the end

■ TOK Links

Conformity involves changing your behaviours in order to 'fit in' or 'go along' with the people around you. In some cases, this social influence might involve agreeing with or acting like the majority of people in a specific group, or it might involve behaving in a particular way in order to be perceived as 'normal' by the group.

Why do we conform?

Researchers have found that people conform for a number of different reasons. In many cases, looking to the rest of the group for clues for how we should behave can actually be helpful. Other people might have greater knowledge or experience than we do, so following their lead can actually be instructive.

In some instances, we conform to the expectations of the group in order to avoid looking foolish. This tendency can become particularly strong in situations where we are not quite sure how to act or where the expectations are ambiguous.

Deutsch and Gerard (1955) identified two key reasons that people conform: *informational influence* and *normative influence*.

Informational influence happens when people change their behaviour in order to be correct. In situations where we are unsure of the correct response, we often look to others who are better informed and more knowledgeable and use their lead as a guide for our own behaviours. In a classroom setting, for example, this might involve agreeing with the judgments of another classmate whom you perceive as being highly intelligent.

Normative influence stems from a desire to avoid punishments (such as going along with the rules in class even though you don't agree with them) and gain rewards (such as behaving in a certain way in order to get people to like you).

How does conformity influence our individual decisions and our pursuit of truth? Discuss the examples of conformity below. Can you think of other examples?

- A woman reads a book for her book club and really enjoys it. When she attends her book club meeting, the other members all disliked the book. Rather than go against the group opinion, she simply agrees with the others that the book was terrible.
- A student is unsure about the answer to a particular question posed by the teacher. When another student in the class provides an answer, the confused student concurs with the answer believing that the other student is smarter and better informed.

www.verywellmind.com/what-is-conformity-2795889

CREATIVITY, ACTIVITY, SERVICE

For a Creativity project, what about designing a uniform or a logo for your community (school, club, and so on)? Speak to the members and find out what everyone wants to include in the uniform or logo and use your creativity to design something to encompass it all. Once completed, make a presentation to the group and get feedback from the members.

4 Dead Men's Path

'Dead Men's Path' is a short story written by the Nigerian writer Chinua Achebe. In this story, Michael Obi is tasked with reforming Ndume Central School, a place known for its unprogressive or backwards ways. Michael and his wife, Nancy, arrive at the village with the intention of forcing it into the modern age. Their two goals are to enforce a high standard of education and to turn the school campus into a place of beauty. The following passage is from the second half of the short story.

'I was thinking what a grand opportunity we've got at last to show these people how a school should be run.' Ndume School was backward in every sense of the word.

5 Mr Obi put his whole life into the work, and his wife hers too. He had two aims. A high standard of teaching was insisted upon, and the school compound was to be turned into a place of beauty. Nancy's

10 dream-gardens came to life with the coming of the rains and blossomed. Beautiful hibiscus and allamanda hedges in brilliant red and yellow marked out the carefully tended school compound from the rank

15 neighbourhood bushes.

One evening as Obi was admiring his work he was scandalized to see an old woman from the village hobble right across the compound, through a marigold flower-

20 bed and the hedges. On going up there he found faint signs of an almost disused path from the village across the school compound to the bush on the other side.

'It amazes me,' said Obi to one of his

25 teachers who had been three years in the school, 'that you people allowed the villagers to make use of this footpath. It is simply incredible.' He shook his head.

'The path,' said the teacher apologetically,

30 'appears to be very important to them. Although it is hardly used, it connects the village shrine with their place of burial.'

'And what has that got to do with the school?' asked the headmaster.

35 'Well, I don't know,' replied the other with a shrug of the shoulders. 'But I remember there was a big row some time ago when we attempted to close it.'

'That was some time ago. But it will not

40 be used now,' said Obi as he walked away. 'What will the Government Education Officer think of this when he comes to inspect the school next week? The villagers might, for all I know, decide to use the

45 schoolroom for a pagan ritual during the inspection.'

Heavy sticks were planted closely across the path at the two places where it entered and left the school premises. These were further

50 strengthened with barbed wire.

Three days later the village priest of *Ani* called on the headmaster. He was an old man and walked with a slight stoop. He carried a stout walking-stick which he

55 usually tapped on the floor, by way of emphasis, each time he made a new point in his argument.

'I have heard,' he said after the usual exchange of cordialities, 'that our ancestral

60 footpath has recently been closed…'

'Yes,' replied Mr Obi. 'We cannot allow people to make a highway of our school compound.'

'Look here, my son,' said the priest bringing

65 down his walking-stick, 'this path was here before you were born and before your father was born. The whole life of this village depends on it. Our dead relatives depart by it and our ancestors visit us by it.

70 But most important, it is the path of children coming in to be born…'

Mr Obi listened with a satisfied smile on his face.

'The whole purpose of our school,' he said

75 finally, 'is to eradicate just such beliefs as that. Dead men do not require footpaths. The whole idea is just fantastic. Our duty is to teach your children to laugh at such ideas.' 'What you say may be true,' replied

80 the priest, 'but we follow the practices of our fathers. If you re-open the path we shall have nothing to quarrel about. What I always say is: let the hawk perch and let the eagle perch.' He rose to go.

85 'I am sorry,' said the young headmaster. 'But the school compound cannot be a thoroughfare. It is against our regulations. I would suggest your constructing another path, skirting our premises. <u>We can even</u>
90 <u>get our boys to help in building it</u>. I don't suppose the ancestors will find the little detour too burdensome.'

'I have no more words to say,' said the old priest, already outside.

95 Two days later a young woman in the village died in childbed. A diviner was immediately consulted, <u>and he prescribed heavy sacrifices</u> to <u>propitiate</u> ancestors insulted by the fence.

Obi woke up next morning among the ruins
100 of his work. The beautiful hedges were torn up not just near the path but right round the school, the flowers trampled to death and one of the school buildings pulled down … That day, the white Supervisor came to
105 inspect the school and wrote a nasty report on the state of the premises but more seriously about the 'tribal-war situation developing between the school and the village, arising in part from the misguided
110 zeal of the new headmaster'.

Excerpt from 'Dead Men's Path' by Chinua Achebe

Answer the following questions:

1 'I was thinking what a grand opportunity we've got at last…' (lines 1–2). What does *a grand opportunity* refer to?

2 Which of the following is **not** Mr Obi's professional aim?
   a To have high-quality teaching
   b To make the school compound presentable
   c To eradicate paganism through education
   d To persuade villagers to trust his educational ethos

3 Which one of the following is the closest in meaning to 'came to life' in line 10?
   a came to sight
   b was invigorated
   c relived
   d appeared

4 Which one of the following is the closest in meaning to 'scandalized' in line 17?
   a shocked
   b bemused
   c confused
   d enchanted

5 Which phrase between lines 16 and 23 indicates that the path is not used frequently?

6 'But it will not be used now' (lines 39–40). To what does 'it' refer?

7 'What will the Government Education Officer think of this when he comes to inspect the school next week?' (lines 41–44). To what does 'this' refer?

8 Mr Obi's attitude towards the ancestral footpath is…
   a sympathetic
   b dismissive
   c offensive
   d zealous

9 'The whole purpose of our school … is to eradicate just such beliefs as that' (lines 74–76). What kind of beliefs does 'such beliefs as that' refer to?

   a religious

   b spiritual

   c pagan

   d Christian

10 'We can even get our boys to help in building it.' (lines 89–90). To what does 'it' refer?

11 '… and he prescribed heavy sacrifices…' (line 97). To whom does 'he' refer?

12 Which one of the following is the closest in meaning to 'propitiate' in line 98?

   a assuage

   b worship

   c assume

   d adore

13 Which of the following words does **not** describe Mr Obi?

   a enthusiastic

   b arrogant

   c ambitious

   d ambiguous

UNIT **7** Lifestyles

- Look at the photos above. Discuss in a small group which photos you feel reflect a healthy lifestyle. Then, explain what you do to find balance in your own life and to stay healthy.
- What does the second photo illustrate about our relationship with technology? How might this affect our health?

1 Health

Take this survey: https://psychcentral.com/quizzes/internet-addiction-quiz/. In pairs, discuss your habits and results. How do you compare with your peers?

A **In small groups, discuss what you think it means to be healthy in the 21st century.**

Your overall physical and mental health is vital for success in your studies and for finding happiness in life. One of the IB Learner Profile attributes is 'balanced'. In this unit, you will explore lifestyle choices and how those choices affect your health and overall life balance.

Using the internet to access the world of ideas no doubt has many benefits. According to Common Sense Media, using the internet also helps young people build friendships, find support, express their views and do good in the world through social media and other avenues. The article below, however, explores some of the health issues that arise from the modern technology on which we have become so dependent.

B **Look up the following words and categorize them by part of speech (noun, verb, adjective, and so on). Write the word in your own language in a personal dictionary you create for yourself.**

- exorbitant
- alter
- neurological
- excessive

- addicted
- imbalance
- depression

---

http://happysciencemom.com

How Smartphone Addiction Is Affecting Teens' Brains

Kids today are spending an exorbitant amount of time glued to their electronics. A 2015 survey published by Common Sense Media found that American teenagers (ages 13 to 18) averaged six and a half hours of screen time per day on social media and other activities like video games. In addition, a 2015 report from Pew Research Center found that 24% of teenagers ages 13 to 17 reported being online 'almost constantly,' and that 73% had a smartphone or access to one.

Sadly, more teens are also starting to get addicted to their phones and other devices. There is even now a term – 'nomophobia' – to describe such people who can't handle being away from their phone. One study found that 66% of people in the United Kingdom have some form of nomophobia.

With all of this excessive phone use, a group of neuroscientists wanted to find out if the exposure is damaging neurological health, especially in children and teens whose brains are still developing. The research team from Korea University in Seoul, South Korea, recently published a study that found that being addicted to smartphones creates a chemical imbalance in the brain linked to depression and anxiety in young people.

About 20 teens being treated for smartphone or internet addiction, half boys and half girls with an average age of 15, were recruited to participate in the study. First, researchers evaluated the seriousness of the teens' addiction by looking at their productivity, feelings, social life, and daily routines. They noted that teens addicted to their phones had higher rates of anxiety, depression, impulse control problems, and sleep disorders than other teens their age.

Next, researchers used a technology called magnetic resonance spectroscopy (MRS) to track the movement of biochemicals in the teens' brains. They looked at a chemical called gamma aminobutyric acid (GABA) that's involved in motor control and vision, and regulates brain function. Too much GABA may lead to anxiety.

They also observed levels of glutamate-glutamine (Glx), a neurotransmitter that causes the brain's nerve cells to become excited. The amount of these chemicals that we have in our brains affects our emotions and cognitive ability. Thus addiction, anxiety, and depression can result when these chemicals are out of balance.

The amount of these two chemicals in the study participants clearly showed that the brain was altered from smartphone addiction. They saw how GABA slowed down their brain function, resulting in poorer attention and control. Therefore when people are too attached to their phone, they are essentially destroying their ability to focus. In addition, they noted how the addicted teenagers had significantly higher levels of anxiety, depression, insomnia, and impulsivity.

Finally, the teens went through a nine-week cognitive behavioral therapy program, which included mindfulness, to address their phone addiction. Interestingly, the levels of GABA to glutamate-glutamine normalized after the therapy.

Although the study was limited because of the small sample size used, the results are troubling.

We can clearly see the connection between extensive phone use and negative changes to the brain. No matter what age our children are, we can start to think about how to break their reliance on phones and other electronics before they get too attached, or possibly even addicted.

Here are some ideas.
- Learn more about technology addiction and evaluate if your children are struggling.
- Seek professional help so they can undergo cognitive behavioural therapy.
- Introduce mindfulness to help break their tech habit.
- Enforce tech use rules, such as putting gadgets away during dinner and homework time, and while driving.
- Remove social media apps, like Facebook and Twitter, from their phone and only allow them to check those sites from their laptop.
- Remove chimes from their phone so they are not constantly prompted to look at a new text or post as it arrives.
- Forbid the use of electronics before bedtime, as this can disturb sleep patterns.
- Help your children replace electronics with healthier activities like creative arts, meditating, exercise, and talking to people in person.

Being mindful of our teens' tech habits will help them, and their brains, develop into adulthood.

Sandi Schwartz http://happysciencemom.com and www.sandischwartz.com

 Read the statements below. Which statements are true and which are false?

1 There is a new term to describe people who can't be without their phone.
2 Scientists found that teens addicted to their phones had the same impulse controls as other teens their age.
3 Too much of the brain chemical GABA can improve brain function.
4 Chemical imbalance in the brain contributes to anxiety.
5 Negative impact on one's sleep is a symptom of internet addiction.
6 Being attached to your phone does not affect concentration and focus.
7 The study tested a large pool of participants.
8 Despite the help that the addicts received, they showed no improvement.
9 The writer doesn't think teens need help to curb their phone use.

Grammar

Relative clauses – adjective clauses

Subject (people) – *who*:

- *That boy seems tired.* **He** *is on his phone all the time.* – *That boy* **who** *is on his phone all the time always seems tired.*

  The subject *He* (that boy, a person) is replaced by *who* to make a relative clause and complex sentence.

Subject (things) – *which*:

- *Internet addiction is a real problem for teens.* **It** *is similar to alcohol or drug addiction.* – *Internet addiction,* **which** *is similar to alcohol or drug addiction, is a real problem for teens.*

  The subject *It* (internet addiction, a thing **not** a person) is replaced by *which* to make a relative clause and a complex sentence.

Possessive – *whose*:

- *That teen has real phone-addiction problems.* **His** *phone is always in his hand.* – *That teen* **whose** *phone is always in his hand has real phone-addiction problems.*

  The possessive adjective *His* is replaced by *whose* to make a relative clause and a complex sentence.

 D You can form complex sentences and connect two or more ideas by using relative pronouns like who, whose and which, which describe a noun in the sentence (adjective clause). Match the following sentences, and then combine them using who, whose or which. Finally, check your answers in the preceding text.

1. Finally, the teens went through a nine-week cognitive behavioural therapy programme to address their phone addiction.

2. With all of this excessive phone use, a group of neuroscientists wanted to find out if the exposure is damaging neurological health, especially in children and teens.

3. There is even now a term – nomophobia – to describe people.

a. They can't handle being away from their phone.

b. It included mindfulness.

c. Their brains are still developing.

 E Listen to the podcast from National Public Radio in the United States at https://n.pr/2pxrihW. Then complete the comprehension check and the speaking task below. You can read the transcript of the podcast on the website. For reading and listening tasks, it is a good idea to read the questions first so you know for what purpose you are reading or listening.

Note that you will have three listening tasks on Paper 2 of the IB external exam. The tasks range from 2 to 5 minutes each.

1. Discuss with a partner what you think addiction is. Can the internet be addictive? How frequently do you use your devices?

2. Answer the following short-answer questions. Listen to the podcast again as necessary to find the answers.

   a. Ellen's daughter became more sociable after using her phone more often. True or false?

   b. What was Naomi's motivation for watching more YouTube videos?

   c. How did this affect her school achievement?

   d. What event was very upsetting for Ellen (Naomi's mother)?

   e. What kinds of activities do people do at the rehab centre Naomi attended?

   f. What evidence is there that internet addiction is similar to drug addiction?

   g. What are common effects / symptoms of addiction? Give two.

F ■ Internal assessment: speaking practice – the individual oral (SL)

Look at the graph below. Based on the information in this section, your own experience and the image, make an outline based on the following structure, with ten bullet points.

1 Introduce the topic by describing the image. (1 minute)

Sentence starter: This image features / represents / illustrates / depicts…

2 Give background information / facts on the topic from your own experiences and class activities related to anglophone cultures. (1 minute)

Sentence starter: The image makes us think of the topic / invites us to think about the topic of…

3 Conclude with your opinion about this topic by taking a position / making an argument. (1 minute)

Sentence starter: In my opinion / Finally, I would argue…

Take about 10–15 minutes to make notes. Then, use these notes to give a talk to a partner for 3–4 minutes followed by answering questions that your partner asks you. Record yourself.

Repeat the process, with your partner giving his / her talk.

Now listen to your recordings and score each talk on the individual oral (standard level) rubric given on page 42 of the subject guide. Discuss your scores and why you scored them the way you did.

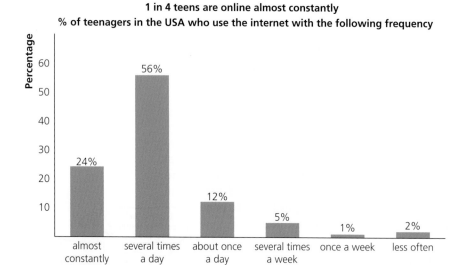

1 in 4 teens are online almost constantly
% of teenagers in the USA who use the internet with the following frequency

G Imagine you are suffering from internet addiction. Write a diary entry based on some of the ideas mentioned in the preceding text 'How Smartphone Addiction Is Affecting Teens' Brains' to describe what one day in your life is like. Include words from the vocabulary list from Exercise B. Share this with a partner to get feedback for improvement when you are done.

■ TOK Links

'Language wraps itself around, in, through and between everything that we teachers and learners do in the classroom.'

Ron Ritchhart, 2002

Language is one of the ways of knowing (WOK) as highlighted in Theory of Knowledge. As noted in this unit, more and more language is presented to us through the medium of screens on our phones and computers. Similarly, text and images often appear together and our increasing habit of reading on screens may mean we have more access to information but less time to understand what it all means.

Discuss these questions or reflect on them in writing in your reflection journal, then go back and check your spelling and grammar as necessary:

- What is the implication for us as teachers and learners?
- What does it mean to know and understand when we can look up information at any time?
- How can we know what is true when there is so much conflicting information online?

CREATIVITY, ACTIVITY, SERVICE

According to IB, CAS enables students to enhance their personal and interpersonal development by learning through experience and working with others.

Organize a committee that researches the topic of technology, and specifically of phones and their effect on teens, within your school community. Consider these points:

- Write a questionnaire or survey to gather information on attitudes to phone use in your school from different members of the school community (students, parents, teachers).
- Research the effects of phone use on teenagers.
- Write a proposal* of schoolwide guidelines based on your findings and include suggestions for students to find balance in their lives.
- Present this to the school leadership and the student body in a schoolwide presentation.

*A proposal will:

- be formal
- note the recipient / audience
- indicate the purpose of the proposal, with a title or heading
- be clearly organized in paragraphs
- show proposed outcomes / results.

2 Physical well-being

The greatest wealth is health.

Virgil

What does the quotation above mean to you? How are health and happiness connected?
Write in your reflection journal or discuss with a classmate.

 A With a partner, discuss and make a list of guidelines (in bullet form) for teenagers to develop good healthy habits. When you are done, share them with the class. Then, preview the text below from livestrong.com to compare you answers to the suggestions there.

How much physical activity should you do?

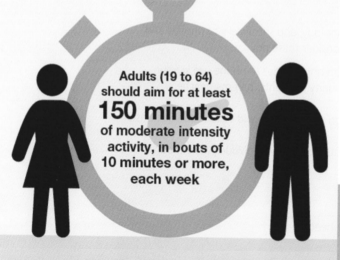

Adults (19 to 64) should aim for at least **150 minutes** of moderate intensity activity, in bouts of 10 minutes or more, each week

This can also be achieved by 75 minutes of vigorous activity across the week or a mixture of moderate and vigorous.

All adults should undertake muscle strengthening activity, such as

exercising with weights

yoga

or carrying heavy shopping

at least 2 days a week

Minimise the amount of time spent sedentary (sitting) for extended periods

Healthy living tips for teenagers

The teenage years are a period of intense physical, emotional, mental and intellectual growth. It's also a time when you develop habits that can last a lifetime. You can reach <u>optimal</u> growth and development by <u>instilling</u> lifestyle habits that support a healthy and happy body.

[1] _____

NHS Choices, a UK-based health website, recommends that teens get at least five servings of fruits and vegetables each day. There is a <u>shortfall</u> for most teens, however. According to the 2007 Australian National Children's Nutrition and Physical Activity survey, teenagers only eat about half of the recommended amount of fruits and vegetables each day. Fruits and vegetables provide important vitamins and minerals that a teen's body needs to grow and function properly. Eating a diet high in fruits and vegetables also helps keep you full without providing excess calories that can lead to weight gain.

[2] _____

Exercise does more than burn calories. Engaging in physical activity helps keep the heart and lungs strong and produces endorphins – chemicals that improve mood. A well-balanced exercise routine includes aerobic exercise, strength training and flexibility training, such as yoga or pilates. According to Kids Health, a website presented by the Nemours

Foundation, teens should <u>engage in</u> at least 60 minutes of vigorous exercise every day.

[3] _____

Your body is almost two-thirds water, so staying hydrated is important. Teenagers should aim to drink six to eight glasses of water per day, according to the British Nutrition Foundation. That number increases for teens who engage in sports or are especially active. Other good sources of fluid include 100 per cent fruit juice and low-fat milk. Sugary and caffeinated drinks should be limited or <u>eliminated</u> from the diet completely as they provide excess sugar and empty calories.

[4] _____

According to the Cleveland Clinic, teenagers need at least nine hours of sleep each night to function at their best during the day. It sounds easy enough, but with early school start times, late afternoon practices and hours of homework, getting enough sleep can be a challenge. Set a regular bedtime time that allows for nine hours of sleep before you have to get up for school. You should also plan for at least an hour of "quiet time" prior to bedtime. The goal is for all electronics to be turned off for the night so that the brain and body relax. Quiet time may involve listening to <u>soothing</u> music or reading a book.

Lindsay Boyers
www.livestrong.com/article/365455-healthy-living-tips-for-teenagers

---

B Choose the heading that best fits each section, numbered 1–4 in the text.
There are more headings than necessary.

a Make time for friends

b Watch your beverage intake

c If you don't snooze, you lose

d Eat right

e Get your behind moving

C Choose a word from the box that best matches the words below from the text.

1 optimal (introduction)

2 instil (introduction)

3 shortfall (section 1)

4 engage in (section 2)

5 eliminate (section 3)

6 soothing (section 4)

a participate	**c** promote	**e** ideal
b remove	**d** comfort	**f** deficit

D Listen to the TED Talk at the following link about how not sleeping enough, or sleep deprivation, can affect your health: www.ted.com/talks/claudia_aguirre_what_would_happen_if_you_didn_t_sleep#t-3687

Tip: Read the questions below first before you listen so you know what you are listening for and predict each answer. Listen as many times as you need. Then, check your answers in the transcript provided online.

1 Seventeen-year-old Randy Gardner experienced which of the following symptoms in his 11-day experiment with sleep deprivation in 1965?

■ What would happen if you didn't sleep for 11 days?

   a He lost his appetite
   b His eyes stopped focusing
   c He attacked his family and friends
   d He could not identify objects by touch
   e He felt moody
   f He was uncoordinated
   g He could no longer read
   h He could not concentrate
   i He hallucinated
   j He died

2 How many hours sleep should teens get each night?

3 What is repaired during sleep?

4 List **one** other health problem linked to a lack of sleep.

5 What happens in the brain when you don't sleep enough? (Or: What happens in the brain when you do sleep enough?)

Grammar

If clauses (conditional clauses)

If clauses are sometimes a difficult structure to master in English. There are three major conditional types:

- Can do, for example:

  *If you **sleep**, you **will feel** better.*

- May be possible to do, for example:

  *If you **slept**, you **might / could / should / would feel** better.*

- Not possible because it's too late, for example:

  *If you **had slept** last night, you **might / would / could / should have felt** better.*

What do you notice about how the verbs change in each type?

E Use the examples in the box above to complete the exercise below, based on the previous listening task, by putting each underlined verb in the correct form.

1 If teens <u>sleep</u>, they <u>do</u> better in school.

2 If Randy Gardner <u>continue</u> to stay awake, he <u>die</u>.

3 If teachers <u>give</u> less homework, perhaps students <u>feel</u> better rested.

4 People don't always realize that if they <u>sleep</u> more; they <u>flush</u> their brains of toxins that damage health and mental performance.

How much sleep do you get?

Some research has indicated that teens might benefit from starting school a little bit later, even just 30 minutes later. This research pointed out that loss of sleep is related to several health problems, and that later school times might not only help with these health issues but might actually help students' academic performance. Others argue that there are learning benefits to starting school earlier and many parents don't agree with later start times.

You can read more here: https://theconversation.com/why-teen-brains-need-a-later-school-start-time-65308

Teenagers need 8½–9¼ hours of sleep each night

2/3 of high-school students get less than 7 hours sleep a night

43% of US public high schools start before 8a.m.

33% of teenagers report falling asleep in school

F Conduct a class debate based on a proposal to start school later each morning. Organize two teams: one for maintaining the current school hours, and the other team arguing for a later start to the school day. Write your speeches first and then practise in teams. Each person should focus on one aspect of your team's argument as well as your opening and closing statements (introduction and conclusion). Allow for spontaneous question-and-answer times to challenge each other's ideas. Consider these tips as you prepare:

■ Use more formal language (formal register).

■ Use rhetorical devices including ethos, pathos, logos (see the following task), as well as repetition and asking questions (where appropriate).

■ Grab the listeners' attention, and leave a strong impression at the end.

■ Strategies for speaking

Rhetorical skills:

■ **Pathos** (emotional appeal) is a way to persuade an audience by bringing out emotions, often through an anecdote (story) or using the audience's emotions (fear, hope, anger, and so on). Some people say this is persuading people with their 'hearts'.

■ **Logos** (logical appeal) is a way of convincing an audience by using evidence such as facts, data and reason. Some people say this is persuading people with their 'minds'.

■ **Ethos** (ethical appeal) is a way to convince an audience through ethical arguments including through how much the audience trusts the speaker and his / her authority.

G Complete this task by selecting whether each sentence on the importance of sleep uses pathos, logos or ethos. Then, go back to your speech from the previous speaking (debate) task, and consider ways you can use these rhetorical techniques in your speech.

1 Research on school strongly indicates that early start times for students have negative impacts on learning.

2 Students who drive to school tired could be at a higher risk of dying in an automobile accident. Do you want kids dying just to get to school?

3 I stand before you today as a concerned parent.

4 Remember, teachers are people too and they need time with their own families, so later times for teachers sadly means less time with their own kids in the afternoons.

5 Data shows that afternoon activities are important for students too, so by starting later you will take away the opportunity for students to find a healthy balance in their lives.

Conduct a survey of students across your school to find out about your peers' sleep habits. Based on that information as well as the conclusions of the preceding tasks and your class debate, write a formal letter to your school leadership supporting the existing school times *or* proposing changes based on the survey results. See the strategies and text-type conventions below.

■ Strategies for writing

Surveys: According to http://zapier.com, you should consider these points when writing survey questions:

- Use simple, direct language.
- Be specific.
- Avoid leading questions (where a specific answer is desired).
- Ask one point per question.

Formal letters: Such letters usually have a formal register since the writer and audience often do not know each other. In addition, you should consider these suggestions:

- Include a date and address at the top.
- After the date and address, start with a salutation / greeting ('Dear X,').
- Organize the main body of your letter by paragraphs, clearly starting with an introductory paragraph of what you hope to achieve or argue (why are you writing this letter?) and then developing paragraphs on your main points.
- Finish with a concluding paragraph summing up your main ideas in light of the evidence you have presented.
- End your letter with 'Sincerely,' or 'Yours sincerely,' and then your name underneath.

■ TOK Links

According to the World Health Organization (WHO), 'health is a state of complete physical, mental and social well-being and not merely the absence of disease or infirmity'. A recent study at Stanford University (www.ncbi.nlm.nih.gov/pubmed/28726475) highlighted that one's mental attitude and belief (and perception) of one's own fitness is strongly related to one's mortality, or death. That means our beliefs about our own health may be as important as physical exercise in living longer. In this way, belief as a way of knowing (WOK) is a powerful placebo (a medicine with no physical effects but that can impact a patient psychologically) in determining one's health.

In your reflection journal, spend some time reflecting in writing on your own health based on the information you have read in this unit. Are you healthy? How much of your health is related to your beliefs surrounding your health and your attitudes to health in general? In what other ways can our beliefs influence our 'reality'?

CREATIVITY, ACTIVITY, SERVICE

Work with your school's health centre or nurses to organize a campaign to encourage students to develop better sleep habits based on the survey results from the previous writing task (Exercise H). Consider carrying out a 'public service announcement' campaign and making flyers with useful information. A flyer will likely:

- address the audience
- have a title or heading(s)
- use bullets and have subheadings
- have an overall attractive visual structure to support the main idea / message
- include contact information.

3 Mental health

What does being *mindful* mean to you? Discuss with a partner and share your ideas with your class. After discussing, try the breathing techniques in the image below. How do they make you feel?

MINDFUL BREATHING

1 Choose a quiet place where you won't be distracted.

2 Take deep, slow breaths, noticing your stomach rise and fall while listening to your breath go in and out.

3 Try this for 5 minutes.

These techniques have been shown to reduce stress and induce a state of relaxation.

Mindfulness meditation and children: An interview with Susan Kaiser Greenland

Today I have the honor of interviewing Susan Kaiser Greenland, who is author of the book *The Mindful Child: How to Help Your Kid Manage Stress and Become Happier, Kinder, and More Compassionate*, designed to teach young kids [1] _____ skills toward a more peaceful and compassionate world.

Elisha: What inspired you to [2] _____ into this important area?

Susan: I practiced meditation myself and saw how it helped me, so it was only natural to wonder if it could help my children too. But the [3] _____ to begin looking in earnest for ways to practice with my children came when I was on a week-long meditation retreat. Looking around the meditation hall one evening, I noticed that many of us were parents and I was struck by the fact that none of us were talking about bringing mindfulness to our kids. Something happened during that retreat and I felt a shift – a desire to [4] _____ mindfulness into my family life in a more direct way.

Elisha: Can you give us a brief summary of some of the skills you teach children?

Susan: The program has evolved over the years and now my primary objective is to teach kids a more mindful [5] _____. This comes through the development of three qualities simultaneously: attention, balance and compassion, what I like to think of as the new ABCs of learning. By learning these new ABCs, kids, teens and their families can develop a more mindful outlook by:

- Approaching new experiences with curiosity and an open mind
- Developing strong and stable attention
- Seeing life experience clearly without an emotional charge
- Developing compassionate action and relationships
- Building communities with kindness and compassion
- Working together to make a difference in the world
- Expressing [6] _____ to others, and

- Planting seeds of peace by nurturing common ground

Elisha: Can you share a specific practice that works well for introducing mindfulness?

Susan: Sure. First, I think helping kids find a physically comfortable [7] _____ is very important. Encouraging kids to lie down while practicing breath awareness is quite useful in being mindful and in the moment, but also is an activity that I use called the Pendulum Swing. The aim of this activity is to help those who find it hard to be still to meditate in a group. Here's how it goes:

- Starting from a seated position, take one or more breaths and notice the sensations associated with breathing.
- Swing your body from side to side slowly, starting to the right (keeping your bottom firmly on a cushion) and then slowly swinging back to the left.
- The object of attention (or focus) is the [8] _____ of swinging from side to side and if you notice that your mind has wandered, just bring it back to the sensation of movement. The goal is to find and establish a repetitive, rhythmic swing that works for you.
- The instruction goes like this: move to one side; shift weight; move back toward center; pause for a moment to feel centered sitting on the cushion. Then, move to the opposite side; shift weight; move back again toward center; pause for a moment to feel centered sitting on the cushion. Repeat.

Elisha: What else can parents do to support their children in being more mindful?

Susan: Hands down, the most powerful thing a parent can do to support his or her children in their practice is to develop their own mindfulness and practise themselves. Kids learn by example and what we do often has a greater impact on our children than what we say.

Elisha: I found this book incredibly insightful as a parent so thanks for taking the time to speak to us.

Elisha Goldstein, PhD
www.huffingtonpost.com/elisha-goldstein-phd/mindfulness-meditation-an_b_611400.html

---

A Choose words from the box below to fill in the blank spaces numbered 1–8 in the text.

a gratitude	**c** posture	**e** venture	**g** integrate
b sensation	**d** worldview	**f** inspiration	**h** vital

Grammar

Pronouns

Subject pronoun	Object pronoun	Possessive adjective	Possessive pronoun
I	me	my	mine
you	you	your	yours
he	him	his	his
she	her	her	hers
it	it	its	–
we	us	our	ours
they	them	their	theirs

B

Pronouns (*I*, *you*, *she*, *he*, *it*, *we*, *they*, *that*, *this*, *these*, *those*, and so on) are words that replace nouns in a text and they can often give a text cohesion, that is they help connect the ideas in the text. Try this task to see which words pronouns refer to in the text. Identify which word in each sentence the underlined pronoun refers to.

1 I practiced meditation myself and saw how it helped me, so it was only natural to wonder if <u>it</u> could help my children too.

2 I noticed that many of us were parents and I was struck by the fact that <u>none</u> of us were talking about bringing mindfulness to our kids.

3 The program has evolved over the years and now my primary objective is to teach kids a more mindful worldview. <u>This</u> comes through the development of three qualities.

4 The aim of this activity is to help those who find it hard to be still to meditate in a group. Here's how <u>it</u> goes.

5 The most powerful thing a parent can do to support his or her children in their practice is to develop their own mindfulness and practise <u>themselves</u>.

C

Life can sometimes be stressful, whether it is studying for an IB exam or balancing other parts of your life including family, friends, activities or work. Take a moment to reflect in writing in your learning journal about what causes you stress in your life. Can stress ever be good for you?

D

Listen to the book review of *The Upside of Stress* by Kelly McGonigal at https://youtu.be/1cfIqjWbVAE

Before you listen, read the questions below so you know what you are listening for, and take notes as you listen. You can go back to listen again as necessary to check your answers.

Note: For more information on this topic, you might consider watching this TED Talk by the author herself: https://youtu.be/RcGyVTAoXEU

1 What is the author's job?

2 List one health problem linked to stress.

3 Which word shows the author's dislike of stress before she changed her mind?

4 According to the author, how can stress make you happier?

5 Which university conducted a study using videos about stress?

6 What neurosteroid (chemical / hormone) helps your brain learn to deal with stress?

7   Select which statements are true, according to the audio.

A military survival study showed that those with more of this hormone had…

a   better sleep

b   more focus

c   weight loss

d   better problem-solving skills

e   fewer post-traumatic stress symptoms

8   Why is oxytocin is called the 'cuddle drug'?

9   What visualization can help improve your attitudes to dealing with stress?

10 According to the author, stress can make you…

a   smarter   d   successful

b   sexier   e   superhuman

c   stronger

11 Does the man talking in the video like this book? Give a short quotation to justify your answer.

E   **Write an email to a friend who is having difficulty dealing with the stresses of life and school. Make suggestions about ways they might better cope with stress. Use the understandings you have developed in this unit and your own experiences to construct your text. A successful email will:**

■   Use an informal register.

■   Use a friendly and, at times, speech-like style.

■   Address a specific issue or concern.

■   Include opening and closing salutations.

■   Use an appropriate layout (including the sender's and recipient's email addresses).

■ TOK Links

Mindfulness

One simple definition of mindfulness is merely the practice (through meditation, breathing, and so on) of clearing one's mind of the daily distractions of life in order to manage stress and achieve health and happiness. The roots of mindfulness come out of ancient practices associated with Buddhism.

Descartes famously said, 'I think, therefore I am.' However, Thich Nhat Hanh, a famous Buddhist monk and peace activist, says that you are truly alive when you stop thinking.

What do you think Thich Nhat Hanh means? Do you agree or disagree with his statement? Write in your reflection journal addressing these questions.

CREATIVITY, ACTIVITY, SERVICE

Bullying and its effects on the mental well-being of students is increasingly becoming a worry. A *bully* is someone who likes to scare or hurt other people. Bullying is a problem particularly for school-age children and there is concern that online bullying is increasing due to the availability of social media. Many studies have confirmed the relationship between bullying, poor mental health and suicidality (the likelihood of killing oneself) for the victims of bullying.

Work with administrators, health officials, teachers and fellow students to organize a support group for students who may become victims of bullying. Create a web page or social media forum where students can access resources or ask questions anonymously.

■ Literature

'Don't judge a book by its cover.' What do you think this quotation means? Discuss with a partner.

4 Wonder

Wonder is novel about a 10-year-old boy called August who lives in New York City. He does all the normal things young boys like to do, but because he was born with a medical condition that has caused his face to be disfigured, other children are often curious at best, or afraid of him at worst, because of the way he looks. One day his parents decide, after years of homeschooling him, that he should go to a real school with other kids and start making new friends. Will he succeed, or will his unusual looks cause him to be excluded?

In this extract (or section of the book), August is attending a camp with some of his school friends when students from another school bump into them in the dark with a torch. August is the victim of teasing and bullying in this scene.

In *Wonder*, the themes of bullying and kindness are explored. Before you read the extract, spend some time reading a few texts online that you can find about the relationship between mental health and bullying to prepare for your practice oral.

Keep time and take 20 minutes to read the extract, making brief notes about it and the topic of bullying and mental health. You can practise this oral with a classmate, questioning each other, or your teacher may ask you to give your talk directly with him / her. Organize your talk in this way:

- **Presentation:**

  Present the extract. You may place the extract in relation to the literary work (in this case, you can read a summary of the book online if you want to), but must spend the majority of the presentation discussing the events, ideas and messages in the extract itself. (3–4 minutes).

- **Follow-up discussion:**

  Your teacher will engage you in questions on the content of the extract that you present, expanding on observations that you provide in the presentation. (4–5 minutes).

- **General discussion:**

  You and your teacher will then have a general discussion using one or more of the five themes of the syllabus as a starting point. (5–6 minutes).

"Oh my God!" she shrieked, holding her hand over her eyes like she was crying. I figured maybe a huge bug had just flown in her face or something…

5 "What is that?" said the kid who was pointing the flashlight at us, and it was only then that I realized that the flashlight was pointed right at my face, and what they were talking about – screaming about – was 10 me.

"Let's get out of here," Jack said to me quietly, and he pulled me by my sweatshirt sleeve and started walking away from them.

"Wait wait wait!" yelled the guy with the 15 flashlight, cutting us off. He pointed the flashlight right in my face again, and now he was only about five feet away. "Oh man! Oh man!!" he said, shaking his head, his mouth wide open. "What happened to your face?"

20 "Stop it, Eddie," said one of the girls.

"I didn't know we were watching *Lord of the Rings* tonight!" he said. "Look, guys, it's Gollum!"

This made his friends hysterical.

25 Again we tried to walk away from them, and again the kid named Eddie cut us off. He was at least a head taller than Jack, who was about a head taller than me, so the guy looked huge to me.

30 "No man, it's Alien!" said one of the other kids.

"No, no, no, man. It's an orc!" laughed Eddie, pointing the flashlight in my face again. This time he was right in front of us.

35 "Leave him alone, okay?" said Jack, pushing the hand holding the flashlight away.

"Make me," answered Eddie, pointing the flashlight in Jack's face now.

"What's your problem, dude?" said Jack.

40 "Your boyfriend's my problem!"

"Jack, let's just go," I said, pulling him by the arm.

"Oh man, it talks!" screamed Eddie, shining the flashlight in my face again. Then one 45 of the other guys threw a firecracker at our feet.

Excerpt from Wonder *by R.J. Palacio*

UNIT 8 Beliefs and values

REFLECTION

How do beliefs and values shape our identities?

Beliefs can be described as ideas we hold to be true, even without evidence. Often religions form the basis of our belief system, and faith is explored as one of the ways of knowing (WOK) in your Theory of Knowledge course.

Values are qualities that we accept as universal, whatever the context. These can be related to ideas ranging from honesty to equality. The IB learner profile includes values and traits that IB candidates strive to develop through their IB courses, the extended essay and Creativity, Activity, Service. They are:
- Inquirers
- Knowledgeable
- Thinkers
- Communicators
- Principled
- Open-minded
- Caring
- Risk-takers
- Balanced
- Reflective

Write out these words in your personal dictionary and on a word wall you make for your class. Next to the English words, write the words out in your mother-tongue languages as a class and then explain what they mean to you and in a small group give examples of how you have aimed to meet these traits.

What values define your culture? What values define you as an individual? How do these value systems clash (if at all)? Write your thoughts in your reflection journal before you complete the following reading.

1 Culture (the influence of culture on identity)

Make a Venn diagram (see www.educationworld.com/tools_templates/venn_diagram2.doc) with a partner on the theme of cultural values. One circle can be focused on your cultural values and the other your partner's cultural values. In the middle, make notes on how your two cultures' values are similar. As you read the following text, see if the values you selected are mentioned there.

Read the blog post and complete the tasks that follow. Note the underlined words as you read.

https://blog.oup.com/2017/03/hofstede-cultural-dimensions

Cultural dimensions and differences across cultures

Geert Hofstede, in his [1] pioneer study looking at differences in culture across modern nations, identified five dimensions, or features, of cultural values: *individualism–collectivism, power distance, uncertainty avoidance, masculinity–femininity,* and *long-term orientation.* According to Hofstede's research, people in individualistic societies are expected to care for themselves and their immediate families only; while in collectivist cultures, people view themselves as members of larger groups, including extended family members, and are expected to take responsibility for caring for each other. With regards to power distance, different countries have varying levels of accepting the distribution of unequal power. [2] Uncertainty avoidance takes into consideration how certain cultures deal with uncertainties. Then, masculinity–femininity examines the [3] dominant values of a culture and determines where these values land on a spectrum in which "masculine" is associated with [4] assertiveness, the [5] acquisition of money and things, as well as not caring for others. Finally, long-term orientation looks at how a society considers respect for tradition and fulfilling social [6] obligations and how one views the future, such as the value of thrift (saving and being careful with money).

Hofstede's cultural dimensions have formed a basic [7] framework for viewing other people and their cultures. International business people, psychologists, communications researchers, and diplomats all benefit from Hofstede's work, as well as everyone else. Using these frameworks leads to a greater understanding of ourselves and others.

To see differences across cultures more clearly, we compiled a list of illustrations of Hofstede's concepts in action.

1   People in collectivistic societies, such as most of Latin American, African, and Asian countries, and the Middle East, emphasize the obligations they have toward their ingroup members, and are willing to sacrifice their individual needs and desires for the benefits of the group. Collectivists emphasize fitting in; they value a sense of belonging, harmony, and conformity (being like others), and are more likely to exercise self-control over their words and actions because they consider it immature or [8] imprudent to freely express one's thoughts, opinions, or emotions without taking into account their impact on others. They care about their relationships with ingroups, often by treating them differently than strangers.

2   In high power distance societies, such as many Latin American countries, most African and Asian countries, and most countries in the Mediterranean area, people generally accept power as an [9] integral part of the society. [10] Hierarchy and power inequality are considered appropriate and beneficial. The superiors are expected to take care of the [11] subordinates, and in exchange for that, the subordinates owe them [12] obedience and loyalty. It is quite common in these cultures that the seniors or the superiors take [13] precedence in seating, eating, walking, and speaking, whereas the subordinates must wait and follow them to show proper respect. The juniors and subordinates [14] refrain from freely expressing their thoughts, opinions, and emotions, particularly negative ones, such as disagreements, doubts, anger, and so on. Most high power distance societies are also collectivist societies, aside from a few exceptions such as France.

3   In low power distance countries such as Israel, Denmark, and Ireland, people value equality and seek to minimize or eliminate various kinds of social and class inequalities. They value democracy, and juniors and subordinates are free to question or challenge authority. Most low power distance cultures are also individualistic societies.

4 People from high uncertainty avoidance cultures, such as many Latin American cultures, Mediterranean cultures, and some European (e.g. Germany, Poland) and Asian cultures (e.g. Japan, Pakistan) tend to have greater need for formal rules, standards, and structures. [15] Deviation from these rules and standards is considered disruptive and undesirable. They also tend to avoid conflict and take fewer risks.

5 In low uncertainty avoidance cultures, such as China, Jamaica, and the United Kingdom, people are more comfortable with unstructured situations. Uncertainty and ambiguity are considered natural and necessary. They value creativity and individual choice, and are free to take risks.

6 In masculine cultures, such as Mexico, Italy, Japan, and Australia, tough values – such as achievements, ambition, power, and self-confidence – are preferred over tender values – such as quality of life and compassion for the weak. Additionally, gender roles are generally distinct, which means that men and women play separate roles in the society and are expected to differ in embracing these roles. For instance, men are expected to be assertive, tough, and focus on material success, whereas women are expected to be modest and tender, and focus on improving the quality of life for the family.

■ Xi'an Bell Tower, Xi'an, China

7 In feminine cultures, such as most Scandinavian cultures, gender roles are flexible: men and women do not necessarily have separate roles, and they can switch their jobs while taking care of the family. Feminine societies care more about quality of life, service, and nurturing others, and such tender values are embraced by both men and women in the society.

8 Based on the teachings of Confucius, long-term orientation deals with a society's search for strengths. Societies with a long-term orientation, such as most East Asian societies, embrace future-oriented qualities such as thrift and effort, ordering relationships by status, and feeling a sense of shame for falling short of expectations.

9 Societies with a short-term orientation, or way of thinking, foster more present- or past-oriented virtues such as stability, respect for tradition, and exchanging greetings, favors, and gifts. Countries with a short-term orientation include Norway, the United Kingdom, and Kenya.

Cassandra Gill

A **What experiences do you have with these cultural dimensions in your travels and studies? Write down your comments.**

B **Find the word (synonym) in the box below that is closest to meaning to each of the underlined words in the text you read on Hofstede's cultural dimensions.**

Tip: Words that match best should be the same part of speech. In other words, a noun should match another noun, an adjective should match another adjective, and so on.

a essential	**e** riskiness	**i** avoid	**m** structure
b confidence	**f** submission	**j** priority	**n** innovative
c rank	**g** vagueness	**k** main	**o** obtaining
d responsibilities	**h** juniors	**l** unwise	

Grammar

Affixes

Many words in English are formed using **affixes**, which are parts of words added to a root word to make a new word. **Prefixes** (word beginnings) change the meaning of a word. **Suffixes** (word endings) change the word form, also known as the *part of speech*.

C Make a copy of the table below and then look back at the underlined words in the text. See if you can identify any common prefixes from the table and then write a definition of the word in your own words. Check your answers in a dictionary.

Prefix	Meaning	Word from text	Your definition
un-			
im-			
sub-			
re-			
pre-			

D The myth of national identity:

What makes up a national identity? How does our nationality influence our sense of identity? Is it possible to have a world without national identity? And would that be good or bad? Discuss with your classmates before the following task.

One of the aims of the International Baccalaureate Organization is to develop global citizens. Watch the following video from the *New York Times* about national identity and then answer the questions below: https://nyti.ms/2F25xPT. Use the closed captions, pause and re-listen as needed.

Tip: In addition to reading the questions before you listen (or read), make predictions of the answers if possible. Good readers and listeners actively try to predict so that when they read and listen, they are merely checking their predictions.

1 Where did people get their identities from before the idea of a national identity?

2 According to this video, what is 'weird' about national identity?

3 According to the video, 'national identity is the myth that built the modern world'. List **two** negative results that can arise from national identity.

4 What is the first factor mentioned that unites France? Has it always been that way?

5 Ethnic groups of Europe match national borders. True or false?

6 According to the video, what were the four big changes of the modern era that led to national identity?

   a Urbanization   **d** Sports

   b Agriculture   **e** Warfare

   c Mass communication and transport (trains, newspapers)   **f** Governments overtook religion in establishing authority

7 According the video, national identity affects us as individuals. How is this shown by the research on the movie *Rocky IV*? How did the people who identified as American feel as they watched the movie when Rocky wins?

8 How does whether or not a country plays in the Football World Cup affect how likely that country is to attack another nation and start a war?

9 According the video, the negative effects of national identity resulted in the Second World War. After this terrible event, the world experimented with a new kind of national identity that started in the USA. What was this new idea of national identity?

10 What shared values were supposed to unite Americans?

E How would the world be different if there were no countries or boundaries?

Considering the question above, as well as the previous tasks and vocabulary in this unit, write a diary entry imagining yourself in a future world with no borders and no nations. Be as creative as you like.

Tip: A successful diary entry will probably:

- start with a date and location
- have a salutation ('Dear diary')
- be written to the writer himself / herself, reflecting on one's experience
- be informal
- use first person narration.

F

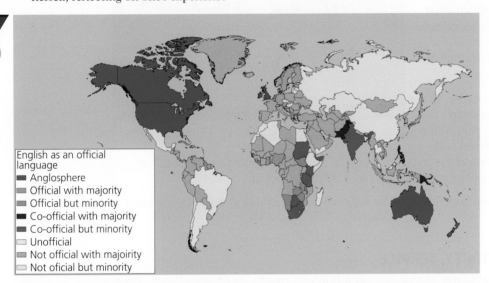

English as an official language
- Anglosphere
- Official with majority
- Official but minority
- Co-official with majority
- Co-official but minority
- Unofficial
- Not official with majoirity
- Not oficial but minority

Follow this link and look up your own country: www.hofstede-insights.com/country-comparison

Look at the bar graph based on the cultural dimensions described in the text you read earlier in this unit and read the descriptions below it for your country. Now, look up an anglophone culture of your choice and do the same. Make notes comparing the two countries based on the value systems highlighted.

Make about ten bullet points that outline your ideas. Using these notes, and the graphs (you can print or show them on screen), give a 3–4 minute talk to your classmates comparing your country's values to an anglophone country's cultural values. You may want to add your own experiences to make your talk more personalized, as well as answer questions from your classmates / groupmates after your talk. Finally, consider recording yourself while you speak and score yourself using the speaking rubric Criterion A.

■ TOK Links

Culture hides much more than it reveals. Strangely enough, what it hides, it hides most effectively from its own members.

Edward T. Hall

Hall referred to culture as the 'silent language'. What did he mean by this? Discuss this question, the quotation above and how it relates your own experiences with a partner.

Culture can be defined as *the shared values of a group of people that influence those people's behaviour.* This is illustrated in the culture iceberg metaphor and graphic on the right. Often what we see and experience as 'culture' is just the manifestations of cultural values and norms that lie at the heart of a culture.

Students in the IBDP explore culture as a way of knowing (WOK) in TOK. Here, using your understandings developed in the previous speaking task and the texts in this unit as well as the iceberg model of culture, answer the following question in writing in your reflection journal:

How much of our knowledge is shaped by our own culture as well as our understanding of other cultures?

■ The culture iceberg metaphor

CREATIVITY, ACTIVITY, SERVICE

Create a travel guide (written or as an audio podcast) to your country for citizens of anglophone countries, based on ideas and understandings you have developed from the texts and tasks in this unit. Then consider publishing your travel guide online with supporting media (images, and so on). A good travel guide will:

- include a country profile (statistics on population, and so on)
- note important geographic information and highlights to see
- note important cultural facts and features as well as highlights (possibly including food)
- include some notes on useful language expressions.

2 Values

Look at the image in the extract below. Discuss with a partner the following question: How can culture cause a plane to crash?

Malcolm Gladwell on culture, cockpit communication and plane crashes

Can cultural issues cause plane crashes? Malcolm Gladwell, the pop intellectual and author of *Outliers: the Story of Success,* has dedicated a whole chapter to this topic in his new book. While it touches on aviation, the book is largely focused on issues concerning what makes people successful. He concludes it's a cocktail of culture, work ethic and luck. We had the chance to sit down with Gladwell and talk about the chapter, "The ethnic theory of plane crashes."

Journalist: *You share a fascinating story about culture and airline safety in your new book. Can you explain a bit about that?*

Gladwell: *Korean Air had more plane crashes than almost any other airline in the world for a period at the end of the 1990s. When we think of airline crashes, we think, Oh, they must have had old planes. They must have had badly trained pilots. No. What they were struggling with was a cultural legacy, that Korean culture is hierarchical. You are obliged to be deferential toward your elders and superiors in a way that would be unimaginable in the USA.*

But Boeing and Airbus design modern, complex airplanes to be flown by two equals. That works beautifully in low-power-distance cultures [like the USA, where hierarchies aren't as important]. But in cultures that have high power distance, it's very difficult.

I use the case study of a very famous plane crash in Guam of Korean Air. They're flying along, and they run into a little bit of trouble, the weather's bad. The pilot makes an error, and the co-pilot doesn't correct him. But once Korean Air figured out that their problem was cultural, they fixed it. And they even require pilots now to speak English to avoid this cultural influence on flight safety.

Gladwell examines the role of culture in plane crashes like Korean Air Flight 801 in 1997 and others. In addition to weather and pilot fatigue, he blames those crashes on crew members whose cultural legacy made them too submissive to communicate clearly that the plane was about to crash. Key problems involve Korea's authoritarian culture, reflected in a hiring and promotion policy that favors former military fliers over normal civilians. Too often, the effect has been friction that hampers the pilot teamwork needed to fly modern jets.

To find out more about the role of culture and success, make sure you pick up a copy of this fascinating book.

Outliers: the Story of Success by Malcolm Gladwell, $25 hardback

Matt Phillips
http://on.wsj.com/1968rQJ

A Read the extract and complete the tasks that follow.

1 Is each of the following sentences true or false? Justify your answers by quoting a relevant phrase from the text.

   a The entire book focuses on a history of plane crashes.

   b Poor training for pilots caused several Korean Air crashes in the 1990s.

   c It is important in Korean culture to show respect to authority.

   d Showing respect is similar in Korean and American cultures.

   e Gladwell suggests that it is more difficult to pilot a plane successfully when the staff come from a culture where showing respect for rank is critical.

   f A well-known crash in Guam was due solely to bad weather.

2 Refer to this sentence for these questions: 'The effect has been friction that hampers the pilot teamwork needed to fly modern jets.'

   a What does 'the effect' refer to?

   b Which word could best replace 'hampers' in the sentence?

i supports	iii aids
ii constrains	iv sustains

3 Select any of the following text types this text *could* be:

   a An interview

   b A newspaper article

   c A review

   d A brochure

   e A blog

Grammar

Mitigating or hedging language

Mitigating or **hedging language** is a way of using language in certain ways to show respect (and sometimes embarrassment). Many cultures use this function of language to show politeness with a more formal register of the language, especially when communicating to someone in a position of authority. One of the assessment aims of English B is to 'understand and use language appropriate to a range of interpersonal and / or intercultural contexts and audiences,' and your understanding of language registers is critical to achieving this aim.

For example, in English, we would **not** ask a stranger 'What time is it?'; instead, we might say, 'Excuse me. Could you tell me the time?' This politeness or 'mitigation' is often achieved by using conditional forms and modal verbs, such as *could, would, might*, and so on. See some examples below.

Direct language	Mitigating (polite) language
Pass me the chips.	**Would** you pass me the chips. or It **would** be great if you passed me the chips.
Do this by Monday.	If you **could** get this done by Monday, I'd really appreciate it.
Turn left now.	I **would** turn left here.
What?	**Could** you say that again?

B Try the following task, which is based on transcripts and translations of the conversation between the pilot and co-pilot of the doomed 1997 Korean Air flight to Guam mentioned in the previous text. Make a copy of the table and complete the final column with mitigated language. How would you politely ask the pilot to change his course of action?

What the co-pilot said	Meaning	Mitigated language
Don't you think it rains more? In this area, here.	**The weather is bad and we can't see the runway. We might crash. We must turn around.**	
It's Guam, Guam.		
Captain, the weather radar has helped us a lot.		

C Watch the following interview with Malcolm Gladwell from 1:19, taking notes as you listen: https://youtu.be/6KYPcHv78tk. Answer the questions, and replay the interview as necessary to check your answers.

1 What is the single most important factor in plane safety?

2 Name two characteristics that define successful communication in planes.

3 Based on the previous question, what is the basis of these qualities according to the interview?

4 Based on the questions and answers above, write a brief summary of the interview.

■ Writer Malcolm Gladwell (*Outliers: the Story of Success*)

Grammar

Question forms

Review these basic **question forms**:

- Move the helping (auxiliary or modal) verb to the front of the sentence:

Statement form	Question form
Korean Air **has** improved its safety record.	**Has** Korean Air improved its safety record?
We **can** see the runway.	**Can** we see the runway?

- If there is only one word in the verb, use *do / does / did* (in the correct tense) at the beginning, then the subject, then the bare infinitive. If the verb *to be* is the main verb, move it in front of the subject:

Statement form	Question form
The plane crashed.	**Did** the plane crash?
A Korean typically shows respect for authority.	**Does** a Korean typically show respect for authority?
Malcolm Gladwell **is** an author.	**Is** Malcolm Gladwell an author?

D First, write questions for an interview with your favourite English-speaking author, musician or artist. Have a classmate check your question forms. Research as much as you can about this author, musician or artist, and then write out your answers to the questions as if you were this person based on what you think he / she would say from his / her perspective.

E Using the previous writing task as a transcript, record your conversation with your partner and upload it to an online forum where your other classmates can listen and comment. Consider listening and reflecting on your language skills (see Criterion A for the internal assessment criteria). Then write your thoughts in your reflection journal.

■ TOK Links

One IB learner profile characteristic is **open-minded**: *We critically appreciate our own cultures and personal histories, as well as the values and traditions of others. We seek and evaluate a range of points of view, and we are willing to grow from the experience.*

If values vary from culture to culture, can there be such things as 'universal values' that apply across all cultures? In your opinion, are some cultural values superior to others, or should cultural relativity (meaning all cultures are a product of their individual histories and contexts, and therefore equal) be respected?

In your reflection journal, explore these questions, expanding on your own experience and the understanding you have developed through exploring ideas and texts in this unit.

CREATIVITY, ACTIVITY, SERVICE

Start a culture club in your school where students meet to discuss cultural values and attributes with the aim of raising student and teacher awareness of how cultures are similar and different. Make a poster to advertise your group. A successful poster will include:

- an aesthetically attractive design
- the name of the club
- the meeting time and location
- contact information.

3 Beliefs

Discuss the following questions with a partner:

- What is truth?
- How do you know something is true?
- How do group identity and beliefs influence knowledge?

One of the philosophical aspects that underpins learning in the IBDP is the idea of **inquiry**, or the act of investigating to learn the truth. In the IB learner profile, the attribute of being an 'inquirer' is described accordingly: *We nurture our curiosity, developing skills for inquiry and research. We know how to learn independently and with others. We learn with enthusiasm and sustain our love of learning throughout life.*

In some ways, there has never been a better time to be a learner. With nearly an infinite amount of information at our fingertips via the internet, students are no longer limited to the monopoly on knowledge that textbooks and teachers once had.

On the other hand, how can you as a student decide what information is accurate and reliable given the amount of information online? The recent coining of the term 'fake news' has made it ever more difficult for readers to feel confident that what they have read is accurate, which may lead to a sense of confusion and dismay.

The following text explores this topic and attempts to answer why people believe untruths and how one's political identity is related to the belief (or lack of belief) in facts.

A Before you read the following article, check your understanding of the words below. If you aren't sure of the meaning, look them up in a dictionary and note the word in your own language. Then read the text to get a general idea of the meaning before going back and filling in the blanks with these words.

a affirm	**c** astray	**e** contradictory	**g** discrepancy	**i** plausible
b aligns	**d** bolster	**f** converge	**h** generalization	**j** partisan

■ Strategies for reading

- **Skimming** is a technique used to get the main idea of a text. The reader quickly runs his / her eyes over the text, picking out topic sentences and key words and looking at headings and graphics to get the 'gist' of the text.

- **Scanning** is a technique used to find specific information. Rather than reading the whole text carefully, the reader looks just for the information he / she needs (to answer questions, for example).

These techniques can help you save time when completing text-handling tasks, such as in your IB exam for English B, as well as to better understand texts.

Fake news and the influence of political parties (why do we believe untrue stuff?)

Fake news is everywhere. However, why we believe it is still unclear. Drawing on neuroeconomics research, psychologists suggest that valuing our identity more than our accuracy is what leads us to accept incorrect information that [1]_____ with our political party's beliefs. This value [2]_____ can explain why high-quality news sources are no longer enough. In addition, understanding it can help us find better strategies to bridge the political divide between people of differing political opinions.

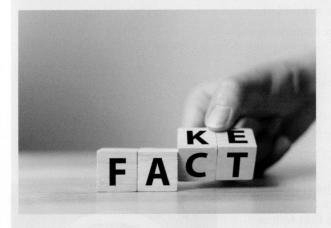

The research

"Neuroeconomics has started to [3]_____ on this understanding of how we calculate value. We're choosing what matters to us and how to engage with the world, whether that's which newspaper we pick up in the morning or what we have for breakfast," says senior author Jay Van Bavel, a psychologist at New York University. "And so we started to think, it's when our goals to fit in with certain groups are stronger than the

goal we have to be accurate that we are more likely to be led [4]_____."

Identity-based beliefs

This is what he calls his identity-based model of belief. The idea is that we assign values to different ideas based on what matters to us most at the moment and then compare those values to decide which idea we believe is true. Our political parties can provide us with a sense of belonging and help us define ourselves, and therefore, agreeing with them can [5]_____ our sense of self. And that can sometimes matter more to us than accuracy about an issue, even if accuracy is something we normally do care about. When that happens, we'll likely believe the ideas that align with our party's views, no matter how [6]_____.

Truth doesn't always matter

This can mean that the sources of information we normally rely on to shape our views have less of an impact. "Having a really high-quality news source doesn't matter that much if we think the people producing it belong to a different group than us," Van Bavel says. "They might have the best writers, the best investigative journalists, the best editorial standards, all the stuff that we would normally care about." But we stop valuing those things, which would normally lead to a high likelihood of accuracy, and instead focus on the group we think the news is aligned with, for example.

Making the truth count

Still, Van Bavel does believe that his model offers strategies that can help bridge the political divide. "Our model really doesn't pick a side," he says. "What it argues for is increasing the value of truth or else finding ways to reduce the effects of identity, whether on the left or the right."

Put your money where your mouth is

Being put into a role that requires someone to be accurate can give people criteria with which to evaluate information and help them be better at thinking critically. Even more simply, Van Bavel says we can increase the value of accurate beliefs by asking people to put their money where their mouth is. "When you are in a disagreement, ask your opponent, 'You wanna bet?' And then their accuracy motives are increased, and you can see right away whether they were engaging in motivated reasoning. Suddenly $20 is on the line, and they don't want to be proven wrong," he says.

Don't criticise

We can also work to reduce the effects of identity. One way is by creating a superordinate identity: getting people to think of themselves as citizens of a nation or the world rather than as members of a political party. But we also have to pay attention to how we engage with people of different political opinions. "It turns out that if you insult them and publicly criticize them, their identity needs increase, and they become threatened and less concerned about accuracy. You actually need to [7]_____ their identity before you present information that might be [8]_____ to what they believe," Van Bavel says.

Currently, Van Bavel is working on empirical studies that will reaffirm the [9]_____ of these neuroeconomics principles to our beliefs. In the meantime, though, and especially in today's political climate, he believes the message is simple: "Our [10]_____ identities lead us to believe things that are untrue. So, we need to step back and critically evaluate what we believe and why." Ultimately, we have to be aware that the truth does not always prevail.

www.sciencedaily.com/releases/2018/02/180220123127.htm

 B Transitions, sometimes called 'discourse markers' or 'transition signals', are used frequently in writing to help the reader understand the structure of the ideas being expressed and to signal the logic and coherence of the written text. See if you can match the following transitions to the correct sentence by matching them to the gaps in the text below. You can check your answers in the previous text when you are done.

> **a** In addition **d** However
> **b** Therefore **e** For example
> **c** Ultimately

Fake news is everywhere. [1]_____, why we believe it is still unclear.

This … can explain why high-quality news sources are no longer enough. [2]_____, understanding it can help us find better strategies to bridge the political divide between people of differing political opinions.

Our political parties can provide us with a sense of belonging and help us define ourselves, and [3]_____, agreeing with them can bolster our sense of self.

But we stop valuing those things, which would normally lead to a high likelihood of accuracy, and instead focus on the group we think the news is aligned with, [4]_____.

[5]_____, we have to be aware that the truth does not always prevail.

 C Is the Earth flat? A group of people known as the Flat-Earthers believe so. Listen to this audio: www.livescience.com/24310-flat-earth-belief.html and answer the questions that follow.

1 What was the name of the photo that depicted the Earth as round, taken by the Apollo space missions?

2 What do the group known as the Flat-Earth Society say about the idea of the Earth being round?

3 What shape do they say the Earth is?
 a A flat square
 b A flat disc
 c A flat rectangle
 d An infinite flat plane

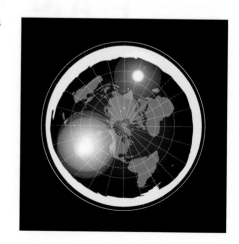

4   List **three** pieces of evidence from the video that explain why the Earth is round.

5   What is meaning of 'falls flat' in the phrase 'this conspiracy theory falls flat'?

D   In your IB studies, you will undoubtedly develop curiosity and conduct research online to find information for your classes as well as for various projects, including the extended essay. Review different sites, take notes and write a set of guidelines for IB students at your school to follow when searching for reliable sources of information online. Your guidelines will:

■   be appropriate to the audience

■   use semi-formal language

■   be concise and clear

■   have a title

■   be clearly organized

■   use subheadings and bullet or numbered points.

E   Using the guidelines you developed in the previous task, give a talk to your class or make a (screencast) video with supporting visuals that can be shared with classmates on how best to find reliable information online.

■ TOK Links

Confirmation bias

A *bias* is simply an unfair judgment or error of judgment based on certain influences. *Confirmation bias* is the habit of looking for and favouring information that 'confirms' one's existing theories or beliefs, as explained in the previous text ('Fake news and the influence of political parties'), where people may choose to ignore facts if those facts go against their political beliefs.

In light of confirmation bias and increasing participation in social media, especially by young people who have online 'friends' with similar beliefs, values and opinions, what are the implications for seeking 'the truth'? How is social media like an 'echo chamber' in reflecting what we already believe and know, and how can this be damaging to society?

Write a response to this question in your reflection journal.

CREATIVITY, ACTIVITY, SERVICE

Academic honesty

Academic integrity is becoming a serious concern for academic institutions, and academic honesty is something that IB takes very seriously. Producing independent academic work and avoiding plagiarism are goals IB students should strive for.

Some schools have 'honour committees' composed of a mix of teachers, administrators and fellow students who deal with cases of alleged academic dishonesty or other disciplinary issues that occur at school. Students might hear testimony from students, assess evidence and suggest a consequence, where appropriate.

If such a system does not already exist at your school, propose this to the school administration. If it does exist, propose to the administration how such a committee can support academic honesty at the school.

■ **Literature**

4 The Curious Incident of the Dog in the Night-Time

In English B higher level, you will read at least two works of literature, and for the individual oral (internal assessment) you will have a choice of one of two excerpts your teacher gives you from these works to discuss. In addition to exploring topics related to the IB themes in this course, you will explore **characters**, **setting**, **plot** and **themes** from the novel itself:

- **Characters:** the people or roles in a work of fiction
- **Setting:** where (place) and when (time) the story takes place
- **Plot:** the events of the story, and the order in which they happen
- **Themes:** the main idea(s) and underlying meaning developed in a novel that often address human nature or society

In the novel *The Curious Incident of the Dog in the Night-Time* by Mark Haddon, Christopher Boone is a 15-year-old boy who lives with his father in Swindon, England. As Christopher is the narrator of the story, we learn about his unique worldview and talents, including his amazing mathematical ability (he uses prime numbers to number the chapters) as well as his passion for detective novels like the *Sherlock Holmes* series.

Christopher also has challenges, including his inability to read others' emotions and his dislike of certain colours and physical contact, which suggest he may have Asperger's Syndrome, considered to be a high-functioning subtype on the spectrum of autism disorders. Through the investigation of the murder his neighbour's dog, Christopher takes his reader on his adventure of personal growth, giving us insights and challenging our 'neurotypical' beliefs and views that he sometimes finds strangely curious himself, as exemplified in the following excerpt. Christopher tells us in Chapter 199:

People believe in God because the world is very complicated and they think it is very unlikely that anything as complicated as a flying squirrel or the human eye or a brain
5 could happen by chance. But they should think logically and if they thought logically they would see that they can only ask this question because it has already happened and they exist … And there are billions of
10 planets where there is no life, but there is no one on those planets with brains to notice … And people who believe in God think God has put human beings on the earth because they think human beings are
15 the best animal, but human beings are just an animal and they will evolve into another animal, and that animal will be cleverer and it will put human beings into a zoo, like we put chimpanzees and gorillas into a zoo. Or
20 human beings will all catch a disease and die out or they will make too much pollution and kill themselves, and then there will only be insects in the world and they will be the best animal.

Excerpt from The Curious Incident of the Dog in the Night-Time *by Mark Haddon*

In light of your understanding developed in this unit and your IB studies, develop a 3–4 minute talk based on the excerpt above. Practise your talk with a partner and question each other. Consider recording your talk and assessing yourself against the IB interactive assessment rubric.

- **Presentation:**

   Present the extract. You may place the extract in relation to the literary work (in this case, you can read a summary of the book online if you want to), but you must spend the majority of the presentation discussing the events, ideas and messages in the extract itself. (3–4 minutes).

- **Follow-up discussion:**

   Your teacher will engage you in questions on the content of the extract that you present, expanding on observations that you provide in the presentation. (4–5 minutes).

- **General discussion:**

   You and your teacher will then have general discussion using one or more of the five themes of the syllabus as a starting point. (5–6 minutes).

Language and identity

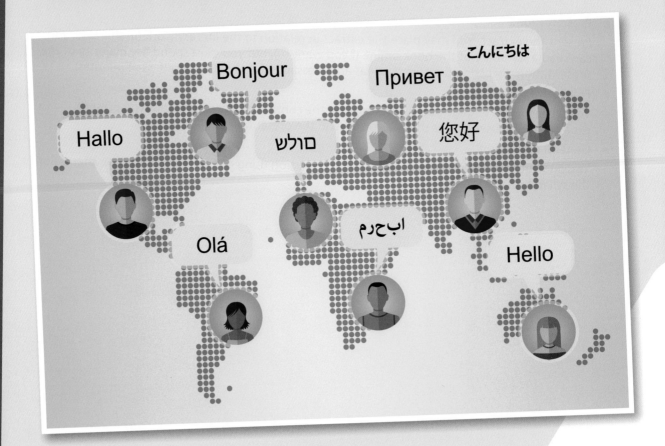

REFLECTION

How does language impact our identity? In simple terms, identity is defined by the characteristics that make us whom we are. Language and identity are interrelated on so many levels since our language(s) is (are) the principal way we interact with others and think. On that level, our languages and culture have a large impact on our identity, either as we see ourselves or as others see us. Two of the readings in this unit explore this notion and how languages can help us, but also how they disadvantage some due to the linguistic dominance of English. But language itself and the words we choose to describe ourselves and others also impact identity. The third text explores this idea.

Ludwig Wittgenstein once said, 'The limits of my language are the limits of my world.' If that is true, does bilingualism or multilingualism expand your world? Discuss with your classmates the advantages of bilingualism.

1 The benefits of bilingualism

With a partner, discuss the advantages (and any disadvantages) of bilingualism. When you are done, skim the next reading passage quickly to check whether any of the advantages you listed are mentioned in the text.

The joys and benefits of bilingualism

More than half the world's population is now bilingual. Now thought to encourage flexibility of mind and empathy, bilingualism is also transforming societies.

1 Everyone knows that it's moving to watch your children change over the years. But to hear them alter their language, over the course of a few weeks and months, is almost surreal. It's as if the precious beings you thought you knew are completely different and the experience is both intriguing and unsettling.

2 Our children were 12, 10 and seven when we moved from England to their mother's country, Italy, last summer. Until then, they had always lived in England and their English was what you would expect: the odd spelling mistake, but otherwise fluent and full of pre-teen playground slang.

3 Now, in Italy, barely a day goes by when they don't inadvertently say something odd: "Mum, I'm eshing [going out]"; "Can we eat pesh? [fish]"; "I've scritten [written] to Grandpa"; "Can you accorten [shorten] my trousers?"; "Have you chiused [closed] the door?"; "Shut up, I'm parling [talking]"; "I've strapped [ripped] the page". Every time it happens we laugh about our private pidgin, called – take your pick – "Engaliano" or "Italish". But behind the laughter is mild astonishment at the speed at which children can overlay and overlap languages in an intelligible way.

4 What's breathtaking isn't just their language acquisition; it's the way their personalities subtly mutate and shift. Benedetta, a bruiser at the best of times, is strangely sweet and gentle in Italian; Emma, our incessant joker in English who is always funny, is precise and serious; and Leo, who has always seemed stereotypically Italian, is even more boisterous. It feels as if our children are different, more mature, but also, because of linguistic struggles, somehow more infantile or vulnerable.

5 Until recent decades, bilingualism was deeply frowned upon and considered bad for a child's development. The received wisdom for much of the 20th century was that there was really only space for one language in a child's brain. It was thought that if, for example, immigrants maintained a mother tongue at home, it would impede integration at school and probably lead to academic failure and confusion.

6 As one journal study put it in 1926: "The use of a foreign language in the home is one of the chief factors in producing mental retardation as measured by intelligence tests." The choice to avoid the mother tongue wasn't simply an educational, but also a social one; the home language was invariably considered a source of shame, a sign of poverty or difference that would almost certainly lead to being singled out and bullied.

7 However, in recent decades academics have been suggesting that, far from being a hindrance, exposure to more than one language could offer a distinct advantage. Aptitude tests have revealed that bilinguals are marginally more competent at problem solving, metalinguistic awareness and symbol manipulation. The more tests have been done, the more neurologists and cognitive scientists focused on "executive control", the cognitive skills in the brain that support high-level thought, memory, attention and multitasking.

8 The effects of bilingualism appear to take place almost from birth. Extraordinary experiments – involving electric sensors in babies' dummies – suggested that infants only a few months old can distinguish one language from the next. If such "enhanced perceptual attentiveness" is evident so early on, it's perhaps not surprising that the bilingual brain seems to be wired differently.

9 At the other end of the life spectrum, there appear to be positive consequences of bilingualism. One researcher from Canada analysed the medical records of patients diagnosed with dementia and discovered that onset symptoms were diagnosed between three and four years later in bilinguals.

10 In November last year, there was a good news story at a school in London that earned the highest exam results in the area. What made it remarkable was the fact that 96% of students were EALs (speaking "English as an additional language"). Here, it seemed, was proof of what academic research had been saying for years: that the maintenance of a "home language" may be beneficial for learning the "community language", that proficiency in that first tongue enables proficiency in the next (English). Antonella Sorace is the director of Bilingualism Matters, a research and information centre at the University of Edinburgh that promotes multilingualism in Scotland and across the globe. "For decades," she says, "there was this notion that learning two languages together, or too soon, would affect children. It would cause problems at school. That's always the message that parents got, but there's absolutely no evidence of that; in fact, quite the opposite."

11 In another language, you don't just learn new words, or sounds, but new notions. It's like putting on different spectacles and seeing the world with different eyes. You become adept at understanding different perspectives and, it seems, you may become more, rather than less, intelligent and eloquent.

Tobias Jones

www.theguardian.com/commentisfree/2018/jan/21/the-joys-and-benefits-of-bilingualism

A Go back through the text and use the context to understand the meaning of the following words. Then, select the option that is closest in meaning to the word from the text.

1 surreal (paragraph 1):
   a decorated
   b weird
   c satisfied
   d added monthly
   e focused only on the area where you live

2 unsettling (paragraph 1):
   a having a baby
   b church-related
   c moved away
   d a harmless thing
   e disturbing

3 intelligible (paragraph 3):
   a shrunken
   b near
   c understandable
   d little parts that can be seen
   e in threes (side by side)

4 breathtaking (paragraph 4):
   a amazing
   b thinking
   c long
   d natural
   e rude

5 subtly (paragraph 4):
   a improve (as much as possible)
   b suffered (from a loss)
   c connection
   d slightly (in a detailed way)
   e pushing forward

6 mutate (paragraph 4):
   a messes up
   b playful
   c numbing with drugs
   d change
   e memorize

7 bruiser (paragraph 4):
   a damaged
   b joys
   c sleep
   d fairly real and clear
   e tough guy

8 incessant (paragraph 4):
   a incredibly valuable
   b fast
   c preferred
   d written
   e constant

9   impede (paragraph 5):
   a   the study of how the human body moves
   b   conditions
   c   collapse from being tired or shocked
   d   hell / afterlife
   e   stop / interfere with

10   hindrance (paragraph 7):
   a   using images
   b   treating something like it's the greatest thing in the world
   c   built up
   d   interference
   e   are liked by most people

11   adept at (paragraph 11):
   a   extremely clean
   b   strongly wanting to
   c   confident
   d   good at
   e   heavily walking

12   eloquent (paragraph 11):
   a   wealthy
   b   very well-spoken
   c   cowardly
   d   getting lots of compliments
   e   quiet

 B   **Write a summary of the text incorporating the main ideas and most important details of the article.**

Grammar

Nominalization

In addition to developing increasing accuracy and fluency in English in this course, you will develop better control of the various *registers* of English. Register is the degree of formality we use to communicate, often determined by whom we are communicating with. This determines choices we make in terms of vocabulary or grammar, for example with your friends you may use slang as your register, whereas in academic tasks you will often use more formal language.

IB students aim towards developing increasing technical, abstract and formal language in their academic writing. One way to achieve this is called **nominalization**. Nominalization is simply transforming words like adjectives and verbs into nouns or noun phrases. Nominalization is often used in academic writing because abstract ideas and processes can be 'packed' into one single word (for example *photosynthesis*) and classified or quantified, whereas spoken language typically uses more verbs and adjectives. In addition, nominalization makes our writing less personal and more objective (avoiding personal pronouns like *I*, *we*, *you*, *they*, and so on) and even more authoritative.

Note that nominalization is used primarily in academic writing, and overusing it can make your writing difficult to read (or even boring at times!).

 C   **Change the emboldened words into nouns and transform the sentences accordingly to develop a more formal style. Compare your answers to the ones in the preceding text.**

Less formal: If you **spoke another language** at home, it was not considered good for children **while they were growing up**, in some people's view.

More formal with nominalization: **Bilingualism** was considered bad for a child's **development**. (paragraph 5)

1 Students wouldn't **integrate** with others at school (if they spoke another language), and they would **fail** and feel **confused**. (paragraph 5)

2 Some **chose** not to speak their mother tongue for educational and social reasons. (paragraph 6)

3 Recently, some academics have been saying that rather than **damaging** children, if you **expose** your children to another language, it actually **helps** them. (paragraph 7)

4 If we **speak another language**, it **causes** us to change, starting from when we **are born**. (paragraph 8)

5 As we **age**, if we **speak another language**, it appears to **affect** us in a good way. (paragraph 9)

 D The Sapir–Whorf Hypothesis suggests that the language you speak affects the way you perceive the world as well as affecting your thoughts. Benjamin Whorf, who studied Native American languages, noticed the Inuits in the Arctic region of North America had dozens of words for snow.

What is suggested in the cartoon on the right? Discuss with your class.

E Watch the video at www.nativlang.com/linguistics/linguistic-relativity.php and answer the questions below. You can check your answers in the transcript on the website.

1 What are universal categories of language? List any **two** mentioned in the audio.

2 'Language and culture are superficial, but language and cognition run deep.' Which statement below best demonstrates the meaning of this sentence in the context of the audio?

   a Language and culture are the same all in humans, but thinking varies depending on where you live.

   b Language and culture are different around the world, but thinking and linguistic processes in the brain are similar for all humans.

   c Language, thinking and culture are all related.

3 What is the name of the view of language and thinking that grew out of Sapir and Whorf's ideas?

4 Give one example of this theory in the real world (using the culture and concept discussed).

5 Complete the following paragraph:

   One practical consequence of linguistic relativity: direct [a]_____ between languages isn't always possible. Since Hopi and English aren't simply ways of expressing the same thing in different words, you can't preserve [b]_____ or [c]_____ when you translate between them.

146

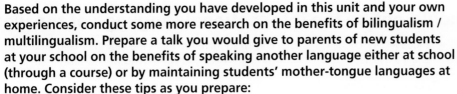

 F Based on the understanding you have developed in this unit and your own experiences, conduct some more research on the benefits of bilingualism / multilingualism. Prepare a talk you would give to parents of new students at your school on the benefits of speaking another language either at school (through a course) or by maintaining students' mother-tongue languages at home. Consider these tips as you prepare:

- Use more formal language (formal register).
- Grab the listeners' attention from the start, and leave a strong impression at the end.
- Use techniques to make a connection with the audience (including humour, questions, use of 'you' and 'we', and so on).
- Present data and anecdotes, from your or other students' experiences.
- Consider using visuals (for example images and graphs) to complement your speech.

 G Write a proposal to your school administration suggesting increasing the number of languages taught at the school and / or ways the school might better support students' mother-tongue / home languages. A successful proposal will:

- be directed at the school administration (audience)
- include formal language (register)
- address the goals of the proposal with a title or heading
- use clear organization, through use of subheadings, numbered bullets, and so on.

■ TOK Links

In TOK, you explore how language is a way of knowing (WOK). In light of the reading on bilingualism and the previous listening task, as well as your own experience, **agree** or **disagree** with the following statement. Write in your reflection journal.

Knowledge is dependent on our language and culture.

CREATIVITY, ACTIVITY, SERVICE

To support students' mother-tongue / home languages, work with a group of students, teachers and administrators at your school to create a mother-tongue peer tutoring system, whereby students in the IBDP are paired and tutor younger students in the school who share the same mother-tongue language so that the younger students' academic achievement and bilingualism are supported.

2 English as a global language

To have another language is to possess a second soul.

Charlemagne

What do you think this quotation means? Discuss with a partner and share your ideas with your class.

Should English be the global language (*lingua franca*)? The following text comes from a blog and explores this question. Before you read it, discuss with a partner the advantages and disadvantages of having a global language. Make a T-chart with advantages on one side and disadvantages on the other as you discuss. Then read the text and see how your ideas compare to the writer's.

Lingua francas are languages that are used across cultures, often those that don't share the same language. In the ancient world, Latin was the *lingua franca* of the Roman Empire of Europe, the Near and Middle East and North Africa. Today, English is often considered the *lingua franca* of our globalized world, where diplomacy, research, business, tourism, media and education are increasingly dominated by English.

Why English should not be the international language of the world

When I was younger I didn't like languages. In school, I hated Irish and thought it was a complete waste of time. Why bother learning it when everyone spoke English? In fact what's the use of any other language when it's obvious that English is the international language? This view is very common among English native speakers and to a certain extent it's true. English is one of the most spoken languages in the world and is [1] so / by far the most common second language in the world. No matter where you travel in the world, you have a decent chance of finding an English speaker. International conferences almost always are held in English and over 90% of academic articles are published in English. So it seems like case closed, English is the global language, everyone speaks it and I should be thankful that I happen to be a native speaker.

Except recently I've been having doubts. I began to reconsider my views when I went travelling through Europe. I was impressed so many people could speak English, but I felt guilty that they had spent years learning my language, yet I couldn't speak a word of theirs. Learning a language isn't easy; it involves months of hard work just to become conversational and years to become fluent. It costs time and money and can be deeply frustrating. Up until that point, I had taken English [2] for / of granted; I never realised how much work the rest of the world goes through. It's not as though English is an easy language to learn; it's incredibly irregular and outright random (especially the spelling and grammar).

Nor did I pay much attention to what happens if you don't speak English. The vast majority of academic papers are published in English and it is required in most of the top universities and businesses. English is a privilege; if you have it, you get access to an elite club of the rich and famous. If you don't, you're left [3] out / behind in the cold.

Language isn't just a tool to communicate; it is also a huge part of our identity. It's how we think and how we view the world. So when English speakers expect the rest of the world to learn our language, we are actually asking a lot. English speakers often treat not knowing English as primitive as not having electricity, but we don't think about what people give [4] out / up to learn our language. Languages carry a lot of cultural and historical baggage, both good and bad. The only reason I (and many others) speak English is that centuries ago my country was invaded, colonised and the native language suppressed. It wasn't for linguistic reasons that English dominated, but political.

To put it [5] in / on perspective, imagine if you had to speak Spanish (presuming you don't already). You still live and work in the same place, but for reasons beyond your control it has been decided that more people speak Spanish than

English so therefore this is the new international language through which you will have to work. Most people would be horrified at the prospect. I'm sure plenty of people in England and America would rather die than do so. It would feel like surrendering our culture, our traditions. Yet this is the very thing that many English speakers expect the rest of the world to do. If we aren't willing to learn even the basics of another language, why should we expect the rest of the world to make such an effort just to suit ourselves?

Imagine if a law was introduced putting major barriers in front of women's careers in the world of business and science. They could still attend university and get good jobs but beforehand they had to undergo years of work to get an additional qualification. Men could go straight to the top, but women were sidetracked by years of extra work. Sure they could still continue their careers but with a serious handicap. Most people would be rightly horrified. It would be deeply unfair and severely damaging as we would lose all they have to contribute to society. Placing extra burdens on some people just due to the luck of birth offends our sense of justice. Imagine still, if the barriers were erected in front of all non-whites in the world. This is even worse. Society would be dominated [6] by / with a small handful, who didn't earn their place, but only got there based on whom they were born to. No one could in any good conscience support such an unjust system.

But this is exactly what expecting everyone to speak English does. It enforces barriers to three-quarters of the world that are difficult to cross and excludes the rest. It is similar to erecting barriers to success based [7] on / at arbitrary classes like race, which like language mostly comes from your parents. Sure, many overcome this barrier and become successful in the world of science and business, but many do not. Even those that do have to spend years learning English that could have been put to better use in their research or at their job. It is the equivalent of a tax on everyone who had the misfortune to be born to parents who didn't speak English. It is the same as asking people to complete an extra qualification before they can make it into the upper levels of business and science (considering how research is almost solely published in English and business so heavily conducted in English).

A world where everyone speaks English and only English would have advantages (I'm deeply aware that this blog would only have a tiny fraction of the number of its views if I blogged [8] with / in any other language) but also major disadvantages. It would be a duller, blander world where we all had the same conversations, watched the same movies and listened to the same music. We would lose a huge amount of the diversity in the world, a huge part of what makes us unique, what makes us who we are.

Robert Nielsen

https://whistlinginthewind.org/2015/02/11/why-english-should-not-be-the-international-language-of-the-world/

A Select the correct option for each of the underlined words in the text.

 B Select which of these statements are true according to the text.

1 Most scholarly work is published in languages other than English.
2 English is an easy language to learn since so many people speak it.
3 English is a major advantage of the wealthy.
4 English speakers sometimes treat non-English speakers with disdain.
5 All people in England and the United States would embrace learning another language if they had to, according to the writer.
6 Expecting everyone to speak English is essentially unfair.
7 The writer thinks that people who don't speak English should be taxed more.
8 The writer thinks the world would be more boring if everyone spoke English.

Grammar

Phrasal verbs

Phrasal verbs are verbs that have two or more parts and are often used in less formal, spoken language. For many phrasal verbs, there are single-word equivalents that have the same meaning, but are used in more formal, sometimes academic, writing or speech. For example:

• You might say to a friend:

*We **found out** who speaks the most languages at school.*

• Whereas you might use more formal language for academic work, such as:

*It was **discovered** who speaks the most languages.* (note use of the passive voice too)

The more formal words often have Greek or Latin roots. Other examples include:

• *ask for = request*
• *set up = establish*
• *lie to = deceive*
• *come down with (an illness) = contract*
• *go before = proceed*

Your mastery through reading and practice of using phrasal verbs and their formal equivalents will aid you in developing your understanding and usage of the various registers of English (slang, informal, semi-formal, formal).

 C Complete this task by finding the appropriate phrasal verb to replace the more formal, underlined one-part verb, or by finding an appropriate formal verb to replace the less formal underlined phrasal verb. You can check your answers in the preceding text when you are done.

1 I began to <u>think again about</u> my views when travelling throughout Europe.
2 I was <u>blown away that</u> so many people could speak English.
3 If you don't [speak English], you're <u>excluded</u>.
4 We don't think about what people <u>sacrifice</u> to learn our language.
5 Most people would be [deeply] <u>offended by</u> the prospect [of working in another language].
6 It would feel like <u>handing over</u> our culture, our traditions.
7 Imagine still, if the barriers were <u>put up</u> in front of all non-whites in the world.

D Watch the film trailer for the award-winning documentary *Sound and Fury* at https://youtu.be/zXNrqKPsac0. The film follows the developing conflict between members of an extended family in New York, which includes several people who are deaf (cannot hear). Peter Artinian, his wife and all his children are born deaf, but his eldest daughter, Heather, wants cochlear implants. This technology can aid a child or adult to hear and to develop speech like hearing individuals by implanting a device into the brain. Peter is hesitant because he is afraid his daughter will lose her deaf culture and sign language. But his brother decides to implant his son (Heather's cousin) after they discover he is deaf too. What should Peter do, and will the decision divide the family?

Answer the following questions as you watch the video. Then consider watching the film with your class or watching Heather Artinian's TED Talk (www.youtube.com/watch?v=jhm5OaXJVMQ) to see how important language and culture are in relation to one's identity.

1 How does the man (Peter) feel about his children's deafness and his own deafness?
2 What is one thing that deaf people can't enjoy according to the video?
3 Complete the following sentence the grandmother says: 'Forget deaf. You do _____.'
4 What does the crowd of deaf people believe will happen to deaf culture if the cochlear implant becomes common?
5 Why is the father (Peter) angry at his mother in the last scene?

 E Imagine you have been asked to produce a radio programme / podcast for your school newspaper or news site. Base your radio programme / podcast on a series of interviews with students in your class or at your school as well as some teachers on the benefits and challenges of learning / speaking another language. A successful radio programme will:

■ have interview questions scripted in advance
■ have a catchy title
■ be well organized and include a brief introduction that precedes the recorded interviews
■ use informal to semi-formal language that is simple and clear in all spoken language (for ease of listening and understanding)
■ be edited for conciseness and may include music.

Note: Your teacher may be able to recommend what software you can use to produce such an audio programme.

 F Imagine your school has developed a new policy with the aim of improving students' language skills that says students must only speak English at school, both in class and in social situations. How would you feel if you were forced to use only English at school?

Write a social media post (such as Facebook) to your 'friends', describing your feelings about this new policy.

For a social media post, it is assumed the writer is expressing his / her views to a larger audience of friends, family and fellow students (in this case). Therefore the language register will likely be informal but might include some formality, depending on the sentiments expressed and who is expected to read it. The purpose of such a social media post is to mention the issue and offer a comment or opinion.

THINK OF YOUR AUDIENCE

Your friends, family and people in your 'network' might read your post, so make sure it is appropriate for the audience in terms of content and register (formality and showing emotion).

STAUS UPDATE

KEEP IT SHORT

Generally speaking, people don't read lengthy texts on social media, so grab your readers' attention and get to the point (explain the topic briefly, as necessary, and give your opinion).

CONSIDER ADDING AN IMAGE, OR LINK TO MORE INFORMATION

If you can add an image that stimulates your readers / followers, or you have a link that explains more on the topic, consider adding that.

LIKE - COMMENT - SHARE

COMMENTS

PROMOTE INTERACTION

Ideally, you are inviting a response from your readers, so encourage them to comment to promote a polite exchange of ideas

CREATIVITY, ACTIVITY, SERVICE

Research has shown that students who develop their mother-tongue / home language to an academic level have a better chance of developing sophisticated language skills in a second language. Similarly, the relationship between reading and language development is very clear: the more one reads, the better one's language becomes in terms of reading, writing, listening, speaking, vocabulary and grammar.

With this in mind, get students from your English B class as well as your teacher to organize a schoolwide campaign for students and parents to donate books in various languages to your school's library to complement the existing book collection, so students have reading materials from all the languages represented and studied at school.

■ TOK Links

Language reflects our brain's evolution and it gives us great insight into human psychology. Language also reflects our culture and experiences. While having a *lingua franca* such as English may have many benefits in our globalized society, consider the disadvantages.

In your reflection journal, consider the question below and write a response based on your understanding from this unit as well as your own experience.

'What would be lost if the whole world shared one common language?'

3 Gender and identity

Come up with a list of words that define your identity, for example brother, son, student, and so on. When you have your list, rank those words from most important to least important relative to your identity. Compare your answers with those of a partner and then discuss these questions:

- Is boy / girl (man / woman) on your list?
- How does gender affect your identity?

In addition to language and culture, much of our identity is formed through our gender, that is whether we are or feel male or female, or in some cases in between. Many languages like English reflect this in our use of pronouns like 'he' or 'she'. Read the blog below about how some parents are rejecting clear genders for their children and how this is even reflected in the language they use when referring to their children.

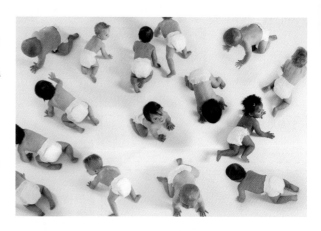

A Before you read the blog, check your understanding of the words below. If you aren't sure of the meaning, look them up in a dictionary and note the word in your own language. Then read the text to get a general idea of the meaning before going back and filling in the blanks with these words.

a defy	**c** stereotypical	**e** shaming	**g** anatomy	**i** patriarchy
b discriminating	**d** gist	**f** doused	**h** expansive	**j** intentionally

The rise of "theybies": How parents are raising children in a genderless world

if you've been reading the news lately, then you might have heard that some parents are calling their newborns a "theyby" instead of "baby". Several couples are [1] _____ – and very thoughtfully – raising their children without assigning gender.

Basically, the [2] _____ of it is this: these parents, known as "gender-creative parents", know the sex of their child based on [3] _____; yet in as many cases as possible, they do not reveal that information to others to avoid someone attaching a gender label based on their child's body parts. From birth, these gender-creative kids are given "they / them" pronouns rather than "he / she".

So why are the parents doing this? As Kyle Myers, parent to a 2-year-old, told us:

I'm very tired of the [4] _____ of our culture telling kids who they should be. A part of why we are parenting this way is because sex and gender occur on a spectrum, yet our culture loves to think people, all 7 billion of them, can and should be reduced to either / or, that is, male or female, with our language limiting them to only "he" or "she".

Other gender-creative parents worry that their child will be boxed into gender stereotypes. They fear that their full potential will be limited based on someone seeing them as either a boy or a girl, and they want to raise a child without gendered ideas of what to wear, play with, or how to exist – at least for the first few years of childhood.

Chances are, you already have a very strong opinion about all of this, one way or another. But whatever your personal opinion, I think the fact that we are having a conversation about gender identity and raising kids who [5] _____ societal gender constraints is a good thing, even an incredible thing.

And whether or not you agree with these parents, it is true that many parents do in fact leave little room for their kids to figure out gender identity on their own. Often, from the moment a parent sees the first image from an ultrasound, there's the leap to assume that their child's gender identity will match their physical body.

From gender reveal parties to over-the-top baby showers (parties for parents to celebrate the upcoming birth of their child) [6] _____ in pink or blue, there are expectations, ideas, and hopes placed on a child simply by labeling them a girl or a boy – long before they even make their way into the world.

However, the assumption that a child's gender will match their biological sex is one based in traditional thinking, and that can be a very [7] _____ way to think. The truth is, sex and gender are two different things, formed through different processes. Most children's gender identity is locked in by age 3 or 4, and most kids will happily tell you if they are a boy or a girl.

Society feels uncomfortable when a person doesn't identify as either a boy or a girl, or when they identify opposite their birth sex. This is especially the case for these transgender children. But if a child knows they are a boy or a girl in preschool, why do we have a problem with a transgender child knowing their gender at the same age?

The gender-creative parents raising their theybies are aware of this, too. As one parent told us, "Around 3, our kid was just like, 'I'm a girl.' And we said, 'Oh, yay, we've always wanted a girl. You're amazing. Welcome.'" This parent also explains that despite being raised without a gender assignment, their child still defined "girl" using many [8]_____ concepts placed on the female gender.

The difference is, this child's view of gender is wider than most. But do we really need to raise our kids without gender to give them an [9]_____ view of it? Personally, I don't think so. If anything, I think challenging gender stereotypes while accepting the fact that our kids may not be what we thought

they were is a more productive and realistic path to a society that thinks outside of the binary of "he" or "she".

We can encourage our kids to wear all colors, play with all kinds of toys, and wear sparkly clothes and nail polish, no matter their gender. We can allow our kids to be kids without [10]_____ them into what we think a "girl" or "boy" should be. So when our kids come to us doubting the label we gave them at birth, it's our job to validate them by listening to the identity they know to be true.

I don't think we need to raise kids without gender to raise kids who are accepting of themselves, others, and gender-creative and non-conforming people. I personally choose raising a kid who knows anything is possible whatever their gender and identity, and I can't wait until the day arrives when all societies take up this view.

www.babble.com/parenting/theybies-gender-neutral-parenting

Grammar

Text cohesion

There are different ways to successfully give a text **cohesion**, that is to connect / link the ideas in the text. You explored how pronouns and transitions do this in previous units. Look at other ways you can build cohesion and make links in your writing in the examples below. Write out the translations for these words in your own language.

Conjunctions:
- Addition: *and, also, too*
- Choice: *or, nor*
- Result: *so, for*
- Contrast: *but, yet*

Subordinate conjunctions / connectors:
- Time order: *after, before, until, when*
- Comparing / contrasting: *while, whereas, although, even though, despite, however*
- Cause and effect: *so that, since, because*

B **Fill in the blanks with the missing linking words from the grammar box above. You can check your answers in the preceding text.**

1 These parents, known as 'gender-creative parents', know the sex of their child based on anatomy; _____ in as many cases as possible, they do not reveal that information to others to avoid someone attaching a gender label.

2 Chances are, you already have a very strong opinion about all of this, one way or another. _____ whatever your personal opinion, I think the fact that we are having a conversation about gender identity is a good thing.

3 There are expectations, ideas, and hopes placed on a child simply by labeling them a girl or a boy. _____, the assumption that a child's gender will match their biological sex is one based in traditional thinking.

4 The gender-creative parents raising their theybies are aware of this, too. As one parent told us, "Around 3, our kid was just like, 'I'm a girl.' _____ we said, 'Oh, yay, we've always wanted a girl. You're amazing. Welcome.'" This parent also explains that _____ being raised without a gender assignment, their child still defined 'girl' using many stereotypical concepts.

5 I personally choose raising a kid who knows anything is possible whatever their gender and identity, and I can't wait _____ the day arrives when all societies take up this view.

C When Neil Armstrong landed on the moon in 1969, what if he had said, 'that was one small step for man, one giant leap for *peoplekind*' (instead of *mankind*)?

The prime minister of Canada, Justin Trudeau, made waves in the news when he once interrupted a woman at a meeting and 'corrected' her by saying that she shouldn't refer to 'mankind' but 'peoplekind' because the latter is more inclusive. What did he mean?

Watch the following news programme up to 3:00, which explores the idea of bias (prejudice in favour of one thing over another; errors in judgment) and sexism in language and how that might offend others and even limit our thinking: https://youtu.be/byn0fBCVeHA. Listen to the interviewer and interviewee discuss how some want the suffix / prefix / root word 'man' to be changed in common English words. Answer the following questions as you watch:

1 Which words should be avoided in writing according to Purdue University? Why?

2 Why does the interviewer say it's ironic that she is in Manhattan?

3 Fill in the blank: 'It's not about spelling; it's about being _____, and "mail" is offensive.'

4 Note examples of words given by the interviewed guest of words that could be changed. Also come up with you own English word and suggested alternative.

Words with 'man'	Suggested alternative without 'man'
a man-made	
b	people
c mailman	
d	

5 The tone of the interviewer's questions is…

    a curious   **b** sarcastic   **c** supportive   **d** angry

    Provide a quotation to support your answer.

D Our name is an important part our identity: it often reflects our family background, our language and our cultural or religious heritage, and for better or for worse, people often make assumptions about others based on their name. Therefore, sometimes students elect to change their name to an 'English-sounding' name when they are in their English classroom or if they study in an English-medium school. This may be to adopt a new identity in their new environment, or even to make their name easier to remember for classmates and teachers who might not speak the student's mother-tongue language.

Conduct a class debate based on the following statement:

'Students should adopt an English name when in an English-speaking environment (class or school), regardless of their language background.'

Organize two teams: one arguing for students to change their names to English names, and the other team for students maintaining their real names. Write your speeches first and then practise in teams. Each person should focus on one aspect of your team's argument as well as your opening and closing statements (introduction and conclusion). Allow for spontaneous question-and-answer times to challenge each other's ideas. Consider these tips as you prepare:

- Use more formal language (formal register).
- Use rhetorical devices including ethos, pathos, logos (see Unit 7), as well as repetition and asking questions (where appropriate).
- Grab the listeners' attention at the start, and leave a strong impression at the end.

■ Strategies for writing

Informal letters:

Such a letter usually has an informal to semi-formal register since the writer and audience are peers (the same age). In addition, you should consider these suggestions:

- Include a date and addresses at the top (see Unit 7).
- After the date and addresses, start with a salutation / greeting ('Hi X,').
- Organize the main body of your letter by paragraphs, clearly starting with an introductory paragraph of what you hope to achieve or argue (why are you writing this letter?) and then develop paragraphs on your main points.
- Consider using 'I', 'we' and 'you' to establish a connection, as well as flashes of humour, slang and other similar informalities.
- Finish with a concluding paragraph summing up your main ideas in light of the evidence you have presented.
- End your letter with 'Regards,' or 'Best regards,' and then your name underneath.

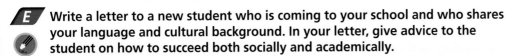

E Write a letter to a new student who is coming to your school and who shares your language and cultural background. In your letter, give advice to the student on how to succeed both socially and academically.

■ TOK Links

How does language allow us to make generalizations and stereotypes, and to what extent are they true?

In the previous section, you listened to a podcast about the Sapir–Whorf Hypothesis. If the theory of linguistic relativity is true, and language does influence our thinking, can **political correctness** help society become more fair and equal? Write in your reflection journal using your understanding developed in this unit as well as your own experience.

> The term *political correctness* is used to describe language, policies or measures that are intended to avoid offense or disadvantage to members of particular groups in society.
>
> *Wikipedia*

CREATIVITY, ACTIVITY, SERVICE

Adolescence is a period of great growth and change for all. In addition to balancing school, social and physical activity, teenagers are figuring out whom they are, and their identity is solidifying through experience. There can be many challenges at this time of life and sometimes teens might not know whom to talk to about their life questions and concerns.

Propose creating a support group with help from the health and counselling staff for students at your school who may struggle with questions around their identity, whether this be based on sexuality and gender, culture and language backgrounds, belief and value systems, or other sub-themes of identity. Consider putting out information (flyers, and so on) about how students can get in touch should they or someone they know need support.

■ Literature

4 The Other Hand

The Other Hand is the story of a young woman who flees conflict in her home village in the oil-rich region of southern Nigeria. She makes her way to the UK as an illegal immigrant and is detained for a long period of time at an immigrant detention centre near London. When she finally gets out, she seeks out the only two people she knows in England, whom she met on a Nigerian beach during a life-changing event a few years before. Will she be able to find them, and if so will they help her? And if not, will she survive in her newly adopted country as an immigrant?

Most days I wish I was a British pound coin instead of an African girl…

How I would love to be a British pound. A pound is free to travel to safety, and we
5 are free to watch it go. This is the human triumph. This is called, globalisation. A girl like me gets stopped at immigration, but a pound can leap the turnstiles, and dodge the tackles of those big men with their uniform
10 caps, and jump straight into a waiting airport taxi. *Where to, sir?* Western Civilisation, my good man, and make it snappy.

See how nicely a British pound coin talks? It speaks with the voice of Queen Elizabeth the
15 Second of England. Her face is stamped upon it, and sometimes when I look very closely I can see her lips moving. I hold her up to my ear. What is she saying? *Put me down this minute, young lady, or I shall call my guards.*

20 If the Queen spoke to you in such a voice, do you suppose it would be possible to disobey? I have read that the people around her – even Kings and Prime Ministers – they find their bodies responding to her orders before their
25 brains can even think why not. Let me tell you, it is not the crown and the sceptre that have this effect. Me, I could pin a tiara on my short fuzzy hair, and I could hold up a sceptre in one hand, like this, and police officers
30 would still walk up to me in their big shoes and say, *Love the ensemble, madam, now let's have quick look at your ID, shall we?* No, it is not the Queen's crown and sceptre that rule in your land. It is her grammar and her
35 voice. That is why it is desirable to speak the way she does. That way you can say to police officers, in a voice as clear as the Cullinan diamond, *My goodness, how dare you?*

I am only alive at all because I learned the
40 Queen's English. Maybe you are thinking, that isn't so hard. After all, English is the official language of my country, Nigeria. Yes, but the trouble is that back home we speak it so much better than you. To talk
45 the Queen's English, I had to forget all the best tricks of my mother tongue. For example, the Queen could never say, *There was plenty wahala, that girl done use her bottom power to engage my number one
50 son and anyone could see she would end in the bad bush.* Instead the Queen must say, *My late daughter-in-law used her feminine charms to become engaged to my heir, and one might have foreseen that it wouldn't
55 end well.* It is all a little sad, don't you think?

Learning the Queen's English is like scrubbing off the bright red varnish from your toe nails, the morning after a dance. It takes a long time and there is always
60 a little bit left at the end, a stain of red along the growing edges to remind you of the good time you had. So, you can see that learning came slowly to me. On the other hand, I had plenty of time. I learned
65 your language in an immigration detention centre, in Essex, in the southeastern part of the United Kingdom. Two years, they locked me in there. Time was all I had.

But why did I go to all the trouble? It is
70 because of what some of the older girls explained to me: to survive, you must look good or talk even better. The plain ones and the silent ones, it seems their paperwork is never in order. You say, they
75 get repatriated. We say, *sent home early.*

Excerpt from The Other Hand *by Chris Cleave*

Answer the following questions:

1 Why does the narrator (Little Bee) tell us she would rather be a British pound coin than an African girl?

2 What appears on a British coin?

3 Which word best means 'ensemble' in line 31?

   a singing

   b costume

   c accent

   d coin

4 Why does Little Bee want to speak like the Queen?

5 Why does the narrator suggest we might think it's not so surprising that she learned the 'Queen's English'?

6 What does she mean in line 56 when she says, 'It is all a little sad, don't you think'?

7 What metaphor does she use to describe learning formal, that is the Queen's, English? What does she mean by this metaphor?

8 Where did she learn the Queen's English?

9 What does she suggest would have happened if she hadn't learned formal English?

10 In what ways is learning formal, academic English versus learning social English (slang, and so on) like Little Bee's experience of learning the 'Queen's English'? Write a short paragraph based on the previous excerpt, your understanding developed in this unit and your own experience. Discuss with a partner when you are finished.

UNIT 10 Artistic expression

Choose one of the pictures above and explain or answer the following:
■ Describe the picture.
■ What might a viewer like or dislike about this image? Explain why.
■ Explain the art form the picture is expressing.
■ How are thoughts and feelings expressed in this art form?

1 Expression through culture

In pairs, find three photographs from three different time periods of a popular clothing fashion. From the pictures, discuss what can be understood about society at that time, simply based on these examples of fashion. Possible questions to ask yourselves are:

■ Why did people dress this way?

■ What could this be related to in society?

■ Why might other people imitate it?

Share your photographs and thoughts with the class.

Visual arts review: "Native Fashion Now" – Tradition and cutting edge, superbly balanced

Even without museum commentary, Native Fashion Now *is an important show – visually, socially, and politically.*

This show will explode your ideas of where Native Americans fit in the world of fashion. Maybe you [1] don't / didn't realize fashion had a Native presence, but it very much does, and this exhibition celebrates Native American artists who [2] had / have found their balance between tradition and cutting edge.

[3] At / In the show's opening, the museum hosted a roundtable discussion with three artists, Jamie Okuma (Shoshone), Patricia Michaels (Taos Pueblo), and Pat Pruitt (Laguna Pueblo), and they helped orient my non-Native thinking [4] for / about their work. First, they are artists who choose to work in bead, fabric, and metal, and they produce clothing, footwear, and jewelry that can be useful as well as beautiful. Native peoples have been creating functional items for millennia, sourcing materials locally or through [5] their / its extensive trade networks, then decorating them with geometric and nature-based designs. Today's artists continue in that tradition, but kick it up several notches, with globally sourced materials and innovative designs.

The first Native American to achieve success with consumer fashion was Lloyd Kiva New, [6] he / who designed dresses and leather goods in the 1950s. For his fabrics, he borrowed colors [7] from / with western riverbeds, cliffs, and scrub plants; he printed the cloths with stylized figures and animals drawn from his Cherokee heritage.

Roughly his contemporary, Frankie Welch designed clothing in Alexandria, Virginia, [8] when / where she rubbed elbows with high level government officials. Her scarf with Cherokee language syllabics was used as an official presidential gift in 1966, and First Lady Betty Ford wore Welch's red and gold embroidered evening dress.

Following [9] this / these auspicious beginning, the excitement about Native fashion tapered off. Two dresses on loan from Phoenix's Heard Museum reflect the stasis of the 1970s and '80s: a wool blanket dress and another embroidered in turquoise and coral are carefully executed but they seem like artifacts, interesting but hardly exciting.

The buzz [10] returned / has returned in the early years of this century. For [11] its / his black-fringed dress, Derek Jagodzinsky printed Cree language syllabics on a white band around the midriff. On its own, the dress would be reminiscent of the straight shift worn by flapper girls in the roaring twenties, but the midriff band and long fringe transform it into a wholly different creation. [12] Other / Another piece, also black and white, comes from Virgil Ortiz's collaboration with Donna Karan – a strapless, gently flared dress with a bold design abstracted from plant and animal figures. It's Cochiti Pueblo meets New York.

In recent years, the work [13] has / had become even more experimental, edgy, even political. Two stand-out dresses are from Bethany Yellowtail (Apsaalooké / Crow and Northern Cheyenne). She layers fine black lace over a beige strapless sheath and stitches a row of white elk teeth down each sleeve. Leather appliqué on the black lace positions a large bell-shaped flower over the breasts. Her long-ago relatives may have worn clothes adorned with elk teeth, [14] but / and this is an entirely modern take. And its attitude is nimbly accentuated by a sunglass accessory – an example of 'Rez Bans' designed by Kevin Pourier (Oglala Lakota) – which is made out of buffalo horn, malachite, mother-of-pearl, coral, lapis lazuli, and sandstone.

The other Yellowtail dress is a simple, short-sleeved shift, using photoprint fabric: black birds in flight over ivory-colored satin. The photo comes from Matika Wilbur (Swinomish and Tulalip) who is photographing contemporary Native Americans for her Project 562 (that's the number of tribes recognized by the federal government). Here, again, the accessory [15] _____ an afterthought. The cuff bracelet by Caroline Blechert (Inuit) makes use of beads, porcupine quills, caribou hide, and antler to create a colorful, abstract design of lines and triangles.

The use of indigenous materials (feathers, furs, beads, leather) and design elements (birds, plants, geometric shapes) are ingredients that link most of the work in the show. But these connections are elastic; each artist [16] _____ them in his or her own way. Some work combines traditional materials with others that are not (silk, Mylar). Other pieces manipulate natural materials in new ways. Lisa Telford, for instance, stitched pieces of red cedar bark into a dress. Her Haida forbearers, [17] _____ cedar forests, may never have used tree bark for a dress, but if they did, it certainly would not be this short, form fitting, and one-shouldered. Sho Sho Esquiro (Kaska Dene / Cree) created a deeply slit dress using seal, beaver, carp, beads, silk, rayon, and rooster feathers. It is modern and gorgeous, with feathers as the main event.

****

Some artists deploy traditional design in entirely new places – a skateboard deck, for instance. Rico Lanaat Worl (Tlingit and Athabascan) makes use of formline design to decorate wooden decks. The black lines of his ravens and eagles are bold yet restrained; they hold something back, [18] _____ there was space needed to let the intricate images breathe. Louie Gong (Nooksack and Squamish) enhances Chuck Taylor sneakers with the formline design of a wolf, [19] _____ a look that is both indigenous and urban. Jared Yazzie (Diné (Navajo)) coined the phrase "Native Americans discovered Columbus" on his T-shirt.

****

Jamie Okuma famously created beaded boots. They are Christian Louboutin boots – the red soles are the giveaway – and they are groundbreaking. They also, [20] _____ sneakers, skateboards, and some of the clothing in the show, inevitably lead to the challenging question of cross-cultural fertilization.

The artists at the roundtable shared thoughts about the specter of assimilation. Most Native artists learn about technique and the spiritual significance of traditional design [21] _____ ceremonial garments and objects for the tribe. When it comes to their own art, they draw on all that makes them whom they are, including tribal traditions, and that motivates them [22] _____ deciding what to use in their artistic and commercial enterprises. "Whatever we're doing as artists is to be seen, and sold." Okuma said. On the other hand, some of their creations must remain out of sight from the public. "Ceremonial life remains private to the pueblo," insists Pruitt.

One audience member raised the tricky issue of cultural appropriation this way: "What advice can I give fashion students who are inspired by Native art?" [23] _____, Okuma pointed out the Isaac Mizrahi dress on display in the gallery: "It's beautifully done, in a respectful manner. [24] _____ a design, an artist should write to the tribe for guidance. Get permission. Your work must bear the integrity of whom you are and where the elements came from."

Michaels offered this as summary: "We are artists, and we are still here, after all the genocides, dislocations, and pillaging. We are proud of whom we are, and want to be part of the larger world, while also celebrating our own culture." The splendid *Native Fashion Now* shows that this vital and complex conversation about cultural inspiration, mingling, borrowing, and appropriation is well underway.

Kathleen C. Stone is a writer pursuing her MFA degree, a lawyer who earned her JD many years ago, and, even before that, was a student of art history. Her blog can be found here: http://artsfuse.org/137624/visual-arts-review-native-fashion-now-tradition-and-cutting-edge-superbly-balanced

A Complete the blanks in the article.

1 For numbers 1–14, choose the word that best completes the sentence.

2 For numbers 15–24, choose a group of words (a–j) from the box below to fill in each blank.

a when answering	**e** makes use of	**i** giving them
b is far more than	**f** when it comes to	**j** as if
c by working on	**g** who lived among	
d but before using	**h** along with	

B Match the person (1–10) with what they have done (a–j).

1 Bethany Yellowtail

2 Caroline Blechert

3 Lisa Telford

4 Jamie Okuma

5 Lloyd Kiva New

6 Louie Gong

7 Frankie Welch

8 Kevin Pourier

9 Derek Jagodzinsky

10 Virgil Ortiz

a Used a tree bark to make a dress

b Designed sneakers with a wolf on them

c Encouraged artists to contact tribes for advice on using native designs

d Made sunglasses out of buffalo horn

e Has ancestors who wore clothes decorated with elk teeth

f Worked with Donna Karan

g Made a bracelet designed with abstract lines and triangles

h Drew animals on cloth

i Designed a dress for a president's wife

j Printed his native language on his clothes

Grammar

Using *who*, *when*, *where* or *which* when giving additional information

We sometimes use ***who***, ***when***, ***where*** or ***which*** to give additional information about a person, time, place or thing. This information is added to the sentence using a comma and one of these words. It is important to remember what each word introducing this **relative clause** is referring to:

- *who* refers to a person
- *when* refers to a time
- *where* refers to a place
- *which* refers to a thing

C Fill in the blanks with the correct word: *who, when, where* or *which*.

1 Jamie has a new job, _____ is much closer to her house than her previous job.

2 They spent the weekend in Chicago, _____ there was a large music festival going on.

3 The dentist's office is next to a large shopping mall, _____ I went for a coffee while I waited for my husband to get his teeth examined.

4 We always travel to Spain in the summer, _____ the weather is warm and we can swim in the sea.

5 After work, they went to see Tom's lawyer, _____ is considered one of the best lawyers in London.

6 Dance is an art form, _____ not a lot of people remember when you ask them to list art forms they are familiar with.

7 I love the hour just before the sun sets, _____ the sky changes colour and the city buildings are simply outlines of themselves.

8 When there is a conflict in the tribe, the solution is found by the village elders, _____ are considered the wisest people in the tribe.

D You will listen to a television report on a young artist from South Africa, whose name is Loyiso Mkize (www.youtube.com/watch?v=6al528MPdhg). Listen to the report and answer the following questions:

1 Why is Mkize's exhibition called 'Black Magic'?

2 Why does Mkize feel that this is an exciting time period?

3 How did social media play a role in Mkize's success?

4 Where is Mkize's exhibition opening that night?

5 What does Mkize's superhero, Quasi, have to do before he can use his powers?

6 What does Kirsten Muller like about Mkize's comic book?

7 What idea does Mikize want to communicate to young South Africans through his comic book?

E In small groups, take turns describing a person, a place or an object that you associate with your culture, while the other students draw that person, place or object. Share your drawings and explain why you drew them the way you did.

 F Create a comic book page for a new superhero. You may draw, describe or borrow images for the visual aspects of the page, but you should accompany your images with your story and dialogue.

■ TOK Links

To what extent is imagination important in art?

What other areas of knowledge use imagination and how is it similar to or different from its use in art?

CREATIVITY, ACTIVITY, SERVICE

Find a community in need close to your school. Discover what forms of art are important to its culture and work with it to produce an exhibition of that art at your school, raising awareness of that community and its needs.

2 Expression through movement

Play a game of charades, where each student takes a turn 'acting out', or communicating, the meaning of a word or phrase through body movements. The person acting out the word or phrase cannot speak. Choose words associated with one of the topics listed in the box:

visual arts	music	literature
theatre	film	architecture

After the game has finished, discuss the following:

- What was most helpful for students guessing the correct meaning of the word?
- What caused the most difficulty?
- What does this tell us about body language and communication generally?

How to Act Shakespeare

Acting Shakespeare, in many ways, is like acting any other style or genre. However, due to the complexity and intricacy of the text it requires a more eager investigation by the actor. It is [1] _____ another language, yet it cannot be performed as such. It must fall onto the ears of the audience with absolute clarity. There is no definitive guide on how to act Shakespeare.

He left us only his plays as a guide and so as you read more about Shakespeare, remember your natural instincts are invaluable. There will be many people who tell you there is a [2] _____ way, but it just isn't the case. I have laid out some personal tips and ideas that may help you on your way to better understanding and performing Shakespeare.

Understand the Words

Understand [3] _____ word and phrase. When we speak in a contemporary play we understand everything we are saying. Yet for some reason actors often think Shakespeare is [4] _____ complicated or out of reach and therefore they don't bother to invest the time in [5] _____ the words, delivering the text without clarity or meaning. Here then, I believe, is the greatest rule in how to act Shakespeare: if you don't know what you're saying, the audience doesn't either. If they don't understand what you're saying, they aren't engaged.

■ Laurence Olivier in the 1948 film version of *Hamlet*.

Work out the Thoughts

As the words become clear you will start to unlock the meaning of [6] _____ line, in turn unlocking each thought and [7] _____ the text as a whole will begin to make sense. Simply put, a thought is a new idea. And you must understand every new idea for the text to come alive.

[8] _____ the punctuation is a great guide in helping you identify the thought: a full stop indicating the end of a thought. [9] _____ punctuation may vary between editions, therefore use your instinct as well [10] _____ your understanding of the text to help you work out the thoughts.

Paraphrase

Now you understand every unfamiliar word and you have marked out the thought shifts, have a go at paraphrasing the text; put the text into your own words. This is common practice in rehearsals for Shakespeare plays and is great to do with audition monologues or scenes you are working on. If you can't speak the monologue in modern English, you can't truly communicate it in Shakespearean English.

Tell the story

Once you understand your thoughts, move on to the rest of the speech. What is it trying to say? Then look to understand the particular scene you are working on and how that scene fits in with the whole play. In Shakespeare everything builds on what precedes it and so understanding the story helps you tell your part more clearly.

Tip: there will always be people who can't understand you. Shakespeare is a two-way street that requires an audience to be fully engaged and listening, but you owe it to those who are truly listening to share the words with clarity and meaning.

Read more Shakespeare

As I mentioned earlier, speaking Shakespearean text is not dissimilar to speaking a foreign language. Many words are unfamiliar and you can read a whole play and not really understand what happened. So, read and go see as many Shakespeare plays as you can to help make his words seem natural to you. Every play you read helps make the next play you read clearer and therefore more enjoyable.

Tip: when working on a soliloquy, look for where the character is using compare and contrast, question and answer or disagreement and agreement in the speech. In soliloquies the character is usually debating what course of action he/she should take next, so try to figure out these changes in thought as this is what is interesting for the audience.

Acting work

Shakespeare's text might be more complex than contemporary text, yet the acting fundamentals are the same. Firstly, don't try to manufacture character. Character comes in what you do, your actions. Oberon (A Midsummer Night's Dream) is a King, but that status comes in how he treats Puck and other characters and how other characters endow him. Not from acting like a King. You can work physically on a role such as Oberon. A King would likely be proud and stand tall; his servant, Puck, perhaps quicker paced and flustered.

Conclusion

Try to listen to great Shakespearean actors speaking the verse. Read as many plays as you can. All this work will help turn Shakespearean from foreign language to beautiful, wonderful text.

Andrew Hearle https://www.stagemilk.com/how-to-act-shakespeare/.

 A **Read the text to get a general idea of the meaning before going back and filling in the blanks (1–10) with one of the following words:**

a every	**e** almost	**i** often
b each	**f** eventually	**j** understanding
c too	**g** right	
d as	**h** however	

Grammar

Verbs using *in*, *on*, *to*, *from* and *into*

Below are verbs that can be used with the prepositions *in*, *on*, *to*, *from* and *into*:

- *hear*
- *keep*
- *put*
- *listen*
- *get*
- *take*
- *come*
- *turn*
- *go*
- *look*

B Put a 'tick' under the section where you would find the information listed in a–j.

Where would you find the following advice:	Understand the words	Work out the thoughts	Paraphrase	Tell the story	Read more Shakespeare	Acting work
a This is helpful for auditions						
b Understand how the scene fits in with the whole play						
c Put the text into your own words						
d Look for characters using compare and contrast						
e A King would act proud						
f Shakespeare is a two-way street						
g Some think Shakespeare is too complicated						
h The acting fundamentals are the same						
i It's like speaking a foreign language						
j Punctuation is helpful						

C What do the following phrases in the text mean?

1 'Fall onto the ears' (paragraph 1)
2 'Out of reach' (paragraph 3)
3 'Have a go' (paragraph 5)
4 'Two-way street' (paragraph 7)
5 'Course of action' (paragraph 9)

Listen to the conversation about break dancing, an athletic style of street dancing, at www.npr.org/templates/transcript/transcript.php?storyId=546323243 and answer the following questions.

1 Which of the following statements are true?
   a   The name 'break dancing' was started by Richard Colon's manager.
   b   Break dancing became an Olympic sport in the 1970s.
   c   People are 'lucky' if they are in New York at the time of the broadcast because the city is hosting its biggest break dancing competition.
   d   Colon has been to refugee camps where he's seen people break dance.
   e   Break dancing was not approved of by most parents in Colon's neighbourhood.
   f   Colon's mother never supported his desire to dance.
   g   When Colon is judging break dancers, he focuses on the rhythms of the movements.
   h   Break dancing grew internationally after the movie Flashdance.
   i   Break dancing began in community centres and as an after-school activity.
   j   Colon considers break dancing more of an art form than a sport.
   k   Colon does not like break dancers to have a particular 'flavour'.
   l   Colon says break dancing began in his community because of a lack of activities for young people.

2 Complete the following sentences with three to five words.
   a   Richard Colon will be watching a lineup of.
   b   Colon said 'If we didn't need a budget for it,.'
   c   The word 'B-Boy' meant.
   d   Colon wants a 'respectable amount of foundation' to complement.
   e   Colon is proud to have contributed to the world that can be considered an American folk dance.

E In small groups, create a role play where you imagine that you are participants on a game show. One student is the show's host and the others are contestants. Create questions based on different artistic genres: visual arts, dance, music, theatre or literature. Use your own ideas as well as some of the information from this unit for your questions and answers. Perform your show for the rest of the class.

F Imagine that you are an actor, a dancer or a musician. Write a diary entry where you describe your thoughts and feelings just before a performance. You may write what you like but some possible ideas are to discuss what it is like just before the curtain rises on stage, or to discuss all of the preparation that has gone into that performance.

■ TOK Links

To what extent is non-verbal language an effective source of knowledge?

What kinds of knowledge are gained from theatre and dance?

CREATIVITY, ACTIVITY, SERVICE

Create a dance competition or a fashion show at your school. Make it entirely student-run. Organize and promote it. Use it to raise money for a good cause.

3 Expression through images

Research the construction of a famous building. Find out what makes this building unique.
Where did the architects' ideas or inspiration come from? Share your answers with the class.

The Sydney Opera House

■ Sydney Opera House

The Spherical Solution

As construction of the podium began in Sydney, Jørn Utzon and his team of architects back in Hellebæk explored how to build the Opera House's shell-shaped roof. Between 1958 and 1962, the roof design for the Sydney Opera House evolved through various iterations as Utzon and his team pursued parabolic, ellipsoid and finally spherical geometry to derive the final form of the shells. The [1] eventual realisation that the form of the Sydney Opera House's shells could be [2] derived from the surface of a sphere marked a milestone in 20th century architecture.

To work out how to build the shells, the engineers at Arup & Partners needed to express the shell shapes mathematically. Asked by the engineers in 1958 to define the curves of the roof, Utzon took a plastic ruler, bent it against a table and simply [3] traced the curves. He sent these drawings to Arup & Partners in London, explaining these were the shapes he wanted. The simplicity and ease of repetition was immediately [4] appealing.

■ Spherical solution model, 1962. Image: State Library of NSW

The building's shape slowly [5] shifted away from Utzon's competition drawings. His new curves were detailed in the Red Book, a complete set of plans, sections and elevations sent to the NSW government in March 1958, which expanded on the schematic drawings from his competition entry. The roof's ridge profiles had become higher and more pointed; the end shell form no longer cantilevered like a cliff over the sea. These higher profiles also allowed for more volume for the stage towers and auditoriums.

Yet the drawings contained in the Red Book were structurally unsound, with difficult bends near the roof's footings. Each shell was different. The lack of a defining geometry would make it impossible for the builders to reuse formwork and would add to the building's costs.

As the years and iterations continued without a satisfactory solution, resolution of the issue went from pressing to critical. By late 1961, three years had passed since Utzon had bent his plastic ruler on a table and a solution to building the shells had still not been found. Utzon was even asked by the NSW government whether he should consider another engineering firm – but the architect refused to look elsewhere, convinced his [6] collaboration with Arup would yield the solution. In the end the solution would come from Utzon himself.

Various [7] myths surround the discovery of the so-called Spherical Solution, the unified answer to the problems of buildable shells. The iconic sculptural form of the Sydney Opera House essentially relies on the form of these shells, so the importance of finding the best solution to the roof cannot be [8] underestimated. As one of the more popular myths has it, Utzon had a eureka moment while peeling an orange. While it's true that the solution can be demonstrated in this way, it had in fact been architect Eero Saarinen who, over breakfast one morning years earlier, cut into a grapefruit to describe the thin shell structure of the roof of his TWA Building, and later used an orange to explain the shape of the shells to others.

By his own [9] account, Utzon was alone one evening in his Hellebæk office with a number of the most intractable Sydney Opera House problems weighing heavily on his mind.

Utzon was [10] stacking the shells of the large model to make space when he noticed how similar the shapes appeared to be. Previously, each shell had seemed distinct from the others. But now it struck him that as they were so similar, each could perhaps be derived from a single, constant form, such as the plane of a sphere.

The simplicity and ease of repetition was immediately appealing. It would mean that the building's form could be [11] prefabricated from a repetitive geometry. Not only that, but a uniform pattern could also be achieved for tiling the exterior surface. It would become the single, [12] unifying discovery that allowed for the distinctive characteristics of Sydney Opera House to be finally realised, from the vaulted arches and timeless, sail-like silhouette of the Opera House to the exceptionally beautiful finish of the tiles.

For Utzon, this realisation was an epiphany. His assistants were [13] stunned when he explained the idea and set out to provide drawings that would prove its [14] validity.

By finding the parts of a sphere that best suited the existing shapes of the shells, each new form could be extracted.

Furthermore, only one side of each profile was required as this would be mirrored to complete the arch.

The Spherical Solution would become the binding discovery that allowed for the unified and distinctive characteristics of the Sydney Opera House to be realised finally.

By any standard it was a beautiful solution to crucial problems: it elevated the architecture beyond a mere style – in this case that of shells – into a more permanent idea, one inherent in the universal geometry of the sphere. It was also a timeless expression of the [15] fusion between design and engineering.

In January 1962 Utzon submitted his Yellow Book: 38 pages of plans, sections and elevations setting out the shells, details of the precast ribs and the tiling. Its cover showed the principles of the spherical geometry that would allow the Opera House to finally be realised.

www.sydneyoperahouse.com/our-story/sydney-opera-house-history/spherical-solution.html

A **V** **Match each word from the text (numbers 1–15) on the left, with its meaning on the right (a–o).**

1	eventual	a	drew
2	derived	b	work together
3	traced	c	thought unimportant
4	appealing	d	explanation
5	shifted	e	created
6	collaboration	f	bringing together
7	myths	g	mixture
8	underestimated	h	made beforehand
9	account	i	correctness
10	stacking	j	final
11	prefabricated	k	amazed
12	unifying	l	placing on top of each other
13	stunned	m	stories
14	validity	n	attractive
15	fusion	o	moved

B Choose the correct answer (a–d) for Questions 1–5.

1 The Sydney Opera House was a 'milestone' in architecture because:
   a It was made from shells
   b It was designed between 1958 and 1962
   c Its roof could be derived from the surface of a sphere
   d Utzon had to bend a ruler to draw the initial design

2 What did Arup & Partners like about Utzon's design?
   a It shifted away from his competition's drawings
   b The roof's ridges were higher and more pointed
   c Each shell was different
   d Its simplicity and ease of repetition

3 How did Utzon discover the solution to building the roof?
   a By stacking shells from the model
   b By peeling an orange
   c By eating a grapefruit
   d By studying the plane of a sphere

4 How did Utzon's assistants respond to his final solution for the roof?
   a They were worried about the costs
   b They wanted Utzon to consider another engineering firm
   c They were amazed
   d They were unsure if it would work

5 Why was the design called 'timeless'?
   a It took a long time to construct
   b It combined elements of design and engineering
   c It still exists today
   d It was finally 'realised'

Grammar

The use of *as*

As can be used in several ways:

- It can be used to mean *because*:
  As *I was tired, I sat down.*
  *I sat down, **as** I was tired.*

- It can be used to mean *at the same time*:
  As *I was walking down the street, I suddenly saw a large crowd coming towards me.*

- It can be used to compare two people, places or things:
  *He is not **as** fast **as** his sister.*

- It can be used in the phrase *as if* to describe how someone looks / sounds / feels:
  *She looks **as if** she's been exercising.*
  *They sound **as if** they are excited.*

- It can be used with *such* to mean 'for example':
  *The school offers the opportunity to join a variety of clubs, **such as** the chess club, the French club or the cooking club.*

C Write one sentence of your own for each of the five possibilities listed above
for using *as*.

D Listen to the discussion on how we view images, both in paintings and in films,
at https://youtu.be/0pDE4VX_9Kk. Listen from 0:48 to 5:29 and answer the
following questions:

1 What's the difference between how light works in a lighthouse and how the eye sees
light?
   a The light in a lighthouse is not real
   b The light travels in, not out
   c The light in a lighthouse blinks off and on
   d Every person's eye is different

2 What changed with the invention of the camera?
   a We could see things that were not in front of us
   b It allowed us to travel the world
   c We could see things as they really were
   d We no longer needed light to see

3 Which point of view is being described in Dziga Vertov's quotation?
   a A machine's
   b The image's
   c A Russian's
   d The camera's

4 How is a painting, in a way, like a human eye?
   a It can only be in one place at one time
   b It can be seen by anyone
   c What is painted is what we see
   d It stays in one room

5 What's the difference between a camera and a painting on a wall?
   a The painting was done before the invention of the camera
   b The camera's images are more realistic
   c The camera can make a painting appear in any size for any purpose
   d The painting is part of a person's home

6 What does the narrator say about Botticelli's painting 'Venus and Mars'?
   a The camera has changed Botticelli's intention
   b There are now millions of paintings like it
   c Now it can be viewed in different people's rooms, within different contexts
   d The original has lost its value

7 What point does the narrator make about Renaissance churches?
   a The movie camera has made them less unique
   b The paintings on the walls were a part of the building's life
   c The paintings on the walls no longer give viewers a feeling
   d Their meaning depends on a person's memory

E Imagine that you are a tour guide. Take your class, or a small group of students, on an architectural tour of a city. Show them pictures of significant or creatively designed buildings and explain the ideas behind them.

F Write a dialogue between two people who are looking at a work of art. Have each person discuss the different possible interpretations of the artwork. They can discuss what they like or don't like, what the artist's intentions might have been and how, and how effectively, the artist achieved his / her purpose.

■ TOK Links

To what extent is artistic knowledge dependent on historical knowledge?

What is the value of subjective knowledge?

CREATIVITY, ACTIVITY, SERVICE

Organize an architectural competition at your school where students submit plans and a model for a new building or space. This could be on your school's campus, or it could be a building or space for people in need.

■ Literature

HIGHER LEVEL

4 Sonny's Blues

'Sonny's Blues' is a short story written by James Baldwin in 1957. It is the story of two brothers who are trying to reconnect after a long separation. Sonny wants to be a blues musician. Sonny's older brother is his only living relative. After their mother dies, Sonny's brother is asked to care for him. In this scene, Sonny's brother, who is the narrator, is trying to find out what Sonny wants to do with his life after graduation from high school.

With just Sonny and me alone in the empty kitchen, I tried to find out something about him.

"What do you want to do?" I asked him.

"I'm going to be a musician," he said.

For he had graduated, in the time I had been away, from dancing to the juke box to finding out who was playing what, and what they were doing with it, and he had bought himself a set of drums.

"You mean, you want to be a drummer?" I somehow had the feeling that being a drummer might be all right for other people but not for my brother Sonny.

"I don't think," he said, looking at me very gravely, "that I'll ever be a good drummer. But I think I can play a piano."

I frowned. I'd never played the role of the oldest brother quite so seriously before, had scarcely ever, in fact, asked Sonny a damn thing. I sensed myself in the presence of something I didn't really know how to handle, didn't understand. So I made my frown a little deeper as I asked: "What kind of musician do you want to be?"

He grinned. "How many kinds do you think there are?"

"Be serious," I said.

He laughed, throwing his head back, and then looked at me. "I am serious."

"Well, then, for Christ's sake, stop kidding around and answer a serious question. I mean, do you want to be a concert pianist, you want to play classical music and all that, or – or what?" Long before I finished he was laughing again. "For Christ's sake. Sonny!"

He sobered, but with difficulty. "I'm sorry. But you sound so – scared!" and he was off again.

"Well, you may think it's funny now, baby, but it's not going to be so funny when you have to make your living at it, let me tell you that." I was furious because I knew he was laughing at me and I didn't know why.

"No," he said, very sober now, and afraid, perhaps, that he'd hurt me, "I don't want to be a classical pianist. That isn't what interests me. I mean" – he paused, looking hard at me, as though his eyes would help me to understand, and then gestured helplessly, as though perhaps his hand would help – "I mean, I'll have a lot of studying to do, and I'll have to study everything, but, I mean, I want to play with – jazz musicians." He stopped. "I want to play jazz," he said.

Well, the word had never before sounded as heavy, as real, as it sounded that afternoon in Sonny's mouth. I just looked at him and I was probably frowning a real frown by this time. I simply couldn't see why on earth he'd want to spend his time hanging around nightclubs, clowning around on bandstands, while people pushed each other around a dance floor. It seemed – beneath him, somehow. I had never thought about it before, had never been forced to, but I suppose I had always put jazz musicians in a class with what Daddy called "goodtime people."

"Are you serious?"

"Hell, yes, I'm serious."

He looked more helpless than ever, and annoyed, and deeply hurt.

I suggested, helpfully: "You mean – like Louis Armstrong?"

His face closed as though I'd struck him. "No. I'm not talking about none of that old-time, down home crap."

"Well, look, Sonny, I'm sorry, don't get mad. I just don't altogether get it, that's all. Name somebody – you know, a jazz musician you admire."

"Bird."

"Who?"

"Bird! Charlie Parker! Don't they teach you nothing in the goddamn army?"

I lit a cigarette. I was surprised and then a little amused to discover that I was trembling.

"I've been out of touch," I said. "You'll have to be patient with me. Now. Who's this Parker character?"

"He's just one of the greatest jazz musicians alive," said Sonny, sullenly, his hands in his pockets, his back to me. "Maybe the greatest," he added, bitterly, "that's probably why you never heard of him."

"All right," I said, "I'm ignorant. I'm sorry. I'll go out and buy all the cat's records right away, all right?"

"It don't," said Sonny, with dignity, "make any difference to me. I don't care what you listen to. Don't do me no favors."

I was beginning to realize that I'd never seen him so upset before. With another part of my mind I was thinking that this would probably turn out to be one of those things kids go through and that I shouldn't make it seem important by pushing it too hard. Still, I didn't think it would do any harm to ask: "Doesn't all this take a lot of time? Can you make a living at it?"

He turned back to me and half leaned, half sat, on the kitchen table. "Everything takes time," he said, "and – well, yes, sure, I can make a living at it. But what I don't seem to be able to make you understand is that it's the only thing I want to do."

"Well, Sonny," I said gently, "you know people can't always do exactly what they want to do –"

"No, I don't know that," said Sonny, surprising me. "I think people ought to do what they want to do, what else are they alive for?"

Excerpt from 'Sonny's Blues' by James Baldwin

Answer the following questions:

1 What does the narrator mean when he says 'I didn't really know how to handle'?
2 Why does the narrator become 'furious'?
3 Why would the word 'jazz' sound 'heavy' to the narrator?
4 What are two words that describe how Sonny feels?
5 What does the writer mean that Sonny's face 'closed as though I'd struck him'?
6 Who is the 'cat' the narrator refers to?
7 What does the narrator mean when he says 'those things kids go through'?
8 Why might the narrator be 'surprised' by Sonny's response at the end of the passage?
9 How does the conversation change from the beginning to the end?
10 How would you describe the relationship of the brothers?

UNIT **11** Communication and media

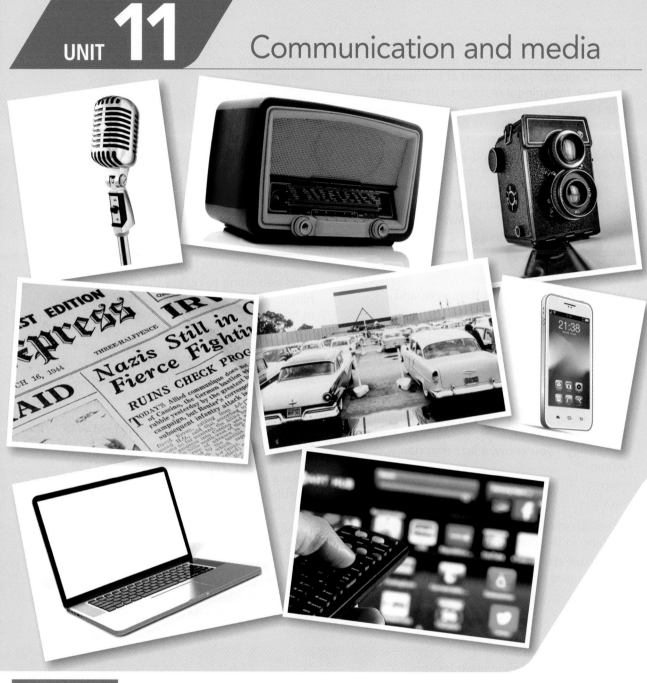

Look at the pictures above and use them to explain how the media and forms of communication have evolved.

- Look at today's newspaper front pages online (this URL on the BBC is a useful link: www.bbc.co.uk/news/blogs/the_papers). How are the pages similar or different? Are there any that can be grouped together?

- What can readers understand simply by looking at a newspaper's front page?

- In pairs or small groups, tell each other stories you have heard. Imagine that the story you were told will appear on the front page of a newspaper. Write the headline for that story. Note that headlines in newspapers are:

short	focused on key words
written in the present tense	sometimes humorous
written in the active voice	sometimes a play on words.

1 Mobility

In small groups, list all the uses of a phone, then organize your list from most useful to least useful. Does your list surprise you in any way? Discuss as a class:

■ When and why do people use phones?

■ What are the advantages and disadvantages of phone use?

What will your phone be like in 20 years?

From batteries that charge in minutes to screens that let you feel

1 If you look back 20 years in terms of phones, you're going back to the likes of the Nokia 8110, and that should tell you all you need to know about the rapid pace at which we're going – so will the jump be just as big, or even bigger, over the next two decades?

2 That Nokia 8110 phone had a monochrome LCD display, and, with no touchscreen, had a keypad for a keyboard. It may have been featured in one of the scenes in The Matrix but it couldn't do much more than send and receive phone calls and text messages.

3 Could the phones of 2036 be as far ahead of the iPhone 7 as the iPhone 7 is from the Nokia 8110? We've spent some time gazing into the T3 crystal ball and these are the changes we expect to see when we're unwrapping a brand new handset some 20 years from now.

Better batteries

4 Battery life remains the biggest bugbear among phone users. With our phones becoming more powerful and boasting better displays, it's understandable that the batteries have always struggled to keep up.

5 The good news is that better battery technology is coming, from nanobatteries (featuring tiny tower structures that are hundreds of times smaller than the bits in current power packs) to improved, more efficient materials (like lithium metal foil).

6 It's not inconceivable that in 20 years' time we might be talking about topping up while the kettle boils rather than leaving phones plugged in overnight. Wireless charging should also become standard too, so that any surface is a charger.

7 Want something even more out-there? How about a phone battery that's powered by water? Hydrogen fuel cells, first proposed by Samsung back in 2008, use the reaction between water and a metal element in the phone to produce hydrogen gas, which then powers the cell. We're still waiting for a Samsung–Evian tie-in, though.

Folding phone displays

8 We've now got used to phones with curved edges on their displays, and you can expect this technology to improve substantially over the next two decades.

9 Will we see a phone you can fold up and put in your pocket by 2036? It's hard to say, but it's almost certain that the display technology will be ready – it's just a question of whether phone manufacturers can get all the other bits and pieces to flex too.

10 There's going to be plenty more happening in the field of phone displays over the next few years too: think screens powered by solar energy, or holographic displays that can project an image a few centimetres above your phone (which might make your favourite endless runner that bit easier to play).

11 We're also going to see screens become more intelligent and more responsive, screens that can mimic paper or other kinds of textures. Devices like the Apple Watch already have basic haptic feedback, and so in 20 years' time it's going to be much more advanced – imagine the kind of tactile response you might get from games and apps.

Console-killing graphics

12 Back in the day, we dreamed about home consoles beating arcade-machine graphics. Then it was all about seeing how long it would take PCs to flatten console graphics. Now we're in the big race to see how long it'll take phones to outdo the consoles.

13 Given its prowess in the graphics-card space, it's no surprise that Nvidia is pushing forward to make the mobile phone a real rival for your console, with the brand confirming to us that the tech is advancing at a rate of knots.

14 Every year the graphics capabilities of our smartphones get better, and the devices of 2036 should easily outpace the PlayStation 4s of today. Quite how advanced our home consoles will have become by then remains to be seen, but based on the pace of change over the last 5–10 years we'd say there's a lot to look forward to.

15 Let's not forget virtual reality, already around on smartphones in limited form. Better graphics and better screens will mean better virtual worlds and maybe wearable headsets that are barely noticeable.

Super network speeds

16 Most of us are just [1]_____ with 4G, but 5G is already revving its engine. You probably won't get to taste its goodies until around 2020, but they're set to revolutionise the way we use phones, offering speeds up to 70 times [2]_____ what's currently available.

17 Want a movie in three seconds? Done. Fancy that Spotify album but not sure if you've got time to download it? It's already happened in the time it took to read that sentence. Not only is that mind-bendingly fast, it's about [3]_____ than your old computer hard drive could even save stuff.

18 Streaming console-grade games to your phone will no longer have that annoying lag, so remotely playing console games on the bus will finally be a reality. And as long as the servers and websites on the other end are quick enough, browsing the web and watching streamed videos will be [4]_____ as looking at content stored on your phone.

19 It's hard to over-emphasise what a difference a super-fast, ubiquitous mobile network could make – imagine having high-speed Wi-Fi all the time, wherever you go. By 2036, you won't have to imagine.

Digital assistants

20 The likes of Cortana, Siri and Google Assistant already play big roles on the phones of today but it's nothing [5]_____ the influence they'll have in 20 years' time.

21 This really is where the innovation is going to happen over the next couple of decades, as these assistant apps become smarter and learn more and more about us. The traditional rows and columns of apps will go away to be replaced by a simplified interface that shows us what we want to see before we know we want to see it.

22 Siri and its rivals will be almost indistinguishable from the friends and family you talk to via your phone, and if you've seen the movie *Her* then you know how that might turn out. It may sound scary but it should be hugely useful.

23 The whole concept of the phone might go away as we use small microphones and earpieces to communicate with the cloud instead, though there's still likely to be a screen of some kind, even if it is an optional, foldable one – otherwise how else are you going to battle through the *Star Wars Episode XVIII* spin-off game?

www.t3.com/features/your-phone-in-20-years

A **Which word or phrase means the same as the following?**

1 fast (paragraph 1)
2 looking (paragraph 3)
3 had difficulty (paragraph 4)
4 normal (paragraph 6)
5 unreal (paragraph 7)

B **Choose the best answer to the following questions:**

1 Why has battery life always been a problem?
   a Because of the reaction between water and metal
   b Because of new wireless capabilities
   c Because of improved display screens
   d Because of nanobatteries

2 The writer says future screens might do all of the following **except...**
   a be powered by solar energy
   b be like paper
   c be a health indicator
   d be foldable

3 What will be one result of better screen graphics?
   a Better arcade machines
   b Better PlayStations
   c Better home consoles
   d Better virtual worlds

4　Why will it be easier to play console games while travelling?

   a　Because of increased network speeds

   b　Because of Wi-Fi integration on buses

   c　Because of better websites

   d　Because you won't have to save it on your computer's hard drive

5　How will the role of digital assistants change?

   a　They will no longer be like Siri or Google Assistant

   b　They will know what we want before we ask for it

   c　They will interact with your friends and family

   d　They will use foldable screens

Grammar

Like, would like* and *would have liked

- The verb ***like*** can be used with the *-ing* form of a verb or the infinitive *to*. For example:

  *I **like playing** football.*

  *I **like to spend** time with my friends.*

- ***Would like*** is usually followed by the infinitive *to*. For example:

  *I **would like to** ask you something.*

  The infinitive *to* also usually follows *would love, would hate* and *would prefer*.

- ***Would have liked*** means that you regret that you did not or could not do something. For example:

  *I **would have liked** to have gone to the party, but I had too much homework.*

  Would have loved / hated / preferred are also followed by the infinitive *to*.

 C Use the phrases in the box to complete the blanks (1–5) in the article.

> **a** compared to   **d** getting to grips
>
> **b** just as quick   **e** faster than
>
> **c** ten times quicker

D Use the following words to create sentences using *would* and *would have*, along with the appropriate forms of the verbs. For example:

We / not like / go / on holiday by car.

We would not like to go on holiday by car.

1　Parents / prefer / eat / in quiet restaurants.

2　The police / help / the man if / know / he / need / help.

3　What / you like / drink?

4　Spencer / like / play / board games.

5　I / love / have / a phone like hers.

6　Christopher / prefer / read / the novel but he / have / read / the play.

175

E You will hear a discussion on 'mobile journalism', which is when a journalist uses a mobile phone to do all of his or her reporting (www.youtube.com/watch?v=a0Uwx6nN-6I). Listen to the discussion and answer the following questions:

Which of the following statements are true and which are false?

1 The narrator refers to a mobile phone as a Swiss army knife because it can do so much.
2 Nick Garnet believes people need confidence that a phone can get them great results.
3 Garnet has been doing radio recordings with a smartphone since 2009.
4 The first tape recorder made sounds like a newborn baby.
5 To be a mobile journalist, you cannot invade a person's space.
6 Garnet prefers to have a few apps on his phone that he knows really well.
7 It's important to buy the best apps for your phone.
8 Some people don't know that what's shown on TV is shot from a mobile phone.

Choose the best answer for the following questions:

9 Nick Garnet first got involved in mobile journalism because…
  a everyone was doing it
  b he didn't like carrying heavy equipment
  c he didn't know there were so many media platforms
  d he already had an iPhone

10 Why does Garnet say we are only limited by our imaginations?
  a Because if people think of new ways to use a phone someone will develop an app for it
  b Because we demand apps that people can't build
  c Because we're on a journey that we create with our dreams
  d Because we don't have to think about how heavy a phone is anymore

11 Why would Garnet like to start calling mobile journalism simply 'journalism'?
  a Because it is not mobile anymore
  b Because people realize they're already doing it
  c Because we need to stop depending on technology
  d Because using a phone is the same as using a notepad and a camera

12 Which 'deep set' skills do people need to be a mobile journalist?
  a They need the best camera available
  b They need to know what they're carrying
  c They need to be able to file a story from anywhere
  d They need to see a story developing and know how to film and record it

13 The 'trick' Garnet describes for interviewing someone from certain cultures is…
  a to know if women are not supposed to be too close to men
  b to interview them standing shoulder to shoulder
  c to interview them face-to-face
  d to know which kind of microphone to use

F In groups, choose one of the following oral activities and do a presentation to the class.

■ Discuss the similarities and differences between phones your grandparents used, phones your parents used and phones you use. Do a presentation for the class on these similarities and differences where you show the evolution of the phone from then to now.

■ Create a role play where you see a news story developing and you use your mobile phone to film and record that story. Some group members can act as news producers or editors discussing what to keep and delete and how to present it to a viewing or listening audience.

■ Record and edit a story with your phone, show it to the class and explain the decisions you made and the techniques you used to create the final result.

Write a blog entitled 'A day in the life of a mobile journalist'. Explain what you do to prepare to cover a story. Give an example of a story you reported for a news station. Describe some of the audio, video and editing techniques you used.

■ TOK Links

To what extent does our access to knowledge depend on our culture?

To what extent can the future be predicted?

CREATIVITY, ACTIVITY, SERVICE

Think of an idea for a phone application that allows CAS students from all over the world to share and participate in each other's projects.

2 Social media

In small groups, create a table similar to the one below, where you list 'social' in one column and 'media' in the other. Underneath each heading, write as many words as you can think of that you associate with either 'social' or 'media'. When you are finished, look at your list and choose one aspect of each word that you think exists in today's forms of social media, and one aspect that does not exist.

Social	Media

What is Pinterest: A database of intentions

Evan Sharp, one of the co-founders of Pinterest, delves into what the wildly popular image-collecting site is really about, and what it's likely to do in the future.

[1] _____

Today, I define it as a place where people can go to get ideas for any project or interest in their life. And as you encounter great ideas and discover new things that you didn't even know were out there, you can pin them and make them part of your life through our system of boards.

Best of all, as you're creating a board on Pinterest, other people can get inspiration from your ideas, so there's this cycle where what you're creating for yourself also helps other people make their lives.

I think of it as a kind of utility. People use it to save and organize things for later. And then it turns out that integral to saving things is discovering new things.

[2] _____

I didn't have grand plans. I don't think Ben [Silbermann] did either in the beginning. It was just the tool I used in my job. I was in school for architecture and when you're in school for a creative discipline, so much of what you produce comes out of inspiration from other people. The more you're exposed to architecturally, the better you can develop your own language out of that history of architectural thought.

So I had thousands of images that I had saved in folders on my computer. But they were all named like databasestrings. jpg and I had no idea what any of them were. So Pinterest was a way for me to create a link: let's bookmark an image so that when I go look at it later, I go to where it came from. *This is this architect's building. This is what it is.* And collections are a natural way of organizing that sort of inspiration.

So for me, it was very much a professional tool in my industry. For Ben, it was slightly different. Ben used it in ways that you see the broader cross-section of people using it. He used it for recipe ideas, products he was in love with, planning travel. He had a kid. He got married. He did all those things on Pinterest.

[3] _____

You build something and it's like, what can I build on top of that and what can I build on top of that and what can I build on top of that. Great companies, I think, are the ones that *see* what they've built and can build on top of it and iterate their product.

I don't remember exactly when we were like "Holy crap! Pins aren't just images. They are representations of things and we can make them rich and we can make them canonical and link back to the best source and we can attribute this properly to the creator." (Which is a huge problem that I'm personally interested in.)

I would say we saw that pretty early on, but we're still pretty early on in executing against that the vision of making Pinterest the largest inventory of the world's objects.

What's cool is that every object was put there by a person. It's not the largest inventory in the way that maybe a nerd like me would get excited about. But everything that's on there, at least one human found interesting, so there is a very good chance that at least one other human is going to find that interesting. So, it's a good set of objects. It's the world's largest set of objects that people care about.

[4] _____

My background industry is design – I code a lot, too – but there's been this narrative of design in technology becoming more prominent. What the user interface enables on Pinterest is this human activity that ends up creating a great database. And it's that knitting of front-end and back-end abilities that will power our products. We're not going to be exclusively the best engineering company – though we have some of the best engineers – and we're not going to be the world's prettiest, best designed company. What's interesting is how those things interact, over and over, and back and forth. That's where the magic comes out. That's where the best new products are coming out on the internet.

[5] _____

I used to work at Facebook. And fundamentally, Pinterest is about inspiration. And inspiration is a word that doesn't resonate with people until they use Pinterest and get what that means, but that's fundamentally about connecting to other people. Other people end up being people's source of inspiration, which also happens on Facebook. So, we're like Google in the data model way, but we're like Facebook in the more experiential way. The way you discover is a combination of the two.

[6] _____

Zuck describes Facebook in the press, I might butcher his words, but he's like people have a psychological need to spend time and know about and learn about the people they care about. It's built into our brains and it's Facebook's job to remove as much effort as possible from that, so you can fulfill it any time you want to. Pinterest is not about your friends, it's about yourself. It's about the things you want in your life, the possibilities. What can my kid's first birthday party look like? It's very future-looking in a way that Twitter and Facebook are very right now or backwards looking.

Pinterest is about connecting you with people who manifest one thing you want your life to be like. So, if you are getting into photography, what do you do? You read photography blogs because these guys or girls are really into photography. They love their photos. They're talking about how to do it. People develop taste through other people, whether that's celebrities or people they know. And we have the data to understand – in a very non-creepy way, honestly – who are the people on Pinterest that manifest and express the things you look like you're interested in.

That's why Pinterest doesn't just show an image. It's an image with a person. That was a very deliberate decision. Everything on Pinterest was put there by a human being and – in aggregate – we can figure out who are the human beings who are the enthusiasts in the thing that really interests you. And those are the people who can guide your journey in that interest or project you're planning.

People are fundamental not just for our data model, but because eventually, we'll be able to connect you with the people who really share your taste and express whom you want to be. And that's something that's happened for decades in magazines and on blogs and on TV.

Alexis C. Madrigal

www.theatlantic.com/technology/archive/2014/07/what-is-pinterest-a-database-of-intentions/375365

A **The questions (1–6) in this interview have been removed and placed below. Match the correct question with Evan Sharp's answers.**

a How much do you think the design of the interface has defined what Pinterest does?

b So, how do you see yourself opening up the social potential of Pinterest?

c You were once the only service that actually worked to let us save images from across the web. What did you think Pinterest was then?

d How would you compare yourself to Facebook?

e How do you think about what Pinterest is? How do you define it now?

f So when did you know that you had something bigger than a bookmarking site?

B **Which of the following statements are true? For each true statement, write out the part of the sentence from the article that justifies this. The first one is done for you.**

Pinterest allows its users to influence others. **True**

Justification: 'other people can get inspiration from your ideas'

1 Great companies copy what other companies do.
2 Ben used Pinterest like an architect.
3 Pinterest is built on the interests of individual people.
4 Sharp originally created Pinterest to organize his stored images.
5 Pinterest is different from Facebook because it's not based on the people you care about.
6 Pinterest is more similar to Facebook than Google.
7 Pinterest is similar to Facebook because people get ideas from one another.
8 Pinterest, Twitter and Facebook are always looking towards the future.
9 Pinterest knows people with similar interests to you.

C **In your own words, define the following words from the text:**

1 grand
2 discipline
3 cross-section
4 inventory
5 interact
6 fundamentally

Grammar

So and such

- We use **so** with an adjective or adverb, for example:
  so *gentle*
  so *accurately*
- We use **such** with a noun, for example:
  such *a nice man*
- We can also use *so much* and *so many* to express quantity, for example:
  there was **so much** *traffic*
  there were **so many** *people there*

D **Create one sentence from the two given below using *so*, *such*, *so many* or *so much*. For example:**

The exam was difficult. I could not answer one question.

The exam was so difficult that I could not answer one question.

1 We had a good time at your house. We want to do it again soon.
2 There were a lot of people in line. I did not want to wait that long for a ticket.
3 The boss gave us a lot of work. We did not have time to finish it.
4 John is fast. No one can beat him.
5 That child is intelligent. I think she will become a scientist.
6 My grandfather never becomes angry when we are late. He is a patient man.
7 The music was loud. We could not hear ourselves speak.

E **Listen to the discussion about the negative and positive aspects of social media at https://n.pr/2IOWkfe. Answer the following questions:**

1 Answer the following comprehension questions:

   a Has the host, Mary Louise Kelly, quit Facebook?

   b Why does Ms Tufekci mention seatbelts and car emissions?

   c What does Ms Tufekci mean when she says 'I'm being sold' when using Facebook?

   d If Ms Tufekci were creating a new app, how would it be different from Facebook?

   e Why does Ms Tufekci think people shouldn't feel guilty about using Facebook?

   f Why is Ms Tufekci an optimist?

   g Why does she say Silicon Valley is a very boring place right now?

2 Use three to five words to complete the sentences from the conversation.

   a The question for me is, how do we make the good _____?

   b It's quite plausible to have this level of connectivity that is affordable almost _____.

   c So you're talking about designing a social media platform with a fundamentally different business model _____.

   d So this should be _____ that we shouldn't allow this to continue.

   e _____ for this landscape to change quite a lot.

   f Let's keep all the good, and let's get rid of _____ as we possibly can.

F **Organize yourselves into groups of three or four. Each group will look at the statements below, and, as a group, organize them from 'most important' to 'least important' in regards to the issues facing social media platforms and their users today. Once your order is complete, share it with another group and explain why you made the choices you did.**

- Social media gives people innovative ideas.

- Social media gives anyone a chance to become influential.

- Social media allows people to be more caring towards the people they love.

- Social media allows people with similar interests to connect.

- Social media platforms need to be controlled so that people are not exploited.

- Social media can give people false impressions of reality.

- Social media has made people less social in face-to-face situations.

- Social media platforms are businesses that only care about making money.

G **Create a post for a social media site where you discuss the advantages and disadvantages of social media. Along with the post, create comments on it from different readers. Try to have a variety of points of view. There can be one or two dialogues that develop between those who have posted.**

■ TOK Links

How can we evaluate a psychological truth?

To what extent is a computer program's intuition similar to a human's intuition?

CREATIVITY, ACTIVITY, SERVICE

Create a Pinterest board that you feel will connect people in a positive way.

3 Entertainment

In small groups, find two short videos that you will play for another group. For one video, first play only the sound and not the video. Ask the other group to guess what is happening in the video, based on what they hear. Then show them the real video. For the second video, first show the other group the video without the sound and ask them what they think is being said or talked about. Then play them the video with sound. As a class, discuss what you discovered from this activity.

Why TIFF matters, and 3 other things to know about the Toronto International Film Festival

The world of film insiders is known for its tiffs – petty quarrels about whether a director's work is pretentious or brilliant, tempests in teapots over editing choices and special effects. But every fall, right after Labor Day, a bigger TIFF takes over film conversation for a few weeks: the Toronto International Film Festival, which most people call by its acronym.

Since it launched in 1976, the 10-day festival has become one of the largest and most prestigious in the world, propelling emerging filmmakers onto the international scene and awards hopefuls toward the big fall movie season. But there's plenty about it that an average movie fan might not know.

Why does TIFF matter?

For your average moviegoer, there's one big reason: The 10-day festival is the unofficial kick-off to the "prestige movie season" – which means keeping an eye on what's buzzy at TIFF may tell you a lot about what performances and movies will be part of awards chatter later in the year.

The festival's timing – right after Labor Day – positions it as the de facto opening of awards season, a marathon of mostly serious dramas that lasts about six months, until the Oscars finally wrap it all up in early March.

But is TIFF as important a festival as, say, Cannes, which happens in late May? That depends on who you ask. Cannes is the reigning title holder of "most prestigious festival" and most filmmakers aspire to have their work play in competition there someday. (Cannes also has more than 30 years of existence on TIFF.) But Cannes films often skew toward more rarefied and international films, while at Toronto – which programs many more movies – you can find bigger crowdpleasers that might also find more money at the box office and wind up bigger awards-season contenders. (American Beauty, Slumdog Millionaire, The King's Speech, and Silver Linings Playbook, for instance, all premiered at TIFF.)

For people who love movies, or who follow awards keenly, that's what makes TIFF interesting. Just because a film doesn't play at TIFF doesn't mean it won't win awards. (2014 Best Picture winner Birdman, for instance, didn't make an appearance in Toronto.) But Cannes winners are rarely Oscar winners, while TIFF sets the pace for the year's awards chatter.

Who goes to TIFF?

Unlike a festival like Cannes, which is only open to about 30,000 accredited film industry professionals, the general public can buy tickets to TIFF – and boy, do they ever. In 2016, an estimated 480,000 attendees showed up and only about 5,000 of those were in the industry (which includes filmmakers, distributors, publicists, and journalists).

That is huge. Sundance, by contrast, drew 71,600 attendees in 2017. This year's Berlin Film Festival, generally considered the world's largest public festival, ended with 496,471 theater visits, which includes tickets sold to the public as well as the 20,000 film industry professionals in attendance, who carry badges instead of buying tickets. TIFF is one of the world's most well-attended festivals – likely in part because of the reasonable cost of staying in Toronto and the favorable early-autumn weather.

The fact that so many members of the public attend TIFF bodes well for the movies there. If buzz builds around a TIFF movie, it's not just because of the critics who are writing about it – hundreds of thousands of movie lovers may also be talking about the film in restaurants, bars, and cafes, and posting about them on social media. That means the barometer for a film's popularity can be spread out more broadly – and filmmakers have the chance to gauge how the public, in addition to critics, will react when their film hits theaters later on.

What kind of movies play at TIFF?

In 2016, nearly 400 films screened at TIFF, picked by the festival's well-respected programming staff. For contrast, Sundance screened 181 in 2017; the number of movies in the three official programs at Cannes was only 46, though many more played in parallel sections held alongside the official festival.

Those films are programmed by the festival's staff in 14 sections, each of which has its own goals and flavor. Some of those include:

- Gala Presentations – films with a high profile and stars on the red carpet
- Special Presentations – other high-profile films, and sometimes world premieres
- Discovery – directors' first or second feature film
- Midnight Madness – genre films (mostly horror and thrillers) that open at midnight and play again the following day
- Masters – movies made by the world's most influential 'art-house' filmmakers
- Contemporary World Cinema – movies by international directors who are established, but not household names
- Platform – a competition section for narrative and documentary features that have not yet been acquired for distribution in North America. An international jury chooses a winner, which receives $25,000 CAD. Last year's winner was Jackie.

There are sections for short films, classics, TV episodes, documentaries, movies aimed at kids and teenagers, and experimental films as well.

Some festivals are very prize-focused – think Cannes' Palme d'Or, or the Golden Bear at the Berlin Film Festival – but Toronto is generally less focused on festival-specific awards than on generating buzz. But one that augurs well for the recipient's Oscar chances is the Grolsch People's Choice Award, which filmgoers vote on. Some of the recent winners, like The King's Speech, La La Land, Room, and 12 Years a Slave, have gone on to clean up at year-end awards.

And this makes perfect sense. TIFF is a festival for the public, first and foremost. Its biggest focus is on films that will catch the eye of both critics and moviegoers – crowdpleasers with awards potential, which often play well with Oscar voters later on. So naturally, the award the ticket-holding public votes on – rather than a small number of famous people picked to sit on a jury – is the most important award of the festival.

Oscar Tallies for Festival Prize Winners, 2000 to 2016

Award Type	Berlinale Golden Bear	Cannes Palme d'Or	TIFF People's Choice Award
Best Picture Nominations	0	3	9
Best Foreign Film Nominations	2	3	2
All Oscar Nominations	8	18	91
Best Picture Wins	0	1	4
Best Foreign Film Wins	1	1	1
All Oscar Wins	2	4	30

■ Data from IMDB.com

Alissa Wilkinson www.vox.com/culture/2017/9/5/16184614/tiff-toronto-international-film-festival-explainer-matters-oscars

A **Now that you have read the article, answer the following questions.**

1 When was the first TIFF?
2 Why might the Cannes film festival be considered 'the most prestigious festival'?
3 What advantage does TIFF seem to have over the Cannes festival?
4 When the writer says 'That is huge' in paragraph 8, what does the word 'that' refer to?
5 How might the fact that so many members of the public attend the TIFF be important for the success of a movie?
6 How many 'sections' of films are there at TIFF?
7 What are 'Midnight Madness' films?
8 Which film festival prize had the most 'Best Foreign Film Nominations'?
9 Why does TIFF's 'People's Choice Award' seem to lead to so many Oscar awards?

B **You can increase your vocabulary and your ability to understand and use new words by looking for related forms of a word. The following words are underlined in the article. Write as many related forms of the word as you can. You can do this by adding or subtracting suffixes or prefixes. The first one is done for you.**

Word: Unofficial
Related forms: official, officially, office

1 unofficial
2 performances
3 important
4 interesting
5 unlike
6 considered
7 reasonable
8 popularity
9 well-respected
10 naturally

Grammar

There is and *there was*

- We begin sentences with ***there is*** or ***there was*** when something exists / existed or is / was happening at a particular time and place. For example:

  There is *a light coming towards us on the road.*

  There was *a lot of thunder and lightning last night.*

- If the word after the verb is singular, the verb is singular. If the noun is plural, the verb is plural. For example:

  There was *a crowd of people waiting outside the restaurant.*

  There were *hundreds of people waiting outside the restaurant.*

- We use the same patterns with questions:

  Is there*…*

  Are there*…*

  Was there*…*

  Were there*…*

C Fill in the blanks with *there is, there are, there was* or *there were*.

Sally   I think [1]_____ something wrong with Joseph. Last night, I called him and [2]_____ no answer.

Beverley Maybe he went out. You do know that [3]_____ a lot of parties last night on campus.

Sally   No. It's not just last night. [4]_____ four or five other occasions this week when I called and he did not answer.

Beverley I'm sure [5]_____ an explanation. Maybe he's busy. Maybe he went on a trip. [6]_____ some reason you are so worried?

Sally   Yes. He told me last week to call him because he said [7]_____ something very important he wanted to tell me.

Beverley [8]_____ any of his friends around whom you could talk to about this?

Sally   [9]_____ one person I can think of. Maybe I will try to locate him.

Beverley I think that's a good idea. [10]_____ probably a very good explanation for his absence.

Sally   I hope so. [11]_____ so many things I would like to say to him.

D You will hear an interview with Netflix founder Reed Hastings. Listen to the interview at www.ted.com/talks/reed_hastings_how_netflix_changed_ entertainment_and_where_it_s_headed/transcript up to 3:38 and answer the questions below.

1 What does the interviewer mean when he says Netflix was 'growing like a weed'?

2 What does he mean by a 'bet-the-company' decision?

3 Why was acquiring *House of Cards* the 'breakthrough' for Netflix?

4 What is 'binge-viewing'?

5 What can Netflix do that linear TV can't do?

6 How did *House of Cards* help make the Netflix brand stronger?

Match the beginning of each sentence on the left with its ending on the right.

7 You were basically a streaming service

8 It was a fantastic investment and

9 If you got that wrong

10 With episodic content

11 It's really about making the brand stronger

a it might have been really devastating for the company.

b it's so powerful to have all the episodes at once.

c for other people's films and TV content.

d so that more people want to join.

e it was in competition with HBO.

E **In pairs, do some research on an interesting innovation in one of the following areas:**

- Radio
- Film
- Television
- Phone applications
- Social media sites

Then imagine that you two are sitting somewhere having a conversation about this innovation. Write some notes for this imaginary conversation and then have the conversation in front of the class.

F **Write the script for a radio show, where one person is interviewing another and there are two or three listeners who call in and ask questions. You may include notes in the script for when there is music, sound effects or an advertisement.**

■ TOK Links

To what extent are our senses personal and / or shared knowledge?

To what extent are patterns in human behaviour reliable?

CREATIVITY, ACTIVITY, SERVICE

Create new media to broadcast, stream or highlight important events at your school, such as sporting events, artistic performances or shows, projects or group events. Publicize how students can view or listen to these events.

■ Literature

4 The Ballad of the Landlord

In 1940, Langston Hughes wrote the following poem. Hughes lived in Harlem, a poor African-American district of New York City, and attempted to depict racial inequalities in his poetry. Read the following poem and answer the questions at the end.

Landlord, landlord,
My roof has sprung a leak.
Don't you 'member I told you about it
Way last week?

Landlord, landlord,
These steps is broken down.
When you come up yourself
It's a wonder you don't fall down.

Ten Bucks you say I owe you?
Ten Bucks you say is due?
Well, that's Ten Bucks more'n I'll pay you
Till you fix this house up new.

What? You gonna get eviction orders?
You gonna cut off my heat?
You gonna take my furniture and
Throw it in the street?

Um-huh! You talking high and mighty.
Talk on-till you get through.
You ain't gonna be able to say a word
If I land my fist on you.

Police! Police!
Come and get this man!
He's trying to ruin the government
And overturn the land!

Copper's whistle!
Patrol bell!
Arrest.
Precinct Station.
Iron cell.

Headlines in press:
MAN THREATENS LANDLORD
TENANT HELD NO BAIL
JUDGE GIVES NEGRO 90 DAYS IN COUNTY JAIL!

Langston Hughes
https://allpoetry.com/The-Ballad-Of-The-Landlord

Answer the following questions:

1 What are two complaints made by the tenant in the poem?
2 What is the landlord's response?
3 Give two examples of the tenant's informal style of speaking. Why would Hughes do this?
4 How many questions does the tenant raise? Why do you think we do not hear the direct response of the landlord?
5 When the landlord does speak, why do you think he says the tenant is 'trying to ruin the government and overturn the land'?
6 Why do you think the seventh stanza is written so differently from the other stanzas?
7 What is ironic about the headlines in the press? What does this imply about the media at this time?

UNIT 12 Innovation in science and technology

REFLECTION

Choose one of the images above and, with a partner, do the following:

■ Describe the picture.
■ Explain what that image is trying to express.
■ Explain how it might be connected to innovations in science and technology.

Use the image of the cell as a metaphor for another subject in science or technology. Explain that subject in the way that the cell is explained; how one part is connected to another. Try to connect four parts of the topic as it is done in the image.

1 Benefits to society

To what extent are advances in science and technology helping, or harming, society? Create a list of the benefits and harmful effects of science and technology. Choose one of your ideas from each list and answer the following questions:

- Who is being harmed or helped? How?
- Why is this happening?
- What could be done to prevent further harm, or to increase the benefits?

Interview of a social entrepreneur: Pete Ceglinski, co-founder of The Seabin Project

At Ye! we support social initiatives [1]_____ possible. There is today a growing number of entrepreneurs [2]_____ the leap and creating their startups because they [3]_____ a problem in their local community or society at large, and found a way to solve it. [4]_____ people, putting sustainability at the center of their business model, are called social entrepreneurs.

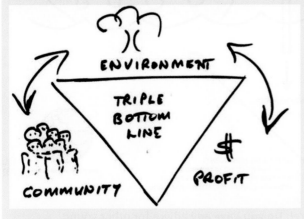

Pete Ceglinski, who kindly [5]_____ to be interviewed by our team, is a good example of a social entrepreneur. [6]_____ with his friend, Andrew Turton, they developed the Seabin.

Pete and Andrew are two Australian boat builders and surfers. They were sick of seeing trash all [7]_____ the beaches, sea and marinas when surfing and sailing. It felt wrong to them. Indeed, polluted oceans are wrong for the planet as a [8]_____ : plastics and trash pollute the sea and destroy the ecosystems. It is the whole equilibrium that is at stake here and the [9]_____ are terrible: it provokes diseases, malformations and death for marine wildlife. [10]_____ it is dangerous for humans, as consumers of sea products.

The two friends came up with the idea of a trash can that would collect debris in the water. It took them four years to develop what would later become the Seabin. The concept is pretty simple: similar to skimmer boxes in swimming pools, the Seabin is located in the water and fixed to a floating dock. There is a water pump that creates a flow of water into the can, bringing with it all floating trash. The debris is caught in a catch bag and the water is sucked out of the can and pumped back into the sea. The Seabin is designed for marinas, harbors, private pontoons, inland waterways, residential lakes and ports.

The project was incubated by Australian company Shark Mitigation Systems and was later crowdfunded on the Indiegogo website. They raised more than $260,000 in two months.

As of today the project is successful. In March 2016, The Seabin Project partnered with Poralu Marine, a French manufacturer of pontoons and marina equipment. Shortly after, they signed a contract with the city of La Grande Motte, in France. The city agreed to implement the Seabin in its marinas as well as developing an awareness campaign on ocean pollution.

The Seabin Project is now located in Palma de Mallorca, Spain, and has big plans for the future.

Below, Pete Ceglinski delivers his inspiring point of view:

Ye!: What drove you to become an entrepreneur and to start your company / organization?

Pete: I wanted to follow the day dreams I was having all day at my "proper" job. I wanted to make a difference in the world and I didn't want to wear shoes … Simple as that.

Ye!: What was the biggest challenge you experienced in your entrepreneurship journey and how did you overcome it?

Pete: Trying to sell a dream to the world. Selling a product that 99% of populations cannot use or touch but benefits every single living thing on Earth. I overcame this with total dedication, lack of sleep and not taking no for an answer when deep down my gut feeling told me the opposite…

Ye!: What is your vision for your company / organization in the next three years?

Pete: We would like to have our flagship product, the Seabin, spread all over the world and making a difference. We'd like to reinvest into newer models and better educative programs that relate directly to the Seabin.

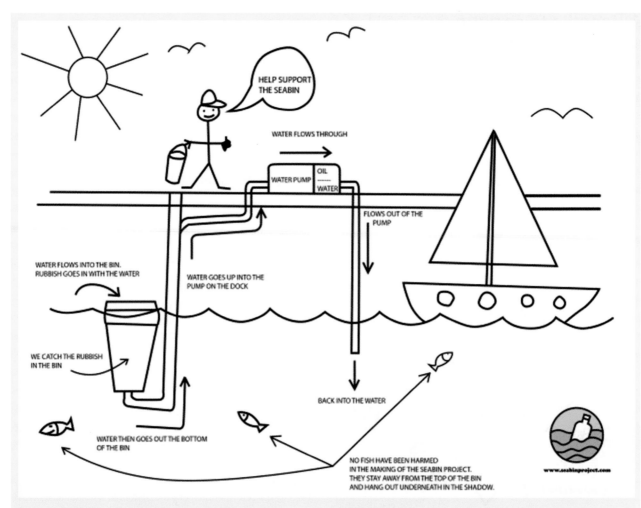

Ye!: Is there anything that you would have done otherwise?

Pete: No … Not a thing. I'm a firm believer that everything happens for a reason and that you are exactly where you should be in life right now. And to an extent that you make your own luck.

Ye!: Do you have any advice for other young entrepreneurs?

Pete: Follow your own dreams and gut feelings. If you day dream about the same things everyday, take the plunge, make a plan to support yourself and then quit everything and just do it! I spent one year secretly saving my money and working out a plan. Then I quit my job and made it happen. I had enough tools and money to last me one year while I renovated a factory and set up the project.

https://yecommunity.com/en/blog/interview-of-a-social-entrepreneur-pete-ceglinski-co-founder-of-the-seabin-project

 A **Use the words in the box to fill in the blanks 1–10 in the passage. There are more words than necessary.**

a accepted	**f** along	**k** over
b around	**g** such	**l** taking
c whenever	**h** jumping	**m** also
d recognized	**i** moreover	**n** consequences
e whole	**j** total	**o** wanted

B Which of the following statements are true?

1 Pete Ceglinski and Andrew Turton came up with their idea when they were sick.
2 Pete Ceglinski would one day like to move to France or Spain.
3 Pete and Andrew's product cannot be used by most people but benefits everyone.
4 Pete was not interested in a 'proper' job.
5 Pete's advice is not to daydream and waste time.
6 The Seabin is compared to a swimming-pool cleaner.
7 Pete wishes they had better luck at the beginning of their project.
8 The entrepreneurs were originally boat builders.
9 Plastic and trash destroy ecosystems.
10 Shark mitigation systems invested $260,000 into the company.
11 Pete believes you have to follow your gut feelings.
12 The Seabin is designed for the deepest parts of the ocean.

C What is the meaning of the following words or phrases as they are used in the text?

1 awareness campaign
2 trying to sell a dream
3 deep down
4 everything happens for a reason
5 take the plunge

Grammar

Some, any, someone, something, anyone or anything

- We use **some** with plural and uncountable nouns, for example:
  *There were **some people** in the car I did not recognize.*
  ***Some acts** of kindness really touch your heart.*
- We use **any** when we use a negative in a sentence, such as *not*, *hardly* or *never*:
  *There is **never any** food in his refrigerator.*
  *I am **not** ready to give him **any** credit for the project.*
- **Someone**, **something**, **anyone** and **anything** follow the same rules as above.

D Complete the sentences with *some, any, someone, something, anyone* or *anything*.

1 She wanted to talk to him, but he was talking to _____ else.
2 Doesn't _____ care that we are not respecting the rights of certain individuals?
3 He didn't do _____ to deserve that award.
4 I know you don't have _____ to do, but I will think of _____.
5 Would you like _____ sugar with your coffee?
6 _____ of my friends are attending a meeting to discuss developing our community services.
7 I didn't see _____ that I knew at lunch, so I did not stay.
8 _____ very interesting happened to me today.
9 Can _____ please help me find my glasses. I cannot see without them.
10 If you need bus money, there are _____ coins in the jar in the kitchen.

Watch the discussion on innovation in Australia at https://youtu.be/ Zz1RyY9vO6o from the start to 0:29 and from 3:37 to 6:40 and answer the questions that follow.

Open questions

Answer the following questions:

1 Why didn't the speaker's daughter want to go to robotics camp?

2 What changed her daughter's mind?

3 According to the speaker, what is the image the media gives of innovation or entrepreneurship?

4 Which role models does the speaker think should be promoted?

True or false

Which statements are true and which are false?

5 Australia is now looking for more investment from overseas.

6 In the past, Australia was not interested in investing in robotics.

7 The speaker does not think her daughter would be inspired by the current role models presented in the media.

8 The mainstream media promotes too many start-up companies.

9 The speaker thinks Australia's innovation has been quite positive recently.

10 The speaker reminded her daughter of the woman who saved her life.

11 The speaker found out her daughter will attend robotics class from an SMS text from her husband.

12 The speaker does not think something is broken in the innovation system in Australia.

 In groups of three or four, have a round-table discussion where you discuss the question: 'What are the challenges facing society today that can be overcome by innovations in science and technology?'

 Research an innovation that has benefited society, and write a blog about it. You can write the blog from your point of view as a student, or you can imagine you are the innovator and write it from his / her point of view. Think about the audience for your blog.

■ TOK Links

To what extent do the natural sciences have an ethical obligation towards society?

How might our perception of science be subjective?

CREATIVITY, ACTIVITY, SERVICE

Find an environmental problem in your area and think of possible solution for it. Contact an organization that you can work with on this solution, or begin working on the solution with others at your school.

2 Privacy

Your rights end where another's begin.

The quotation above is often used to discuss the difficulties in creating laws, discussing freedom and establishing ethical beliefs. In small groups, think of examples where this quotation is true. Discuss the difficulties in creating clear lines where one person's rights begin and another's end. Share your thoughts with the class.

Is it ethical to have a national DNA database?

The National DNA Database has proved to be a valuable tool in the fight against crime. However, [1] much / many *people are concerned about how it has evolved* [2] for / from *a database containing genetic information on convicted criminals to one that* [3] has / had *information from a much wider group of people.*

The UK National DNA Database holds the DNA profiles and relevant DNA samples from [4] the / a select number of UK individuals. It is the [5] largest / larger database of its kind in the world and is continuing to grow each year. Every profile in the UK National DNA Database is derived from a sample [6] of / with human material, such as saliva or hair, collected from a crime scene or police suspects.

[7] Although / However, many people are against the idea of extending the DNA database because of the potential threat it has [8] to / on our privacy. While a DNA profile provides very little information about [9] everyone / someone, their DNA sample contains information that can reveal their ethnicity or how susceptible they [10] are / were to disease. The risk of data abuse [11] is / are therefore potentially high.

Below are some of the pros and cons of having a national DNA database.

Is a national DNA database useful for police investigating crimes?

Yes

- The information derived from each DNA profile can be a powerful tool in the fight against crime. If a match is made between a DNA profile at a crime scene and a DNA profile on the database, it can help police to identify a possible <u>suspect</u> quickly. They can then use this information as strong evidence to demonstrate an individual is guilty of a crime.
- Searching the database to find a DNA profile match helps identify a suspect in around 60 per cent of cases in the UK.
- Information can be shared between databases held in different countries to help identify criminals who commit crimes in more than one country.
- It is easier to travel internationally <u>enabling</u> potential criminals to escape police and conviction. A DNA database may help to keep track of criminals around the world.
- A DNA database of everyone may make it easier for police to identify missing people and <u>unidentified</u> remains.

No

- There is little evidence to support that more crimes would be solved if a national DNA database is extended to contain samples from people who have not previously been convicted of a crime.
- If a national DNA database contains more samples it may increase the possibility of false matches being made and innocent people being arrested.
- Because samples are stored and compared against DNA collected at crime scenes, police may be more likely to <u>pursue</u> crimes committed by members of overrepresented groups. This may lead to discrimination, while underrepresented groups may more easily evade detection.
- If police can't find a database match for DNA taken from a crime scene, they may then look at <u>partial</u> DNA matches. This could lead to innocent relatives of criminals being wrongfully pursued for a crime.

Does having a national DNA database help eliminate discrimination?

Yes

- The 2012 UK Protection of Freedoms Bill addressed the fact that the details of many innocent people were held on the database. This resulted in 1,766,000 DNA profiles from innocent people being deleted from the UK national DNA database.

No

- At one time, the UK National DNA Database contained genetic information from around one million people who had not been convicted of a crime, and about half a million from juveniles. As a consequence, specific groups, such as young people and black men, made up an unequal number of those included on the UK National DNA Database.

- Extending a national DNA database to include the whole population could eliminate current ethnic and gender bias, for example towards young, black men.
- It would make solving crimes quicker and more accurate as forensic material from a crime scene could be automatically screened against information in the database to identify potential suspects.

- Individuals on the DNA database may be seen as potential offenders rather than law-abiding citizens. If the database is extended beyond just convicted criminals, everyone would be seen as possible suspects.
- DNA records are linked to other computer records such as records of arrest, which can be used to refuse someone a visa or job. This opens up the potential for discrimination.

Do national DNA databases take into consideration an individual's human rights?

Yes
- The Forensic Genetics Policy Initiative seeks to set international standards for DNA databases that respect and protect human rights.
- We all have the right to live in a society free from crime.

No
- Keeping a DNA database is seen by many as a further infringement of privacy and human rights.
- It is debatable whether the benefits to society of having a national DNA database outweigh an individual's right to privacy.

Is the privacy of the individuals on a national DNA database protected?

Yes
- Personal information is already held by groups in the private sector; if people can trust the private sector then they should be able to trust the Government.
- In 2010, the UK Government pledged to make changes to the length of time DNA samples are kept in the UK National DNA Database. These were included in the 2012 Protection of Freedoms Act. These changes ensure that the DNA (and fingerprints) of individuals arrested but not convicted of an offence is retained for a maximum of 5 years.

No
- Individuals who provide their own personal information to the private sector, do so voluntarily and usually in exchange for a service. An individual has no choice on whether their DNA sample is included in a national DNA database.
- Currently there are no comprehensive privacy regulations that would prevent governments sharing DNA profiles with other groups, such as insurance companies.
- DNA samples are rarely destroyed, meaning that the information derived from a sample could potentially be accessed by anyone.
- The information contained in DNA is limitless. Information about hair colour, eye colour and genetic diseases can all be found in our DNA.
- Who owns the genetic information and who controls what happens to it and how it is used? Who is responsible for the genetic information isn't clear and is a cause for concern for individuals who have records on the database.
- The 2008 Counter-Terrorism Act allows security personnel to 'biologically' track and identify individuals.

www.yourgenome.org/debates/is-it-ethical-to-have-a-national-dna-database

 Choose the word for numbers 1–11 that best completes the sentence grammatically.

B Copy and complete the following table. Put a × in the box under either 'Pro' or 'Con' to indicate whether the statement is from the pro or con argument in the debate.

Statement	Pro	Con
1 Young people and black men are unequally represented in the database.		
2 DNA samples are never destroyed.		
3 DNA profiling helps police identify 60% of suspected criminals.		
4 DNA samples from innocent people are deleted from the database.		
5 DNA of individuals is held for a maximum of five years.		
6 Innocent relatives of criminals could be wrongly pursued.		
7 We have a right to live in a society free of crime.		
8 An individual has a right to privacy.		

C Match the word from the text on the left with the word closest in meaning on the right.

1 suspect	a unknown
2 enabling	b looks
3 unidentified	c created
4 pursue	d kept
5 partial	e possible criminal
6 potential	f follow
7 seeks	g making it possible
8 retained	h possible
9 derived	i workers
10 personnel	j incomplete

Grammar

If … not, unless, whether, as long as and *provided that*

- **Unless** can replace *if … not* in conditional sentences:
  Unless *the government changes its mind, the law will pass.* (If the government does not…)
- We use **if … not** when we talk about unreal situations (situations that did not happen), emotions and in most questions:
  *He would be more excited about the holiday, **if** his cousin was **not** coming.*
  ***If** you do **not** attend the meeting, what will happen?*
  ***If** I had **not** been born in this country, my life would have been very different.*
- We use **unless** as an afterthought:
  *There is no reason for you to attend the meeting, **unless** you want to.*
- We use **whether** or **if** when we talk about two possibilities:
  *We do not know **whether** / **if** it is a good idea or not.*
- We usually use **whether** with *not*:
  ***Whether** or **not** he accepts the invitation, it is his decision.*
- **Provided that** and **as long as** can also replace *if* in certain conditional sentences, which can vary your word choice to enrich your sentences. For example:
  *The restaurant will keep your reservation, **provided that** you call one week in advance.*
  *You may share these documents with your co-workers **as long as** you give credit to their creators.*

193

D Rewrite the sentences below using *if … not, unless, whether, as long as* and *provided that*. Use each possibility only once.

1 The planet will continue to be destroyed. We must do something about it.
2 They may add an extra theatre performance to the calendar. It is not certain.
3 You can debate that topic. Simply use respectful language.
4 We will give him a second chance. However, he must apologize.
5 The police would not have solved the case without the DNA sample.

E Watch the TED Talk on facial recognition from 4:57 to 10:36 at www.ted.com/talks/alessandro_acquisti_why_privacy_matters/transcript and answer the questions that follow.

Matching

The speaker asks his audience several questions. Match the question he asks the audience with the topic he is discussing.

1 What will this future without secrets look like?

2 Which group do you think was more likely to judge harshly our subject?

3 Why should that be always the case?

4 Do you think that you would be equally likely to call either candidate for an interview?

5 How long a delay do you think we had to add in order to nullify the inhibitory effect of knowing that faculty would see your answers?

a Groups viewing online data about job candidates.

b Information about us will always be used in a positive manner.

c Strangers knowing you through Google Glasses.

d Students answering a question on whether they have ever cheated on an exam.

e An HR director looking for more information based on people's résumés.

Comprehension questions

6 Why does the speaker say the example of Google Glasses might produce 'a future without secrets'?

7 Why does the speaker say that 'privacy is not about having something negative to hide'?

8 How were US companies discriminating through social media?

9 How is the scene in *Minority Report* different from the reality today?

10 According to the speaker, how might an advertiser use your list of Facebook friends to sell you a product?

11 Why does the speaker say the current protection policies we have are 'like bringing a knife to a gunfight'?

12 Why isn't transparency sufficient for protecting personal information?

F In small groups, create a scenario where a person, or people, are being questioned because of data that has been collected on them. Include ideas such as 'protection', 'privacy' or 'bias'. Possible scenarios are:

- Someone being stopped at an airport because of racial profiling.
- A student being questioned about posts on Facebook.
- Students being questioned about online bullying.
- A job interview where someone is asked about their social media posts.
- A mistaken identity because of the use of facial recognition.
- A court case where DNA samples are being used as evidence.

Write a five-paragraph essay where you argue for or against the following claim: 'Technology has done more harm than good for society'. The paragraphs can be organized as follows:

- Paragraph 1: Introduction
- Paragraph 2: First point with example
- Paragraph 3: Second point with example
- Paragraph 4: One possible argument from the opposing side with your counter-argument to this point
- Paragraph 5: Conclusion

■ TOK Links

To what extent is faith in the natural sciences necessary?

How can we know when a knowledge claim is valid?

CREATIVITY, ACTIVITY, SERVICE

Find out about your school's data protection policy. If there isn't one, ask to help create one. If there is one, think of ways to communicate this policy to everyone in the school community.

3 The future

Work in pairs. You and your partner are scriptwriters, and you have been asked to come up with an idea for a science-fiction film. Think of an idea for the film and then pitch it to the class. *Pitch it* means to present the idea with the intention of convincing or persuading someone to buy, or make, your film idea. Common science-fiction film plots involve:

- Robots
- Space travel
- Time travel
- Alien invasions
- Our world in the future

You can base your idea on one of those above, or create your own. When everyone has shared their ideas, discuss which ones you liked the best and why.

So how does AI actually work?

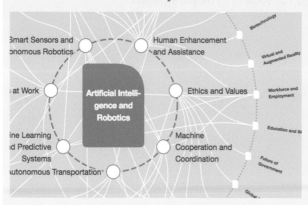

Artificial intelligence and robotics

Tech entrepreneur Elon Musk argues that artificial intelligence (AI) poses a greater threat to humanity than nuclear weapons, while Facebook CEO Mark Zuckerberg believes AI will save lives.

Regardless of whether you agree with Musk's or Zuckerberg's argument, what is clear is that AI is reshaping the world we live in. It's driving advances in medicine and autonomous vehicles and disrupting industries from manufacturing to marketing. And although we may not be aware of it, we are already using it in our Facebook news feeds, when we talk to Siri on our iPhones or ask our Alexa-enabled speakers to play a track.

Yet although it's powering products and services we use every day, AI remains a mystery to many of us. So Facebook AI experts Yann LeCun and Joaquin Quiñonero Candela have set about simplifying this complex field of computer science in a series of educational videos and blog posts.

"Not magic, just code"

"Artificial intelligence is not magic," write LeCun, head of Facebook's AI research, and Candela, Facebook's Director of Applied Machine Learning, in their blog. "But we have already seen how it can make seemingly magical advances in scientific research and contribute to the everyday marvel of identifying objects in photos, recognizing speech, driving a car, or translating an online post into dozens of languages."

How does it do this? Many intelligent machines and systems use algorithmic techniques loosely based on the human brain. These neural networks can learn to recognize patterns, translate languages, do simple logical reasoning, create images and even come up with ideas.

"All of this happens at blinding speed through a set of coded programs designed to run neural networks with millions of units and billions of connections," write LeCun and Candela. "Intelligence emerges out of the interaction between this large number of simple elements."

If, for example, you want to teach a computer to tell the difference between a car and a dog, instead of programming it to carry out the task, you can train it to recognize objects in images so that it learns for itself.

So what is deep learning?

Deep learning is a type of machine learning that structures neural networks in multiple processing layers. This helps a computer to identify what is in an image or learn to recognize speech and text.

"In a park we can see a collie and a chihuahua, but recognize them both as dogs, despite their size and weight variations," write LeCun and Candela. "To a computer, an image is simply an array of numbers. Within this array of numbers, local motifs, such as the edge of an object, are easily detectable in the first layer.

"The next layer would detect combinations of these simple motifs that form simple shapes, like the wheel of a car or the eyes in a face.

"The next layer will detect combinations of shapes that form parts of objects, like a face, a leg, or the wing of an airplane.

"The last layer would detect combinations of parts that form objects: a car, an airplane, a person, a dog, etc. The depth of the network – with its multiple layers – is what allows it to recognize complex patterns in this hierarchical fashion."

Deep learning is helping to push forward research in fields including physics, engineering, biology and medicine. It is also at the heart of the development of autonomous systems such as self-driving vehicles.

■ Many intelligent machines and systems use algorithmic techniques loosely based on the human brain

What about AI's impact on jobs?

Despite growing anxiety over automation eliminating jobs, LeCun and Candela believe that AI will create new roles for humans in manufacturing, training, sales and maintenance and management of intelligent robots.

"AI and robots will enable the creation of new services that are difficult to imagine today. But it's clear that health care and transportation will be among the first industries to be completely transformed by it," they write.

"Increasingly, human intellectual activities will be performed in conjunction with intelligent machines. Our intelligence is what makes us human, and AI is an extension of that quality."

■ Self-driving cars are being tested on highways around the world

Maryam Munir

www.weforum.org/agenda/2017/09/so-how-does-ai-actually-work-these-videos-by-facebook-experts-explain-everything

A Answer the following questions:

1 What are two industries that artificial intelligence is already being used in?
2 What are two examples that make artificial intelligence seem like 'magic'?
3 How can a computer tell the difference between a car and a dog?
4 List what a computer does in the four layers of recognition that LeCun and Candela describe.
5 What will be AI's effect on jobs, according to LeCun and Candela?

B Complete the following sentences using three to five words from the text each time:

1 Mark Zuckerberg believes that _____.
2 We are already using AI when we talk _____.
3 AI machines use algorithmic techniques _____.
4 Deep learning helps a computer _____.
5 To a computer, an image is _____.
6 Deep learning is the heart of the development of autonomous systems _____.
7 AI will create new services that _____.

Grammar

Each **and** *every*

- We can use ***each*** or ***every*** for singular countable nouns: ***Each*** *day...* or ***Every*** *day...*
- A singular verb is used after both *each* and *every*: ***Every*** *hospital has...*, ***Each*** *university provides...*
- We use *every* with *almost* and *nearly*, when we are talking about a large group and if the plural noun has a number in front of it:

  *We completed **almost every** exercise.*

  ***Every six months**, you should take a young child to a doctor for a check-up.*

- We use *each* when we are talking about individual members of a group or when we are talking about a pair:

  *We were **each** assigned a partner.*

  ***Each** teacher is expected to have his / her own website.*

  *They are identical twins, but they **each** have their own distinct personality.*

197

C Fill in the blanks with either *each* or *every*.

1 _____ year, I set a new goal for myself.

2 It is clear that _____ of us must create an individual proposal.

3 There are several flats to let in the city, and _____ of them is expensive.

4 It is up to _____ one of us to decide what we believe is right or wrong.

5 Almost _____ candidate mentioned unemployment in their speeches.

6 The director divided the actors into two groups and asked _____ group to create a scene based on the word 'comfort'.

7 He looked at the checklist, and they had ticked nearly _____ box.

8 Each group consists of four members, however, _____ member is required to speak in the presentation.

D You will hear a news report on how NASA is using high-school students to develop new virtual reality (VR) programs for space and Earth exploration. Listen to the report at https://n.pr/2mMr2j7 and answer the following questions:

1 There is a list of comments (a–h) on the left, about the different speakers in the report. Copy and complete the table to identify the name of the person who matches each comment.

Who...	Rebecca Hersher	Jackson Ames	Thomas Grubb
a said the VR headset should not be too tight?			
b became dizzy when looking up while using the headset?			
c said 'Onward' adds new layers to VR's realism?			
d has no time for video games any more?			
e wants NASA scientists to be using VR headsets?			
f can't remember a time when he didn't use computers?			
g is 28 years old?			
h thinks VR is an improvement over 2D screens?			

2 Below are sentences from the report with two to five words missing from each. Find the words from the report that complete the sentences.

a A lot of games involve _____.

b 'Onward' makes players feel like _____.

c Ames landed _____ over the summer at NASA.

d High-school students were valuable because they _____ and what doesn't in the virtual world.

e Herscher found the virtual lava tube _____.

E Research an innovation involving virtual reality or artificial intelligence. After reading about it, think of a question it raises in your mind on its positive or negative effects. Do a presentation to the class where you:

■ explain your example

■ ask the question it raised in your mind

■ explain the possible positive and negative answers to this question.

F Create a dialogue between a machine and a human, where the machine is trying to help the human do something. Demonstrate how helpful the machine can be but also where confusion or misunderstanding occurs. You may begin by explaining where the person talking / writing to the machine is, before the dialogue begins. You may also describe what the person does after the dialogue ends.

■ TOK Links

To what extent are models based on human behaviour accurate?

To what extent are emotions important in obtaining knowledge?

CREATIVITY, ACTIVITY, SERVICE

Research an organization or person who is using technology or science to help a certain group of people. Invite someone to your school to speak about this project and build a relationship with the person or organization so that students at your school can contribute to its success.

HIGHER LEVEL

■ Literature

4 The War of the Worlds

The War of the Worlds is a science-fiction novel, written by H.G. Wells in 1897. It is the story of the invasion of the Earth by Martians, and it was one of the first stories of its kind, where the writer imagined what it would be like if aliens landed on and invaded the Earth. The story begins in Surrey, not far from London. The scene below describes the arrival of the Martians' spaceship. At first, it is thought to be a meteor that has fallen to Earth, but strange movements indicate that someone, or something, is inside the unusual spaceship.

Then came the night of the first falling star. It was seen early in the morning, rushing over Winchester eastward, a line of flame high in the atmosphere. Hundreds must have seen it, and taken it for an ordinary falling star. Albin described it as leaving a greenish streak behind it that glowed for some seconds. Denning, our greatest authority on meteorites, stated that the height of its first appearance was about ninety or one hundred miles. It seemed to him that it fell to earth about one hundred miles east of him.

I was at home at that hour and writing in my study; and although my French windows face towards Ottershaw and the blind was up (for I loved in those days to look up at the night sky), I saw nothing of it. Yet this strangest of all things that ever came to earth from outer space must have fallen while I was sitting there, visible to me had I only looked up as it passed. Some of those who saw its flight say it travelled with a hissing sound. I myself heard nothing of that. Many people in Berkshire, Surrey, and Middlesex must have seen the fall of it, and, at most, have thought that another meteorite had descended. No one seems to have troubled to look for the fallen mass that night.

But very early in the morning poor Ogilvy, who had seen the shooting star and who was persuaded that a meteorite lay somewhere on the common between Horsell, Ottershaw, and Woking, rose early with the idea of finding it. Find it he did, soon after dawn, and not far from the sand pits. An enormous hole had been made by the impact of the projectile, and the sand and gravel had been flung violently in every direction over the heath, forming heaps visible a mile and a half away. The heather was on fire eastward, and a thin blue smoke rose against the dawn.

The Thing itself lay almost entirely buried in sand, amidst the scattered splinters of a fir tree it had shivered to fragments in its descent. The uncovered part had the appearance of a huge cylinder, caked over and its outline softened by a thick scaly dun-coloured incrustation. It had a diameter of about thirty yards. He approached the mass, surprised at the size and more so at the shape, since most meteorites are rounded more or less completely. It was, however, still so hot from its flight through the air as to forbid his near approach. A stirring noise within its cylinder he ascribed to the unequal cooling of its surface; for at that time it had not occurred to him that it might be hollow.

He remained standing at the edge of the pit that the Thing had made for itself, staring at its strange appearance, astonished chiefly at its unusual shape and colour, and dimly perceiving even then some evidence of design in its arrival. The early morning was wonderfully still, and the sun, just clearing the pine trees towards

Weybridge, was already warm. He did not remember hearing any birds that morning, there was certainly no breeze stirring, and the only sounds were the faint movements from within the cindery cylinder. He was all alone on the common.

Then suddenly he noticed with a start that some of the grey clinker, the ashy incrustation that covered the meteorite, was falling off the circular edge of the end. It was dropping off in flakes and raining down upon the sand. A large piece suddenly came off and fell with a sharp noise that brought his heart into his mouth.

For a minute he scarcely realised what this meant, and, although the heat was excessive, he clambered down into the pit close to the bulk to see the Thing more clearly. He fancied even then that the cooling of the body might account for this, but what disturbed that idea was the fact that the ash was falling only from the end of the cylinder. And then he perceived that, very slowly, the circular top of the cylinder was rotating on its body. It was such a gradual movement that he discovered it only through noticing that a black mark that had been near him five minutes ago was now at the other side of the circumference. Even then he scarcely understood what this indicated, until he heard a muffled grating sound and saw the black mark jerk forward an inch or so. Then the Thing came upon him in a flash. The cylinder was artificial – hollow – with an end that screwed out! Something within the cylinder was unscrewing the top!

"Good heavens!" said Ogilvy. "There's a man in it – men in it! Half roasted to death! Trying to escape!"

Excerpt from The War of the Worlds *by H.G. Wells*

Answer these comprehension questions.

1 What did most people first think the Thing was?

2 How did Albin and Denning describe it?

3 Why was the narrator's window blind up at night?

4 Why do you think the narrator first describes Ogilvy as 'poor Ogilvy'?

5 How did the area around the fallen object look?

6 What were Ogilvy's first thoughts about the Thing?

7 What is the writer implying when he writes 'dimly perceiving even then some evidence of design in its arrival'?

8 What does the narrator mean by 'suddenly he noticed with a start'?

9 How did Ogilvy understand that the top of the cylinder was moving?

10 Why did Ogilvy's final realization frighten him?

UNIT 13 The environment

REFLECTION

Think individually about the questions below. Then pair with a partner and discuss the questions. Share your ideas with the rest of the class.

- Which words spring to mind when you hear the words 'green power'?
- What are the sources of your electricity?
- What is renewable / green energy?
- How important is plastic?
- How is plastic made?
- How is plastic harmful to our environment?
- What would the world be like without plastic?
- What is climate change?
- Should we be worried about climate change and global warming?
- Can we reverse the effects of man-made climate change?

1 Green power

'Green power' refers to renewable energy resources that provide the highest environmental benefit. Energy sources such as the sun, wind, moving water, organic plants, waste material and the Earth's heat can all be defined as renewable energy, as they restore themselves over short periods of time and do not diminish.

In pairs, think about this question: Why should we care about green power / renewable energy resources?

Conventional power sources include the combustion of fossil fuels. Fossil fuels have environmental costs from mining, drilling or extraction and emit greenhouse gases and air pollution during combustion, and they do not restore themselves as quickly as we use them up. One day, we may run out of fossil fuels. With the ever-increasing world population, we need to find cleaner alternative energy resources so that we can mitigate some of the negative human impacts on our one and only planet.

A **Before reading the article below, discuss the meaning of the following words:**

- harness
- grid
- distil
- integrated

- maintenance
- inverter
- convert
- intensify

- quantum physics
- nanotechnology
- emission
- hazardous

● ● ●

← → C   www.greenmatch.co.uk/blog/2014/08/5-advantages-and-5-disadvantages-of-solar-energy   ≡

What are the advantages and disadvantages of solar energy?

Solar energy is derived from the sun's radiation. The sun is a powerful energy source, and this energy source can be harnessed by installing solar panels. Did you know that the energy that it provides to the Earth in one hour could meet global energy needs for one year? We are able to harness only 0.001 per cent of that energy.

Advantages of solar energy

[1] _____

Among all the benefits of solar panels, the most important is that solar energy is a truly renewable energy source. It can be harnessed in all areas of the world and is available every day. We cannot run out of solar energy, unlike some other sources of energy. Solar energy will be accessible as long as we have the sun, therefore sunlight will be available to us for at least 5 billion years when, according to scientists, the sun will die.

[2] _____

Since you will be meeting some of your energy needs with the electricity your solar-panel system has generated, your energy bills will drop. How much you save on your bill will depend on the size of the system and your electricity or heat usage. Moreover, not only will you be saving on your electricity bill, but if you generate more electricity than you use, the surplus will be exported back to the grid and you will receive bonus payments for that amount (assuming your solar-panel system is connected to the grid). Savings can grow further if you sell excess electricity at high rates during the day and then buy electricity from the grid during the evening when the rates are lower.

[3] _____

Solar energy can be used for diverse purposes. You can generate electricity (solar photovoltaics) or heat (solar thermal). Solar energy can be used to produce electricity in areas without access to the National Grid, to distil water in regions with limited clean water supplies and to power satellites in space. Solar energy can also be integrated into materials used for buildings. Not long ago Sharp introduced transparent solar energy windows.

[4] _____

Solar-energy systems generally don't require a lot of maintenance. You only need to keep them relatively clean; cleaning them a couple of times per year will do the job. If in doubt, you can always rely on specialist cleaning companies, which offer this service from around £25–£35. Most reliable solar-panel manufacturers give 20–25 years' warranty. Also, as there are no moving parts, there is no wear and tear. The inverter is usually the only part that needs to be changed, after 5–10 years, because it is continuously working to convert solar energy into electricity and heat. Apart from the inverter, the cables also need maintenance to ensure your solar-power system runs at maximum efficiency. So, after covering the initial cost of the system, you can expect very little spending on maintenance and repair work.

[5] _____

Technology in the solar-power industry is constantly advancing and improvements will <u>intensify</u> in the future. Innovations in <u>quantum physics</u> and <u>nanotechnology</u> could potentially increase the effectiveness of solar panels and double, or even triple, the electrical input of solar-power systems.

Solar energy disadvantages

1 Cost

The initial cost of purchasing a solar-panel system is fairly high. Although the UK Government has introduced some schemes for encouraging the adoption of renewable energy sources, for example the Feed-in Tariff, the consumer still has to cover the upfront costs. <u>This includes paying for the solar panels</u>, inverter, batteries, wiring and for the installation. Nevertheless, solar technologies are constantly developing, so it is safe to assume that prices will go down in the future.

2 Weather dependent

Although solar energy can still be collected on cloudy and rainy days, the efficiency of the system drops. Solar panels depend on sunlight to gather solar energy effectively. Therefore, a few cloudy, rainy days can have a noticeable effect on the energy system. You should also take into account that solar energy cannot be collected during the night. On the other hand, if you also require your water-heating solution to work at night or during wintertime, thermodynamic panels are an alternative to consider.

3 Solar energy storage is expensive

Solar energy can be used right away, or it can be stored in large batteries. These batteries, used in off-the-grid systems, can be charged during the day so that the energy can be used at night. This is a good solution for using solar energy at all hours but it is also quite expensive. In most cases, it is smarter just to use solar energy during the day and take energy from the grid at the night (you can only do this if your system is connected to the grid). Luckily our energy demand is usually higher during the day <u>so we can meet most of it with solar energy</u>.

4 Uses a lot of space

The more electricity you want to produce, the more solar panels you will need because you want to collect as much sunlight as possible. Solar panels require a lot of space and some roofs are not big enough to fit the number of solar panels that you would like to have. An alternative is to install some of the panels in your garden, as long as it accesses sunlight. If you don't have the space for all the panels you want, you can get fewer and they will still satisfy some of your energy needs.

5 Associated with pollution

Although pollution related to solar-energy systems is far lower compared to other sources of energy, solar energy can be associated with pollution. Transportation and installation of systems is associated with the <u>emission</u> of greenhouse gases. There are also some toxic materials and <u>hazardous</u> products used during the manufacturing process of solar photovoltaics, which can indirectly affect the environment. Nevertheless, solar energy pollutes far less than alternative energy sources.

B **Read the article and answer the following questions:**

1 Choose an appropriate heading from the list below for each of the paragraphs numbered 1–5.
   a Low maintenance costs
   b Reduces electricity bills
   c Renewable energy source
   d Technology development
   e Diverse applications

2 To whom or to what do the following underlined words refer? Answer using words as they appear in the text.
   a Did you know that the energy that <u>it</u> provides to the Earth in one hour… (introduction)
   b <u>It</u> can be harnessed in all areas of the world… (first part, paragraph 1)
   c You only need to keep <u>them</u> relatively clean… (first part, paragraph 4)
   d … because <u>it</u> is continuously working to… (first part, paragraph 4)
   e <u>This</u> includes paying for the solar panels… (second part, paragraph 1)
   f … so we can meet most of <u>it</u> with solar energy. (second part, paragraph 3)

3 Are the following sentences true or false? Justify your answers by quoting a relevant phrase from the text.
a The sun will be available to us forever.
b The size of the solar-energy system you use, and your electricity usage, will affect your savings on electricity bills.
c Solar panels on roofs are the only solar-energy system currently available to us.
d The Feed-in Tariff is one of the government schemes to boost the adoption of renewable energy sources.
e The efficiency of the system is non-existent on rainy days.
f We consume more electricity at night.

Grammar

Prepositions of time

For

For refers to a length of time and shows how long something lasted. For example:

• Sunlight will be available to us **for** at least 5 billion years when, according to scientists, the sun will die.

In / during

In or **during** describes a shorter period of time within a longer period. For example:

• Savings can grow further if you sell excess electricity at high rates **during** the day and then buy electricity from the grid **during** the evening when the rates are lower.

From ... to / between ... and

Use **from ... to** to describe the length of a period of time by stating the start and end points. For example:

• I read the book **from** two o'clock **to** three o'clock. (= I read for an hour)

Use **between ... and** to say that an action happened at some point in a period of time. For example:

• What time was Rachel woken up? Sometime **between** two **and** three o'clock. (= we don't know exactly what time)

By / until (till) / before

Use **by** to talk about an action or event that was completed at some point previously, or at a point in time. For example:

• **By** the evening, she'd fallen hopelessly in love.

Use **until / till** to describe an action or event that will continue from the time of speaking to precisely the point in time. For example:

• She stays on the beach **until (till)** five o'clock.

Use **before** to describe an action or event that is completed at some time previous to the time given. For example:

• I always read a book **before** I go to bed.

After / since

Use **after** to describe an action or event that happened at some time later than the point in time given. For example:

• She woke up **after** midnight.

Use **since** to refer to the time at which an action (which continues to the present) started. For example:

• She hasn't been able to sleep **since** midnight. (= she is still awake)

C Complete this part of a famous story by choosing the appropriate preposition for numbers 1–7.

[1] By / From / To sunset, all the guests had arrived along with the King, the Queen and the Prince. The dancing began. [2] Before / After / During the evening, many young single ladies tried to attract the attention of the Prince. But [3] for / since / between the beginning of the ball, he had shown no interest in anything or anybody.

However, [4] during / after / since some time, a new, unexpected guest arrived at the ball. The Queen whispered to the King, 'Who is the girl in the white dress and glass slippers? She's beautiful.' [5] By / In / Until that moment, the Prince hadn't moved from his seat, but instantly, he invited the guest to dance and could not be separated from her [6] for / to / before the rest of the evening.

But suddenly, just [7] to / in / before midnight, the mysterious visitor began to run from the castle with no explanation. The Prince followed her as the castle bell began striking twelve. But outside, there was no sign of her – except a glass slipper.

Practical Grammar by John Hughes and Ceri Jones

D Working with a partner, create a role play about renewable energy sources.

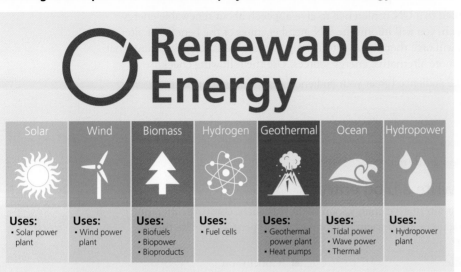

Student A: You think solar energy is the ultimate form of a renewable energy source. Your role is to convince your partner to install solar panels. Base your argument on the text you've just read.

Student B: You are not convinced about solar energy. Try to convince your partner that other renewable energy sources such as biomass, hydropower, geothermal and wind are better alternatives.

E Read aloud the transcript of a speech given by the Secretary of State for Energy and Climate Change in New Delhi (or ask a volunteer) www.gov.uk/government/speeches/clean-energy-is-the-energy-of-today-and-tomorrow). Listen to the audio twice and answer the following questions:

1 Complete the following gaps. Use no more than three words for each gap.

Notes on the speech by the Secretary of State for Energy and Climate Change in New Delhi.

 a The UK and India have a strong and growing collaboration on ____.
 b Both countries' priority is ____.
 c Both countries have ambitious plans for ____.

2 Which of the following does **not** qualify for the existing commercial collaboration between the UK and India?

 a BP's joint venture with Reliance Energy
 b Cyan Technologies and Tata working for smart grid pilot projects
 c Indian businesses raising capital for clean energy in London

3 Which of the following is **not** one of the reasons that the UK was able to assemble £45 billion of private investment in electricity generation and networks?

 a World class expertise in R&D, technology, finance and business
 b The strength of London as an international financial centre
 c Strong policy frameworks that give confidence to investors

4 Which of the following is **not** one of the benefits clean energy can bring to India?

 a Cleaner air
 b Improved trade deals
 c Energy security
 d Wider access to water and electricity

5 In what area can the City of London help India and Indian companies in their transition to clean energy and low carbon infrastructure?

6 What helped form India's pioneering policy for industrial energy efficiency?

7 What did the government of India recently approve?

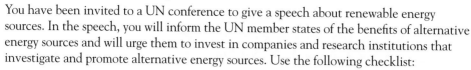

F ■ Task 1: To write a speech

You have been invited to a UN conference to give a speech about renewable energy sources. In the speech, you will inform the UN member states of the benefits of alternative energy sources and will urge them to invest in companies and research institutions that investigate and promote alternative energy sources. Use the following checklist:

- ■ Awareness of the audience (greet your audience, grab their attention, etc.)
- ■ Formal register
- ■ Clear structure
- ■ Rhetorical devices
- ■ Strong impression at the end

■ Task 2: To write a blog entry

You run a blog about alternative energy sources. In this entry, compare different alternative energy sources. Be engaging, informative and persuasive! Use the following checklist:

- ■ Eye-catching title
- ■ Introduction
- ■ Body paragraphs
- ■ Conclusion
- ■ Awareness of the audience

■ TOK Links

If you decide to use alternative energy sources for yourself and your family, you are willing to be 'brave' enough to be different, as the word *alternative* means 'different'. How difficult is it for you to choose a path that is not well trodden? If it is difficult, why is it so?

What role does peer pressure play in your decision making? Would you be able to do something that you think is right even though you know that you will not be liked by others if you choose to do it? If people around you do not like it, how convinced are you as to whether you are doing the right thing? Do you find it easy to be different sometimes but not other times? When is it more difficult to be different? When is it easy?

Art is I; Science is We

Claude Bernard, 1813–78

What does this quotation mean? Is your personal knowledge more valued in some areas of knowledge than in others?

CREATIVITY, ACTIVITY, SERVICE

Does your school community use any 'green power'? If not, why not? One possible reason people are not yet using cleaner energy sources might be that they are not fully informed. For your CAS project, what about making a presentation about green energy sources for your school community?

2 Plastic pollution

When plastic was first invented, it was revolutionary. This light, versatile and durable material transformed the packaging industry. Due to their low cost and ease of manufacture, plastics have seeped into every corner of our lives – from packaging to toys. We now live in a world where we would be hard pressed to find products that do not contain any plastic.

After decades of using plastic in our daily lives, we have realized that this convenient material has been destroying ocean wildlife beyond belief. Did you know that more than 8 million tons of plastic are dumped in our oceans every year? That over 90 per cent of all seabirds have pieces of plastic in their stomachs?

Once in the ocean, plastic litter affects the safety of sea transport, fisheries, tourism and recreation. When broken up into tiny pieces, plastic attracts toxic chemicals released over decades from industry and agriculture, the concentration of which increases as they move up the food chain.

It has been suggested that exposure to these chemicals contributes to some cancers and infertility, as well as immune, metabolic, cognitive and behavioural disorders. The entry of plastic into our food chain is of concern to human health.

 A

V

Before reading the article below, discuss the meaning of the following words:

- marine
- debris
- havoc
- juxtaposition
- derived

- durability
- detrimental
- persist
- obstruct
- ingested

- accumulate
- contaminated
- incentivise

Film review: *A Plastic Ocean* shows us a world awash with rubbish

We live in a world of plastic. Shopping bags, drink bottles, your toothbrush and even your clothes are among the everyday items made from plastic. But plastic isn't fantastic, and [1] _____ is the current state of our environment.

Humans have been mass-producing plastic since the 1950s. We produce hundreds of millions of tonnes of plastic every year and production is only increasing. [2] _____, most of it is used only once and then thrown away.

Only a small proportion of plastic is recycled. The majority ends up in landfill or, in the worst case scenario, our oceans.

A Plastic Ocean is a documentary film directed by the Australian journalist Craig Leeson. It dives into and investigates the devastating impacts that plastic has caused to our environment, [3] _____ our marine life.

What starts off as an adventure to film the blue whale, the largest animal on the planet, leads to the shocking discovery of a thick layer of plastic debris floating in the middle of the Indian Ocean. Craig, alongside Tanya Streeter, a world record-breaking free diver and environmental activist, [4] _____ travel across the globe to report on the havoc caused by decades of plastic use.

The film presents beautiful shots of the marine environment. This contrasts with footage of heavily polluted cities and dumps full of plastic rubbish. The juxtaposition between these images sends the message that our actions and choices can severely impact the planet. [5] _____ the film, experts are interviewed to provide further insight into some of the problems derived from plastic.

Impacts of plastic use

Plastic is so widely used because it is durable and cheap. Unfortunately, this durability is the same quality that makes

it so detrimental to the environment. Most plastics do not break down chemically. Instead, they break into smaller and smaller pieces that can persist in the environment for an extensive period of time.

Because it is so affordable, developing countries use plastics extensively. However, many regions lack proper waste management, and much of the rubbish is washed into the ocean when it rains. As a result, a large percentage of all plastics in the ocean are due to only a handful of countries. Scientists estimate that more than 5 trillion pieces of plastic are currently floating in our oceans.

Throughout the film, we are shown footage of numerous marine species that have been affected by plastic debris. Marine animals and sea birds often mistake floating plastic for food. Large pieces of plastic, when eaten, can obstruct the animals' digestive tracts, essentially starving them to death.

When smaller "microplastics" are ingested, toxins are released and become stored in their tissue. These toxins accumulate up the food chain and can eventually end up on our dinner tables. The consumption of the contaminated seafood can cause many health problems including cancer, immune system problems, and even childhood developmental issues. This is a major problem, as almost a fifth of the world's population relies on the ocean for their primary source of protein. Society's huge appetite for plastic is literally poisoning us.

The future of plastics

There is no quick fix for a problem that has grown hugely over the last few decades. The use of plastics is so ingrained in society that it is all but impossible to eliminate them completely.

The film does, however, offer various strategies that can be implemented to reduce the impact of plastics.

3   Make a copy of the table below and list the things that Lauren did to stop producing any trash and the benefits of her actions.

Things that Lauren did	The benefits of her actions

4   Which of the following is **not** one of the three simple steps suggested by Lauren Singer?
   a   Look at your trash and understand it
   b   Pick fruit that is easily reachable
   c   Use a reusable bag
   d   Learn how to make your products yourself

5   The tone of the speech is…
   a   encouraging
   b   condescending
   c   regretful
   d   unconcerned

Task 1: To write a report

The amount of single-use plastic in your community has increased dramatically over the last few years. You have been volunteering for the organization Plastic Oceans Foundation, which works to raise awareness of the danger of continuing to perceive plastic as disposable. You are involved in one of projects it has organized, and you have been asked to write a report on single-use plastic to share on its website. Use the following checklist:

■   Heading and subheadings
■   Introduction (purpose, problem)
■   Discussions (divided into sections)
■   Formal register
■   Conclusions
■   Recommendations

Task 2: To write an essay

Plastic bags are the preferred mode of packaging for many products in the markets of today. This is due to their being light, inexpensive and easy to produce. They are also utilized in agriculture for cultivating crops in controlled environments, besides being used in the manufacture of protective material. However, the nature of the plastic material makes its disposal a challenge that leads to pollution. Write an essay on the dangers brought about by the use of plastic bags and possible solutions to the problem. Use the following checklist:

■   Title
■   Clear introduction, body and conclusion
■   Formal register
■   Clear viewpoint
■   Development of your ideas

■ TOK Links

Why do people litter?

There are people who clean up the streets and others who litter the streets. What kind of mindset does it take, and what must one be thinking, to litter? Wouldn't the world be a better place if nobody littered?

Why do some people persistently litter? Is it because they don't know it is morally wrong and bad for the environment? Is it because they don't care? Is it because it's too much of a hassle to find a rubbish bin?

According to self-interest theory, human beings are universally selfish. If we consider littering to be a selfish behaviour, does the theory imply that human beings will always litter due to our nature of selfishness?

CREATIVITY, ACTIVITY, SERVICE

Altruism and CAS

Altruism refers to selfless behaviour in which we put other people's welfare before our own. If the above-mentioned self-interest theory is completely true, there is no true altruism, as self-interest theory implies that even our altruistic actions are carried out with self-interest. However, can you think of anyone in our history who was truly altruistic? How about people who go through major surgery to donate their kidney to a stranger? Do you really think true altruism doesn't exist?

We don't yet know why some people are more altruistic than others. However, do we know that we as a society are more sympathetic to others' sufferings now than previously? Perhaps our knowledge fed by our education, media, and so on helps us develop our altruistic nature? If kindness is contagious, can we make ourselves and others more altruistic by doing more selfless good deeds?

One of the aims of the CAS programme is to develop students who understand they are members of local and global communities with responsibilities towards each other and the environment. Doing a good deed could be the first step towards fulfilling your responsibilities as a citizen. What is your good deed of the day?

3 Climate change

Climate is what we expect, weather is what we get.

Mark Twain

'Climate' refers to the average weather conditions in a certain place over many years. For example, the climate in Minnesota is cold and snowy in the winter, and the climate in Honolulu, Hawaii, is warm and humid all year long. The climate in one area, like the Midwest or Hawaii, is called a 'regional climate'. The average climate around the world is called 'global climate'.

When scientists talk about global climate change, they're talking about the global climate and a pattern of change that's happening over many years. One of the most important trends that scientists look at is the average temperature of the Earth, which has been increasing for many years. This is called 'global warming'.

Rising global temperatures lead to other changes around the world, such as stronger hurricanes, melting glaciers and the loss of wildlife habitats. This is because the Earth's air, water and land are all related to one another and to the climate, which means a change in one place can lead to other changes somewhere else. For example, when air temperatures rise, the oceans absorb more heat from the atmosphere and become warmer. Warmer oceans, in turn, can cause stronger storms.

 A Before reading the article below, discuss the meaning of the following words:

- sweltering
- culprit
- cumulative
- ominous
- inexorably
- blinkered

This heatwave is just the start. Britain has to adapt to climate change, fast

1 Much of the world is in the grip of a heatwave. Britain is so hot and dry that we have Indonesia-style peat fires raging across our moorlands. Montreal posted its highest temperature ever, with the deaths of 33 people in Quebec attributed to the scorching heat. And if you think that's hot and dangerous, the town of Quriyat in Oman never went below a frightening 42.6°C for a full 24 hours in June, almost certainly a global record. While many people love a bit of sun, extreme heat is deadly. But are these sweltering temperatures just a freak event, or part of an ominous trend we need to prepare for?

2 Earth's climate system has always produced occasional extreme weather events, both warm and cold. What is different about now is that extra short-term warmth – from the jet stream being further north than usual – is adding to the long-term trend of rising global temperatures. The warming trend is very clear: the US National Oceanic and Atmospheric Administration shows that all 18 years of the 21st century are among the 19 warmest on record; and 2016 was the warmest year ever recorded. Overall global surface air temperatures have risen by 1°C since the industrial revolution. It is therefore no surprise that temperature records are being broken. And we can expect this to become a feature of future summers.

3 The long-term warming trend is driven by the release of greenhouse gases, chiefly carbon dioxide. Many alternative causes have been tested by scientists: the effects of sunspots, volcanic eruptions and other natural events. Only greenhouse gas emissions, dominated by fossil fuel use, explain the warming over the last century. This understanding isn't just retrospective: 30 years ago this summer, climate scientist James Hansen told a US Senate committee that the climate was changing and fossil fuels were the main culprit. He made headlines worldwide with predictions that if emissions continued our planet would continue to warm, which it inexorably has.

4 So what is to be done? The amount of warming we see is directly related to the cumulative emissions of carbon dioxide. Stopping the warming requires moving to zero emissions of carbon dioxide. Despite the Paris Agreement on climate change being designed to do exactly that, progress has been slow. Today 80% of world energy use is from fossil fuels. While the share of renewables is rising rapidly, so is energy use, meaning that globally, carbon emissions are flatlining, not declining. Commitments made so far under the Paris Agreement show that we are on track for an additional 2°C warming this century. Such large and rapid change will make it very difficult for societies to cope.

5 We will therefore also need to adapt. There is a lot we can do. At an individual level, we can cool our homes by keeping the curtains and windows shut on the sunny side of our house during the day to slow the rate at which it heats up, and then open windows at night to cool it down. We also need to keep a close eye on the very young and very old because they cannot regulate their temperatures very well, and suffer most in the heat. The major 2003 European heatwave killed 70,000, mostly older people. Changes to social care, for example, to attend to the needs of

people who are vulnerable to high temperatures, can help avoid such death tolls in the future.

6 Beyond this, many aspects of society will require deep and difficult changes, including to our own mindsets. In the summers of the future, particularly in the south of England, we will regularly live in Mediterranean-type conditions. Adapting our national infrastructure, particularly around maintaining our water supplies, updating our housing stock as it is built to retain heat, and altering how we manage our land to avoid further catastrophic fires, will all be required. It is under-appreciated that climate change will transform the very fabric of the experience of living in the UK.

7 This coming new reality is not high on the political agenda. Climate change is a greater threat to the UK than EU directives, terrorism or a foreign power invading. Yet the scope of our political discussion on future threats is limited to Brexit and spending on defence. Instead of this <u>blinkered</u> view where the future is the same as the past, we need to step out of the intense heat and take a cool look at what we are doing to our home planet.

8 The development of farming and rise of civilisations occurred within a 10,000-year window of unusually stable environmental conditions. Those stable interglacial conditions are over. Human actions are driving Earth to a hot new super-interglacial state. What scientists call the Anthropocene epoch, this unstable time, is a new chapter of history. Today's heat is a forewarning of far worse to come. To live well in this new world needs political action to catch up with this changing reality. Fast.

Simon Lewis

Simon Lewis is professor of global change science at University College London and the University of Leeds
www.theguardian.com/commentisfree/2018/jul/06/britain-heatwave-worse-to-come-water-climate-change

B **Read the article and answer the following questions:**

1 List two pieces of evidence from the text of extreme heat.
2 Which word in the first two paragraphs is used to indicate the dangers of extreme heat?
3 Which of the following is the most distinctive feature of the current climate trend?
   a Extreme weather events
   b Extra short-term warmth
   c The warming trend
   d Rising global surface air temperatures
4 What does 'this' refer at the end of paragraph 2?
5 Which word in paragraph 3 or 4 is closet in meaning to 'directed to the past'?
6 What is the cause of the global warming over the last century?
7 Despite the rapid rising of renewable energy sources, what is the reason that carbon emissions are not declining?
8 Why do very young and very old people suffer most in the heat?
9 Which of the following is **not** one of things we must change to cope with the warming trend?
   a Water supplies   c How to heat up the house
   b Housing stock   d How to manage our land
10 Find a word in the text that is closest in meaning to 'narrow-minded'.
11 Which phrase in paragraph 4 or 5 indicates a dystopian future?
12 Which words or phrases go in the gaps? Choose the words from the box below.

The text discusses the [a]＿＿＿＿ of climate change and the severity of it. The writer predicts that extra short-term warmth such as a heatwave will continuously add to the long-term trend of rising global temperatures in the future. [b]＿＿＿＿ the rapid increase of renewable energy sources, carbon emissions are not declining due to increasing energy use. The writer urges us to take action at an individual level as well as at a [c]＿＿＿＿ level to [d]＿＿＿＿ with this changing reality.

i experience	iii political	v liberal	vii although	ix cope
ii impact	iv communal	vi despite	viii owing to	x handle

Grammar

Dependent prepositions

Some verbs need a preposition to introduce their objects. Many of these verbs are always followed by the same preposition. These prepositions are called **dependent prepositions**.

- I'm **listening to** the new Coldplay album.
- What do you **think of** it?
- **Look at** the cover.

(*Listen*, *think* and *look* can also be used with other prepositions, but their meanings change.)

Some verbs have more than one dependent preposition. The preposition changes depending on the nature of the object, but the meaning of the verb stays the same:

- I don't **agree with** you. (agree with + person)
- I **agree about** the cover. (agree about + something)
- We **went to** their concert last week. (go to + place)
- We **went with** Jake and Casi. (go with + person)

Sometimes you can use both prepositions at the same time:

- I **agree with** you **about** the cover.
- We **went to** the concert **with** Jake and Casi.

Prepositions are normally followed by a noun or pronoun:

- Listen to **this**.
- Look at **the rain**.
- We were just talking about **you**!

Many of these verbs can be used without an object. In this case, do not use the dependent preposition:

- Can you be quiet and just **listen**?
- Open your eyes and **look**.

However, you must include dependent prepositions:

- at the end of questions with *who*, *what* or *which*:
  What are you listening **to**?
  What are you talking **about**?
- in relative clauses:
  This is the album that I was talking **about**.
- with adjectives followed by an infinitive:
  This music is very easy to listen **to**.

C **Add dependent prepositions to the sentences below.**

1 I love listening music when I'm on my bike.
2 Hey! What are you looking? Can I have a look?
3 Look, that's the car I was telling you. It's great, isn't it!
4 So, what did you think the film? I thought it was great!
5 You go on ahead. Don't wait me. I'll join you later.
6 I really think Ronnie worries work too much. She needs to learn to relax more.
7 Here's the report you asked. I finished it last night.
8 He's a difficult person. He really isn't very easy to live.

Practical Grammar Level 3 by John Hughes and Ceri Jones

D **Discuss the following statements in small groups or pairs. Justify your opinion as much as you can with facts and examples.**

1 Climate change is the most serious threat to our planet at the moment.
2 All countries should be forced to apply serious regulations to reduce carbon emissions.
3 Normal people can't do much to stop global warming.
4 Climate change isn't as serious as people say. People like to worry about something!
5 There are simply too many people living on planet Earth!
6 We are going to lose many animal species and areas of low land in the very near future because of global warming.

E **Read aloud the transcript of Spiegel's interview with Naomi Klein (or ask a volunteer) www.spiegel.de/international/world/global-warming-interview-with-naomi-klein-a-1020007.html. Listen to the audio twice and complete the following exercises:**

1 Which of the following is **not** Klein's opinion about climate change?
   a Capitalism is much to be blamed for climate change
   b It is impossible to stabilize rising global temperatures
   c Wealthier countries should take a greater part in reducing carbon emissions
   d Most individuals would willingly make changes to their lifestyle to protect the climate

2   Which of the following has **not** contributed to climate change?
  a   Capitalism
  b   Consumerism
  c   Growth mindset
  d   Ideology

3   Several years ago, what was set as a goal for climate protection by the international community?

4   To achieve the target set by the international community, by how much do we have to reduce global emissions?

5   Are the following statements true or false?
  a   Klein believes that unregulated capitalism is much to be blamed for carbon emissions
  b   Klein believes that a new era of consumption and energy use has helped the world to be more sustainable
  c   In 2000, carbon emissions started to go up by 1 per cent per year
  d   Consumerism requires a lot of energy
  e   Klein's view of the future is generally pessimistic

6   Fill in the following gaps. Use only one word in each.

Klein believes that we need to make a [a]_____ change both in policy and [b]_____ to reduce global carbon emissions. She emphasizes the responsibility of the [c]_____ and governments in climate protection, stating that individuals already know that climate protection requires reasonable [d]_____: less driving, less flying and less [e]_____.

F 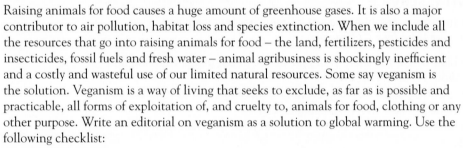 Task 1: To write an editorial

Raising animals for food causes a huge amount of greenhouse gases. It is also a major contributor to air pollution, habitat loss and species extinction. When we include all the resources that go into raising animals for food – the land, fertilizers, pesticides and insecticides, fossil fuels and fresh water – animal agribusiness is shockingly inefficient and a costly and wasteful use of our limited natural resources. Some say veganism is the solution. Veganism is a way of living that seeks to exclude, as far as is possible and practicable, all forms of exploitation of, and cruelty to, animals for food, clothing or any other purpose. Write an editorial on veganism as a solution to global warming. Use the following checklist:

- Heading
- Introduction, body and conclusion
- Objective explanation of the issue
- Opinions from the opposing viewpoint
- A solid and concise conclusion
- Formal or semi-formal register

Task 2: To write a formal letter

You realize your government is not making enough effort to tackle global warming. As a concerned citizen, write a letter to your Prime Minister / President / Head of State. In the letter, explain the severity of global warming and suggest solutions to stabilize rising global temperatures. You believe that we require social responsibility and collective action to tackle the issue. Use the following checklist:

- Appropriate conventions of a formal letter such as 'Dear…', date of writing, recipient's address, sender's address, formal sign-off
- Formal register
- Clear paragraphs
- Serious tone
- Progression of your ideas

■ TOK Links

Natural sciences vs human sciences

The natural sciences are the fields of science that deal with the physical world, for example physics, chemistry, geology, biology. Since the scientific revolution of the 17th century, we have made tremendous progress that shows no sign of coming to an end. Due to extraordinary success in the natural sciences, some believe that science is the only road to knowledge and even the only solution to all our problems. There has been talk of technologies that remove greenhouse gases from the atmosphere. Is the development of technology the way forward for climate protection? How do we know the new technologies will be successful? Since history has proven that science is fallible, and it has its limitations, we have to wonder how far the natural sciences really do give us certainty.

The human sciences study the philosophical, biological, social and cultural aspects of human life. Subjects such as psychology, economics, anthropology and sociology come under the human sciences, which are all based on observation and seek to discover laws and theories about human nature. Due to the complexity of human nature, there are many challenges in studying human beings in a scientific way. Despite the scientific evidence of global warming, it is hard to predict how its impact will influence human behaviour. What makes some people care more about the environment than others? What scientific evidence of global warming would encourage people, organizations and governments to make positive changes to the status quo?

CREATIVITY, ACTIVITY, SERVICE

To raise awareness of climate change, organize an event in your school community. The following is a suggestion of ideas for a CAS project:

- **Creativity:** Design a blog where you share your knowledge about global warming and make practical suggestions on taking action.
- **Activity:** Organize and participate in a cycling event or a running event to fundraise for 'Campaign against Climate Change': www.campaigncc.org
- **Service:** Make useful products for a local school out of recycled materials such as storage cans or boxes.

Remember that the primary purpose of the CAS project is to ensure participation in sustained collaboration. Through the project, you need to show initiative, demonstrate perseverance and develop skills such as those of cooperation, problem-solving and decision-making.

■ Literature

4 The Coming Race

The Coming Race is a science-fiction novel written by Edward Bulwer-Lytton in 1871 and hailed as one of the first of its genre. The novel follows the narrator (later named as Tish) as he accompanies an engineer, who believes he has discovered signs of life underground, into a chasm. The engineer is fatally wounded in the descent and the narrator is confronted by a huge monster, from whom he must flee. He enters the new underworld alone where he discovers a race named Vril-ya – a race of humans who retreated beneath the earth's surface to survive a huge flood. They have formed a utopian society where crime is non-existent and men and women are equal, with female members among the most learned in society. They are powered by 'Vril', a limitless source of energy used for all forms of living: communication, healing, power and, occasionally, destruction.

The following excerpt is taken from where the narrator and the engineer enter the chasm.

We descended, one after the other, till we reached the place at which my friend had previously halted. From this spot the chasm widened rapidly like the lower end of a vast
5 funnel, and I saw distinctly the valley, the road, the lamps which my companion had described. We now proceeded to attach the end of the rope we had brought with us to the ledge on which we stood, by the aid of
10 clamps and grappling hooks.

We were almost silent in our work. We toiled like men afraid to speak to each other. One end of the rope being thus apparently made firm to the ledge, the
15 other, to which we fastened a fragment of the rock, rested on the ground below, a distance of some fifty feet. I was a younger and more active man than my companion, and having served on board ship in my
20 boyhood, this mode of transit was more familiar to me than to him. I claimed the precedence, so that when I gained the ground I might serve to hold the rope more steady for his descent. I got safely to the
25 ground beneath, and the engineer now began to lower himself. But he had scarcely accomplished ten feet of the descent, when the fastenings, which we had fancied so secure, gave way; the unhappy man was
30 precipitated to the bottom, falling just at my feet, and bringing down with his fall splinters of the rock, one of which, fortunately but a small one, struck and for the time stunned me. When I recovered my
35 senses I saw my companion an inanimate mass beside me, life utterly extinct.

While I was bending over his corpse in grief and horror, I heard close at hand a strange sound between a snort and a hiss; and
40 turning instinctively to the quarter from which it came, I saw emerging from a dark fissure in the rock a vast and terrible head, with open jaws and dull, ghastly, hungry eyes – the head of a monstrous reptile
45 resembling that of the crocodile or alligator, but infinitely larger than the largest creature of that kind I had ever beheld in my travels. I started to my feet and fled down the valley at my utmost speed.
50 I stopped at last, ashamed of my panic and my flight, and returned to the spot on which I had left the body of my friend. It was gone; doubtless the monster had already drawn it into its den and devoured it.
55 The rope and the grappling-hooks still lay where they had fallen, but they afforded me no chance of return; it was impossible to re-attach them to the rock above, and the sides of the rock were too sheer and smooth
60 for human steps to clamber. I was alone in this strange world, amidst the bowels of the earth.

Slowly and cautiously I went my solitary way down the lamplit road and towards a
65 large building. The road itself seemed like a great Alpine pass, skirting rocky mountains like the one through whose chasm I had descended. Deep below to the left lay a vast valley, which presented to my astonished
70 eye the unmistakeable evidences of art and culture. There were fields covered with a strange vegetation, similar to none I have seen above the earth; the colour of it not green, but rather of a dull and leaden hue
75 or of a golden red.

There were lakes and rivulets which seemed to have been curved into artificial banks; some of pure water, others that shone

217

like pools of petroleum. At my right hand,
80 ravines and gorges opened amidst the
rocks, with passes between. They were
evidently constructed by art, and bordered
by trees resembling, for the most part,
gigantic ferns, with exquisite varieties of
85 feathery foliage, and stems like those of
the palm-tree. Others were more like the
cane-plant, but taller, bearing large clusters
of flowers. Others, again, had the form
of enormous fungi, with short thick stems
90 supporting a wide dome-like roof, from
which either rose or drooped long slender
branches. The whole scene behind, before,
and beside me far as the eye could reach,
was brilliant with innumerable lamps. The
95 world without a sun was bright and warm
as an Italian landscape at noon, but the air
less oppressive, the heat softer. Nor was the
scene before me void of signs of habitation.
I could distinguish, at a distance, buildings
100 that must surely be the homes of men.
I could even discover, though far off, forms
that appeared to be human moving amidst
the landscape. Right above me there was
no sky, but only a cavernous roof. This roof
105 grew higher and higher at the distance
of the landscapes beyond, till it became
imperceptible, as an atmosphere of haze
formed itself beneath.

Continuing my walk from a bush that
110 resembled a great tangle of sea-weeds,

I saw a curious animal about the size and
shape of a deer. After bounding away a
few paces, it turned round and gazed at
me inquisitively. I perceived that it was not
115 like any species of deer above the earth,
but it brought instantly to my recollection a
plaster cast I had seen in some museum of a
variety of the elk stag, said to have existed
before the Deluge. The creature seemed
120 tame enough, and, after inspecting me a
moment or two, began to graze on the
singular herbage around undismayed and
careless.

I now came in full sight of the building.
125 Yes, it had been made by hands, and
hollowed partly out of a great rock.
I should have supposed it at the first
glance to have been of the earliest form
of Egyptian architecture. It was fronted
130 by huge columns, tapering upward from
massive plinths, and with capitals that,
as I came nearer, I perceived to be more
ornamental and more fantastically graceful
that Egyptian architecture allows. And now
135 there came out of this building a form –
was it human? It stood and looked around,
beheld me and approached. It came within
a few yards of me, and at the sight and
presence of it an indescribable awe and
140 tremor seized me, rooting my feet to the
ground.

Excerpt from The Coming Race by Edward Bulwer-Lytton

A **Answer the following questions.**

1 Find two words in the second paragraph that convey the meaning 'no longer in existence'.

2 Find two similes in paragraph 5.

3 Which word used to describe the deer is closest in meaning to 'strange'?

4 'I started to my feet and fled down the valley at my utmost speed. I stopped at last, ashamed of my panic and my flight, and returned to the spot on which I had left the body of my friend. It was gone; doubtless the monster had already drawn it into its den and devoured it.' (lines 48–54) Judging by these statements, how do you think the narrator felt at the time?

a Guilty

b Impotent

c Afraid

d Confused

B

Copy and complete the following table by indicating to whom or to what the underlined word refers.

In the phrase …	the word …	refers to …
1 it was impossible to re-attach them to the rock above (lines 57–58)	'them'	
2 the colour of it not green (lines 73–74)	'it'	
3 it turned round and gazed at me inquisitively (lines 113–114)	'it'	
4 They were evidently constructed by art (lines 113–114)	'They'	

C

Choose the correct answer from a, b, c or d.

1 toiled (line 12) means…

   a fought

   b worked hard

   c failed

   d disagreed

2 tame (line 120) means…

   a not dangerous

   b unintelligent

   c dull

   d healthy

3 ornamental (line 134) means …

   a mysterious

   b useless

   c decorative

   d frightening

4 With a partner, discuss the effect the following phrases and sentences have on the reader.

   a 'I saw emerging from a dark fissure in the rock a vast and terrible head, with open jaws and dull, ghastly, hungry eyes …'

   b 'I was alone in this strange world, amidst the bowels of the earth.'

   c 'The whole scene behind, before, and beside me far as the eye could reach, was brilliant with innumerable lamps.'

   d 'It came within a few yards of me, and at the sight and presence of it an indescribable awe and tremor seized me, rooting my feet to the ground.'

UNIT **14** Human rights

To deny people their human rights is to challenge their very humanity.

Nelson Mandela

All human beings are born free and equal in dignity

Universal Declaration of Human Rights

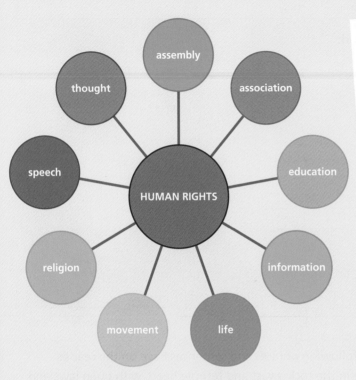

REFLECTION

Think individually about the questions below. Then pair with a partner and discuss the questions. Share your ideas with the rest of the class.

- What are human rights?
- Do you think all people in the world are equal and deserve the same rights?
- What human rights do you know about?
- Which human right is the most important?
- Do unborn children have human rights?
- What is the most important human right for children?
- Do men and women always and everywhere have equal rights? If not, why not?
- Do some people have 'more equal rights' than others?
- How would the world be different if all human rights were respected at all times?
- Do religions respect human rights?

1 Freedom of speech

Article 19 of the Universal Declaration of Human Rights, adopted in 1948, states that everyone has the right to freedom of opinion and expression; this right includes freedom to hold opinions without interference and to seek, receive and impart information and ideas through any media and regardless of frontiers.

We often take freedom of speech for granted, but we didn't always have this basic right in history. During the medieval period under the tyranny of monarchy, people were prohibited from speaking ill of their monarch as it was considered treason. To this day, some countries have state-sponsored censorship, monitoring and surveillance of the internet. Even in a liberal democratic country, there are groups of people who feel marginalized and restricted when it comes to accessing information and expressing their opinions.

A **Before reading the article below, discuss the meaning of the following words:**

- discrimination
- repressive
- participation
- restrictions
- marginalised

- flourish
- deployed
- illiteracy
- constraints

Why is access to freedom of expression important?

All over the world today, both in developing and developed states, liberal democracies and less free societies, there are groups who struggle to gain full access to freedom of expression for a wide range of reasons including poverty, discrimination and cultural pressures. While attention is often, rightly, focused on the damaging impact discrimination or poverty can have on people's lives, the impact such problems have on free expression is rarely addressed.

We are not talking about the classic examples of challenges to freedom of expression where repressive regimes attempt to block, limit and inhibit it across a population as a whole. Rather we are looking at cases where in both more and less free societies particular groups face greater barriers to free expression than the wider population. Such groups can often be denied an equal voice, and active and meaningful participation in political processes and wider society. Poverty, discrimination, legal barriers, cultural restrictions, religious customs and other barriers can directly or indirectly block the voices of the already marginalised. How much do these barriers and lack of access to freedom of expression matter? A lot – as the examples below tell us.

Why is access to freedom of expression important? Freedom of expression is a fundamental human right. It also underpins most other rights and allows them to flourish. The right to speak your mind freely on important issues in society, access information and hold the powers that be to account play a vital role in the healthy development process of any society.

The lack of access to freedom of expression is a problem that particularly affects the already marginalised – that is, minorities facing discrimination both in developed and developing countries, from LGBT people in African countries, to disabled people in Western Europe. While the scale of their struggles varies greatly, the principle is the same: within the context of their society, these groups face greater barriers to

freedom of expression than the majority. If they are unable to communicate their ideas, views, worries and needs effectively, it means they are often excluded from meaningful participation in society, and from the opportunity to better their own circumstances. In other words, discrimination is one of the core elements of unequal access to freedom of expression.

Access to free expression is also vital both to support the development process and as a development goal in its own right. The connection was perhaps most famously put forward by Amartya Sen in his widely cited book – *Development as Freedom* – where he argued that expansion of freedom is both the primary end and the principal means of development.

It is striking to note the way in which cultural and religious customs are sometimes used to clamp down on various minorities' rights to expression and assembly in many countries around the world. Human Rights Watch's latest world report states that "traditional values are often deployed as an excuse to undermine human rights." One example of this is the caste system still in place in countries including India, Nepal and Pakistan. This is culturally based discrimination on a major, systematic scale. A significant proportion of the Dalits (lower-caste people, or "untouchables") are barred from participation in public life and have a limited say in policies that directly affect them. In May 2008, the Dalit community in the Nesda village in the state of Gujarat attempted to stage a protest after being excluded from the government's development funds allocation, by refusing to fulfil their historic "caste duty" of disposing of dead animals. The dominant caste in the region promptly blocked the protest through a "social boycott", forbidding any social or economic interaction between Dalits and non-Dalits. This is only one example of Dalits being barred from having a say in development matters directly relating to them. When they attempted to stage a peaceful protest, they were only further marginalised, and their weak economic, social and political position further cemented. It's a vicious cycle.

Full access to freedom of expression is difficult to achieve in the absence of universal education and literacy. Around the world, illiteracy and inadequate (or non-existent) education hits the poorest hardest – both because education is often private, and because in poor countries where it is provided by the state, the standard of education can be low. Women and girls in the developing world are the groups most affected by illiteracy. There are a number of factors contributing to this, including higher levels of poverty among women, with culture and tradition also playing a significant part. There are still a number of societies around the world where it simply is not accepted that girls should receive education at all, and certainly not higher education. While the gender gap in education has been decreasing over time, in 2009 there were still around 35 million girls out of primary education, compared to 31 million boys. Lack of education is still the single biggest contributing factor to high and persistent levels of illiteracy – making it the most basic barrier to freedom of expression. It stops people from participating in society effectively, as it hinders them from being able to read, write and share written information, and thus fully engage with

a range of issues or debates. Women make up the majority (64 per cent) of the nearly 800 million illiterate people in the world today. UNHCR resolution 2003/42 identified this as a contributing factor to constraints on women's rights to freedom of expression.

As well as the impact of poverty, discrimination and religious and cultural factors, governments and local authorities often put in place more formal mechanisms that result in significant restrictions on access to freedom of expression for minority groups. This can come in the form of restrictions on minority languages, such as Kurdish in Turkey, or barriers to political participation, such as the Bosnian constitutional ban on Jews and Roma running for high office.

The barriers to free expression discussed here show why exercising our right to free expression is not as simple as living in a democratic society that broadly respects rights. Barriers that block or inhibit access to freedom of expression exist all over the world, in various forms and to varying degrees. Through being denied a voice, these groups are being denied a fundamental right, are facing barriers to their active participation in society, and, in many cases, are facing additional limits on their ability and opportunity to play a part in improving their own lives. Tackling the barriers from poverty to discrimination to laws that limit access to freedom of expression is vital.

www.indexoncensorship.org/2013/03/why-is-access-to-freedom-of-expression-important

B **Choose the correct answer. Your answers should be solely based on the text.**

1 Which of the following is **not** one of the reasons that some groups of people have limited access to freedom of expression?

   a Poverty
   b Discrimination
   c Prejudice
   d Law

2 Which one of the following is **not** related to freedom of expression?

   a It supports most other human rights
   b It gives you the right to speak your mind only on an individual level
   c It underpins the constructive development of a society
   d It allows you to access information

3 Which of the following groups would have limited access to freedom of expression?

   a A gay community in Kenya
   b Working class people in England
   c Less educated people in the United States
   d Shadow government

4 Which of the following could be a result of the lack of access to freedom of expression?

   a Limited participation of the marginalized in society
   b Satisfactory treatment for disabled people
   c Reduced discrimination in society
   d Threats to the majority in society

5 Are the following sentences true or false? Justify your answers by quoting a relevant phrase from the text.

   a Amartya Sen stated in his book that expansion of freedom is the fundamental goal and the essential tool of development
   b Culture and religion enhance freedom of expression in many countries

c Without education and literacy, it is challenging to attain full access to freedom of expression

d More than half of the world's illiterate population are women

e Governments always support freedom of expression for minority groups

f Barriers to freedom of expression only exist in communist countries

6 To whom or to what do the underlined words refer? Answer using words as they appear in the text.

a 'the impact <u>such problems</u> have on free expression…'

b 'and allows <u>them</u> to flourish.'

c 'While the scale of <u>their</u> struggles varies greatly,'

d 'have a limited say in policies that directly affect <u>them</u>.'

e 'making <u>it</u> the most basic barrier to freedom of expression.'

Grammar

Emphasis 1: *do, does, did*

You can add emphasis to affirmative sentences by adding **do / does** before the main verb in the present simple, or **did** before the main verb in the past simple. For example:

• *You look beautiful. – You **do look** beautiful.*

• *She looks beautiful. – She **does look** beautiful.*

• *I told you she'd be late. – I **did tell** you she'd be late.*

For negative sentences using *don't / doesn't / didn't*, add emphasis by using the full form *do not / does not / did not* and stressing **not**. For example:

• *We don't need to hurry. – You do **not** need to hurry!*

• *He didn't have to wait too long. – He did **not** have to wait too long.*

Do not use *do / does / did* for emphasis with the verb *to be* or with continuous or perfect tenses. Add emphasis to these forms by using the full form – do not use the contracted form. For example:

• *We're late. – We **are** late!*

• *We aren't late. – We are **not** late!*

• *Everyone's waiting. – Everyone **is** waiting.*

• *I've remembered the ring. – I **have** remembered the ring.*

You can add emphasis to an imperative sentence with *do*. It is often used to express anger or annoyance. For example:

• *Hurry up! – **Do** hurry up!*

• *Clean up your mess! – **Do** clean up your mess!*

C **Fill in the gaps with present simple or past simple forms of the verbs in the box. Where you think it is appropriate, add emphatic *do, does* or *did*.**

come	get	have	offer
decide	give	look	see
do	go	meet	travel

Dick doesn't have a car and [1] _____ to work by bus every day. He doesn't have to wait very long for the bus, but he [2] _____ to change buses once.

On Friday, the bus drivers [3] _____ to go on strike for the day, so there were no buses. Now it was Saturday and Dick was working in his garden. His next-door neighbour Tom leant over the garden fence.

"So you won't have managed to get to work yesterday, then?" he said.

"Actually, I [4] _____ to work," said Dick, "A colleague [5] _____ me a lift."

Then Tom's wife Marge came out to call Tom in for tea. "Hello Dick", she said, "I must say your garden [6] _____ beautiful now you've added the pond and the waterfall. Did you do it all yourself?"

"Well, I [7] _____ most of it myself, yes, but to be honest I [8] _____ a bit of help from my brother, Harry."

"Oh, was Harry here? [9] _____ him my regards next time you [10] _____ him, won't you."

"Will do," said Dick.

"My sister Betty has just popped round to see us, I think you [11] _____ her at our drinks party, didn't you? We're just about to have some tea. [12] _____ in and join us." said Marge.

"Love to," replied Dick, blushing slightly and hoping that Marge wouldn't notice.

http://random-idea-english.blogspot.com/2012/04/emphatic-do-does-did-and-other.html

 D **For this task, you'll be working in pairs. The visual stimuli below are all related to the topic 'Human rights'.**

Student A: Choose one of the photos and prepare a talk for 15 minutes. Once ready, talk to your partner about the stimulus for 3–4 minutes.

Student B: Prepare questions related to the stimulus and the theme for 15 minutes. When your partner's talk is finished, ask questions to follow up. Include a general discussion on at least one additional theme from the five themes (Social organization, Experiences, Identities, Human ingenuity, Sharing the planet). Note that the topic 'Human rights' belongs to 'Sharing the planet'. This follow-up and general discussion should last about 9–11 minutes.

Swap roles and repeat the process.

Watch the interview with Professor Paul Hunt, former UN Special Rapporteur, at https://youtu.be/P-oWpXNWOfk and answer the following questions. You are allowed to listen to it twice.

1 Choose the **five** true statements.

a The right to health is not included in the Universal Declaration of Human Rights.

b The right to health can help health workers achieve their professional objectives.

c Human rights lawyers are the only people who can implement the right to the highest attainable standard of health.

d Hunt had to report to the UN Commission on Human Rights every day.

e By putting forward maternal mortality as a human rights issue, Hunt made the UN resonate with him on the matter.

f Some of the mental health institutions Hunt visited were of a poor quality.

g Hunt believes that child mortality is the next issue the human rights community should work on.

h Hunt likes sticking his neck out for emerging issues.

i Mental health is often neglected by the human rights community.

j Many infant deaths are unavoidable around the world.

2 Fill in the gaps below. Use one word only for each gap.

Hunt believes that a [a]_____ between the lawyers and the health workers and many others is necessary to [b]_____ the right to health across the globe. During his time as UN Special Rapporteur on the right to health, he identified two issues that impose barriers for many people to access to health care: [c]_____ and [d]_____. He is also concerned about maternal mortality and mental health as human rights issues. By applying a human rights lens to such problems, Hunt aims to help identify what has to be done as a matter of [e]_____ obligation.

■ Task 1: To write a proposal

You think that your school does not provide enough opportunities for students to voice their opinions on important matters in the school. You also think students whose mother tongue is not English have even more limited access to freedom of expression. Write a proposal to address this issue. Use the following checklist:

- Title
- Subheadings
- Problem and solution clearly explained

- Formal register
- Positive tone (focus on the benefits of your proposal)

■ Task 2: To write an essay

With the use of social media, we now have more and easier opportunities to voice our opinions. At times, there are too many different opinions – some rather polarizing, contrasting, unfounded and even untrue – and it is no surprise the term 'fake news' is brandished everywhere these days.

Internet censorship is the control of what can be accessed, published or viewed on the internet. The extent of internet censorship varies from country to country. While most democratic countries have moderate censorship, other countries go as far as to limit access to information such as news and to suppress discussion among citizens.

Support for and opposition to internet censorship varies. In a 2012 Internet Society survey, 71 per cent of respondents agreed that 'censorship should exist in some form on the internet'. In the same survey, 83 per cent agreed that 'access to the internet should be considered a basic human right' and 86 per cent agreed that 'freedom of expression should be guaranteed on the internet'. What is your opinion? Write an essay on internet censorship. Use the following checklist:

- Title
- Clear introduction, body and conclusion

- Formal register
- Clear viewpoint
- Development of your ideas

■ **TOK Links**

Kantian ethics

German philosopher Immanuel Kant (1724–1804) believed that certain types of actions (including murder, theft and lying) were absolutely prohibited, even in cases where the action would bring about more happiness than the alternative. For Kantians, there are two questions that we must ask ourselves whenever we decide to act: **1** Can I rationally will that *everyone* act as I propose to act? If the answer is no, then we must not perform the action. **2** Does my action respect the goals of human beings rather than merely using them for my own purposes? Again, if the answer is no, then we must not perform the action. (Kant believed that these questions were equivalent.)

So, when you want to say something mean about your friend on social media, think whether you would be happy if everyone did what you are just about to do, or if what you are about to do is good for humankind. If your answer is no to either of them, you should consider your (potential) action unethical.

However, things are not always as simple as this! You may come across a very complicated situation and may decide to act 'unethically' for a better consequence. Does this mean that you are unethical? For example, imagine that you have seen your close friend cheating on his girlfriend. The right thing to do according to Kantian ethics is to tell his girlfriend the truth. However, you decide to talk to your friend instead of telling the truth. Does this mean you are in the wrong?

CREATIVITY, ACTIVITY, SERVICE

Be a voice for the voiceless

Can you think of any groups of people in your country or community who do not have equal opportunities to voice their opinions? How about becoming a voice for the people who need your help to make their opinions heard? There are many ways in which you can help them. For example, you could help them to build their own website and to share their ideas through social media.

2 Children's rights

Most parents and carers love their children and do their best to provide necessary protection, care and education for the children under their care. So why do children need their own rights?

Due to their vulnerability and lack of autonomy, children have been abused, neglected and exploited in various forms in history and at present. The 1989 Convention on the Rights of the Child (CRC) was established to protect vulnerable children from harm. A child is defined as 'any human being below the age of eighteen years, unless under the law applicable to the child, majority is attained earlier', according to the CRC. Children's rights include their right to association with both parents, and human identity, as well as the basic needs of physical protection, food, universal state-paid education, health care and criminal laws appropriate for the age and development of the child, equal protection of the child's civil rights and freedom from discrimination.

The United Nations established Universal Children's Day in 1954 to promote improving children's welfare around the world. Universal Children's Day is celebrated on 20 November each year, while countries around the world have the autonomy to choose a date deemed appropriate for themselves. Despite its various shapes and forms, Children's Day promotes the common goal to advocate, promote and celebrate children's rights.

Children have a right to our protection.

Children have a right to say no to touching that worries them.

Children have a right to be heard.

Children have a right to be taken seriously.

Children have a right to information.

Children have a right to express anger.

Children have a right to talk with us about anything.

Children have a right to the ownership of their bodies.

Children have a right to tell secrets that worry them.

Children have a right to feel good about themselves.

Children have a right to trust their feelings.

Children have a right to feel safe.

■ A child is every human being under the age of 18

How do children around the world celebrate children's day?

Children in Singapore recognize the first Friday of October (it used to be 1 October) as 'Children's Day' – a time to honour and celebrate the joys of childhood through various activities and events catered especially for children. However, did you know that children around the world uniquely celebrate the very same occasion at different times of the year?

In 1954, the United Nations General Assembly recommended that a day should be set aside to celebrate children around the world. The Assembly adopted 20 November as 'International Children's Day' but allowed each country to select for themselves a date they deemed appropriate.

Japan

The Japanese people celebrate Children's Day or *Kodomo no hi* on the fifth day of the fifth month every year. Families fly colourful carp kites called *koinobori* flags from their homes, as carps represent determination and vigour in Japanese folklore. They display figurines of Samurai warriors in their homes to symbolise strength and bravery. Children enjoy sticky rice cakes in oak leaves (*Kashiwa-mochi*) and participate in events around the country like traditional Japanese plays. A 'Kids' Olympics' is also held in Tokyo, attracting thousands of child competitors annually.

Mexico

In Mexico, Children's Day, also known as *El Día del Niño*, is marked on 30 April. Schools, parks and other organizations arrange a variety of special events for the children of Mexico. Classes in schools are replaced by large parties with food, games and fun rides. Traditional and common games like 'Pin the Tail on the Donkey' are played by the children. Flying banners, *piñatas*, live music and puppet shows are some common sights in their local *fiestas*. On this day, Mexican children follow a common culture of singing a song while rolling a *molinillo* (a traditional Mexican wooden whisk) between their palms in a chocolate drink, before enjoying it at breakfast.

Thailand

On the second Saturday of January each year, National Children's Day is observed in Thailand. Children are considered to be the most valuable resource of the nation and this annual celebration serves to stimulate children to be aware of their importance and responsibility towards society. On this special day, Thai children are allowed free travel on buses and free entrance to entertainment parks, zoos and government offices such as Government House, as well as to Army, Navy and Air Force bases. Children are also granted permission by the Royal Thai Air Force to explore their aircraft.

Turkey

In Turkey, National Sovereignty and Children's Day is celebrated on 23 April each year. Children take seats in the Turkish Parliament and symbolically govern the country for a day. They elect a President who will address the nation on television, and for the rest of the day children's festivals take place all across the country. Children from all over the world are invited to participate and perform their traditional dances in their traditional dress for the various festivals as a way to encourage cultural exchange for all children.

So, on this Children's Day may the children of Singapore keep in remembrance their value and place in society as they enjoy and indulge in the range of festivities dedicated just for them.

https://thenewageparents.com/childrens-day-around-the-world

A **Copy and complete the table below.**

Country	Date of Children's Day	How it's celebrated
1 Singapore		
2 Japan		
3 Mexico		
4 Thailand		
5 Turkey		

Are the following sentences true or false?

6 20 November is International Children's Day.

7 Carps symbolize strength and bravery in Japanese culture.

8 A Kids' Olympics is held in Tokyo every four years.

9 Mexican children have a chocolate drink for breakfast.

10 Traditional games such as *piñatas* are played in the national festival on Children's Day.

11 In Thailand, National Children's Day is observed to encourage children to be aware of their importance and responsibility toward the society.

12 Thai children get a free pass to all transport and events apart from government buildings on Children's Day.

Grammar

Emphasis 2: cleft sentences

Cleft sentences are used to help us focus on a particular part of the sentence and to emphasize what we want to say by introducing it or building up to it with a kind of relative clause. Because there are two parts to the sentence it is called *cleft* (from the verb *cleave*), which means 'divided into two'. Cleft sentences are particularly useful in writing where we cannot use intonation for purposes of focus or emphasis, but they are also frequently used in speech.

Cleft sentences with *what*:

- **What I like is / are** the free lunches.
- Fill in this form. – **What you do is** fill in this form.
- He applied for a new job. – **What he did was** apply for a new job.
- I was walking past when I saw your advert in the window. – **What happened was** (that) I was walking past when I saw your advert in the window.

Cleft sentences with *it*:

- *You need to see the manager.* – **It's** the manager (whom) you need to see.
- *You sign your name on this line.* – **It's** on this line (that) you sign your name.

Cleft sentences with *the thing*:

- *I like the holidays.* – **The thing I like** is the holidays.
- *Talk to the manager.* – **The best thing to do** is talk to the manager.

Cleft sentences with *place / person / reason / way*:

- **The place** (where) he works **is** a fast food restaurant.
- **The person** (whom) you need to see **is** the manager.
- **The reason** (why) I'm here **is** that I saw the advert in your window.
- **The way** to do this **is** by filling in this form.

B **Read the dialogues below. Speaker B corrects speaker A using cleft sentences. Write speaker B's sentences using the words in brackets.**

1. **A** Doesn't Martin build model cars?
   B No … (what / builds / aeroplanes)

2. **A** Do I put this in the oven now?
   B No … (what / do / in the fridge)

3. **A** Did they take the wrong train?
   B No … (what happened / the wrong bus)

4. **A** We need to call an electrician.
   B No … (it / plumber / call)

5. **A** We can't afford to go to the museums in London. It'll be so expensive.
   B No … (the good thing about museums in London / they / free)

6. **A** The car's broken down. Call the police!
   B No … (the person / need to call / a mechanic)

Practical Grammar Level 3 by John Hughes and Ceri Jones

C **In small groups, design a perfect country for children. Discuss the following aspects of the country:**

- Social structure
- Law and order
- Children's rights
- Votes and elections
- Government

Once you've agreed on details, share your ideas with the whole group.

D Listen to the interview on children's rights with Milka Pietikainen (www.youtube.com/watch?v=AE-bJLtCtjM) and answer the following questions. You are allowed to listen twice.

1 Choose the **five** true statements.

a Working with children's rights enabled Millicom to prioritize its corporate responsibility work.

b Children's rights impact assessments focus on the impact of child labour only.

c Children's rights impact assessments allow companies to address wider issues of human rights, environment, and so on.

d The business case for children's rights at Millicom includes managing the risks.

e There is a low risk of child labour in the distribution of services.

f Child online protection brings huge opportunities.

g Mobile birth registration in Tanzania provided children with greater access to education.

h Millicom started to conduct children's rights impact assessments in 2012.

i Unicef launched a children's rights and business principles checklist before 2012.

j A children's rights self-assessment for the mobile operator sector is already in use.

Choose the correct answer to each of the following questions:

2 Working with children's rights for Millicom has been…

a rewarding

b tedious

c complicated

3 The spectrum of children's rights impact assessments is…

a narrow

b broad

c undetermined

4 Child online protection can bring huge opportunities, such as…

a more profits for companies

b access to information

c increased birth control

5 The Unicef-launched children's rights and business principles checklist had…

a five principles

b ten principles

c fourteen principles

E Task: To write a speech

As a UN ambassador of children's rights, you are going to make a speech at a UN conference. In the speech, you would like to raise awareness of the lack of children's rights in certain countries such as Syria, Uganda and Sierra Leone. Below is a list of selected articles from the UN Rights of the Child. Focus on a few from the list and persuade the UN member countries to invest in these countries. Use the following checklist:

■ Awareness of the audience (greet your audience, grab their attention, etc.)

■ Formal register

■ Clear structure

■ Rhetorical devices

■ Strong impression at the end

Selected articles from the UN Rights of the Child

Article 3: Adults should do what is best for you.

Article 6: You have the right to be alive.

Article 14: You have the right to think what you like and be whatever religion you want to be.

Article 15: You have the right to make friends.

Article 17: You have the right to collect information from radios, newspapers, television, books, etc. from all around the world.

Article 19: No one should hurt you in any way.

Article 24: You have a right to good health.

Article 27: You have the right to food, clothes and a place to live.

Article 28: You have a right to education.

Article 30: You have the right to enjoy your own culture, practise your own religion and use your own language.

Article 31: You have the right to play.

Article 37: You should not be put in prison.

■ TOK Links

How to measure happiness?

In honour of Children's Day, international NGO Save the Children released its 'End of Childhood Index 2017'.

The ranking highlights the best and worst places for children to grow up across 172 countries, taking into account things like mortality rates, child-labour laws, threats of violence and rates of disease.

The best places for children, the report finds, provide ample access to health care, education and social support. This assessment assumes that greater access to welfare would make children happy. By and large, it's probably true. However, at this point, we might want to ask ourselves how we measure 'happiness', and whether it is even possible.

Jeremy Bentham (1748–1832) defines happiness as the sum of pleasures. The problem is that it is difficult to see how different pleasures can be measured on a common scale. We might also question the idea that a constant stream of pleasures makes for a happy life. You only have to think of the lives of some of the idle rich to see that someone can have a great deal of pleasure and yet still be bored and unhappy.

So when we see Norway voted the best country for children, do we think that children in Norway are happier than those in other countries?

CREATIVITY, ACTIVITY, SERVICE

Poverty is a huge global issue, and it is often a hindrance to implementing children's rights in many countries. Oxfam is a global charity organization of people who share the belief that, in a world rich in resources, poverty isn't inevitable. Find out more about Oxfam and get involved in its fight against poverty: www.oxfam.org

3 Women's rights

International Women's Day is held annually on 8 March to celebrate women's achievements throughout history and across nations. It is also known as the United Nation (UN) Day for Women's Rights and International Peace. On this day, various events including seminars, conferences, luncheons and dinners are organized to remind us of the importance of the half of the population whose equal rights are not yet universally achieved.

Although much progress has been made to protect and promote women's rights in recent times, nowhere in the world can women claim to have all the same rights and opportunities as men, according to the UN. On average, women receive between 30 and 40 per cent less pay than men earn for the same work. Women also continue to be victims of violence, with rape and domestic violence listed as significant causes of disability and death among women worldwide.

The first International Women's Day occurred on 19 March 1911. This inaugural event, which included rallies and organized meetings, was a big success in countries such as Austria, Denmark, Germany and Switzerland. The 19 March date was chosen because it commemorated the day that the Prussian King promised to introduce votes for women in 1848. The promise gave hope for equality, but it was a promise that he failed to keep. The International Women's Day date was moved to 8 March in 1913, and was declared as an annual event by the UN General Assembly in 1977.

A **Before reading the article below, discuss the meaning of the following words:**

- counterparts
- fundamental
- declare
- eligible
- incorporated
- consolidated
- suffrage
- derogatory
- abusive
- custody
- entitlement
- parity

Seven reasons we still need to fight for women's human rights

Human rights are the basic minimum protection that every human being should be able to enjoy. But historically not all people have been able to enjoy and exercise their rights in the same way. The result is unequal treatment.

One such group is women and girls. Throughout history, women have been afforded fewer rights than their male counterparts or have had to work harder to realise their rights in practice. Viewing women's rights as human rights has been fundamental in the struggle to ensure that women are treated fairly. As part of our series for International Women's Day, we are taking a look at how women have fought to be put on an equal footing.

[1] _____

A British court once actually had to declare that women counted as 'persons' in order for them to receive the same treatment as men.

In 1929, a woman named Emily Murphy applied for a position in the Canadian Senate (a house of the Canadian Parliament). She was refused because women were not at the time considered 'persons' under section 24 of the British North America Act 1867. This understanding was based on a British ruling from 1876 that stated that women were 'eligible for pains and penalties, but not rights and privileges'.

Emily Murphy took her case to the Privy Council, the court of last resort in the British Empire.

The judges declared that women were 'persons' who could sit in the Canadian Senate. One of the judges, Lord Sankey, said: 'to those who ask why the word "person" should include females, the obvious answer is why should it not?'

[2] _____

In 1765, a famous legal commentator, Sir William Blackstone, wrote that after marriage, the 'very being or legal existence of the woman is … incorporated and consolidated into that of her husband'. In other words, a married woman did not, legally speaking, exist separately from her husband.

When a woman married, all of her property was automatically placed under the control of her husband. In 1870, an Act of Parliament allowed married women to keep money they earned and to inherit certain property. In 1882, this was extended to allow wives a right to own, buy and sell property in their own right. In 1893 married women were granted control of any property they acquired during marriage.

[3] _____

Before 1918, women were not allowed to vote in parliamentary elections. This meant that they had no say in choosing the people who made law, and those law-makers had no political incentive to care about women, since they did not need to win their votes.

In the early 20th century, activist groups campaigned for women's right to vote ('suffrage'). One such group was the suffragettes. The term 'suffragette' was first used by the *Daily Mail* in 1906. It was intended as a derogatory name for an activist group run by Emmeline Pankhurst and her daughters. In 1913, suffragette Emily Wilding Davison was fatally injured after she ran up to the King's horse, racing at the Epsom Derby.

In 1918, the Representation of the People Act first gave women over the age of 30 the right to vote if they or their husband met a property qualification. The Parliament (Qualification of Women) Act also allowed women to stand for election as Members of Parliament. It took until 1928 (the Equal Franchise Act) for all women in Britain to gain equal voting rights with men.

[4] _____

In 1878, the University of London became the first university in the UK to open its degrees to women. In 1880, four women became the first to obtain degrees when they were awarded Bachelor of Arts by the university. Nowadays, millions of women and girls around the world are still systematically excluded from even basic education.

[5] _____

Before 1839, mothers had no rights at all in relation to their children if their marriage broke down. In 1836, Caroline Norton left her husband, George, who had been abusive towards her. After the separation, George refused Caroline access to their sons. After much campaigning, an Act of Parliament was passed in 1839 giving mothers the right to ask for custody of their children.

In the late 20th century, women gained greater control over whether or not to have children. Initially, it was a criminal offence in the UK to perform an abortion or to try to self-abort. This led to a high number of unsafe back-street abortions – a major cause of pregnancy-related deaths. To address this, Parliament passed the Abortion Act 1967 to permit abortions under medical supervision and subject to certain criteria. In 1974, contraception also became freely available to all women irrespective of marital status through the NHS.

[6] _____

In 1878, the law first said that a woman could obtain an order allowing her to separate from her husband if her husband subjected her to violence. In 1976, an Act of Parliament allowed women in danger of domestic violence to obtain the court's protection from their violent partner.

[7] _____

In 1968, women at the Ford car factory in Dagenham took part in a strike for equal pay, almost stopping production at all Ford UK plants. Their protest led to the passing of the Equal Pay Act 1970, though they had to wait until 1983 (the Equal Pay (Amendment) Regulations) for a legal entitlement to equal pay for work of equal value.

The Equality Act 2010 consolidated the law protecting women from discrimination in the workplace on the grounds of sex or maternity. In 2016, the government published a consultation on proposals for a law to require certain companies in England, Scotland and Wales to publish gender pay gap statistics.

So, how far have we still got to go for equality?

In 1977, the United Nations General Assembly declared International Women's Day an annual event. In 2015, the World Economic Forum predicted that global gender parity would, at the current rate of progress, not be achieved until 2133: 114 years from now. Many women's rights have been hard won over a centuries-long struggle for equality. Do we have to wait another century before we can finally say women are equal?

www.amnesty.org.uk/blogs/yes-minister-it-human-rights-issue/seven-reasons-we-still-need-fight-womens-human-rights

B **Read the article and answer the following questions:**

1 Read the text and choose an appropriate heading from the list below for each of the paragraphs numbered 1–7.

> **a** Women need legal protection from violence, including in the home
>
> **b** Married women were the same legal person … as their husband
>
> **c** Women weren't even people, legally speaking
>
> **d** Women still don't have access to education
>
> **e** Women (still) struggle to achieve equality in the workplace
>
> **f** Women had to fight to access their children and plan their families
>
> **g** Women had to fight really hard for the right to vote

2 To whom or to what do the underlined words refer? Answer using words as they appear in the text.
   a 'work harder to realise <u>their</u> rights in practice.' (introduction)
   b '<u>She</u> was refused because women were not at the time…' (section 1)
   c 'why should <u>it</u> not?' (section 1)
   d 'incorporated and consolidated into <u>that</u> of her husband.' (section 2)
   e 'since <u>they</u> did not need to win their votes.' (section 3)
   f '<u>It</u> was intended as a derogatory name…' (section 3)
   g 'to open <u>its</u> degrees to women.' (section 4)
   h '<u>Their</u> protest led to the passing of the Equal Pay Act 1970, …' (section 7)

3 Find the word in the right-hand column that could meaningfully replace each of the phrases from the text on the left – one word for each phrase. There will be five words left over.

   a   in relation to (section 5)   i   participated
   b   irrespective of (section 5)   ii   took control
   c   took part (section 7)   iii   gap
   d   entitlement (section 7)   iv   related
   e   parity (last section)   v   regardless of
                                         vi   regarding
                                         vii   case
                                         viii   equality
                                         ix   right
                                         x   disrespectful toward

Grammar

Emphasis 3: negative and limiting adverbials

You can put **negative and limiting adverbs or adverbials** at the beginning of a sentence to add emphasis:

- ***Never have*** *I been so scared in all my life.*
- ***Only then do*** *you find yourself saying, 'That was amazing!'*

Negative adverbials are expressions with the word *no, not* or *never*. They include *never before, at no time, no sooner … than, no way, not since* and *not until.*

Limiting (or restrictive) adverbials include *hardly … when, rarely, seldom* and expressions with *only* such as *only when, only after* and *not only.*

- ***No sooner had*** *he attached the elastic rope to me than I was falling…*
- ***Seldom have*** *I been so scared!*
- ***Hardly had*** *I reached the top* ***when*** *I was falling to the bottom…*

Notice the word order of these sentences. It is the same word order as is found in questions.

Rewrite each sentence starting with the adverb or adverbial.

1 I have rarely tasted anything so disgusting!

Rarely…

2 We had hardly started class when the fire alarm rang.

Hardly…

3 It seldom rains at this time of year.

Seldom…

4 My parents never want to go on a cruise again.

Never…

5 You don't often see Michaela work that hard.

Not often…

6 There's no way we're going to work for less money!

No way…

7 There hasn't been an Olympic Gold medallist from our country since 1988.

Not since 1988…

Practical Grammar Level 3 by John Hughes and Ceri Jones

Statements

1 With a partner, discuss the following statements. Limit your time to one minute for each statement.

a Girls get away with more than boys.
b Boys are naturally more violent than girls.
c Girls who wear short skirts are 'asking for it'.
d Girls and boys are always treated equally in this school.
e Everyone should be able to enjoy their human rights.
f Poor people don't have the same rights as rich people.
g Equality is impossible, so it's not worth trying to achieve it.
h Men and women are different, so they can't be equal.
i Being male or female makes no difference to whether you do well at work.
j Pictures of topless women in some newspapers should be banned.
k Doing something 'like a girl' should not be used as an insult.
l Little girls should not be called princesses.

Who said this?

2 Read the following statements. Discuss with a partner and decide whether you think each statement is most likely to have been spoken by a male or a female and try to guess the context in which it is spoken.

	Male / Female / Either?	Context – which country? Why?
a 'Several times my older brother has beaten me up. He also tells me "you go ahead and go to school and I'll throw acid on you".'		
b 'When I complained about not getting paid, he called the police to beat me up.'		
c 'Once I arrived I was introduced to a lady. She took my travel documents and my mobile phone. She said she had bought me, she owned me and that I had to pay back the debt.'		
d 'I wanted to get an education, but my parents were determined to marry me off.'		

e 'When my mother died in childbirth I had to give up school to care for my brothers and sisters.'		
f 'When they gave me the job they said they weren't sure that I'd "hack the pace". So they said they'd pay me less until I'd proved myself.'		
g 'In the morning, I fetch water then I walk to school. One day I arrived late. As punishment my teacher asked me to crawl on my bare knees across the ground from the school gate to the classroom.'		

www.womankind.org.uk

E **Emma Watson's speech at a United Nations event (published by HeForShe) is available on YouTube, entitled 'Emma Watson HeForShe Speech at the United Nations' at www.youtube.com/watch?v=Q0Dg226G2Z8&feature=youtu.be. Listen to her speech and answer these questions:**

1 When she made this speech, how long had Emma Watson been acting as UN Women's Goodwill Ambassador?

2 What has fighting for women's rights become synonymous with?

3 What is the definition of feminism?

4 Emma Watson shares her experience of gender bias. Copy and complete the table below.

Age	Experience of gender bias
8	
14	
15	
18	

5 List at least three words that are negatively associated with feminism.

6 How many countries have achieved gender equality?

7 What do men suffer from as a result of gender bias?

8 What is one main benefit of gender equality?

9 How many more years is it expected to take to achieve gender pay equality?

10 By when are all rural African girls anticipated to receive secondary school education?

11 What two questions does Emma Watson want us to ask ourselves?

12 Which of the following human rights is Emma Watson talking about?
   a Article 1 – Right to Equality
   b Article 4 – Freedom from Slavery
   c Article 18 – Freedom of Belief and Religion
   d Article 26 – Right to Education

F ■ **Task 1: To write an embedded interview**

Imagine you have recently interviewed Emma Watson regarding women's rights. Write the embedded interview (**not** the transcript) for your school newspaper. An embedded interview is essentially an article, based on description and commentary, with liberal quotation that can be either direct quotation or reported speech. Use the following checklist:

■ Heading, byline and date

■ Engaging introduction

■ Engaging tone and appropriate register

■ Body paragraphs based on the interview (focus on the main topic of discussion)

■ Effective direct quotation

Task 2: To write a blog entry

Imagine you have experienced a negative effect of gender bias. (If you think hard enough, you probably don't have to imagine!) Write a blog entry where you share your experience and attempt to raise awareness of prevalent gender inequality. Use the following checklist:

- Eye-catching title
- Introduction
- Body paragraphs
- Conclusion
- Awareness of the audience

TOK Links

Truth

When faced with a truth that betrays our general belief and centuries-long social traditions, people find it hard to believe that truth despite the evidence. This is because people often believe what they want to believe rather than what is justified by the evidence. Some people are reluctant to disturb their peace of mind by questioning their fundamental assumptions and prefer to inhabit their own comfortable illusions rather than face up to harsh and unsettling truths. To protect their beliefs, they may use a variety of *defence mechanisms*, such as **selective attention** (seeing what they want to see), **rationalization** (manufacturing reasons to justify their prejudices) and **communal reinforcement** (mixing exclusively with people who hold similar beliefs).

Theory of Knowledge for the IB Diploma *by Richard van de Lagemaat*

Imagine that you strongly believe in traditional gender roles. You feel uncomfortable about the idea of gender equality, and you think the world would be a better place if we all just fulfilled our gender roles and social rules set by previous generations. How would you feel and what would you do when you were faced with the uncomfortable truth of gender equality? Would you use any of the defence mechanisms mentioned above?

CREATIVITY, ACTIVITY, SERVICE

HeForShe

The HeForShe solidarity movement was created by UN Women including Emma Watson to provide a systematic approach and targeted platform where a global audience can engage and become change agents for the achievement of gender equality in our lifetime. This requires an innovative, inclusive approach that mobilizes people of every gender identity and expression as advocates, and acknowledges the ways that we all benefit from this equality. You can find out more information about this movement at www.heforshe.org. There are many ways in which you can get involved.

■ Literature

4 1984

1984 (*Nineteen Eighty-Four*) is a classic dystopian novel by English author George Orwell, published in 1949. The story is that of Winston Smith, who lives in Oceania, ruled by a totalitarian government called the 'Party' whose leader is Big Brother. Winston Smith is a Party member, but secretly hates the Party. The following excerpt comes from the beginning of this novel.

The hallway smelt of boiled cabbage and old rag mats. At one end of it a coloured poster, too large for indoor display, had been tacked to the wall. It depicted simply an enormous
5 face, more than a metre wide: the face of a man of about forty-five, with a heavy black moustache and ruggedly handsome features. Winston made for the stairs. It was no use trying the lift. Even at the best of times it was
10 seldom working, and at present the electric current was cut off during daylight hours. It was part of the economy drive in preparation for Hate Week. The flat was seven flights up, and Winston, who was thirty-nine and had
15 a varicose ulcer above his right ankle, went slowly, resting several times on the way. On each landing, opposite the lift-shaft, the poster with the enormous face gazed from the wall. It was one of those pictures which are so
20 contrived that the eyes follow you about when you move. BIG BROTHER IS WATCHING YOU, the caption beneath it ran.

Inside the flat a fruity voice was reading out a list of figures which had something
25 to do with the production of pig-iron. The voice came from an oblong metal plaque like a dulled mirror which formed part of the surface of the right-hand wall. Winston turned a switch and the voice sank somewhat,
30 though the words were still distinguishable. The instrument (the telescreen, it was called) could be dimmed, but there was no way of shutting it off completely. He moved over to the window: a smallish, frail figure, the
35 meagreness of his body merely emphasized by the blue overalls which were the uniform of the party. His hair was very fair, his face naturally sanguine, his skin roughened by coarse soap and blunt razor blades and the
40 cold of the winter that had just ended.

Outside, even through the shut window-pane, the world looked cold. Down in the street little eddies of wind were whirling dust and torn paper into spirals, and though the sun
45 was shining and the sky a harsh blue, there seemed to be no colour in anything, except the posters that were plastered everywhere. The blackmoustachio'd face gazed down from every commanding corner. There was one
50 on the house-front immediately opposite. BIG BROTHER IS WATCHING YOU, the caption said, while the dark eyes looked deep into Winston's own. Down at street level another poster, torn at one corner, flapped fitfully in
55 the wind, alternately covering and uncovering the single word INGSOC. In the far distance a helicopter skimmed down between the roofs, hovered for an instant like a bluebottle, and darted away again with a curving
60 flight. It was the police patrol, snooping into people's windows. The patrols did not matter, however. Only the Thought Police mattered.

Behind Winston's back the voice from the telescreen was still babbling away about
65 pig-iron and the overfulfilment of the Ninth Three-Year Plan. The telescreen received and transmitted simultaneously. Any sound that Winston made, above the level of a very low whisper, would be picked up by it, moreover,
70 so long as he remained within the field of vision which the metal plaque commanded, he could be seen as well as heard. There was of course no way of knowing whether you were being watched at any given moment.
75 How often, or on what system, the Thought Police plugged in on any individual wire was guesswork. It was even conceivable that they watched everybody all the time. But at any rate they could plug in your wire whenever
80 they wanted to. You had to live – did live,

from habit that became instinct – in the
assumption that every sound you made was
overheard, and, except in darkness, every
movement scrutinized.

85 Winston kept his back turned to the
telescreen. It was safer, though, as he well
knew, even a back can be revealing.
A kilometre away the Ministry of Truth, his
place of work, towered vast and white above
90 the grimy landscape. This, he thought with
a sort of vague distaste – this was London,
chief city of Airstrip One, itself the third
most populous of the provinces of Oceania.
He tried to squeeze out some childhood
95 memory that should tell him whether London
had always been quite like this. Were there

always these vistas of rotting nineteenth-
century houses, their sides shored up with
baulks of timber, their windows patched with
100 cardboard and their roofs with corrugated
iron, their crazy garden walls sagging in all
directions? And the bombed sites where
the plaster dust swirled in the air and the
willow-herb straggled over the heaps of
105 rubble; and the places where the bombs had
cleared a larger patch and there had sprung
up sordid colonies of wooden dwellings like
chicken-houses? But it was no use, he could
not remember: nothing remained of his
110 childhood except a series of brightlit tableaux
occurring against no background and mostly
unintelligible.

Excerpt from 1984 by George Orwell (1949)

A Answer the following questions:

1 Which phrase between lines 1 and 11 describes a distinctive physical feature of the man in the huge poster displayed in the hallway?

2 Which phrase between lines 1 and 11 best describes the state of the lift?

3 What is the main reason that electricity is not provided during daylight hours?

4 Find four phrases that describe Winston's physical appearance.

5 Which phrase between lines 21 and 31 indicates the ever-present nature of the poster?

B Choose the correct answer from a, b, c or d for each question.

1 The block of flats where Winston lived was…
   a well-maintained   c dysfunctional
   b brand-new   d under-occupied

2 The telescreen was…
   a easy for Winston to switch on   c tailor-made to Winston's needs
   b centrally controlled   d impossible to turn off

3 The police patrol was…
   a looking out for criminals   c controlled by the Thought Police
   b insignificant   d potent

4 The Thought Police…
   a used the telescreen to watch people   c scrutinized your movements only in the darkness
   b was plugged in to the telescreen   d used a method that everyone understood clearly

5 London, chief city of Airstrip One,…
   a had changed dramatically since   c had all the official government buildings
      Winston's childhood
   b was the most populated city in Oceania   d had many modern buildings

C Copy and complete the following table by indicating to whom or to what the underlined word refers:

In the phrase...	the word...	refers to...
1 At one end of <u>it</u> a coloured poster, too large… (line 2)	'it'	
2 the caption beneath <u>it</u> ran… (line 22)	'it'	
3 There was <u>one</u> on the house-front immediately… (line 49)	'one'	
4 would be picked up by <u>it</u>, moreover, … (line 69)	'it'	

UNIT 15 Globalization

REFLECTION

Think individually about the questions below. Then pair with a partner and discuss the questions. Share your ideas with the rest of the class.

- What does 'globalization' mean?
- What are the pros and cons of globalization?
- Do you think it would be a good idea if all barriers to trade were removed from the world and people could freely export and import without customs duties or any other problems? What impact would such a change have?
- Do you think it would be a good idea if people could live and work in any country they liked without restriction? What impact would such a change have?
- 'Protectionism' refers to the practice of putting up trade barriers such as import duties so as to reduce or prevent the importation of goods from poorer countries and protect higher cost industries in more developed nations. What do you think of the morality of excluding goods from poor or developing countries?
- One frequently quoted example of globalization is McDonald's. Some people say that McDonald's restaurants are a bad thing because they mean that everybody eats the same food; others say that they are a good thing because you are always able to eat something you recognize, know and like. What is your opinion?
- Considering that cities around the world are becoming increasingly homogenous (think McDonald's, KFC, Coke, sushi, pizza, kebab, Tesco, Hollywood films, CNN, MTV, E!TV, ESPN, shopping malls, and so on) while simultaneously offering inhabitants greater choice and opportunities than they had before globalization, what opportunities have appeared in your region due to globalization?
- What impact does globalization have on the environment? Is the impact negative or positive, or both?

Globalisation or globalization?

'Globalization' and 'globalisation' both mean the same thing: the process of interaction and integration between people, companies and governments worldwide. The only difference is the spelling: 'globalization' is mostly used in America, while 'globalisation' is used in Britain. You often see differences in spelling of American and British English, for example 'colour' in British English is 'color' in American English. Can you think of more examples of differences between British English and American English spelling?

1 Cultural globalization

Globalization is the process by which the world is becoming increasingly interconnected as a result of massively increased trade and cultural exchange. Globalization has been taking place for hundreds of years but has sped up enormously over the last half-century mainly due to technological advances.

As a result of globalization, we now exchange our ideas and cultures more easily. This cultural globalization has been seen as a trend toward homogeneity that will eventually make human experience everywhere essentially the same. Will we really have one single world culture in the future? Or will we have more diverse cultures all around the world influenced by global cultures?

A Before reading the article below, discuss the meaning of the following words:

- accoutrements
- hubris
- benign
- belligerent
- totalitarian

- obliterated
- concertinaed
- engendering
- personification
- paradox

We are globalized, but have no real intimacy with the rest of the world

The underlying assumption with globalization is that the whole world is moving in the same direction, towards the same destination: it is becoming, and should become, more and more like the west. Where once democracy was not suitable for anyone else, now everyone is required to adopt it, with all its western-style accoutrements.

In short, globalization has brought with it a new kind of western hubris – present in Europe in a relatively benign form, manifest in the US in the belligerent manner befitting a superpower: that western values and arrangements should be those of the world; that they are of universal application and merit. At the heart of globalization is a new kind of intolerance in the west towards other cultures, traditions and values, less brutal than in the era of colonialism, but more comprehensive and totalitarian.

The idea that each culture is possessed of its own specific wisdom and characteristics, its own novelty and uniqueness, born of its own individual struggle over thousands of years to cope with nature and circumstance, has been drowned out by the hue and cry that the world is now one, that the western model – neoliberal markets, democracy and the rest – is the template for all.

The new attitude is driven by many factors. The emergence of an increasingly globalized market has engendered a belief that we are all consumers now, all of a basically similar identity, with our Big Macs, mobile phones and jeans. In this kind of reductionist thinking, the distance between buying habits and cultural/political mores is close to zero: the latter simply follows from the former. Nor is

this kind of thinking confined to the business world, even if it remains the heartland. This is also now an integral part of popular common sense, and more resonant and potent as an international language because consumption has become the mass ideology of western societies. The fact that television and tourism have made the whole world accessible has created the illusion that we enjoy intimate knowledge of other places, when we barely scratch their surface. For the vast majority, the knowledge of Thailand or Sri Lanka acquired through tourism consists of little more than the whereabouts of the beach.

The net effect of all this is a lack of knowledge of and respect for difference. Globalization has obliterated distance, not just physically but also, most dangerously, mentally. It creates the illusion of intimacy when, in fact, the mental distances have changed little. It has concertinaed the world without engendering the necessary respect, recognition and tolerance that must accompany it. Globalization is itself an exemplar of the problem. Goods and capital may move far more freely than ever before, but the movement of labour has barely changed. Jeans may be inanimate, but migrants are the personification of difference. Everywhere, migration is a charged political issue. In the modern era of globalization, everything is allowed to move except people.

We live in a world that we are much more intimate with and yet, at the same time, also much more intolerant of – unless, that is, it conforms to our way of thinking. It is the western condition of globalisation, and its paradox of intimacy and intolerance suggests that the western reaction to the remorseless rise of the non-west will be far from benign.

www.theguardian.com/commentisfree/2006/apr/17/comment.globalisation

B **Answer the following questions:**

1 What are the factors driving globalization?

2 Why do you think the writer uses the phrase 'with our Big Macs, mobile phones and jeans'?

3 Choose the correct phrases from the text to complete the following sentences. Base your answers on information as it appears in the text. Use no more than five words for each sentence.

    a Western hubris has brought the idea that Western values should be _____.

    b An increasingly globalized market has encouraged a belief that our identities are now _____.

    c Television and tourism have created the illusion that we know other places well, but really we _____.

    d Globalization means everything should be allowed to move freely but that migration has become _____.

4 From statements a to d, select the two that correspond to the paragraph that starts 'In short, globalization has brought with it…'.

    a America is more powerful in its belief that Western values should be those of the world than Europe.

    b Western values can still be applied differently across the continents.

    c Other cultures have been marginalized since colonialism.

    d Western values are the easiest to adopt and that is why Europe and America believe they should be the values of the world.

5 From statements a to d, select the two that correspond to the paragraph that starts 'The new attitude is driven…'.

    a Items such as Big Macs, jeans and mobile phones symbolize the idea that consumers all have the same identity.

    b We can learn everything we need about other cultures through television.

    c Tourism is being reduced to just visiting beaches, not discovering new cultures.

    d Consumption is the mass ideology of western societies, but only applies to the business world.

6 From statements a to d, select the two that correspond to the paragraph that starts 'The net effect of all this…'.

    a Globalization brings people physically closer so we are able to connect more.

    b Physically the world has changed quickly but our tolerance of difference and other cultures hasn't evolved at the same rate.

    c Migration has become a symbol of the intolerance to difference.

    d Labour, goods and capital all move freely due to globalization.

7 From statements a to d, select the two that correspond to the whole article.

    a The writer believes that the negatives of globalization can be changed.

    b The writer believes the West will celebrate the rise of other cultures and powers.

    c The writer believes the opposite ideas of intimacy and intolerance are a factor of globalization.

    d The writer believes that individual and unique cultures are slowly being squashed by the values of the West.

Grammar

Reduced relative clauses

If the verb in the **relative clause** is in the active form, use the present participle (-*ing*):

- **Relative clause:** *Passengers who travel without a valid ticket will receive a fine.*

- **Reduced relative clause:** *Passengers **travelling** without a valid ticket will receive a fine.*

If the verb in the relative clause is in the passive form, use the past participle form:

- **Relative clause:** *Metro police will remove and destroy any bags that are left unattended.*

- **Reduced relative clause:** *Metro Police will remove and destroy any bags **left** unattended.*

C Complete the sentences using only the verb in brackets in the correct form.

1 Anyone _____ (drive) over the speed limit will be stopped.

2 Any employee _____ (work) hard could receive a bonus this month.

3 Passengers _____ (wait) for trains can use the waiting room on Platform 2.

4 Letters _____ (send) with a 1st class stamp arrive the following day.

5 Any items _____ (leave) in the classroom at the end of term will be thrown away.

6 Glass _____ (put) in green bins is recycled.

7 The people _____ (live) in this house have been here for years.

8 Many products _____ (buy) online are much cheaper than in the shops.

9 There is a fine for any library books _____ (return) late.

10 We'll give a reward to anyone _____ (provide) the police with information about the missing jewels.

Practical Grammar Level 3 by John Hughes and Ceri Jones

D Cultural globalization is the process of global cultural exchange among countries as a result of globalization. If your country's cultural globalization was in your control, what parts of the cultures would you keep, remove and import?

- **Think:** Copy and complete the table below. Think carefully, as culture is a broad concept.
- **Pair:** Once you've filled in your table, share your ideas with a partner.
- **Share:** Share your ideas with the rest of the group, if possible.

Three parts of the culture of your country that you would like to keep	Three parts of the culture of your country that you would like to remove	Three parts of the cultures of other countries that you would like to import to your country

E Listen to the beginning of the lecture on Globalization and the Cultural Exception and answer the following questions (www.coursera.org/lecture/america-through-foreign-eyes/chapter-5-globalization-and-the-cultural-exception-hiSzV). You are allowed to listen twice.

1 What is globalization often misunderstood as?

2 What do many Americans think the French are against?

3 What do the French believe should be exempted from the laws of supply and demand?

4 List at least two things that the French do to ensure culture is not commercialized.

5 What did Jack Valenti, the American head of Hollywood's Motion Picture Association, compare culture with?

6 Choose the **five** true statements.

a We all understand the same meaning of globalization.

b There are many French multinational corporations.

c The United States doesn't protect its economy as much as France.

d As an EU member state, France rarely negotiates its global partnerships independently.

e France is a strong advocate of cultural exception.

f Cultural exception is the French government policy that is not supported by the French public.

g The French government protects its culture through taxes, subsidies, quotas and regulations.

h In France, quotas are imposed in television and music.

i France is the only EU member state that allows cultural exception in trade agreements.

j France and America have opposing ideas when it comes to culture.

■ Task 1: To write an essay

Write an essay based on the following stimulus:

'It is important to preserve global cultural diversity from the homogenization or the uniformization that happens naturally with globalization when its supply of cultural goods is made to appeal to the largest, therefore lowest, common denominator of mass opinion.' Use the following checklist:

- Title
- Clear introduction, body and conclusion
- Formal register
- Clear viewpoint
- Development of your ideas

■ Task 2: To write an editorial

You have recently noticed that your community is obsessed with American culture. An increasing number of young people watch American TV, listen to American music, eat at American fast-food restaurants and are interested in American politics far more than their own. Write an editorial to express your concerns and raise awareness of cultural homogenization. You may suggest ways in which we can ensure global cultural diversity. Use the following checklist:

- Heading
- Introduction, body and conclusion
- An objective explanation of the issue
- Opinions from the opposing viewpoint
- A solid and concise conclusion
- Formal or semi-formal register

■ TOK Links

Emotions as an obstacle to knowledge

If you see globalization as a move towards global homogeneity and if you do not like the idea of a homogenous world, you may develop a strong dislike of the word 'globalization'. Your dislike may be intensified by the dominant American culture presiding all over the world. Once you develop a strong emotion, you are likely to be biased, as strong emotions can distort your perception. For example, if you like somebody, you are likely to be blind to their faults; if you hate them, you are likely to see only their faults. Your emotions can hinder your objective perception.

We need to acknowledge our emotions as an obstacle to knowledge and put them aside when we wish to truly understand something.

CREATIVITY, ACTIVITY, SERVICE

Creativity

For a CAS project, you and your classmates can plan, design and create a poster or a mural based on the theme of globalization. What would be your learning outcome(s)? You are always welcome to modify expected outcomes during the CAS project and / or its completion. Remember a minimum of one month is recommended for a CAS project, from planning to completion.

2 Trade globalization

Trade globalization is a type of economic globalization through which an individual, a company or a country can expand its market and integrate into the global economy. A much-improved infrastructure and transport system after the Second World War helped multinational companies grow substantially in the world market. We now see such global brands all over the world: McDonald's, Starbucks, Gucci, Chanel, and so on.

Further to these significant changes brought by multinational companies, online businesses are now re-shaping the global market. While we have huge multinational online retailers such as Amazon, we also have small online businesses that thrive in the global market. Individuals and big or small companies take advantage of the broader outreach of an online customer base. With the benefits of technology, you can now set up a business in your own house or garage that could reach out to customers all over the world. How do you think the global market will change in the next phase?

 A **Before reading the article below, discuss the meaning of the following words:**

- sprawling
- decimated
- imperialist capitalism
- anonymous
- sinister
- prophesied

- forged
- outsourcing
- offset
- undercut
- monopoly

 B **Read the article and answer the following questions:**

1 Match the first part of each sentence on the left with the appropriate ending on the right. There are more endings than necessary.

Impact of globalization on small businesses

The following is a classic story, often used by socialists to highlight the 'evils of a capitalist society' – the small-town grocer gets mercilessly taken out by the new Wal-Mart in town. The small-town grocer may have an established customer base and friendly relations with the community, but it simply can't match the low prices offered by Wal-Mart. Being a large national company, Wal-Mart has sprawling global resources and is willing to sacrifice margins to take out local competitors. In the end, customer loyalty means nothing, and the grocer goes bankrupt; decades of hard work decimated overnight. This is a well-known anecdote referring to the impact of globalization on small businesses. Once you start up a new business, you plunge into an ocean populated by a few smaller fish, which compete with you for food, and lots of bigger ones, eager to eat you alive. The big fish in the sea tend to be well-connected, multinational beasts taking full advantage of the perks of globalization – such as outsourcing, uneven exchange rates and low-margin high-volume sales models – making them nearly impossible to compete against. What are the impacts of globalization on the small-business owner, and how can you defend yourself from the blows that will inevitably come your way?

Globalized brands

In *The Communist Manifesto*, Karl Marx famously warned that small local businesses will inevitably be wiped out by large multinational companies in a form of imperialist capitalism. According to him, the destruction of local businesses leads to the loss of local culture, and the rise of a singular anonymous corporate culture that varies only slightly from country to country. Visiting China today, it's hard to argue with Marx's words. The urban landscape is littered with KFCs, Pizza Huts, McDonald's and Starbucks. A trip to a Chinese department store is virtually identical to one in America, with the same multinational brands – Armani, Coach, Chanel, Gucci – lining the halls like an anonymous duty-free airport shop.

However, at a closer glance, today's multinational companies are a far cry from the sinister imperialists that Marx prophesied. Brands are highly localized to accommodate local tastes, and companies have forged mutually beneficial relationships with foreign countries to further their sales. Foreign governments are also quick to kick out offenders who don't play by the rules.

While some small businesses – such as the aforementioned local grocer – have suffered, there are those that have avoided being crushed by a large, globalized company. In China, there are still plenty of successful small restaurants and coffee shops, despite the rise of American multinational eateries. How did these restaurants survive? By providing local menu items – such as dumplings, noodles, Peking duck – that those chains lack the expertise to make. The lesson for a small business is simple – don't keep making hamburgers when a McDonald's comes to town. Sell something else.

Exchange rates and outsourcing

There was a time, decades ago, that 'Made in the USA' meant well-made products that you could be patriotically proud of. Today, 'Made in the USA' usually means paying high labor costs, dealing with labor unions and earning hopelessly tiny profits on slim product margins. It was due to this that outsourcing – or shifting your production base to another country – became attractive. Lower material and labor costs in a country with a weaker currency boosts profits considerably.

Small businesses usually don't have the advantage of forging outsourcing partnerships with overseas factories, and are at a severe disadvantage in pricing. Multinational corporations, such as Wal-Mart, tend to exploit this business model to the fullest, creating extremely cheap goods in China, marking them up only slightly and earning only a slim margin on each product. The goal of this business model is to use high sales volume to offset its low profit per product. A more immediate goal is to undercut any local competitors, who are physically unable to match those low prices due to the lack of an outsourcing infrastructure, and wipe them out with a pricing war. After all these local competitors have been eliminated, Wal-Mart is free to raise prices again, since it has established itself as a local monopoly.

As a small business, it's nearly impossible to protect yourself from this kind of assault. If you want to stand your ground and fight, then the best strategy is to ally yourself with other local businesses and pool your resources. Offer free cross-advertising campaigns and attack the large multinational threat together. While you can't offer discounts on all your products to fight back, offering rotating sales on select products can attract customers. In an all-out war against the big guys, the enemy of your enemy is your best friend.

Stay defensive

Small businesses often drop like flies when targeted by a multinational corporation with strong globalized ties. However, forging a strong identity and solid alliances with small competitors can increase your chances of survival, so that your small business lives to see the day that it matures into a globalized company.

Leo Sun

www.businessdictionary.com/article/583/impact-of-globalization-on-small-businesses

a The story of the small-town grocer getting taken over by the new Wal-Mart in town

b The competitive prices offered by large multinational companies

c Outsourcing is one of the important strategies deployed by

d Karl Marx predicted that

e Today's multinational companies

iii are unbeatable by the small local businesses.

iv highlights the evils of a capitalist society.

v dominate their relationships with foreign countries.

vi globalized companies to cut costs of production.

vii imperialist capitalism would wipe out large multinational companies.

viii is irrelevant to imperialist capitalism.

ix the destruction of local businesses would lead to cultural homogenization.

x small businesses to compete against large companies.

2 Are the following sentences true or false? Justify your answers by quoting a relevant phrase from the text.

a Foreign governments have no say in how multinational companies operate in their country.

i are willing to sacrifice margins to take out local competitors.

ii localize their brands to accommodate local culture.

b Small restaurants in China that serve local menu items survived the rise of the American multinational restaurants.

c Multinational corporations compensate their low profit margin per product by high sales volume.

d Small businesses are advised to create partnerships with global companies and work together.

e Small businesses would always wish to stay local.

Grammar

Alternatives to *if*

Unless (= if … not or only if):
- She won't go to sleep **unless** you tell her a story.

Providing / provided (that), on condition that, as / so long as (= only if):
- She will go to sleep **providing that** you tell her a story.

But for (= if it had not been for, if … not):
- **But for** your warning, we wouldn't have realized the danger.

Whether … or not (= it doesn't matter which of these situations):
- **Whether** governments like it **or not**, they have to give more aid to the developing world.

Suppose / supposing, what if (used to talk about imaginary situations):
- **What if** your plan fails – what then?
- **Suppose** you won the Lottery, what would you do?

Assuming that (= in the possible situation that):
- **Assuming (that)** you're right, we should turn left here.

In case (as a way of being safe from something that may happen):
- Take your umbrella **in case** it rains.

Otherwise (= if not):
- Let's hope the weather improves, **otherwise** we'll have to cancel the picnic.

http://elearning.masterprof.ro/lectiile/engleza/lectie_26/4alternatives_to_if.html

---

 C Rewrite the sentences using the underlined word or words.

1 I'll get the bus if Glen can't take me in the car.
   <u>unless</u>

2 Give me $5 and I'll clean your car for you.
   <u>provided</u>

3 You can come in, but you have to leave before my parents get back.
   <u>as long as</u>

4 If it had not been for your call, I would have had no idea about his arrival.
   <u>but for</u>

5 If the waves stay strong, we will have to cancel today's session.
   <u>otherwise</u>

 D Work with a partner and agree which of the options below you are going to work on. Give yourselves a few minutes to prepare your questions and answers. Once the interview is conducted, choose another option and swap roles.

Student A: You are a journalist. You are going to have an interview with one of the people below. Come up with interesting questions to ask. You would like to ask the interviewee 10 questions to find out as much as you can about what he / she does, what he / she thinks about the current global market and the future one, how his / her business has adapted to changes in the global market, and so on.

Student B: Choose one of the following roles. Answer the interview questions in as much detail as possible.

- You are the owner of a multinational company. You own a household brand name and many branches around the world. Although you are successful now, you are worried that you are not well enough prepared for future changes to the market.

- You own a successful online business that has been making substantial profits over the last two years. Although you are happy with your success, you are worried about the increasing number of competitors.

- You are an entrepreneur whose business model has just begun to take shape. You are beginning to feel that your business can grow into a multinational company. You are thrilled, but you are also worried about the risk of failure.

- You are the owner of a local business that has run successfully over the last decade. You have established a friendly relationship with your customers and you believe in their loyalty. However, you feel that you are losing customers and you are unsure what to do to keep them loyal to your service.

 Listen to the interview with Ben Francis up to 4:30 (www.youtube.com/ watch?v=MpftE7RwQnM), the founder of Gymshark, and answer the following questions. You are allowed to listen twice.

1 How old was Ben when he founded Gymshark?

2 What did Ben Francis's first website sell online?

3 What kind of website is two-tone.com?

4 Who is Lewis?

5 Choose the **five** true statements.
   a Gymshark is the UK's fastest-growing company.
   b All the iPhone apps Ben Francis created were fitness apps.
   c In the early days of Gymshark, Ben Francis did not stock any of the products he sold through the website.
   d Within the first two months, he made an immediate success of Gymshark.
   e Ben Francis thinks creativity is very important when setting up a business.
   f Gymshark started to make its own clothes because the founding members did not like other people's brands of clothing.
   g From the very beginning, Gymshark mass-produced its clothing range.
   h Gymshark's 'influencer marketing' was successful.
   i Early orders of the Luxe tracksuit were low.
   j Ben received the first sample on his birthday.

Choose the correct answer.

6 Two-tone.com was not successful because…
   a there were not enough members
   b there were not enough people visiting the website
   c there were not enough investors

7 Ben had already achieved success …
   a by graduating from university
   b creating four apps, two of which made it into the top charts in the UK
   c as a YouTube coding influencer

8 Gymshark started creating clothing because …
   a it was low cost and profitable
   b the market didn't have anything they wanted to wear themselves
   c they wanted something manual to do

 Task 1: To write a set of guidelines

You are a successful young entrepreneur who has overcome several failures. Write a set of guidelines for other young adults to help them realize their fresh business ideas. Use the following checklist:

- Title / heading
- Subheadings
- Logical order of information
- Short sentences and paragraphs
- Supportive and sympathetic tone

◼ Task 2: To write a proposal

You have a brilliant business idea, but you are young and inexperienced. You need a more experienced business partner who can also invest in your start-up. Write a business proposal for potential business investors. The proposal can be written in a letter format. You will need to explain your business ideas clearly and in detail. It would be a good idea to include costs of the start-up and estimated profit margins. Use the following checklist:

- Title
- Subheadings
- Ideas clearly explained under each subheading
- Formal register
- Persuasive tone

◼ TOK Links

The internet

The internet has become the most important channel for global trade as well as entrepreneurship. With internet access in our handheld mobile devices, we are now able to access shared knowledge anywhere and at any time. The internet has enabled individuals to set up websites and blogs, post their opinions on social media, read news and discuss current issues online. The internet has made shared knowledge more accessible, fluid, connected and pluralistic.

It is great that you can find out about anything anywhere and at any time. Does this mean everyone is knowledgeable? Surely not! The problem with shared knowledge on the internet is that there is too much information – lies as well as truth. For example, uninformed individuals can believe fake news. We have to be mindful of the drawbacks of shared knowledge readily available on the internet. The rise of personalization online has now created filter bubbles that isolate us even further from accessing a broad range of information. To be well-informed and knowledgeable, we have to be aware that what we see and read online is not the full truth.

CREATIVITY, ACTIVITY, SERVICE

Entrepreneurship

Creativity is at the heart of entrepreneurship. CAS will provide you with a perfect opportunity to try out your ideas and enhance your creativity. For example, if you wanted to sell clothes online, try designing clothing or fashion accessory items. By doing this, you can actually trial your ideas and get feedback from your friends and family, and get CAS points!

3 Environmental globalization

How does globalization affect the environment? Globalization has certainly helped the immense growth in international trade and finance. It has made countries work more closely with one another and has led to several innovations in science and technology. Some argue this process of globalization has also contributed to environmental degradation. More transport of goods across borders certainly means more carbon dioxide emissions. Does this mean deglobalization would have the reverse effect on the environment? Could deglobalization be a solution to global warming?

A Before reading the article below, discuss the meaning of the following words:

- fraught
- premise
- exploitation
- depletion

- proponent
- adverse
- race-to-the-bottom
- pollutants

- degradation
- stipulate
- complying

Globalization may actually be better for the environment

The increasing pace of globalization and how it affects the environment has been a major global concern. Although the research has been fraught with contrasting results, there are many who strongly believe that increased globalization has been harmful to the environment.

A large number of environmentalists who support this view base their arguments on the premise that globalization leads to an increase in global demand, resulting in increased production. This indirectly contributes to the exploitation of the environment and the depletion of natural resources.

Amid rising environmental concerns, an important question is whether deglobalization would have the opposite impact on the environment. Put differently, if globalization is harmful, then should we expect that the current deglobalization trend will be less harmful for the environment?

It's an important question to ask right now, considering the mounting anti-globalization sentiments that have engulfed the Global North.

We have not only witnessed Brexit, the election of Donald Trump, the Belgian opposition to the trade agreement between the European Union and Canada in the recent past, but more recently, we have seen anti-globalization sentiments heating up even in the United States, once the strongest architect and proponent of globalization in the world.

[1]_____

The adverse effect of globalization on the environment is supported by what's known as the race-to-the-bottom hypothesis. This school of thought argues that increased gains from globalization are achieved at the expense of the environment because more open economies adopt looser environmental standards.

Those who support this bleak view of globalization argue that it creates global competition, resulting in a boost in economic activities that deplete the environment and its natural resources.

The increased economic activity leads to greater emissions of industrial pollutants and more environmental degradation. The pressure on international firms to remain competitive forces them to adopt cost-saving production techniques that can be environmentally harmful.

[2]_____

But in fact, deglobalization may not necessarily translate into reduced emissions of harmful gases such as CO_2, SO_2, NO_2, but could actually worsen it. Through what's known as the technique effect, we know globalization can trigger environmentally friendly technological innovations that can be transferred from countries with strict environmental regulations to pollution havens.

Globalization doesn't just entail the movement of manufactured goods, but also the transfer of intermediate, capital goods and technologies. That means multinational corporations with clean state-of-the-art technologies can transfer their green know-how to countries with low environmental standards.

It's widely recognized that multinational firms use cleaner types of energy than local firms, and therefore have more energy-efficient production processes. Deglobalization could mean these environmentally friendly technologies aren't passed on to countries that are trying to go green.

[3] _____

Globalization achieved through multilateral negotiations via the World Trade Organization has also demonstrated that although environmental protection is not part of the WTO's core mandate, it has spurred enthusiasm within its member countries for sustainable development and environmentally friendly trade policies.

There are several WTO trade-related measures that are compatible with environmental protection and sustainable use of natural resources. For instance, the green provisions of the WTO direct countries to protect human, animal or plant life and conserve their exhaustible natural resources.

Apart from the WTO, regional trade agreements, known as RTAs, are another feature of globalization that promote environmentally sustainable policies. As countries seek to join RTAs, they are also made to simultaneously embrace environmental cooperation agreements.

Many countries, including Canada and those in the European Union, have developed national policies that stipulate that prior to signing any trade agreement, environmental impact assessments must be carried out. That means that any country that signs trade agreements with those countries must also automatically sign environmental cooperation deals.

[4] _____

We've seen over the years how countries like China, once pollution havens, are making tremendous gains in reducing their emissions, especially after becoming more integrated into the world economy.

Because of the incentives to increase global market access for its products, China has moved from the position of one of the world's top polluters into a global leader spearheading the fight against climate change and pollution.

In 2017, China closed down tens of thousands of factories that were not complying with its environmental standards.

In contrast, we have seen countries like the USA slowly drifting away from the climate change fight in part because of the anti-globalization inclinations of Donald Trump. He pulled the USA out of the Paris Agreement on climate change in keeping with his anti-globalization rhetoric during the 2016 US election campaign.

Through its America First Energy Plan, the Trump administration has outlined its preference for polluting industries, the use of fossil fuels and the revival of the coal industry. This signals that deglobalizing countries may drift away from sustainable development practices towards industrial policies that are devastating to the environment.

Deglobalization isolates countries, making them less likely to be responsible for the environment. The gains associated with globalization, on the other hand, can be used as effective bargaining strategies or an incentive to demand environmental accountability from countries hoping to benefit from global trading systems.

Sylvanus Kwaku Afesorgbor (Assistant Professor, Agri-Food Trade and Policy, University of Guelph) & Binyam Afewerk Demena (Teaching and Research Fellow, International Institute of Social Studies) https://theconversation.com/globalization-may-actually-be-better-for-the-environment-95406

B **Read the article and answer the following questions:**

1 Match each heading with the correct paragraphs in the text. There are more headings than necessary.
   a China leading while the USA lagging?
   b Is deglobalization the answer?
   c Top pollutants of the world
   d Is globalization bad for the environment?
   e Deglobalization may worsen emissions
   f Ending the global 'race-to-the-bottom'
   g WTO and RTAs help protect the environment
   h WTO is key to environmental protection

2 Are the following sentences true or false? Justify your answers by quoting a relevant phrase from the text.
   a Research on the environmental impact of globalization has yielded consistent results over the last few years.
   b The deglobalization trend does not exist anymore.
   c Anti-globalization tendencies are increasing in more developed countries.
   d The United States has never been an advocate of globalization.

For each question, choose the correct answer from a, b, c or d.

3 Increased economic activity leads to…
   a balanced distributions of natural resources
   b strict environmental standards
   c more environmental degradation
   d cost-saving production techniques

4 One of the positive environmental effects of globalization is…

   a sharing environmentally friendly technologies between countries

   b the movement of manufactured goods

   c more energy-efficient production processes by local firms

   d the transfer of capital

5 Regional trade agreements ensure that…

   a the member states sign environmental cooperation deals

   b the member states develop their own trade agreements

   c the member states trade with Canada and the EU

   d the member states are exempt from environmental impact assessments

6 In a bid to fight against climate change and pollution, China…

   a has been integrated into the world economy

   b isolates countries that support deglobalization

   c has outlined its preference for polluting industries

   d has closed down factories that did not comply with its environmental standards

Grammar

Omission of *if*

In conditional clauses, ***if*** can be **omitted** and the auxiliary verb moved in front of the subject (inversion). This structure is formal.

- *If you should ever find yourself in Oxford, we would be glad to see you.* – ***Should*** *you ever find yourself in Oxford, we would be glad to see you.*

- *If the company collapsed, many people would lose their savings.* – ***Were*** *the company* ***to collapse****, many people would lose their savings.*

- *If I had known that you wanted to join the team, I'd have put your name on the list.* – ***Had*** *I* ***known*** *that you wanted to join the team, I'd have put your name on the list.*

http://elearning.masterprof.ro/lectiile/engleza/lectie_26/5omission_of_if.html

 Rewrite the following conditional clauses without using *if*:

1 If I'd known this would happen, I'd have been more careful.

2 If he found out about your lies, you'd lose your job.

3 If his business closed down, it'd be very hard for him to open another business in this area.

4 If you'd phoned me earlier, I'd have had everything ready for you.

5 If the firm hadn't met all the environmental standards, it'd have closed down.

6 If you should find alternative ways, we'd be happy to use them.

7 If we could start again, things would be so much better.

8 If the United States hadn't pulled out of the Paris Agreement, we would have made greater progress in stabilizing the rising global temperature.

 Divide your group into two. One group supports globalization and sees it as an opportunity to share natural resources, technologies, wealth, and so on. The other group is against globalization and sees it as a negative phenomenon. Before the debate, copy and complete the table below in preparation.

Advantages of globalization	Disadvantages of globalization

E Listen to the beginning of the lecture up to 2:50 (www.youtube.com/watch?v=NPMUQh_FRok) on the impacts of globalization on the environment and fill in the gaps below. Use no more than three words for each gap.

Positives of globalization	Negatives of globalization
1 More companies will use _____ such as wind farms and solar power. 2 General economic growth of all governments will lead to mutually _____ . 3 Globalization harmonizes countries _____ . 4 Transnational problems require _____ .	5 The increased consumption causes depletion of _____ . 6 Increased consumption will increase _____ to the global environment. 7 Increased consumption and pollution will result in a loss of variety of _____ . 8 Companies will try to maximize their financial gain by relocating their production to countries with less stringent _____ .

F ■ Task 1: To write a journal entry

Having listened to the lecture on the impacts of globalization on the environment, your teacher has asked you to write a journal entry about this lecture, focusing on both the positives and the negatives of globalization. You want to write the summary of the lecture as well as your thoughts and feelings about the topic. Use the following checklist:

- Date of entry
- Summary of the lecture
- Your opinion
- Progression of your ideas
- Semi-formal register

■ Task 2: To write an article

Your local newspaper is covering globalization as a feature. You are particularly concerned about the environmental impact of globalization and you wish to include your article on the topic in the feature. Write an article about the environmental impact of globalization, focusing either on the positives or on the negatives. Use the following checklist:

- Heading, byline and date
- An engaging introduction
- Main facts
- Follow-up of main facts with additional information
- One or two direct quotations from reliable sources
- Effective conclusion

■ **TOK Links**

Learning from other cultures?

Globalization brings the world closer. It is now easier to learn about other cultures through the internet, advanced transport and easier communication. Does this mean we are more culturally diverse or culturally knowledgeable? Is it even possible truly to learn about a culture without being part of it? It is commonly acknowledged that we look at other cultures through the lens of our own, which can be multifaceted and diverse in itself. However, we have to be mindful of our own bias when learning about other cultures.

CREATIVITY, ACTIVITY, SERVICE
3Rs: Reduce, Reuse, Recycle

If we recognize increased consumption as a negative consequence of globalization, shouldn't we try our best to mitigate the negative impact? Increased consumption brings increased waste. So, what can we do to reduce waste? Have you heard of the 3Rs (Reduce, Reuse, Recycle) campaign? The idea is very simple – we cannot stop waste production entirely, but everyone can make a significant contribution. Think before you bin! It saves energy and natural resources, helps to reduce pollution and reduces the need for landfill. Why not organize the 3Rs campaign in your school community for CAS?

■ Literature

4 Of Mice and Men

Of Mice and Men is a novel written by John Steinbeck. It is the story of two displaced migrant ranch workers, George Milton and Lennie Small, who move from place to place in California in search of new job opportunities during the Great Depression. Lennie is a big, strong man with learning difficulties. George is an intelligent but uneducated man who is Lennie's guardian and best friend. The following excerpt comes from the beginning of the book where the pair are taking a long walk to find work in a ranch. They both dream of a better future…

For a moment the place was lifeless, and then two men emerged from the path and came into the opening by the green pool.

They had walked in single file down the path,
5 and even in the open one stayed behind the other. Both were dressed in denim trousers and in denim coats with brass buttons. Both wore black, shapeless hats and both carried tight blanket rolls slung over their shoulders.
10 The first man was small and quick, dark of face, with restless eyes and sharp, strong features. Every part of him was defined: small, strong hands, slender arms, a thin and bony nose. Behind him walked his opposite, a huge
15 man, shapeless of face, with large, pale eyes, and wide, sloping shoulders; and he walked heavily, dragging his feet a little, the way a bear drags his paws. His arms did not swing at his sides, but hung loosely.
20 The first man stopped short in the clearing, and the follower nearly ran over him. <u>He took off his hat</u> and wiped the sweat-band with his forefinger and snapped the moisture off. <u>His huge companion dropped his blankets</u>
25 and flung himself down and drank from the surface of the green pool; drank with long gulps, snorting into the water like a horse. The small man stepped nervously beside him.

"Lennie!" he said sharply. "Lennie, for God'
30 sakes don't drink so much." Lennie continued to snort into the pool. <u>The small man leaned over</u> and shook him by the shoulder. "Lennie. You gonna be sick like you was last night."

Lennie dipped his whole head under, hat and
35 all, and then he sat up on the bank and his hat dripped down on his blue coat and ran down his back. "That's good," he said. "You drink some, George. You take a good big drink." He smiled happily.

40 George unslung his bindle and dropped it gently on the bank. "I ain't sure it's good water," he said. "Looks kinda scummy."

Lennie dabbled his big paw in the water and wiggled his fingers so the water arose in little
45 splashes; rings widened across the pool to the other side and came back again. <u>Lennie watched them go.</u> "Look, George. Look what I done."

George knelt beside the pool and drank from
50 his hand with quick scoops. "Tastes all right," he admitted. "Don't really seem to be running, though. You never oughta drink water when it ain't running, Lennie," he said hopelessly. "You'd drink out of a gutter if you was
55 thirsty." He threw a scoop of water into his face and rubbed it about with his hand, under his chin and around the back of his neck. Then he replaced his hat, pushed himself back from the river, drew up his knees and embraced
60 them. Lennie, who had been watching, imitated George exactly. He pushed himself back, drew up his knees, embraced them, looked over to George to see whether he had it just right. He pulled his hat down a little
65 more over his eyes, the way George's hat was.

George stared morosely at the water. The rims of his eyes were red with sun glare. He said angrily, "We could just as well of rode clear to the ranch if that bastard bus driver knew what
70 he was talkin' about. 'Jes' a little stretch down the highway,' he says. 'Jes' a little stretch.' God damn near four miles, that's what it was! Didn't wanta stop at the ranch gate, that's what. Too God damn lazy to pull up. <u>Wonder
75 he isn't too damn good</u> to stop in Soledad at all. Kicks us out and says 'Jes' a little stretch down the road.' I bet it was more than four miles. Damn hot day."

Excerpt from Of Mice and Men *by John Steinbeck*

A Answer the following questions:

1 The two men are wearing the same clothes. What are they wearing?

2 Which phrase between lines 1 and 10 indicates that the two men did not walk side by side?

3 Why is George worried about Lennie drinking a lot of water?

4 Why does George think the water is not suitable for drinking?

5 What is 'Jes' in line 70 in standard English?

B Choose the correct answer from a, b, c or d for each question.

1 Lennie 'walked heavily' (line 16–17) because…

 a his arms were too heavy

 b he was a heavy man

 c he was tired and thirsty

 d he did not swing his arms at his sides

2 George's attitude to the water shows that he is generally…

 a cautious

 b scared

 c nervous

 d worried

3 Lennie's attitude to the water shows that he is generally…

 a generous

 b careful

 c unhappy

 d childish

C Copy and complete the following table by indicating to whom or to what the word/s underlined refer/s:

In the phrase...	the word/s...	refer/s to...
1 He took off his hat… (line 21)	'He'	
2 His huge companion dropped his blankets… (line 24)	'His huge companion'	
3 The small man leaned over… (line 31)	'The small man'	
4 Lennie watched them go. (line 46)	'them'	
5 Wonder he isn't too damn good… (line 74)	'he'	

Grammar summary

Verbs

Tenses

Present simple, past simple and present perfect

Notice the tenses in the following sentences.

Present simple tense:

We use the **present simple tense** when you talk about something habitual.

- She **collects** knives with her family.
- He **dons** a suit and **walks** through Central Park to get there.
- In his spare time, the Google cofounder **likes** to push his body to the limit in any way he can.

Past simple tense:

We use the **past simple tense** when you describe an event that happened in the past.

- Her mom **introduced** her to daggers.
- Bush **took** up painting after leaving office in 2009.
- The Project Runway co-host and mentor **told** the New York Times that he spends every Sunday at the Metropolitan Museum.

Present perfect tense:

The **present perfect tense** is used to describe something that happened in the past, but the exact time it happened is not important. It has a relationship with the present.

- Branson says he **has** likely **played** thousands of games in his lifetime.
- The actor and filmmaker **has been collecting** vintage typewriters since 1978.
- The Yahoo CEO **tells** San Francisco magazine that she **has** always **loved** baking.

Past perfect simple and past perfect continuous

We use the **past perfect simple** to talk about:

- single, complete events:

  A few **had gone** the extra mile and **shaved** their legs.

- repeated actions when we give the number of times the action is repeated:

  He **had done** a lot of different jobs in his lifetime.

We use the **past perfect continuous** to talk about how long an action, or a series of actions, was in progress:

- He **had been working** hard all his life.
- He **had been riding** his bike for five hours without stopping.

Parallelism

Parallelism is used to balance the structure of a sentence so that pairs or groups of words are written in a similar form.

Parallelism is used in a list or a series:

- **Incorrect:** Sofia likes to ride a bike, play the piano and talking to her friends.

  The verbs have to follow the same pattern: to ride … play … and talk.

- **Correct:** Sofia likes to **ride** a bike, **play** the piano and **talk** to her friends.

Parallelism is also used when things are compared:

- **Incorrect:** He is more interested in acting in a play than he is to play basketball.

- **Correct:** He **is** more **interested in acting** in a play than he **is in playing** basketball.

Parallelism is used with linking words that connect two ideas, such as: not only … but also; Although…; Even though…; and Despite the fact that…:

- **Incorrect:** Margaret not only sings in a choir, but she is also organizing two after-school clubs.

- **Correct:** Margaret not only **sings** in a choir, but she also **organizes** two after-school clubs.

Conditionals

The conditionals

The following sentences are taken from the text 'Two Kinds' (pages 76–77). Discuss the meaning of the sentences.

- It made me feel proud, **as if** it **were** a shiny trophy I had won back.

- She lamented, **as if** I **had done** this on purpose.

We use if + past simple to talk about imaginary or hypothetical situations in the present or future.

We use if + past perfect to talk about situations that did not happen in the past. The situation described is often the opposite of what really happened.

If clauses (conditional clauses)

If clauses are sometimes a difficult structure to master in English. There are three major conditional types:

- Can do. For example:

  If you **sleep**, you **will feel** better.

- May be possible to do. For example:

  If you **slept**, you **might / could / should / would feel** better.

- Not possible because it's too late. For example:

  *If you **had slept** last night, you **might / would / could / should have felt** better.*

What do you notice about how the verbs change in each type?

Alternatives to *if*

- *Unless* (= if … not or only if):

  *She won't go to sleep **unless** you tell her a story.*

- *Providing / provided (that), on condition that, as / so long as* (= only if):

  *She will go to sleep **providing that** you tell her a story.*

- *But for* (= if it had not been for, if … not):

  ***But for** your warning, we wouldn't have realized the danger.*

- *Whether … or not* (= it doesn't matter which of these situations):

  ***Whether** governments like it **or not**, they have to give more aid to the developing world.*

- *Suppose / supposing, what if* (used to talk about imaginary situations):

  ***What if** your plan fails – what then?*

  ***Suppose** you won the Lottery, what would you do?*

- *Assuming that* (= in the possible situation that):

  ***Assuming (that)** you're right, we should turn left here.*

- *In case* (as a way of being safe from something that may happen):

  *Take your umbrella **in case** it rains.*

- *Otherwise* (= if not):

  *Let's hope the weather improves, **otherwise** we'll have to cancel the picnic.*

http://elearning.masterprof.ro/lectiile/engleza/ lectie_26/4alternatives_to_if.html

Omission of *if*

In conditional clauses, **if** can be **omitted** and the auxiliary verb moved in front of the subject (inversion). This structure is formal.

- *If you should ever find yourself in Oxford, we would be glad to see you. – **Should** you ever find yourself in Oxford, we would be glad to see you.*

- *If the company collapsed, many people would lose their savings. – **Were** the company **to collapse**, many people would lose their savings.*

- *If I had known that you wanted to join the team, I'd have put your name on the list. – **Had** I **known** that you wanted to join the team, I'd have put your name on the list.*

http://elearning.masterprof.ro/lectiile/engleza/ lectie_26/5omission_of_if.html

If … not, unless, whether, as long as and *provided that*

- **Unless** can replace *if … not* in conditional sentences:

  ***Unless** the government changes its mind, the law will pass.* (If the government does not…)

- We use ***if … not*** when we talk about unreal situations (situations that did not happen), emotions and in most questions:

  *He would be more excited about the holiday, **if** his cousin was **not** coming.*

  ***If** you do **not** attend the meeting, what will happen?*

  ***If** I had **not** been born in this country, my life would have been very different.*

- We use **unless** as an afterthought:

  *There is no reason for you to attend the meeting, **unless** you want to.*

- We use **whether** or **if** when we talk about two possibilities:

  *We do not know **whether / if** it is a good idea or not.*

- We usually use **whether** with not:

  ***Whether** or **not** he accepts the invitation, it is his decision.*

- **Provided that** and **as long as** can also replace *if* in certain conditional sentences, which can vary your word choice to enrich your sentences. For example:

  *The restaurant will keep your reservation, **provided that** you call one week in advance.*

  *You may share these documents with your co-workers **as long as** you give credit to their creators.*

Like, would like and *would have liked*

- The verb **like** can be used with the *-ing* form of a verb or the infinitive *to*. For example:

  *I **like playing** football.*

  *I **like to spend** time with my friends.*

- **Would like** is usually followed by the infinitive *to*. For example:

  *I **would like to** ask you something.*

  The infinitive *to* also usually follows *would love, would hate* and *would prefer*.

- **Would have liked** means that you regret that you did not or could not do something. For example:

  *I **would have liked** to have gone to the party, but I had too much homework.*

  Would have loved / hated / preferred are also followed by the infinitive *to*.

Would

We use **would**:

- when we imagine something:

  *I **would** like to become a doctor.*

- when we can't do something:

  *I **would** go to the party, but I can't.*

- sometimes as the past tense of 'will':

  *'I will drive you to the cinema.' – Jack said he **would** drive us to the cinema.*

We use **would have** when we imagine actions in the past:

- *I **would have** done my homework earlier, but I had tennis practice after school.*

Mitigating or hedging language

Mitigating or **hedging language** is a way of using language in certain ways to show respect (and sometimes embarrassment). Many cultures use this function of language to show politeness with a more formal register of the language, especially when communicating to someone in a position of authority. One of the assessment aims of English B is to 'understand and use language appropriate to a range of interpersonal and / or intercultural contexts and audiences,' and your understanding of language registers is critical to achieving this aim.

For example, in English, we would **not** ask a stranger 'What time is it?'; instead, we might say, 'Excuse me. Could you tell me the time?' This politeness or 'mitigation' is often achieved by using conditional forms and modal verbs, such as *could, would, might,* and so on. See some examples below.

Direct language	Mitigating (polite) language
Pass me the chips.	***Would** you pass me the chips.* or *It **would** be great if you passed me the chips.*
Do this by Monday.	*If you **could** get this done by Monday, I'd really appreciate it.*
Turn left now.	*I **would** turn left here.*
What?	***Could** you say that again?*

Modals

Modals

A **modal verb** is a verb used with another verb to express an idea such as possibility that is not expressed by the main verb. The modal verbs in English are:

- *can*
- *could*
- *may*
- *might*
- *must*
- *ought*
- *shall*
- *should*
- *will*
- *would*

Modal verbs are useful when you express your opinion.

Notice the modal verbs used in the following sentences.

- *I think we **must** (have to) take greater individual responsibility.*

  Meaning: *Must* and *have to* are both used to express obligation.

- *We **may** not be an infestation yet.*

  Meaning: *May* is used to express possibility.*

- *Travel **can** narrow the mind too.*

  Meaning: *Can* is used to express possibility.**

*May can also be used to express permission. For example: *You **may** borrow my computer.*

Can* is also used to express permission. For example: ***Can I have some more water, please?*

Note: Although *may* and *can* are interchangeable when used for permission, *may* is more polite than *can*.

Verb phrases

Verb + *-ing* or verb + infinitive

Have a look at the following sentences:

- *Even people who **want to go** to heaven don't **want to die** to get there.*

- ***Keep looking** until you find it.*

Have you noticed that we use the *-ing* form after certain verbs and the **infinitive** after other verbs? Sometimes we can use either form and there is no change in meaning. Occasionally we can use either form and there is a change in meaning. So what's the rule for whether we use the *-ing* form or the infinitive? Sorry, there isn't a rule. You have to learn which verbs go with which pattern.

Verbs followed by **-ing** include:

- *stop*
- *finish*
- *imagine*
- *suggest*
- *recommend*
- *avoid*
- *mind*
- *miss*
- *urge*
- *enjoy*

Verbs followed by the infinitive include:

- *hope*
- *need*
- *fail*
- *agree*
- *forget*
- *say*
- *learn*
- *afford*
- *wait*
- *ask*
- *seem*
- *would like*
- *choose*
- *hurry*
- *promise*
- *want*
- *invite*

The following verbs can be followed by either form:

- *start*
- *bother*
- *love*
- *like*

There are some more verbs that can be followed by *-ing* or the infinitive, but **the two options have different meanings**. For example, *remember* and *stop*:

- *I **forgot to meet** my friend on her birthday.*

  (forget + infinitive = didn't remember to do something you needed to)

- *I **forgot meeting** my friend on her birthday.*

  (forgot + *-ing* = to have no memory of something you have done)

- *She **stopped drinking coffee** six weeks ago.*

  (stop + *-ing* = to not do something any more)

- *It was raining, so we **stopped to** find some shelter.* (we stopped walking)

  (stop + infinitive = to not do something in order to do something else)

Used to / be used to / get used to

We use ***used to*** to talk about past habits, and situations or states:

- *The school was not far from my home and I **used to** walk.* (habit)

- *I **used to** live in Swat.* (situation)

- *She **didn't use to** like the country lifestyle.* (state)

We use ***be used to*** to explain that someone is familiar with a situation or a routine:

- *I **am used to** staying in bed late.*

We use ***get used to*** in the present continuous to explain that someone is in the process of becoming familiar with a situation:

- *I **am getting used to** working early in the morning.*

Use the past simple to show that the process is complete:

- *I quickly **got used to** the new routine.*

Phrasal verbs

Phrasal verbs are verbs that have two or more parts and are often used in less formal, spoken language. For many phrasal verbs, there are single-word equivalents that have the same meaning, but are used in more formal, sometimes academic, writing or speech. For example:

- You might say to a friend:

  *We **found out** who speaks the most languages at school.*

- Whereas you might use more formal language for academic work, such as:

  *It was **discovered** who speaks the most languages.* (note use of the passive voice too)

The more formal words often have Greek or Latin roots. Other examples include:

- *ask for = request*
- *set up = establish*
- *lie to = deceive*
- *come down with (an illness) = contract*
- *go before = proceed*

Your mastery through reading and practice of using phrasal verbs and their formal equivalents will aid you in developing your understanding and usage of the various registers of English (slang, informal, semi-formal, formal).

Passive

Passive voice

Notice how the **passive voice** is used in the following sentences:

- *For example, in dance, distance running, gymnastics and cycling, weight and body composition **are believed to** influence physical performance and the aesthetics of performance.*

- *Use of body mass index (BMI) in athletes **is not recommended**, because it falsely classifies some teens who are of normal weight as being overweight.*

We use the passive voice when we want to focus attention on the person or thing affected by the action. Normally, we use the passive voice when the performer of the action, or the *agent*, is too obvious or ambiguous or not important enough to be mentioned.

The passive forms are made up of the verb ***be*** with a **past participle**:

	be	Past participle	
English	*is*	*spoken*	*all over the world.*
Apples	*have been*	*grown*	*for many years in Asia and Europe.*
The room	*was being*	*cleaned.*	
The work	*will be*	*finished*	soon.
You	*must have been*	*invited*	to the party.

Prepositions

Verbs with the prepositions *about, for* and *of*

Many English verbs are joined with prepositions to create new meanings of those verbs. For example, *to care **for** someone* or *to care **about** them*.

Verbs and dependent prepositions

Some verbs are usually followed by prepositions before the object of the verb. These are called **dependent prepositions** and they are followed by a noun or a gerund (*-ing* form).

- *All golfers must **adhere to** the dress code.* (*to* is the dependent preposition for *adhere*)
- *Members, guests and visitors are reminded not to **engage in** any form of sexual, racial or religious discrimination or harassment.* (*in* is the dependent preposition for *engage*)

Here are some other verbs with their dependent prepositions.

For:

- *He **apologized for** being late.* (You can also 'apologize to' someone.)
- *I **applied for** the job but I didn't get it.*
- *How do you **ask for** a coffee in Polish?*
- *She spent many years **caring for** her aged parents.*
- *I can't go out tonight because I have to **prepare for** my interview tomorrow.*

From:

- *This spray should **protect** you **from** mosquitoes.*
- *Has he **recovered from** his illness yet?*
- *He won an award because he **saved** someone **from** drowning.*
- *I **suffer from** hay fever.*

In:

- *She **believes in** ghosts.*
- *Our company **specializes in** computer software.*
- *You have to work hard if you want to **succeed in** life.*

Of:

- *I don't **approve of** your language, young man.*
- *Our dog **died of** old age.*
- *This shampoo **smells of** bananas.*

On:

- *The film is **based on** the novel by Boris Pasternak.*
- *If you make so much noise I can't **concentrate on** my work.*
- *Come on! We're **relying on** you!*
- *We don't **agree on** anything but we're good friends.*

To:

- *Can I **introduce** you **to** my wife?*
- *Please **refer to** the notes at the end for more information.*
- *Nobody **responded to** my complaint.*

With:

- *I **agree with** everything you've said.*
- *My secretary will **provide** you **with** more information if you need it.*

There are many more verb + dependent preposition combinations – make a note of them as you meet them.

https://learnenglish.britishcouncil.org/en/
quick-grammar/verbs-prepositions

Dependent prepositions

Some verbs need a preposition to introduce their objects. Many of these verbs are always followed by the same preposition. These prepositions are called **dependent prepositions**.

- *I'm **listening to** the new Coldplay album.*
- *What do you **think of** it?*
- ***Look at** the cover.*

(*Listen, think* and *look* can also be used with other prepositions, but their meanings change.)

Some verbs have more than one dependent preposition. The preposition changes depending on the nature of the object, but the meaning of the verb stays the same:

- *I don't **agree with** you.* (agree with + person)
- *I **agree about** the cover.* (agree about + something)
- *We **went to** their concert last week.* (go to + place)
- *We **went with** Jake and Casi.* (go with + person)

Sometimes you can use both prepositions at the same time:

- *I **agree with** you **about** the cover.*
- *We **went to** the concert **with** Jake and Casi.*

Prepositions are normally followed by a noun or pronoun:

- *Listen to **this**.*
- *Look at **the rain**.*
- *We were just talking about **you**!*

Many of these verbs can be used without an object. In this case, do not use the dependent preposition:

- *Can you be quiet and just **listen**?*
- *Open your eyes and **look**.*

However, you must include dependent prepositions:

- at the end of questions with *who, what* or *which*:
  *What are you listening **to**?*
  *What are you talking **about**?*
- in relative clauses:
  *This is the album that I was talking **about**.*
- with adjectives followed by an infinitive:
  *This music is very easy to listen **to**.*

Verbs using *in, on, to, from* and *into*

Below are verbs that can be used with the prepositions **in, on, to, from** and **into**:

- hear
- keep
- put
- listen
- get
- take
- come
- turn
- go
- look

Time

Prepositions of time

For:

For refers to a length of time and shows how long something lasted. For example:

- Sunlight will be available to us *for* at least 5 billion years when, according to scientists, the sun will die.

In / during:

In or *during* describes a shorter period of time within a longer period. For example:

- Savings can grow further if you sell excess electricity at high rates *during* the day and then buy electricity from the grid *during* the evening when the rates are lower.

From … to / between … and:

Use *from … to* to describe the length of a period of time by stating the start and end points. For example:

- I read the book *from* two o'clock *to* three o'clock. (= I read for an hour)

Use *between … and* to say that an action happened at some point in a period of time. For example:

- What time was Rachel woken up? Sometime *between* two *and* three o'clock. (= we don't know exactly what time)

By / until (till) / before:

Use *by* to talk about an action or event that was completed at some point previously, or at a point in time. For example:

- *By* the evening, she'd fallen hopelessly in love.

Use *until / till* to describe an action or event that will continue from the time of speaking to precisely the point in time. For example:

- She stays on the beach *until (till)* five o'clock.

Use *before* to describe an action or event that is completed at some time previous to the time given. For example:

- I always read a book *before* I go to bed.

After / since:

Use *after* to describe an action or event that happened at some time later than the point in time given. For example:

- She woke up *after* midnight.

Use *since* to refer to the time at which an action (which continues to the present) started. For example:

- She hasn't been able to sleep *since* midnight. (= she is still awake)

Prepositions and conjunctions of time

For:

We use *for* with a period of time to say how long something happened. For example:

- *for* a week
- *for* a long time

- *for* the summer

During:

We use *during* with a noun to explain when something happened:

- *during* class
- *during* my summer holiday
- She received a call *during* the speech.

While:

We use *while* with a subject and a verb:

- I was listening to the radio *while* I was cleaning.
- *While* you were having fun, I was studying.
- We visited a lot of museums *while* we were in Italy.

By:

Using *by* in reference to time means 'no later than':

- The new shopping centre should open *by* the end of June.
- We will complete the project *by* Monday.
- *By* the time you arrive, the game will be over.

Until:

We use *until* to explain how long something continues:

- People must work *until* they are 65 years old.
- *Until* a new law is passed, people will continue to suffer.
- You can use my car *until* yours is fixed.

For and *since*

We use *for* and *since* to say how long something happened.

- We use *for* for a period of time:
  I have lived here *for* seven years.
- We use *since* with the start of a period of time:
  I have lived here *since* 2005.

For and *since* are used with the present perfect:

I have been playing football *since* I was young.

I have played the saxophone *for* years.

Still, *yet* and *already*

- We use *still* to say that a situation or action is ongoing and has not stopped. For example:
  He is *still* in the library.
- We use *yet* to mean *until now*. For example:
  Have you finished your homework *yet*?
- It can be used in negative sentences:
  He hasn't answered my email *yet*.
- *Still* can also be used in negative sentences, but it usually shows more surprise or impatience than *yet*. For example:
  He hasn't arrived *yet*, and I'm worried.
  He *still* hasn't arrived, and I'm upset.
- We use *already* to say that something has happened, sometimes sooner than expected. For example:
  He has *already* finished all of the tasks I assigned him.

I'm really impressed.

Place

Prepositions of place

In	On	At
Inside an area or space: *in the city*, *in the sky*, *in* bed	In contact with a surface: *on the wall*, *on the table*, *on the floor*	Close to: *at the table*, *at the bus stop*
Forms of transport: *in a car*, *in a taxi*, *in a helicopter*	Forms of transport: *on a bike*, *on a bus*, *on a train*, *on the Metro*, *on a plane*, *on a ship*	
		Before nouns referring to a place or position: *at the top*, *at the bottom*, *at the front*, *at the back*, *at the beginning*, *at the end*, but *in the middle*
Arrive in a city or country: *arrive in London*, *arrive in France*		Arrive at a small place: *arrive at the station*, *at the meeting*, *at the office*
		To express 'towards': *look at something*, *point at something*, *smile at someone*

Time and place

There is and *there was*

- We begin sentences with **there is** or **there was** when something exists / existed or is / was happening at a particular time and place. For example:

  There is *a light coming towards us on the road.*

  There was *a lot of thunder and lightning last night.*

- If the word after the verb is singular, the verb is singular. If the noun is plural, the verb is plural. For example:

  There was *a crowd of people waiting outside the restaurant.*

  There were *hundreds of people waiting outside the restaurant.*

- We use the same patterns with questions:

  Is there…

  Are there…

  Was there…

  Were there…

Nouns and pronouns

Nominalization

In addition to developing increasing accuracy and fluency in English in this course, you will develop better control of the various *registers* of English. Register is the degree of formality we use to communicate, often determined by whom we are communicating with. This determines choices we make in terms of vocabulary or grammar, for example with your friends you may use slang as your register, whereas in academic tasks you will often use more formal language.

IB students aim towards developing increasing technical, abstract and formal language in their academic writing. One way to achieve this is called **nominalization**. Nominalization is simply transforming words like adjectives and verbs into nouns or noun phrases. Nominalization is often used in academic writing because abstract ideas and processes can be 'packed' into one single word (for example *photosynthesis*) and classified or quantified, whereas spoken language typically uses more verbs and adjectives. In addition, nominalization makes our writing less personal and more objective (avoiding personal pronouns like *I*, *we*, *you*, *they*, and so on) and even more authoritative.

Note that nominalization is used primarily in academic writing, and overusing it can make your writing difficult to read (or even boring at times!).

A / an and *the*

- We use *a* when we are talking about one item, event or action:

  He bought **a** *litre of milk.*

- We use *an* when it precedes a word beginning with a vowel:

  An *elephant likes to eat hay.*

- We use *a* when it is the first time we mention something:

  A *man approached me and asked me for directions.*

- We use *the* after the first time we mention something:

  The *man needed directions because he had never been to New York.*

- We use *the* when referring to something specific:

  You will find an extra blanket in **the** *closet.*

- We use *the* when we are familiar with the person, place or thing:

  The *floor needs to be cleaned.*

- We use *the* with the verb forms of *go to*:

  He went to **the** *bank to deposit some money.*

Pronouns

Subject pronoun	Object pronoun	Possessive adjective	Possessive pronoun
I	me	my	mine
you	you	your	yours
he	him	his	his
she	her	her	hers
it	it	its	–
we	us	our	ours
they	them	their	theirs

Some, any, someone, something, anyone or anything

- We use **some** with plural and uncountable nouns. For example:

  *There were **some people** in the car I did not recognize.*

  ***Some acts** of kindness really touch your heart.*

- We use **any** when we use a negative in a sentence, such as *not*, *hardly* or *never*:

  *There is **never any** food in his refrigerator.*

  *I am **not** ready to give him **any** credit for the project.*

- **Someone**, **something**, **anyone** and **anything** follow the same rules as above.

Relative clauses – adjective clauses

Subject (people) – **who**:

- *That boy seems tired. **He** is on his phone all the time. – That boy **who** is on his phone all the time always seems tired.*

  The subject *He* (that boy, a person) is replaced by *who* to make a relative clause and complex sentence.

Subject (things) – **which**:

- *Internet addiction is a real problem for teens. **It** is similar to alcohol or drug addiction. – Internet addiction, **which** is similar to alcohol or drug addiction, is a real problem for teens.*

  The subject *It* (internet addiction, a thing **not** a person) is replaced by *which* to make a relative clause and a complex sentence.

Possessive – **whose**:

- *That teen has real phone-addiction problems. **His** phone is always in his hand. – That teen **whose** phone is always in his hand has real phone-addiction problems.*

  The possessive adjective *His* is replaced by *whose* to make a relative clause and a complex sentence.

Reduced relative clauses

If the verb in the **relative clause** is in the active form, use the present participle (-ing):

- **Relative clause:** *Passengers who travel without a valid ticket will receive a fine.*

- **Reduced relative clause:** *Passengers **travelling** without a valid ticket will receive a fine.*

If the verb in the relative clause is in the passive form, use the past participle form:

- **Relative clause:** *Metro police will remove and destroy any bags that are left unattended.*

- **Reduced relative clause:** *Metro Police will remove and destroy any bags **left** unattended.*

Using who, when, where or which when giving additional information

We sometimes use **who, when, where** or **which** to give additional information about a person, time, place or thing. This information is added to the sentence using a comma and one of these words. It is important to remember what each word introducing this **relative clause** is referring to:

- *who* refers to a person
- *when* refers to a time
- *where* refers to a place
- *which* refers to a thing

Adverbs and adjectives

Compound adjectives

Stress-inducing is a **compound adjective**, as two words, *stress* (mental or emotional strain or tension) and *induce* (to bring about), are combined to create a new adjective. It is often very easy to guess what these compound adjectives mean – have a go at the following:

- an **English-speaking** country
- a **time-saving** gadget
- a **well-known** writer
- a **short-sighted** man

Try creating a few of your own compound adjectives and share them with your class.

Each and every

- We can use **each** or **every** for singular countable nouns: **Each** day… or **Every** day…

- A singular verb is used after both *each* and *every*: **Every** hospital has…, **Each** university provides…

- We use *every* with *almost* and *nearly*, when we are talking about a large group and if the plural noun has a number in front of it:

  *We completed **almost every** exercise.*

  ***Every six months**, you should take a young child to a doctor for a check-up.*

- We use *each* when we are talking about individual members of a group or when we are talking about a pair:

  *We were **each** assigned a partner.*

  ***Each** teacher is expected to have his / her own website.*

  *They are identical twins, but they **each** have their own distinct personality.*

263

Adjectives or adverbs?

Have a look again at the following sentences from the text '8 best weird and wacky British traditions' (page 97):

- *There are **wonderfully eccentric** traditions all over the British Isles.*
- *Spectators join the race **involuntarily**.*
- *There is a **spectacular** firework show.*

We use **adjectives** to describe **nouns**. They come before the noun or after a copular verb. For example:

- *appear*
- *be*
- *become*
- *get*
- *feel*

- *seem*
- *sound*
- *look*
- *taste*
- *smell*

We use **adverbs** to describe **verbs**, **adjectives** and other **adverbs**.

Some words can be used as both adjectives and adverbs. For example:

- *clean*
- *daily*
- *deep*
- *early*
- *far*
- *fast*
- *free*
- *high*

- *hourly*
- *late*
- *loud*
- *hard*
- *weekly*
- *well*
- *yearly*

- *The test was **hard**.* (adjective: it describes the test)
- *He works **hard**.* (adverb: it describes the way he works)
- *You don't look **well**.* (adjective: well = in good health)
- *She plays the piano **well**.* (adverb: it describes how she plays the piano)

Hardly and lately:

The adverbs *late* and *hard* have a different meaning from the adverbs *lately* and *hardly*. **Lately** means 'recently'. **Hardly** means 'almost not / almost never'.

- *I worked **late** last night.*
- *I've been doing a lot of work **lately**.*
- *He worked **hard** for his exam.*
- *He **hardly** did any work for his exam.*

So and *such*

- We use **so** with an adjective or adverb. For example:

  so *gentle*

  so *accurately*

- We use **such** with a noun. For example:

  such *a nice man*

- We can also use *so much* and *so many* to express quantity. For example:

  *there was **so much** traffic*

  *there were **so many** people there*

Conjunctions

Text cohesion

There are different ways to successfully give a text **cohesion**, that is to connect / link the ideas in the text. Pronouns and transitions also do this. Look at other ways you can build cohesion and make links in your writing in the examples below. Write out the translations for these words in your own language.

Conjunctions:

- Addition: *and, also, too*
- Choice: *or, nor*
- Result: *so, for*
- Contrast: *but, yet*

Subordinate conjunctions / connectors:

- Time order: *after, before, until, when*
- Comparing / contrasting: *while, whereas, although, even though, despite, however*
- Cause and effect: *so that, since, because*

Questions

Question forms

Review these basic **question forms**:

- Move the helping (auxiliary or modal) verb to the front of the sentence:

Statement form	Question form
Korean Air **has** improved its safety record.	**Has** Korean Air improved its safety record?
We **can** see the runway.	**Can** we see the runway?

- If there is only one word in the verb, use *do / does / did* (in the correct tense) at the beginning, then the subject, then the bare infinitive. If the verb *to be* is the main verb, move it in front of the subject:

Statement form	Question form
The plane crashed.	**Did** the plane crash?
A Korean typically shows respect for authority.	**Does** a Korean typically show respect for authority?
Malcolm Gladwell **is** an author.	**Is** Malcolm Gladwell an author?

Comparatives

Comparatives with *-er* or *more*

When we want to **compare two things**, in general, we add *-er* to a short word of one syllable and we use *more* for words with two or more syllables. For example:

-er	more

fast – faster	slowly – more slowly
kind – kinder	interesting – more interesting
big – bigger	enjoyable – more enjoyable

The use of *as*

As can be used in several ways:

- It can be used to mean *because*:

  As I was tired, I sat down.

  I sat down, **as** I was tired.

- It can be used to mean *at the same time*:

  As I was walking down the street, I suddenly saw a large crowd coming towards me.

- It can be used to compare two people, places or things:

  He is not **as** fast **as** his sister.

- It can be used in the phrase *as if* to describe how someone looks / sounds / feels:

  She looks **as if** she's been exercising.

  They sound **as if** they are excited.

- It can be used with *such* to mean 'for example':

  The school offers the opportunity to join a variety of clubs, **such as** the chess club, the French club or the cooking club.

Speech

Direct and indirect (or reported) speech

- When **dialogue** is written, or a journalist quotes someone, the speaker's words are put in quotation marks ('…' or "…") and it is noted who said it. For example:

  'I saw a man wearing a green hat enter the building,' the witness said.

  Notice there is a comma inside the quotation mark, before 'the witness said'. You always use a comma before indicating who spoke.

- **Indirect, or reported, speech** is when someone retells, or reports, what was said. For example:

  The witness said that he saw a man wearing a green hat enter the building.

  Often this form begins with a structure like 'He said that…'.

- Note that when someone speaks in the present tense in a quotation, the verb of the reported speech is changed to the past tense. Reported speech is always in the past tense. For example:

  Direct speech: *'I'm going to the cinema,' she said.*

  Reported speech: *She said that she was going to the cinema.*

Emphasis

Emphasis 1: *do, does, did*

You can add emphasis to affirmative sentences by adding **do / does** before the main verb in the present simple, or **did** before the main verb in the past simple. For example:

- *You look beautiful. – You **do look** beautiful.*
- *She looks beautiful. – She **does look** beautiful.*
- *I told you she'd be late. – I **did tell** you she'd be late.*

For negative sentences using *don't / doesn't / didn't*, add emphasis by using the full form *do not / does not / did not* and stressing *not*. For example:

- *We don't need to hurry. – You do **not** need to hurry!*
- *He didn't have to wait too long. – He did **not** have to wait too long.*

Do not use *do / does / did* for emphasis with the verb *to be* or with continuous or perfect tenses. Add emphasis to these forms by using the full form – do not use the contracted form. For example:

- *We're late. – We **are** late!*
- *We aren't late. – We are **not** late!*
- *Everyone's waiting. – Everyone **is** waiting.*
- *I've remembered the ring. – I **have** remembered the ring.*

You can add emphasis to an imperative sentence with *do*. It is often used to express anger or annoyance. For example:

- *Hurry up! – **Do** hurry up!*
- *Clean up your mess! – **Do** clean up your mess!*

Emphasis 2: cleft sentences

Cleft sentences are used to help us focus on a particular part of the sentence and to emphasize what we want to say by introducing it or building up to it with a kind of relative clause. Because there are two parts to the sentence it is called *cleft* (from the verb *cleave*), which means 'divided into two'. Cleft sentences are particularly useful in writing where we cannot use intonation for purposes of focus or emphasis, but they are also frequently used in speech.

Cleft sentences with ***what***:

- ***What I like is / are*** the free lunches.
- *Fill in this form. – **What you do is** fill in this form.*
- *He applied for a new job. – **What he did was** apply for a new job.*
- *I was walking past when I saw your advert in the window. – **What happened was** (that) I was walking past when I saw your advert in the window.*

Cleft sentences with ***it***:

- *You need to see the manager. – **It's** the manager (whom) you need to see.*
- *You sign your name on this line. – **It's** on this line (that) you sign your name.*

Cleft sentences with *the thing*:

- *I like the holidays. –* **The thing I like** *is the holidays.*
- *Talk to the manager. –* **The best thing to do** *is talk to the manager.*

Cleft sentences with *place / person / reason / way*:

- **The place** *(where) he works* **is** *a fast food restaurant.*
- **The person** *(whom) you need to see* **is** *the manager.*
- **The reason** *(why) I'm here* **is** *that I saw the advert in your window.*
- **The way** *to do this* **is** *by filling in this form.*

Emphasis 3: negative and limiting adverbials

You can put **negative and limiting adverbs or adverbials** at the beginning of a sentence to add emphasis:

- **Never have I** *been so scared in all my life.*
- **Only then do** *you find yourself saying, 'That was amazing!'*

Negative adverbials are expressions with the word *no, not* or *never.* They include *never before, at no time, no sooner … than, no way, not since* and *not until.*

Limiting (or restrictive) adverbials include *hardly … when, rarely, seldom* and expressions with *only* such as *only when, only after* and *not only.*

- **No sooner had** *he attached the elastic rope to me than I was falling…*
- **Seldom have** *I been so scared!*
- **Hardly had** *I reached the top when I was falling to the bottom…*

Notice the word order of these sentences. It is the same word order as is found in questions.

Affixes

Many words in English are formed using **affixes,** which are parts of words added to a root word to make a new word. **Prefixes** (word beginnings) change the meaning of a word. **Suffixes** (word endings) change the word form, also known as the *part of speech.*

Acknowledgements

The publisher would like to thank the following for permission to reproduce copyright material.

Every effort had been made to trace or contact all copyright holders, but if any have been inadvertently overlooked the Publisher will be please to make the necessary arrangements at the first opportunity.

Photo credits

t = top, *l* = left, *c* = centre, *r* = right, *b* = bottom

p.2 © Slow Walker/Shutterstock.com; **p.6** *t* © A Wider Circle, Inc., *r* A Wider Circle, Inc.; **p.15** © Burdun/stock.adobe.com; **p.16** © Pololia/stock.adobe.com; **p.20** © Tierney/stock.adobe.com; **p.25** © Featureflash Photo Agency/Shutterstock.com; **p.30** *tl, tc, tr, cl, cr, bl, br* from Charade, 1963; **p.44** *tl* © Luckybusiness/stock.adobe.com, *tr* © And_rue/stock.adobe.com, *c* © Auremar/stock.adobe.com, *bl* © Csaba Peterdi/stock.adobe.com, *br* © Twinsterphoto/stock.adobe.com; **p.45** © Mark Greenberg/ZUMA Wire/Alamy Live News/Alamy Stock Photo; **p.46** © Larry W Smith/EPA/REX/Shutterstock; **p.50** *l* © Anyaberkut/stock.adobe.com, *r* © EdNurg/stock.adobe.com; **p.54** *tl* © Hadkhanong/stock.adobe.com, *tr* © Monkey Business/stock.adobe.com, *bl* © Riccardo/stock.adobe.com, *br* © Wollertz/stock.adobe.com; **p.55** © Chocostar/stock.adobe.com; **p.57** *tl* © Gary/stock.adobe.com, *tr* © Actionpics/stock.adobe.com, *bl* © Rafal/stock.adobe.com, *br* © Pavel Losevsky/stock.adobe.com; **p.67** *tl* © Africa Studio/stock.adobe.com, *tr* © Monkey Business/stock.adobe.com, *b* © IVASHstudio/stock.adobe.com; **p.77** © Xinhua/Alamy Stock Photo; **p.80** © Paolese/stock.adobe.com; **p.83** *tl* © Artem Varnitsin/stock.adobe.com, *tr* © Gorodenkoff/stock.adobe.com, *bl* © Hero/stock.adobe.com, *br* © GutesaMilos/stock.adobe.com; **p.89** *tl* © yolya_ilyasova/stock.adobe.com, *tr* © David Carillet/stock.adobe.com, *b* © WavebreakMediaMicro/stock.adobe.com; **p.90** © Guy Corbishley/Alamy Stock Photo; **p.91** © Mrallen/stock.adobe.com; **p.93** © Pizzastereo/Shutterstock.com; **p.96** © Somchaikhun/stock.adobe.com; **p.101** © Apex News and Pictures; **p.104** *tl* © Africa Studio/stock.adobe.com, *tr* © Greg Blomberg/stock.adobe.com, *bl* © Sergey Skryl/stock.adobe.com; **p.105** © Kadmy/stock.adobe.com; **p.110** *tl* © Jacek Chabraszewski/stock.adobe.com, *tr* © Antonioguillem/stock.adobe.com, *cl* © Jumlongch/stock.adobe.com, *cr* © Highwaystarz/stock.adobe.com, *b* © .Shock/stock.adobe.com; **p.111** © Bogdan/stock.adobe.com; **p.113** © Sandra de Haan; **p.116** *t* © Adrian_ilie825/stock.adobe.com, *b* How Much physical activity should you do? from Public Health England; **p.118** © Sabphoto/stock.adobe.com; **p.121** © Fizkes/stock.adobe.com; **p.125** © Buzzfuss/123RF; **p.127** © Dpyancy/stock.adobe.com; **p.128** © Annie Spratt on Unsplash; **p.129** © lin qiang on Unsplash; **p.130** © BillionPhotos.com/stock.adobe.com; **p.133** © © Ezra Shaw/Getty Images; **p.135** © Cheese Scientist/Alamy Stock Photo; **p.136** © Coloures-Pic/stock.adobe.com; **p.137** © Monster Ztudio/stock.adobe.com; **p.138** © Nmarques74/stock.adobe.com; **P.140** © GL Portrait/Alamy Stock Photo; **p.142** © Burtsevserge/stock.adobe.com; **p.146** © Dave Coverly; **p.152** © Biker3/stock.adobe.com; **p.154** *t* © NASA/Donaldson collection/Getty Images; **p.156** © Hodder & Stoughton; **p.158** *l* Courtesy Pest Control Office, Banksy, New York, 2013, *tr* © Master1305/stock.adobe.com, *br* © Caspar Benson/fStop Images GmbH/Alamy Stock Photo; **p.163** © Granger Historical Picture Archive/Alamy Stock Photo; **p.166** *t* © Mj - tim photography/Shutterstock.com *b* © Arne Magnussen; **p.172** *tl* © U.P.images/stock.adobe.com, *tc* © Giuseppe Porzani/stock.adobe.com, *tr* © Jasminzejnic/stock.adobe.com, *cl* © Stephen VanHorn/stock.adobe.com, *c* © Everettovrk/stock.adobe.com, *cr* © Norman75/stock.adobe.com, *bl* © Rod5150/stock.adobe.com, *br* © Alextype/stock.adobe.com; **p.173** *t* © Metamorworks/stock.adobe.com, *b* © Maksym Yemelyanov/stock.adobe.com; **p.181** © Zou Zheng/Xinhua/Alamy Live News/Alamy Stock Photo; **p.186** *tr* © Leo Lintang/stock.adobe.com, *cr* © Mopic/stock.adobe.com, *br* © Audrius Merfeldas/123RF; **p.187** © VisionDive/stock.adobe.com; **p.188** Image Courtesy of: Seabin Project www.seabinproject.com; **p.191** © Andrey Burmakin/stock.adobe.com; **p.196** © Julien Tromeur/stock.adobe.com; **p.197** © Andrey Popov/stock.adobe.com; **p.201** *tl* © Alphaspirit/stock.adobe.com, *tr* © somchai rakin-123RF, *bl* © Nokhoog/stock.adobe.com, *br* © Stnazkul/stock.adobe.com; **p.202** © Nd700/stock.adobe.com; **p.207** *l* © sablin/123Rf, *r* © Richard Carey/stock.adobe.com; **p.212** *l* © Tom Wang/stock.adobe.com, *r* © Imaginis/stock.adobe.com; **p.220** © JG Photography/Alamy Stock Photo; **p.224** *tl* © PARESH NATH, *tr* © JG Photography/Alamy Stock Photo © Alpha Historica/Alamy Stock Photo, *bl* © Soupstock/stock.adobe.com, *br* © Gabriel Hackett/Staff/ Hulton Archive/Getty Images; **p.227** © Luis Louro/stock.adobe.com; **p.232** *l* © Everett Collection Inc/Alamy Stock Photo, *r* © Olha/stock.adobe.com; **p.138** © CSU Archives/Everett Collection Historical/Alamy Stock Photo; **p.240** *tl* © Boyko.Pictures/stock.adobe.com, *r* © PARESH NATH, *bl* © WavebreakMediaMicro/stock.adobe.com; **p.241** © What4ever/stock.adobe.com; **p.245** *l* © Kbuntu/stock.adobe.com, *c* © Nnudoo/stock.adobe.com, *r* © Cybrain/stock.adobe.com; **p.250** *l* © R. Gino Santa Maria/stock.adobe.com, *c* © Leo Lintang/stock.adobe.com, *r* © Daniel Berkmann/stock.adobe.com

Acknowledgements

Text credits

p.2 Extract from Australia at 24 million: The challenges facing a growing and ageing nation by Matt Wade, The Sydney Morning Herald © 2016. The use of this work has been licensed by Copyright Agency except as permitted by the Copyright Act, you must not re-use this work without the permission of the copyright owner or Copyright Agency; **pp.6-7** Interview with Sarah Soloane from www.ngopulse.org/article/2015/05/13/interview-sarah-soloane, 22 March, 2018 © 2015 Positive Planet International (www.positiveplanet.ngo). Reprinted with permission; **p.10** Our History, A Wider Circle, Inc. reprinted with the permission of Mark Bergel, Executive Director to Founder, President & CEO; **pp.13-14** From Animal Farm by George Orwell, Published by Martin Secker & Warburg Ltd., Reprinted by permission of The Random House Group Limited © 1945; **pp.16-17** First day of school: It's the parents crying - not the children www.irishtimes.com/news/education/first-day-of-school-it-s-the-parents-crying-not-the-children-1.3203368 by Carl O'Brien Accessed: 30/11/2017 reprinted with permission of THE IRISH TIMES; **pp.20-1** Why learning a language is hard and how to make it easier from www.ef.com/blog/language/why-learning-a-language-is-hard / Accessed: 30/11/2017. Reprinted with permission of EF Education First Ltd.; **p.25** Very Good Lives: Copyright © J.K. Rowling 2008; **pp.28-9** Excerpt from Narrative of the Life of Frederick Douglass; **pp.31-2** "The Truth About Criminal Cases": http://open.justice.gov.uk/courts/criminal-cases Accessed: 02/02/2018, Ministry of JUSTICE; **pp.35-6** © 1957 THE ESTATE OF HENRY FONDA AND DEFENDER PRODUCTIONS, INC. ALL RIGHTS RESERVED. Courtesy of MGM Media Licensing; **p.39** One Year Down, reprinted with the permission of Leigh Sprague; **pp.42-3** Excerpt from Peter James' Want You Dead, Pan Macmillan. Reproduced with permission of the Licensor through PLSclear; **p.48** IB learner profile attributes, International Baccalaureate Foundation; **p.48** Why do we collect things? Love, anxiety or desire, Christian Jarrett 9 Nov 2014, The Guardian. Reprinted with permission; **pp.51-2** Mass tourism is at a tipping point – but we're all part of the problem, Martin Kettle 11 Aug 2017, The Guardian. Reprinted with permission; **pp.58-9** Extract from HealthyChildren.org article, "Weigh-Ins, Weight Gain & Rules for Teen Athletes, American Academy of Pediatrics. Reprinted with permission; **pp.60-1** Hadrian's Wall, www.lingolia.com. Reprinted with permission; **p.63** IB DP Programme Creativity, Activity, Service Guide for students graduating in 2017 and after, International Baccalaureate Foundation; **pp.64-5** Extract from Notes From A Small Island: Journey Through Britain by Bill Bryson, reprinted with permission of Random House UK; **p.67** Elon Musk's 10 rules for success; **pp.69-70** 'Be Happy at Work – Bruce Daisley, Vice President of Twitter Europe' https://lectureinprogress.com/journal/bruce-daisley; **pp.74-5** "Two Kinds" from THE JOY LUCK CLUB by Amy Tan, copyright © 1989 by Amy Tan. Used by permission of G. P. Putnam's Sons, an imprint of Penguin Publishing Group, a division of Penguin Random House LLC. All rights reserved.; "Two Kinds" from THE JOY LUCK CLUB by Amy Tan, copyright © 1989 by Amy Tan. Used by permission of Penguin Random House UK. All rights reserved.; **p.76** Republished with permission of Heinle Cengage Learning, from Practical Grammar 3 : Student Book with Key, John Hughes and Ceri Jones and 2010; permission conveyed through Copyright Clearance Center, Inc.; **p.79** Stereotypes, Lagemaat, R. v. d., 2015. Labels and stereotypes. In: Theory of knowledge. Cambridge: Cambridge University Press, p. 97; **p.81** Extract from I Am Malala, Copyright © 2013 Salarzai Limited; **p.83** Republished with permission of Heinle Cengage Learning, from Practical Grammar 3 : Student Book with Key, John Hughes and Ceri Jones and 2010; permission conveyed through Copyright Clearance Center, Inc.; **p.84** 'The Tall Woman and Her Short Husband' Der wundersame Zopf : Erzählungen, by Feng Jicai; **p.86** Theory of Knowledge for the IB diploma, written by Richard van de Lagemaat, published by Cambridge University Press; **p.86** © Mind. This information is published in full at www.mind.org.uk; **p.87** © Khaled Hosseini, 2003, The Kite Runner, Bloomsbury Publishing Plc.; Excerpt(s) from THE KITE RUNNER by Khaled Hosseini, copyright © 2003 by TKR Publications, LLC. Used by permission of Riverhead, an imprint of Penguin Publishing Group, a division of Penguin Random House LLC. All rights reserved.; Excerpt(s) from THE KITE RUNNER by Khaled Hosseini, Copyright © 2003 Khaled Hosseini. Reprinted by permission of Anchor Canada/Doubleday Canada, a division of Penguin Random House Canada Limited. All rights reserved.; **pp.89-90** Strange traditions from https://garfors.com/2016/12/25-strange-customs-and-traditions-html. Reprinted with permission; **pp.90-1** 10 Best Weird and Wacky British Traditions, FERNE ARFIN, 12/15/2018. reprinted with permission of TripSavvy; **p.92** Republished with permission of Heinle Cengage Learning, from Practical Grammar 3 : Student Book with Key, John Hughes and Ceri Jones and 2010; permission conveyed through Copyright Clearance Center, Inc.; **p.93** www.englishgrammar.org; **p.98** Verbs and dependent prepositions, British Council. Reprinted with permission; **pp.101-2** Teenage boys wear skirts to school to protest against 'no shorts' policy, Steven Morris, 22 June 2017, The Guardian. Reprinted with permission; **p.104** Republished with permission of Heinle Cengage Learning, from Practical Grammar 3 : Student Book with Key, John Hughes and Ceri Jones and 2010; permission conveyed through Copyright Clearance Center, Inc.; **p.106** Conformity and Behavior, Kendra Cherry, 13 March 2019. Reprinted with permission from Verywell; **pp.107-8** Dead Men's Path By Chinua Achebe by The Wylie Agency. Reprinted with permission; "Dead Men's Path" from GIRLS AT WAR: AND OTHER STORIES by Chinua Achebe, copyright © 1972, 1973 by Chinua Achebe. Used by permission of Doubleday, an imprint of the Knopf Doubleday Publishing Group, a division of Penguin Random House LLC. All rights reserved; **p.111-12** © Sandi Schwartz, science writer; **p.114** 1 in 4 teens are online almost constantly from http://infographic.statista.com/normal/chartoftheday_3387_internet_use_teenagers_n. jpg. Reprinted with permission of Statista; **p.117** Healthy Living Tips for Teenagers www.livestrong.com/article/365455-healthy-living-tips-for-teenagers/ Accessed Feb 14, 2018. Reprinted with permission; **p.119** Republished with permission of Association for Supervision and Curriculum Development, from Education Update, Sarah McKibben, Wake-Up Call, Vol 56, Number 4, April 2014; permission conveyed through Copyright Clearance Center, Inc.; **p.120** Writing survey questions from https://zapier.com/learn/forms-surveys/writing-effective-survey/. Reprinted with permission of Zapier; **p.122** Mindfulness Meditation and Children: An Interview With Susan Kaiser Greenland. Reprinted with permission of Dr. Elisha Goldstein (https://elishagoldstein.com), creator of A Course in Mindful Living (https://acourseinmindfulliving.com); **pp.125-6** Wonder by R.J. Palacio, Random House UK; **p.127** IB learner profile attributes, IBO, International Baccalaureate Foundation; **pp.128-9** Cultural dimensions and differences across cultures from https://blog.oup.com/2017/03/hofstede-cultural-dimensions/, Oxford University Press. Reproduced with permission of the Licensor through PLSclear; **p.132** From http://opengecko.com/interculturalism/visualising-the-iceberg-model-of-culture/, Reprinted with permission of James Penstone; **p.133** The Wall Street journal by Dow Jones & Co ; News Corporation Reproduced with permission of DOW JONES COMPANY in the format Book via Copyright Clearance Center; **p.136** Open-minded learner profile attribute, International Baccalaureate Foundation; **p.136** Inquirer learner profile attribute, International Baccalaureate Foundation; **pp.137-8** Cell Press. "How political parties influence our beliefs, and what we can do about it." ScienceDaily. ScienceDaily, 20 February 2018; **p.140** The Curious Incident of the Dog in the Night-Time by Mark Haddon, published by Jonathan Cape (Penguin) Chapter 199, pages 164-65; **p.143** The joys and benefits of bilingualism by Tobias Jones, The Guardian, 21 Jan 2018. Reprinted with permission; **p.148** Why English Should Not Be The International Language Of The World by Robert Nielsen; **pp.152-3** THE RISE OF "THEYBIES": HOW PARENTS ARE RAISING CHILDREN IN A GENDERLESS WORLD. Reprinted with permission of Amber Leventry; **p.156** From LITTLE BEE: A Novel by Chris Cleave. Copyright © 2008 by Chris Cleave. Originally published as The Other Hand in Great Britain 2008 by Sceptre, an imprint of Hodder & Stoughton. Reprinted with the permission of Simon & Schuster, Inc. All rights reserved; Extract from Little Bee by Chris Cleave, ICM Partners. Reprinted with permission.; **pp.159-60** Visual Arts Review: "Native Fashion Now"—Tradition and Cutting Edge, Superbly Balanced, Kathleen C. Stone. Reproduced with permission; **p.163** © Andrew Hearle www.stagemilk.com/how-to-act-shakespeare/ **p.166** The Spherical Solution www.sydneyoperahouse.com/our-story/sydney-opera-house-history/spherical-solution.html Accessed: 13/05/2018 Reprinted with permission; **pp.170-1** Sonny's Blues by James Baldwin, Penguin Books; **pp.173-4** What will your phone be like in 20 years? www.t3.com/features/your-phone-in-20-years Accessed: 26 July, 2018. Reprinted with permission of T3; **pp.177-8** © 2014 The Atlantic Media Co., as first published in TheAtlantic.Com All rights reserved. Distributed by Tribune Content Agency; **pp.181-2** Why TIFF matters, and 4 other things to know about the Toronto International Film Festival, www.vox.com/culture/2017/9/5/16184614/tiff-toronto-international-film-festival-explainer-matters-oscars. Reprinted with permission of Vox media Inc.; **p.185** Poem The Ballad of the Landlord by Langston Hughes, David Higham Associates. Reprinted with permission; "Ballad of the Landlord" from THE COLLECTED POEMS OF LANGSTON HUGHES by Langston Hughes, edited by Arnold Rampersad with David Roessel, Associate Editor, copyright © 1994 by the Estate of Langston Hughes. Used by permission of Alfred A. Knopf, an imprint of the Knopf Doubleday Publishing Group, a division of Penguin Random House LLC. All rights reserved; **pp.187-8** Ye! Community "Interview of a Social Entrepreneur: Pete Ceglinski, Co-founder of The Seabin Project"; **pp.191-2** Is it ethical to have a national DNA database?, YourGenome.Org, 23 June 2018; **pp.196-7** 08 Sep 2017, www.weforum.org/agenda/2017/09/so-how-does-ai-actually-work-these-videos-by-facebook-experts-explain-everything/; **pp.199-200** Extract from The War of the Worlds by H.G. Wells, December 1897; **pp.202-3** What are the Advantages and Disadvantages of Solar Energy?, www.greenmatch.co.uk, 19 December 2018. Reprinted with permission; **p.204** Republished with permission of Heinle Cengage Learning, from Practical Grammar 3 : Student Book with Key, John Hughes and Ceri Jones and 2010; permission conveyed through Copyright Clearance Center, Inc.; **p9.207-8** Film review: A Plastic Ocean shows us a world awash with rubbish, The Conversation Media Group Ltd.; **p.209** Sourced from speakspeak.com, all rights reserved; **pp.212-13** This heatwave is just the start. Britain has to adapt to climate change, fast by Simon Lewis, The Guardian, 6 Jul 2018. Reprinted with permission; **p.214** Republished with permission of Heinle Cengage Learning, from Practical Grammar 3 : Student Book with Key, John Hughes and Ceri Jones and 2010; permission conveyed through Copyright Clearance Center, Inc.; **p.217-18** The Coming Race by Baron Edward Bulwer Lytton Lytton, 1871; **p.220** All human beings are born free and equal in dignity Universal Declaration of Human Rights, United Nations Publication; **pp.221-2** Index on Censorship; **p.223** Emphasis exercise by Warsaw Will; **p.227** Reprinted with permission of The New Age Parents; **p.229** Republished with permission of Heinle Cengage Learning, from Practical Grammar 3 : Student Book with Key, John Hughes and Ceri Jones and 2010; permission conveyed through Copyright Clearance Center, Inc.; **pp.232-3** Seven reasons we still need to fight for women's human rights from www.amnesty.org.uk/blogs/yes-minister-it-human-rights-issue/seven-reasons-we-still-need-fight-womens-human-rights © Corallina Lopez-Curzi and RightsInfo; **p.235** Republished with permission of Heinle Cengage Learning, from Practical Grammar 3 : Student Book with Key, John Hughes and Ceri Jones and 2010; permission conveyed through Copyright Clearance Center, Inc.; **p.235** Quotes taken from stories on Womankind worldwide website through their partner organisations. www.womankind.org.uk; **p.237** Truth Theory of Knowledge for the IB Diploma by Richard van de Lagemaat published by Cambridge University Press; **pp.238-9** From Nineteen Eighty-Four by George Orwell. Published by Martin Secker & Warburg Ltd. Reprinted by permission of The Random House Group Limited. © 1949; **p.241** We are globalised, but have no real intimacy with the rest of the world by Martin Jacques, The Wylie Agency; **p.243** Republished with permission of Heinle Cengage Learning, from Practical Grammar 3: Student Book with Key, John Hughes and Ceri Jones and 2010; permission conveyed through Copyright Clearance Center, Inc.; **pp.245-6** Impact of Globalization on Small Businesses by Leo Sun from www.businessdictionary.com/article/583/impact-of-globalization-on-small-businesses; **p.247** Alternatives to if http://elearning.masterprof.ro/lectiile/engleza/lectie_26/4alternatives_to_if.html Lectii online; **pp.250-1** Globalization may actually be better for the environment https://theconversation.com/globalization-may-actually-be-better-for-the-environment-95406 The Conversation; **p.252** Omission of if http://elearning.masterprof.ro/lectiile/engleza/lectie_26/5omission_of_if.html Lectii online; **p.254** Excerpt from OF MICE AND MEN by John Steinbeck, copyright 1937, © renewed 1965 by John Steinbeck. Used by permission of Viking Books, an imprint of Penguin Publishing Group, a division of Penguin Random House LLC. All rights reserved.